James Quinter, Mary N. Quinter

Life and Sermons of Elder James Quinter

James Quinter, Mary N. Quinter

Life and Sermons of Elder James Quinter

ISBN/EAN: 9783337160234

Printed in Europe, USA, Canada, Australia, Japan

Cover: Foto ©Lupo / pixelio.de

More available books at **www.hansebooks.com**

LIFE AND SERMONS

OF

ELDER JAMES QUINTER,

LATE EDITOR OF

GOSPEL MESSENGER, PRESIDENT OF BRETHREN'S
NORMAL COLLEGE, AND AUTHOR OF
"TRINE IMMERSION."

BY HIS DAUGHTER,

MARY N. QUINTER.

MT. MORRIS, ILL.:
BRETHREN'S PUBLISHING CO.

DONOHUE & HENNEBERRY,
PRINTERS AND BINDERS,
CHICAGO.

TO THE BLESSED MEMORY
OF HIM
WHOSE LIFE WAS A CONSTANT BENEDICTION
AND WHO HAS LEFT AS
A SACRED LEGACY
AN INSPIRATION TO A HIGHER,
HOLIER LIFE,
THIS WORK IS AFFECTIONATELY
INSCRIBED
AS THE LOVING TRIBUTE OF A DAUGHTER
TO HER FATHER'S LIFE.

PREFACE.

The kind indulgence of the reader is asked for the work herewith presented. The writer is a novice in work of this kind, and has undertaken it with great reluctance, and only at the earnest solicitation of the friends who so much desired that the story of this "Life" might be preserved to the church and the people whose welfare was so dear to his heart. We have hesitated, because we felt entirely unable to perform the work as it should be done, and because much that we might desire to say might be criticised as too eulogistic. That some little good may be accomplished is our only motive. It is scarcely expected that the work will find many readers outside of those in some way acquainted and in sympathy with the life portrayed. It is believed that such will accept it simply as a loving attempt to truthfully and faithfully delineate the scenes and incidents in a life filled with arduous toil in varied fields of Christian labor.

No diary or journal recorded the facts of his life, and death came to him so suddenly, that, though it did not find him unprepared, yet there had been so little decline in his powers that no specific preparation for a work of this kind had been made. Had it been otherwise, though he would scarcely have made any preparation himself, yet his friends might have gathered from his lips a more complete account of his life.

From his published work, and from the memory of those who knew him best, have been drawn the facts and incidents here imperfectly sketched. Whenever it has been possible his own account of the scenes and incidents of his life has been used. Much worthy of record has no doubt passed beyond recall, but of this life it can be truthfully said,

"To live in hearts we leave behind is not to die."

His truest life is written in the hearts of those who have been strengthened and quickened anew to spiritual life and to higher desires for holiness by contact with his consecrated life.

To all who have in any way contributed to the interest of the work and without whose aid and assistance it could not have been published, the warmest thanks and deepest gratitude are hereby tendered. Especially are thanks due to Brother H. B. Brumbaugh, whose interest and encouragement so kindly manifested have proved so helpful.

What has been written of his life may seem to his friends to be but a shadowy outline through which they may catch glimpses of the man they knew. But if the glimpses of so pure a life may prove an encouragement and help to any one, the purpose for which it was written shall have been accomplished.

In the sermons those who knew and loved him and whose hearts have been "touched for good and for God" by him, may again come into close contact with a heart warm with the love of Christ and zeal for His cause. They are the true expression of the life of the man. May they prove messages of peace and comfort to many hearts.

That our Father in Heaven may graciously bless the work; that His children who read it may be strengthened anew in their spiritual life and built up in their most holy faith; that some one, yet a stranger to the Master's love, may be led to the acceptance of His truth by a word or sentence here read is the earnest desire and sincere prayer of the author and compiler.   H. N. Q.

HUNTINGDON, Pa., February, 1891.

INTRODUCTION.

The book herewith presented to the Brotherhood and the public is one of no ordinary character, as we have none like it in the literature of the Brethren Church. But it will be none the less appreciated on this account, as for several years there has been a continued and pressing demand for its appearance. At the Annual Meeting held at Harrisonburg, Va., in the year 1889, we presented the propriety of its publication before the Standing Committee of that Meeting, and it was voted a unanimous approval. Since then a large number of inquiries have been received, and the demand for its publication has become so urgent that his daughter, the author and compiler, finally decided to undertake the work, which she has now completed in a very satisfactory manner.

On account of our intimate acquaintance with him for the last twelve years of his eventful life, we have been solicited to write this Introduction. We do it with a considerable degree of reluctance, knowing our inability to do it as we feel it should be done. And yet it affords us great pleasure to be able to introduce to the Church and to the public the author of a ministry that has proved so great a blessing to the world.

In trying to bear an humble testimony to a life that was so noble, so grand and yet so gentle and unpretending, we are made to feel as we felt when standing in the presence of the Niagara Falls, amidst the roar and plunging of the dashing water, the uprising clouds of mist and the circling rainbows that spanned the awe-inspiring scene.

There are times when we have feelings which are beyond our power of expression; ideals that we can neither paint nor describe. Such an one we have before us now, and most gladly would we set it before you, could we do so. A lifelong servant of Jesus, a Bible student, a defender of the Church in her practices and doctrines, and in character God's nobleman; yet, in practical experience, as humble as a loving child.

Our acquaintance with Elder Quinter, prior to his removal to Huntingdon, was from his reputation rather than from personal knowledge, outside of that which we had learned from his writings and editorial labors. His reputation as a successful minister and his known sympathy with the educational movements of the Church led to the consolidation of the two weekly church papers then being published at Myersdale, Pa., and at this place. And on his removal here, in the fall of 1876, he at once became identified with us in both Church and School. From this time on to the close of his life his relations with us as a church were most pleasant, and his fatherly counsels and ministerial labors greatly appreciated by all.

He was a man who commanded the respect and esteem of all, and no one could associate with him without feeling that their lives were made better by coming in contact with his life, and hundreds, in giving him the parting hand, were made to thank God that such a man as Elder Quinter lived. But while he was great and good in his home associations, as a neighbor and citizen, and in his relations to the College as its president, he was especially great in the pulpit and in his ministry. His sermons were accompanied with an inspiration that could be felt only by hearing them. And, often, as we sat weeping under his ministrations, we were made sad to feel that only so few could enjoy that which afforded us so much joy and peace. But we are now made to rejoice in the thought that, though the tongue and the lips that voiced forth with so much eloquence and zeal the riches of the Gospel of Christ have been silenced in death, the messages that were thus given we still have, and now send them forth in this volume to spiritually energize and gladden the hearts of thousands of others who, though they can not hear him speak, can receive his words as they flowed from lips inspired and sanctified by the Holy Ghost.

The object in publishing this volume is three-fold. First, to place before the church and the public a short sketch of the life of a man who has made the world better by his living in it. It is said that bad men are dead while they live, but good men live after they die. This may be truthfully said of Elder Quinter. Though he is dead yet he liveth and will continue to live until all the golden sheaves are gathered.

Second. That a part of his sermons that were prepared with so much care and hard study, and at the dictation of the Spirit, may be preserved for the benefit and instruction of the ministry. They are examples of sermonizing worthy of careful study by our ministers, as from them they can not fail to get form and matter that will greatly aid in the preparation of sermons.

And a third object in publishing this book is that it may prove a home ministry in thousands of Christian families, at times when no other opportunity can be had, to have the Gospel preached.

For the infirm, the aged, and the isolated ones, this book may prove a great comfort. When it is made necessary for the family, or part of it, to remain at home on Sunday, or confined in the sick-chamber, have one of these sermons read and it will prove a good substitute for the regular preaching services. It may prove a household service as did the singing and praying of Paul and Silas in the prison. In the book will be found sermons especially adapted to the family, the afflicted and to the isolated ones. And we are sure that there are hundreds of homes in which this ministry will be gladly welcomed and appreciated. And unto every Christian home it will prove a power for good.

In the brief biography will be found the history of a life that has made the world better—one that ought to give zeal, earnestness and inspiration to the young; to church workers, determination and perseverance in the good cause, and to the aged a solid rock which will make sure the faltering step until the end comes.

The sermons will be adapted to every loving child of Jesus, and to the sinner as well. In them will be found the Bread of Heaven, the Holy Manna, the unsearchable riches of Christ. My prayer is that this volume, freighted, as it is, with messages of peace and salvation from a loving heart, may, everywhere, find an open door. Take it into your homes and, like the Ark in the house of Obed Edom, it will prove a blessing to the household.

Every book, like every person, goes forth into the world on a special mission. So goes forth this unpretentious volume with its special aim which we, in part, at least, have attempted to set forth in this brief Introduction.

It gives the writer pleasure to join in offering to the Brotherhood, and to the Christian world, a work which is intended to be helpful to others, in scattering the seeds of the Gospel of the Son of God to all nations. Go forth on thy mission of love, attended with the prayers of all who love Jesus, and may "this life" and "these words" prove a blessing to generations yet unborn.

H. B. BRUMBAUGH.

HUNTINGDON, PA., February, 1891.

PART I.

A SKETCH OF THE LIFE

OF

ELDER JAMES QUINTER.

TOGETHER WITH

MEMORIAL SKETCHES.

A SKETCH OF THE LIFE

OF

ELDER JAMES QUINTER.

"James, son of John and Mary Quinter, born February 1, A. D. 1816."
This record from the old family Bible tells of the beginning of a life which, measured by its written chronicles, may be briefly told. Of those associated with him in his boyhood and early manhood, few, if any, are left to recall the incidents of those years. A few reminiscences scattered through his editorials or his notes of travel are all that remain to guide us in sketching his life's story.

His mother was a native of New Jersey. Her maiden name was Mary Smith. His father was a native of Philadelphia. In this city they made their first home. Here two of their children were born—Ann Eliza, July 4, 1809, and James, in 1816. The family were poor, dependent on the father's daily labor for their support. In 1824 they removed to Phœnixville, a manufacturing town on the Schuylkill, about twenty-five miles from Philadelphia. The father found work at the iron mills. His work consisted in hauling the finished nails and iron to Philadelphia. There was at this time no railroad and no bridge across the river. The boy James, in the intervals between the short school terms, also was employed; he drove a donkey attached to a cart between the long rows of machinery, gathering the work as it was finished.

In 1829 the father died, the result of his exposure during his trips to and from the city. His little family—a wife, son, and two daughters—were now left with little means for support. Though but a boy of thirteen, the duty of helping to care for his mother and sisters now rested upon this son.

The educational advantages of the time were rare, particularly for the poor. The opportunities, though small, were improved, and the children were sent to school whenever it was possible. The schools of those times are in marked contrast with those of the present. Yet with the lessons of the school book were inculcated lessons of truth, purity and nobility. The Bible was in daily use in many of the schools and the influence of its lessons is ever toward that which is highest. The reading books of the time contained selections from the best writings of the standard authors. In the sketches of biography and history, in essays and poems, the pupils came into constant contact with the pure, the noble, and the good. In the old "English Reader" and its "Sequel" may be found choice selections from Milton, Addison, Young, Gray, Montgomery, Dr. Johnson, Goldsmith, Philip Doddridge, Dr. Hugh Blair, the Scotch divine, and many others. Could such selections as "The Importance of a Good Education," "Happiness Founded in Rectitude of Conduct," "Virtue, Man's Highest Influence," "The Value of Religious Retirement," "The Man of Integrity," and others of a similar character, have else than a salutary influence? The love of books and the desire for an education were fostered, if not awakened, by such lessons. This fact is mentioned as no doubt it had an important influence in forming and developing those noble purposes and high ideals which ever characterized the subject of this sketch.

In his boyhood he manifested a desire and a determination to obtain an education. His mother shared his desire and did all she could to help him. She obtained a situation for him in the family of Philip Rosenberger, at the Perkiomen Stone Bridge, near to which Freeland College — now Ursinus — was located.

After leaving school, he first obtained a situation in the store of Brother Isaac Price, of Corner Stores, near Phœnixville. Brother Price said: " I soon found he was too reserved to make a good storekeeper and asked Brother Fitzwater to take him on the farm." The request was granted and we next find him in the family of Brother Abel Fitzwater. To the influence of this kind Christian family he attributed his early conversion and they were ever kindly and gratefully remembered.

In the surrounding community were the homes of brethren John Umstad, George Price, Samuel Supplee; and. although not in the immediate neighborhood, the home of Brother Isaac Price was not far away. These brethren, with Brother Fitzwater, were among those who came into the Church during a religious revival in the community in 1831. As there was no Church of the Brethren in the neighborhood, they were baptized in the Coventry Church, near Pottstown, Through the efforts of these brethren meetings for public worship were held in the school-houses, and prayer meetings were held at their homes, During a meeting held in the old Green Tree school-house, he was convicted and his mind aroused upon the subject of his salvation. It engaged his thoughts deeply for a time, and one day as he was working at the barn he suddenly stopped, exclaiming, " I've got—I've got it," and ran to the house. "I've got it—peace with God!" He was baptized in the Coventry Church. He was at this time in his seventeenth year.

Later, through the efforts of the brethren, a little church was organized in the village of Lumberville, now Port Providence. The first love-feast was held in Brother Umstad's barn. By the blessing of God and the zeal of the members the little church grew and increased in numbers and power. It was in this church that prayer meetings and protracted meetings were first held among the brethren. In an editorial, written in February, 1888, in which he gives an account of a visit to the Green Tree church, he refers to a number of incidents connected with the early history of the church. In referring to the prayer meetings, he says: " Our prayer meetings that we held in the beginning of the church here afforded us very good opportunities for exercising our gifts. While those meetings were excellent promoters of our spiritual life, they were good schools for our improvement in many ways. In these meetings we exercised somewhat freely as did the brethren and sisters generally."

From the beginning of his Christian experience his life was characterized by deep piety. His exemplary character, his earnestness and his sincerity won for him the love and confidence of all that knew him.

Though he had been obliged to leave school he had not given up study. His determination to obtain an education strengthened with his years. By his diligence and earnestness in improving his few opportunities he accomplished much in the way of self-improvement.

His friends, noting his zeal and his manifest disposition to learn, were interested in him, and by their assistance he was enabled to prepare himself for teaching. He attended for a time a private boarding-school at West Bradford, Chester county, Pa. The school was kept by Jonathan Gause, a Friend.

He began teaching in Limerick township, Montgomery county, Pa., in what was called Hobson's school-house, situated about one mile from Royer's Ford. While teaching here he found a pleasant home in the family of Francis Hobson.

About the time the first love-feast of the Lumberville

church was held the project of building a union meetinghouse in Lumberville was started. In a short time a two-story structure was erected; the lower story was furnished for church services, the second as a school-room.

In the spring of 1834 he came to Lumberville and began teaching in this room. He continued to teach here for seven years, from 1834 to 1841. To his work in the school-room he devoted all his energies, and not only labored to impress upon the minds of his pupils the temporal truths of their daily lessons, but also by precept and example endeavored to lead them to the higher truths of the spiritual life.

While teaching in Lumberville he made his home for a time in Brother Fitzwater's family, and in the family of Joseph Pennypacker. Later he moved his mother and sisters to the village. His elder sister, Ann, had married, and had been left with three little boys. She came with her children to find again a home with her mother, brother and sister. She found love and sympathy among the home hearts, and remained with them till her death, in October, 1842.

Shortly after his conversion he was impressed with a call to follow his Master in the work of the ministry. His conviction of this duty grew stronger, yet in this, as in all things else, he was willing to submit the time to the Lord's will. In 1838, in a council meeting, held at the home of Brother George Price, he was called by the Church to the ministry. The following letter, written to Sister Sarah Price, is interesting as referring to the scenes and incidents of his early life:

COLUMBIANA, O., March 31, 1865.

DEAR SISTER SARAH: I am happy to know there are those among my Christian friends who still retain the friendship and kind feelings toward me that were formed many years ago. And still happier am I to believe that the Christian friendships and acquaintances formed here on earth will continue to exist, and be a source of enjoyment to us in another and higher state of being; and that friends separated here will rejoin one another there, where our friendship and union will be perfected. I assure you, dear sister, I reciprocate the kind regard you have manifested to me, and I deeply sympathize with you in your bereavement, and in all your afflictions, though I may seem to have been somewhat unmindful of you by not writing to you before this. I will not now occupy time or space in making explanations as an apology for my delay. I am sure if you knew my engagements and how often I have thought of you, with other dear friends who are engraven so deeply upon my heart that I can not forget them, your censure would not be severe.

Your letter, dear sister, brought many things connected with the childhood of my Christian life to mind. It is a peculiarity of the human mind to retain in the memory with remarkable freshness those occurrences which happened in childhood. These are remembered while things which occurred later in life are forgotten. It is very much so in being born again, or in our new life. How vividly do many things appear, which are connected with their conversion or their espousal to the Lord, to the minds of believers. How distinctly do I remember the meeting in the old school-house not far from your residence where the bow, though "drawn at a venture," sent arrows of conviction into my poor heart, which produced pain and sorrow from which I could find no relief, until I found it in the healing virtues contained in the stream which flowed from the pierced side of the dying Saviour. That same night, after the meeting alluded to, we stopped, as I well remember, at the Pilgrim's Rest, the homestead of Brother Umstad. Here we had further devotional services, for more besides myself felt very miserable on account of our sins, and the kind and zealous Christian friends knew it, and were willing to labor at a late hour of the night for our comfort and salvation. How solemn was that night to me, when journeying homeward along the romantic Schuylkill, alone, "without Christ . . . having no hope and without God in the world." Lonely and lost I indeed felt. And I regard it as a fortunate circumstance for me, and much to my advantage, that my home was in a Christian family, that of Brother Fitzwater. This was another Bethel—a place that was often felt to be the "house of God and the gate of Heaven." In relation to this place it may, with propriety, I think, be said: "The Lord shall count when he writeth up the people, that this man was born there." Here we found, I humbly trust, peace in believing, and experienced the power of God unto salvation.

And what blessed meetings we had in those days of the planting of the church at "Green Tree!" How simple and child-like were our exercises! How warm our zeal! How ardent our Christian love to one another! How closely were our hearts drawn together in Christian fellowship! And we loved God because he first loved us. Those were happy times, oases, or green and watered spots in the land of our pilgrimage. Our sky was bright, and our sea, with the exception of some little breezes that would ruffle the surface occasionally, smooth.

But within the thirty years that have come and gone since those halcyon days, many changes have taken place. Many of those who then worshiped with us, and encouraged us with their prayers, their exhortations, and their exemplary lives, have left us—have gone away. "They are not lost but have gone before." They are yet remembered—they are yet loved, and will be loved still more, when the value of the soul is seen in the light of Heaven, and when the fullness of salvation is enjoyed in the glorified state, for not until then shall we fully realize what Christ and his Church have done for us. The crown of rejoicing of Christian laborers will be the souls saved through their humble instrumentality. And the Church," without spot or wrinkle," presented as a "chaste virgin to Christ," will be the brightest jewel in King Messiah's crown, and will manifest before the great congregation of universal intelligences the glory of the great work of redemption.

And others who have survived their departure have passed through many trials, conflicts and afflictions, for these are unavoidable in a world that lies in wickedness as ours does. But as our Lord and Master was made "perfect through suffering" before us, we should not object to walk in the way which he himself walked in, since there are still rays of glory reflected from his holy footsteps. And the way of conflict, and trial, and suffering, is further recommended to us by a consideration of the glorious state to which it leads. Of our divine Master it is beautifully and encouragingly said, "he humbled himself, and became obedient unto death, even the death of the cross. *Wherefore* God also hath highly exalted him and given him a name which is above every name." In his case was fulfilled the promise, "he that humbleth himself shall be exalted." And it shall likewise be fulfilled to all his followers who humble themselves and take up their cross. "We are encompassed about with a great cloud of witnesses," and among them perhaps are those to whom we have already referred as having once worshiped with us in our assemblies on earth, "with whom we took sweet counsel together and with whom we walked unto the house of God in company." They are looking down upon us with indescribable interest, watching us with emotions peculiar to the redeemed inhabitants of Heaven, and beckoning us on, and pointing us to the prize of immortality, and waiting to welcome us to everlasting habitations, and to receive us to their number, that we may share in their joys. O, my sister, can any of us be so unfaithful to those sainted ones whom we have loved and who have loved us, as to forsake those holy principles of theirs in which they lived and died, and thus forego a renewal of those tender connections with them which once afforded us so much pleasure, and which will hereafter afford us infinitely more pleasure, when we shall have been brought into that heavenly state so congenial to our immortal natures in developing all the hidden powers of the soul, and thus increase its susceptibilities for the enjoyment of all the blessings of the "purchased possession?" This consideration, the consideration of losing the society of the saints, and especially of those whom we have looked upon as the safest, the purest, and the best of all companions, whose friendship we have tested, and whose society we have enjoyed, should in itself be a strong incentive to urge us to perseverance. But alas! This and all the other numerous considerations which are presented to us to lead us to a "patient continuance in well doing," seem insufficient to keep some in the narrow path, and they break over all the barriers that kind Heaven has thrown in their way to prevent their destruction, and make shipwreck of their faith, and madly pursue their own ruin. Eliphas, the friend of Job, describes the character of such, thus: "He stretcheth out his hand against God, and strengtheneth himself against the Almighty. He runneth upon him, even on his neck, upon the thick bosses of his bucklers."

I am also reminded that it was at your house, and in that room where we often gathered together for religious services, that I was called by the Church to the ministry. The call was unexpected to me at that time. Soon after my conversion I thought I had indications that the Lord would have me at some time to preach the Gospel, and although I had reason to believe the Church had quite as much confidence in me, and indeed much more than I was deserving of, still I did not think that the time had yet come for the Church to confirm what I had thought were the impressions of the spirit of God in regard to my duty to labor in the ministry. I believed that if the impressions I felt were produced by the spirit of the Lord, and if I would continue faithful, the time would come when the Church, in furthering the purposes of the Lord, would set me apart to the ministry. But I felt it was my duty to wait until that time should come, not, however, in idleness, but in such exercises and labors in the service of the Lord as circumstances required and as prudence warranted. And never have I felt my insufficiency for the work to which I was then called, more sensibly than I did at the time in which I was called. And although I then felt that the responsibility connected with the Christian ministry was very great, I appreciate that responsibility, I think, at this time much more correctly, and feel it to be proportionately greater.

We can not properly estimate the responsibility of the Christian ministry without forming at least an approximate value of the immortal souls that the ministry was designed to save and purify for heaven. And as we can not fully or properly estimate the value of a soul, neither can we fully estimate the great responsibility that rests on those who are called to perform the work of the ministry of the Gospel. But we know the value of the soul is great, or it would not have justified the price of redemption which was paid for it, which was not "silver and gold" but "the precious blood of Christ." The responsibility, therefore, must be indeed great.

You call my attention to some beautiful hymns. I thank you for your suggestions as I know your taste is good. I believe all you have named I approve of, and had them all marked for insertion in a new collection of hymns. Especially do I love the hymn you have alluded to — "Nearer My God to Thee" — and which is sometimes called "Upward." I am pleased that it has commended itself to your mind as a beautiful hymn. It shows you want to rise higher and higher in holiness, and thus approach nearer and nearer to God. This is well. I would to heaven that this was the ardent desire of every member of the Church. The sentiments of the hymn are so evangelical and in such perfect harmony with the genuine spirit of Christianity. I wonder if you are familiar with another hymn somewhat similar to the one you have expressed some partiality for? I admire it. It expresses the hope of the Christian and is called "Nearer Home" —

> "One sweetly solemn thought
> Comes to me o'er and o'er,
> I'm nearer home to-day
> Than I have been before," etc.

When we are approaching nearer to God in holiness of character, and in sameness of feeling, as it is our glorious privilege to do, since a growth in grace is a gospel doctrine, or rather a gospel duty; and when by the course of nature, and by the effect of the numerous diseases to which we are all liable, and by some of which many are affected we are borne forward to death, and through death to our Father's house of many mansions,

> "Where the saints of all ages in harmony meet,
> Their Saviour and brethren, transported to greet,"

how glorious is our hope! It is indeed a "lively hope," and it is as "an anchor to the soul."

> "Oh, what a blessed hope is ours!
> While here on earth we stay,
> We more than taste the heavenly powers,
> And antedate that day."

You allude to your bereavement and still seem to feel it sorely. Time and the balm of Gilead we trust will heal the wound, though a sensitiveness will remain, and when reminiscences of your dear son occur to the mind, the waters of your spirit may still be troubled. But remember that our holy Christianity teaches us to look forward rather than backward. And this lesson, with all others which it inculcates, is founded in wisdom, and adapted to our wants, since the joys awaiting us in the future are superior to what we have experienced in the past. In the apostle's beautiful development of Christian life, hope occupies a higher place than experience. He says, "We glory in tribulations also; knowing that tribulation worketh patience; and patience, experience; and experience, hope." Then let us not sorrow over friends that we have lost, over joys that have fled, and over wrecked and shattered constitutions, but "forgetting the past, press forward," "looking for that blessed hope, and the glorious appearing of the great God and our Saviour Jesus Christ."

"We glory in tribulations," says the apostle. This is a great thing to do. But Christians can do great things, for "Christ strengthening me," says Paul, "I can do all things."

We do not glory in tribulations because they are pleasant, but because they are useful. "Tribulation worketh patience."

Among the reminiscences of those happy meetings to which I have alluded, held in your congregation, is the singing of the "Garden Hymn." I am reminded of a verse of it in this connection—in connection with the idea of tribulation:

> "Our troubles and our trials here
> Will only make us richer there,
> When we arrive at home."

Do you sing this expressive hymn yet? You no doubt often think of the sentiments it contains. It always affects my mind pleasantly. We used to sing the closing verse upon the admission of persons into the Church, you will remember:

> "Now here's my heart, and here's my hand,
> To meet you in that heavenly land,
> Where we shall part no more."

You allude in your letter to some meetings that were being held in your church for the benefit of the members and the good of the community. And you seemed to think the members were edified and profited by them. If this was the case, then the labors were not in vain. In these times of temptation and trial, Christians need all the means of grace with which the Church has been intrusted. "Feed my sheep," "Feed my lambs," was the charge of the Saviour to Peter, and through him to the Church. And though the minister, with all believers,

> "Longs to see the season come
> When sinners shall come flocking home,"

yet, if denied this desirable sight, how pleasant it is for them to see "the brethren dwell together in unity," the Church alive, active, humble and joyful. And while it is a pleasant sight for those to see that are ministering in the Gospel to the Church, it is very pleasant for the Church itself to experience those heavenly emotions of joy, which it does experience when it is in a heathly state and when there is a healthy circulation of the Holy Spirit through all its members. And if there is joy in Heaven when a sinner repents, there is joy there when pardoned sinners are faithful to the Lord that redeemed them, and faithful to the Church that adopted them. And if the Church is alive and active, the work of the Lord will be very likely to prosper. The mission of the "Green Tree" branch of the Church is an important one, and I hope the members all will appreciate it, and labor with fidelity in the cause of Christ for the redemption of the world. "He that hath an ear, let him hear what the Spirit saith unto the churches."

Please remember me kindly to Brother George, and all your dear children, and to all the dear Christian friends. May God bless you and keep you faithful unto death. Farewell.

Yours in Faith and Hope,

JAMES QUINTER.

The following extract from a letter from Sister Susan Sidle, late of the Coventry Church, also contains some interesting reminiscences of his early ministry. "Brother Quinter was brought here to Lawrenceville by a dear sister, Sarah Reinwalt, about fifty years ago. She engaged the old school-house and had the brethren come and preach. We lived only a few rods from the school-house at that time, and Brother Quinter often stopped with us under our roof and gave us encouraging and cheering words. How glad we were of his company, and his earnest prayers did us so much good. In connection with his prayers he kept the fast. No wonder he was enabled to show forth such a good example. and such a bright and shining light that he was beloved by the brotherhood. Through the efforts of Sister Sarah Reinwalt, and the labors mostly of Brother Quinter, the first protracted meeting was held in this church.

He had never relinquished his habit of private study, and now with a determined purpose he set himself more earnestly to the task of thoroughly preparing his mind and heart for the sacred work. It became the inspiration of his life. Henceforth the duties of his holy office held the first place in his heart. A deep sense of the great responsibility he had accepted was ever present with him. It was about this time that he adopted the custom of setting apart certain days for fasting and prayer. This habit was continued throughout his life. The days so set apart were passed, as far as possible, in solitude. From them he always came with renewed strength and zeal for his work.

At the annual meeting held in the Aughwick church in 1839, Brother John Umstad arranged to visit a number of the churches in the valleys of Pennsylvania during the fall of the same year. On this journey he was accompanied by Brother Quinter. This was his first preaching tour after entering the ministry. They traveled on horseback and, as the journey extended to the western part of the State, much of it was laborious. The churches were scattered. Many of them were long distances apart, yet as the labor was undertaken with a desire to strengthen and build up the churches and to promote the cause of Christ it proved to be both pleasant and profitable. The visit to the George's Creek church led to his removal there a few years later.

All his visits among the brethren were marked by a devotional spirit, and many have testified to the encouragement they received from his words of Christian counsel and his earnest prayers. An incident which occurred on this first tour among the churches illustrates the prayerful spirit of his life. While the brethren were in the Hopewell Church, Bedford county, they were called one night to visit a home in which the daughter was afflicted with epileptic fits. As they stood looking upon her suffering, he said: "Brethren, let us pray;" and, kneeling, he prayed fervently in her behalf. She was relieved at the time, and her affliction never returned. This incident and the spirit manifested did much to dispel the prejudice which many were disposed to feel against him on account of his youthful appearance.

Every opportunity to promote the cause of Christ and to present the theme of salvation was gladly improved. Though the calls of duty ofttimes involved personal sacrifice, he was none the less ready to heed them. At one time, while teaching in Lumberville, he was called to visit and pray with a young woman who was suffering with smallpox. As he could not bring upon his pupils the danger of infection, he closed his school and responded to the request. He felt it to be a call of duty, and, though fully aware of the danger incurred, he trusted that the Lord would protect him. He escaped, and when all danger of infection was past he reopened his school.

In the spring of 1842, in response to the request of the George's Creek Church, Fayette county, Pa., he came thither from his home in Montgomery county, Pa. In the late fall of the same year he brought his mother, sister and nephews to his new home. The Church gave him as a home a small farm, on which, with much labor and economy, with the assistance of his nephews, he was able to earn a very moderate livelihood. Here also for some years he taught during the winter months. As there was no school-house in the district, the school was kept in the Mennonite meeting-house. He was also selected by the board of directors of Nicholson township to examine the teachers of that township with reference to their qualifications for teaching.

In addition to his ministerial work at home, he accepted calls from the surrounding churches, and often traveled many miles on horseback over the mountains to fill distant appointments. The following extract from a letter from Brother John Wise refers to his ministry in the Ten-mile Church :

"In the spring of 1842 he came to western Pennsylvania. An arrangement was made by which he was to devote a part of his time to the Ten-mile congregation. June 14, 1842, I and my sister were baptized, and between that date and October 18th, there were fifty-two persons baptized in that congregation under his ministry. He was also present when I was chosen to the ministry and gave much encouragement by his kindly talk. To his fatherly care for me I owe much of my success in the ministry. We traveled together and I labored with him as a son with a father in the Gospel. Many excellent lessons were learned from his example. So pious, so meek, he impressed all with his piety."

On September 17, 1850, he was married to Mary Ann, daughter of Brother Daniel Moser. A daughter, Lydia Isabella, was born to them April 15, 1854. She was married September 20, 1877, in the Pilgrim chapel, Huntingdon, Pa., by her father, to Elder J. T. Meyers, of the Green Tree Church, Montgomery county, Pa. A son, named for his grandfather James Quinter, was born to them January 23, 1882, and a daughter, Grace Quinter, July 6, 1885.

In 1851 Elder Henry Kurtz began to publish the *Gospel Visitor* in Poland, Mahoning county, Ohio. It was designed as a religious monthly, "devoted to the exhibition and defense of Gospel-principles and Gospel-practice in their primitive purity and simplicity in order to promote Christian union, brotherly love, and universal charity." So meager were the mechanical facilities for its publication that it was said, and with a good deal of truth, that "The *Gospel Visitor* is published in the loft of a milk-house in the backwoods of Ohio, and three miles from the post-office."

This was the beginning of periodical literature in the Church of the Brethren. While it was bitterly opposed by some, by many it was gladly welcomed as affording wider opportunities for spreading the truths of the Gospel. Among the earliest contributors was Brother Quinter. Under the name *Clement* he contributed a series of articles on "The Elements of the Christian Character."

The *Visitor* increased in size and circulation until the burden of its publication became too great for one editor, and Brother Kurtz desired an assistant. In his editorial, in January, 1856, he says: "The constant increase of labor became exceedingly burdensome and grievous to us, and long already we looked around for assistance. We durst not make our own choice. We waited patiently for some token of Providence. The Lord graciously granted such a token at the last Yearly Meeting. There our dear Brother James Quinter was nominated as our assistant in the clerkship, and performed the duties thereof acceptably, as we have reason to believe, to the whole meeting. From this we took courage to call him to our assistance in the editorship, as being pointed out by the finger of God, and we rejoice to say that he has accepted the call, and will shortly enter upon the duties of the same."

"To this arrangement we were led not merely by a desire of being somewhat relieved of a burden. The reflection that our work should depend on such a frail, poor, unworthy being as we are, and would have to stop in case of our sickness, and to cease if we should be called off this stage of action, distressed us. This desire that our Master's work should go on as long as it pleases Him has been our main motive for the arrangement."

In response to Brother Kurtz's request he removed from Fayette county, Pa., to Poland, Mahoning county, Ohio, in the spring of 1856. His removal from the church in which he had labored for so many years, and among whose members he had formed many warm attachments, was attended with no small degree of pain. He says of it: "We felt the grief of separation to bear with weight upon our spirit, but we had counted the cost and weighed the matter maturely, and acted not from an impulse of hasty excitement, but from an impression of duty. Consequently, our sorrow was mingled with joy, for an honest discharge of duty is ever attended with joyful feelings. But, although we took comfort ourselves from the promises of God, and endeavored to administer comfort to those with whom we parted, still we felt, when standing before the congregation before which we had often stood, and at times with trembling anxiety for their good, and for the good of the cause we were pleading, emotions which we had not fully anticipated. We never experienced anything exactly similar. It is true we had on a former occasion removed from friends and scenes endeared to us by the happiest associations, but our ministerial labors there were performed in the childhood of our ministry, and we did not feel the same amount of responsibility rest upon us as we did in our late charge. Here our labors had been many, and our concern for the salvation of souls at times deep. The thought of our relation as pastor and flock ceasing, and the thought that our separation may be a final one on earth, produced feelings of tender and peculiar solemnity. We had asked for our dismission, and received but a silent consent. We knew the minds of many of our dear brethren and sisters, and a knowledge of their grief made ours the greater. But we greatly rejoiced that, although we had taken the preparatory steps to separate ourselves in person from the brethren among whom we had long dwelt, yet they had not withdrawn their affections from us."

His first editorial was published in June, 1856. In this editorial he says: "The Church of Christ should avail herself of every lawful means at her disposal for the promotion of knowledge, purity, union and edification among her members, and for the enlargement of her dominions by the conversion of sinners. These she is under obligation to do both from fidelity to her Lord and Master and from a proper regard to her own prosperity and success. Regarding, then, as I do, the press as an instrumentality which may advantageously be used by the Church for the accomplishment of those noble ends which her own organization in the world was designed to accomplish, I rejoiced at the appearance of the *Gospel Visitor* among us, and hailed its birth as a favorable sign of progress."

"A variety of qualifications is necessary for those whose business it is to provide for the public. The editor of a Christian journal, as well as a minister of the Gospel, should not shun to declare the 'whole counsel of God.' But with Paul, he should endeavor to 'give no offense neither to the Jews, nor to the Gentiles, nor to the Church of God.' And in performing his duty as a public reformer, whether he refutes an error, or reproves the errorist, or instructs the ignorant, or wakes up the sleepy, or rebukes the guilty, or encourages the weary, his words should be baptized with the spirit of ardent love, that they may brand their meaning on the minds addressed. . . . . . It has been with considerable reluctance that I have consented to become assistant editor, but the hope that the relation which I shall sustain to the brotherhood, through the *Gospel Visitor*, may afford me increased facilities for rendering service to the Church, and through the Church to the Lord, has induced me to assume the responsibilities which I have."

In the autumn of 1856, with his wife and little daughter, he made an extended visit to the churches in eastern Pennsylvania. The churches of Green Tree and Coventry, as they were associated with his early life, his first Christian experience, and his first work in the ministry, were always regarded with feelings of deep, prayerful interest and tender affection. A visit to these scenes of his early life was always a source of pleasure. Of this visit he says: "The brethren at Green Tree had made arrangements for meeting some days. It pleased the Lord to hear and answer prayer, and to own and bless his preached word. Christians were built up "on their most holy faith" and made to "rejoice in God their Saviour." Sinners were distressed upon discovering that they were lost, but by exercising repentance toward God, and faith in the Lord Jesus Christ, and by taking up their cross and confessing Christ, they were made to rejoice in the hope of eternal life. A more solemn meeting throughout we never witnessed. The meeting continued about two weeks; during which time, thirty-two were added to the Church by baptism. And at the close of the meeting there were others who offered themselves as candidates for baptism. While angels in heaven rejoiced, fathers and mothers rejoiced at witnessing the pleasing sight they were permitted to see, when their children said by their profession and actions, we will go to heaven with you. And it was pleasant to see what the occasion afforded an opportunity of seeing, a considerable number of men with their bosom companions, entering the gate to walk the way of eternal life together, and thus showing a happy union of feeling and practice in relation to their eternal interests. And it was no less pleasant to see interesting young men and women take up their cross to follow Christ. He will lead them, if they follow him, from the corrupting ways of sin into the pleasant paths of virtue while on earth, and, when they are on earth no more, he will lead them to 'fountains of living waters' in heaven."

"The recollection that several of the converts had in former years been our pupils, and that they had often bowed with us in our school-room, while we endeavored to implore heaven's blessing upon them, gave us increased pleasure at witnessing their 'good confession.'"

"As it was among these brethren that we sought and found the Lord, and among them we commenced our ministry, we felt much at home among them. It was truly refreshing to our hearts to see them, and greet them, and to have communion of spirit with them. Sweet and pleasant was the time we spent among them, and painful was it to part, and much more so would it have been but for the hope that 'we shall meet again' in our Father's house. For this hope let us bless God: for it let us live, and in it may we all die."

In June, 1857, the office of the *Visitor* was removed from Poland to Columbiana. This was done in order to afford better publishing and mailing facilities. Shortly after this, Elder Kurtz retired from the business and his son Henry took his place.

Through the summer and autumn of 1857 his wife was afflicted with consumption. On September 2d, she was anointed, and as she greatly desired to see her parents again he accompanied her shortly afterward to her old home in Fayette county, where she died, October 9th.

His mother and sister, who had remained in Fayette county when he removed to Ohio, now came to care for his home and his motherless little daughter.

April 11, 1861, he was married to Fanny, daughter of Elder John Studebaker. To them two daughters were born —Mary N., January 21, 1863, and Grace, June 10, 1870. These daughters, with their mother, reside in Huntingdon, Pa.

His own desire for an education and his struggles to obtain it developed a deep interest in education. A school under the control and influence of the Brethren, where the youth of the Church might be educated surrounded by the influences of Gospel Christianity was a dream of his youth and a plan of his manhood. Others shared this feeling and in the early years of the *Visitor* may be found references to a high school to be established in the Brotherhood.

In a letter written to the *Visitor* in March, 1856, he mentions the need of suitable teachers—those in the church sufficiently qualified—and suggests a plan by which worthy young brethren might be educated to fill the positions. In an article in September of the same year, in answering some objections to the proposed school, he says:

"If our youth now desire anything more than a common-school education, they are compelled to resort to institutions not under that pure Christian influence which we, as parents, should want our youth placed under, and thus, by failing to afford them the helps desirable for pursuing their studies, we may in some degree endanger their spiritual welfare. And not only so, but we are in danger of losing the influence and talents of many of our youth, as they will not be likely to feel the same respect for, and attachment to, our denomination, should they not find in us an inclination to sympathize with them in their desires for mental culture and a readiness to afford them suitable opportunities for obtaining that culture, that they would if they found the Church ready to encourage them, and to take them under her sheltering wing, and to feed them with useful knowledge. . . . . Knowing that a number of our young people are from home, pursuing their studies in other institutions of learning, and feeling a deep concern for the welfare of our youth, and a growing attachment to the holy doctrines and practices of Christianity as held by our beloved brethren, we confess we feel no little desire to see the Church affording her youth every opportunity necessary for the promotion of their happiness and usefulness. We think that it is not only right that the Church should encourage institutions in which our youth may acquire useful knowledge, but we think it is her duty—a duty she owes to her God, to herself, and to the rising generation—to encourage and build up such institutions."

Toward the close of the same article he describes his ideal of an institution such as he desired to see established: "We would expect such an institution to be under the influence of spiritually-minded Brethren. We would want religious teachers—teachers who would have a regard to the religious as well as to the intellectual improvements of the students,—consequently the students would have religious counsel administered to them. We would have the Bible daily used in the institution. We would have the students to board in a religious family and have them led daily to a throne of grace and Heaven's blessing invoked upon them. In short, we would have the school to resemble a pious family, under such rules as would discountenance whatever is evil, and encourage whatever is good."

At the time of the removal of the *Visitor* to Columbiana, a plan to establish the proposed school in that locality was under consideration. However, after residing here for a time, Brother Kurtz and Brother Quinter concluded that it was not a desirable locality and began to look about for a better one.

A good brick building erected for an academy in New Vienna, Clinton county, Ohio, being offered for sale, and the prospects of a school there being thought favorable, the brethren of the Fall Creek congregation, in the vicinity of New Vienna, proposed to purchase the academy building provided it should be occupied by the Brethren as a school. They examined the location and surroundings, and, being rather pleased with the place, gave the Brethren there some encouragement. The building was purchased, but, as it was impossible to remove the *Visitor* at the time, on account of the depressed state of business, it was decided that Brother Quinter should remove to Vienna and open the school. He was, however, still to work for the *Gospel Visitor*.

The school was accordingly opened on October 14, 1861, and continued for three years with a reasonable degree of success, though begun under unfavorable circumstances and meeting with much opposition. It was closed June 27, 1864, on account of the disturbed condition of the country during the War of the Rebellion. In this enterprise—which was the beginning of educational work in the church—he was assisted by Brother O. W. Miller, who was principal, Sister C. A. Haas and daughter Hattie, and Sisters Mary Craig and Lettie and Rachel Day. The following notice, which may be found in the *Gospel Visitor* during 1861-2-3, shows the plan and nature of the work:

EDUCATIONAL INSTITUTE.
NEW VIENNA, CLINTON CO., O.

This institution for young ladies and young men, situated on the Marietta & Cincinnati railroad, has been in successful operation for some time. Competent teachers are employed, and it will be the aim of these and all connected with the institution to merit a liberal share of patronage.

SESSIONS OF STUDY.

The year will be divided into three sessions of fourteen weeks each. The first session will commence on the first Monday of September.

TERMS.

Primary Department per session	$3.75
Secondary " "	5.00
Grammar " "	6.50
Higher " "	8.00

Boarding can be obtained at $2.25 per week, including room rent, fuel and lights.

For further information address the undersigned at the above place.

J. QUINTER, SUP'T.

After the close of the school at Vienna he returned to Columbiana, and in the fall of 1866 the office of the *Visitor* was removed to Covington, Miami county, Ohio. Of this removal he thus writes: "We have spread our tent and raised our altar among the brethren and friends in this vicinity. And we hope our residence among them, and our associations with them, may be both pleasant and useful to them and to us. This is our wish and our prayer. The change we have made was not made without much reflection and prayer. And when the time came for us to leave those with whom we had associated, and with whom we had worshiped as Christians, we felt the separation to be very painful. How true it is that we do not appreciate the strength of attachments until the chords that bind loving hearts together are sundered. But the future of Christians promises them a happy reunion where the pleasures of friendship, with all other pleasures, will be complete and lasting. We felt reluctant to leave the Mahoning Church, and shall not cease to feel an interest in its welfare and prosperity, and to pray that the great Head of the Church may bless it with His presence, and make it what every branch of the Church and every individual member of the Church should be, a blessing to the world."

"In coming to this place we met with a very kind and Christian reception, and think we shall feel much at home in this community. The town of Covington is pleasantly situated in the midst of a fertile and well-improved country, and possesses many advantages as a place of residence. There are several flourishing congregations of the Brethren in the neighborhood, and one in and around the town. The opportunities for attending public worship are very good."

The *Visitor* was published in Covington until May, 1869, when the office of publication was removed to Dayton, Ohio. The editorial office remained in Covington. In 1873 the editor purchased, from H. J. Kurtz, the publishing interest of the *Visitor*, and at the same time purchased of H. R. Holsinger *The Christian Family Companion*, a church weekly, published at Meyersdale, Somerset county, Pa. The two papers were united under the name *The Christian Family Companion and Gospel Visitor* and the weekly publication continued at Meyersdale. In January, 1876, the name was changed to *The Primitive Christian.* In October, 1876, this paper was united with *The Pilgrim,* also a weekly, published by H. B. and J. B. Brumbaugh at Huntingdon, Pa. A plan to unite the three church periodicals had been proposed in 1870, but as it did not seem to be expedient at the time the union was deferred.

The publication of the united papers under the name *The Primitive Christian and Pilgrim* was continued at Huntingdon by the firm of Quinter & Brumbaugh Bros.

Upon his removal to Huntingdon he thus writes :

"Trusting it has been the providence of God that has so directed events as to bring us here, we shall try to adapt ourselves to our new position and new associations, and hope in the promises of God wherein he has said : 'I am with thee in all places whither thou goest;' 'as thy days, so shall thy strength be;' 'and whatsoever he doeth shall prosper.'

"We find a little company of brethren and sisters here who are not only endeavoring to be faithful, but who seem to be laboring to grow in grace and in the knowledge of the truth. We trust this little church, the members of which frequently come together, in a room in our office prepared for the purpose, to do as the faithful of old did—to speak 'often one to another,' about the Lord and the 'things which concern salvation,' will form a nucleus around which many will be drawn, and from the body thus formed a Christian influence go out that may be widely felt.

"But while our thoughts are much engrossed with our pressing and numerous duties, and with our new surroundings and associations, we find our mind frequently reverting to the dear friends from whom we lately separated with much sorrow. It has been our lot to live in different localities, and in all these to form pleasant acquaintances and to add to our list of friends. And whenever circumstances called for a separation from those friends, the separation has been painful to our feelings. But never did we feel more sorrow at any such separation than when we left the friends of Meyersdale. When the time came for leaving them we felt much worse than we had anticipated. While our connection with the large congregation of the Elk Lick brethren was marked apparently by a reciprocal feeling of kindness between them and ourselves, there was a number of the members of the congregation that lived in and about the town, with whom we often met at our Sunday night meetings, and in the Bible class and in the Sabbath-school, and on other occasions, between whom and ourselves a very tender and warm feeling of brotherly love existed. These dear friends were much grieved and were very reluctant to see us go when the time for leaving came. And their sorrow increased ours, and we confess our separation was to us a cause of much tender grief. The little social gathering in Brother Beachly's parlor the night before we left, and the gathering at the depot of many Christian friends to show their Christian love and to bid us the affectionate farewell, are scenes so fresh in our memory that a reference to them starts the tears from the tender feelings that come over us when we think of those occasions characterized by so much love and tenderness. But such tears are not altogether tears of sorrow. There is joy mixed with them. They show the presence of love and union. Oh, we do not know how much we love one another until by death or removal we are called upon to separate!

"'Hail, sweetest, dearest tie, that binds
Our glowing hearts in one;
Hail, sacred hope, that tunes our minds
To harmony divine.'

"We cherish a kind regard for the brethren and sisters and friends of Meyersdale, and must now regret in being separated from them, that our sojourn among them was not more to their profit, and that we did not labor more diligently and faithfully to do them good. And though circumstances seem to require us to leave them, we hope the Lord will be with them, and richly supply the ministering brethreu with the gifts of the Holy Ghost, that they may feed the flock, and nurse the lambs, and so preach and labor that they may both save themselves and them that hear them. Oh! let us all so live, that we may enjoy the sweet hope of a blessed reunion of all we have loved in Christ, and worshiped with on earth."

In June, 1883, *The Primitive Christian* was consolidated with *The Brethren at Work*, and, as *The Gospel Messenger*, continued to be published by The Brethren's Publishing Company, at Mt. Morris, Ill., and at Huntingdon, Pa. On this paper as on the *Primitive Christian* Brother Quinter held the position of Editor-in-Chief.

The Normal school which had been opened by Brother J. M. Zuck in the Pilgrim building was a strong inducement to Brother Quinter to make his home in Huntingdon. His interest in educational work had grown stronger and he rejoiced to find an educational project again under way among the Brethren and was ready to lend all his influence in its favor. Though the Normal had a small beginning, yet the fervent prayers and earnest zeal of the brave, true hearts interested in her welfare soon had their reward in her growth and prosperity. Opened at first in a room in the Pilgrim building, larger quarters were soon demanded and a house was rented. This also proved too small and an effort was made to secure funds to erect a suitable building. This resulted in 1878 in the erection of a building pleasantly situated on an elevation overlooking the borough of Huntingdon and the surrounding country. The school was chartered the same year under the name of The Brethren's Normal College. The new building was first occupied in April, 1879. Shortly after the school had been so pleasantly opened in its new home, the death of its founder and honored principal, in May, 1879, cast a gloom over its bright prospects. The work was not suffered to decline, however, and at a meeting of the trustees, in June, Brother J. H. Brumbaugh was elected Principal. At the same time Brother Quinter was elected President, which position he held until his death. His interest in the work was deep and in all his associations with the school his influence was a power for good. To see the students ready to follow the Master and accept His teachings as the guide of their lives was to him a cause of deepest joy—for then he felt that the work of the school had accomplished its highest purpose. In his disposition, ever kind and gentle, he was particularly so with the "lambs of the flock." He was patient, forgiving, ready to teach and to lead them in the way of life.

He held a number of debates upon the doctrines of the Church. Although he did not greatly enjoy this work, yet when urged to defend the truth as he believed it to be taught in the Gospel, he was always ready to do so. He had made a careful and thorough study of all the phases of Christian doctrine, and once having settled his convictions no man held them more firmly or was more ready to give a reason for the hope that was in him.

Of a discussion held in Somerset county, Pa., the only account to be found is the following, written in November, 1881, on the occasion of a visit to the Summit congregation : "To some of us this large meeting-house possessed an interest as being the place in which we held a debate about twenty-five years ago with a Mr. Knepper, a minister of the German Reformed Church. We had made an agreement together to discuss the action, and the proper subjects of Christian baptism. We discussed the first proposition pretty thoroughly, but when that was finished Mr. Knepper declined to take up the second. The debate passed off pleasantly, and apparently to the advantage of the brethren who called us to the discussion with Mr. Knepper."

In September, 1866, he held a discussion with a minister of the Disciple Church, Elder Wilkes, in Macoupin county, Ill. In this discussion the following propositions were affirmed by Brother Quinter:

I. The Holy Scriptures teach that trine immersion is valid baptism.

II. Feet-washing is a church ordinance.

III. The Salutation of the Holy Kiss is a church ordinance.

On the 7th and 8th of August, 1867, he held a discussion in Elkhart county, Indiana, with a minister of the Lutheran Church, Rev. Hugh Wells. In this discussion the following proposition was affirmed by Mr. Wells, and denied by Brother Quinter: *Christian baptism may be performed by sprinkling or pouring.*

On the 21st and 22d of the same month he held another discussion in Carroll county, Indiana, with a Lutheran minister also, Rev. P. S. Snyder. The following proposition was affirmed by Brother Quinter: *Is immersion the mode of Christian baptism authorized and approved by the Bible?* This discussion was published in book-form in 1868, by a joint committee from the Churches represented.

In October, 1867, a discussion was held in Linn county, Iowa, with Rev. McConnell, a Disciple minister. The following propositions were discussed:

I. Trine immersion is essential to Christian baptism. Affirmed by Brother Quinter, denied by Rev. McConnell.

II. The Bread and Wine commanded to be taken by the disciples of Christ, in remembrance of Him, are the Lord's Supper. Affirmed by Rev. McConnell; denied by Brother Quinter.

III. The Washing of Feet is an ordinance established

by Jesus Christ, and by Him commanded to be observed by all the saints, in the public assembly of His Church, until His coming. Affirmed by Brother Quinter, denied by Rev. McConnell. This discussion was also published in bookform in 1868, by a joint committee from the Churches represented.

In June, 1868, he held a discussion with a minister of the Disciple Church, in Cumberland county, Pa. In this discussion these propositions were affirmed by Brother Quinter and denied by Rev. I. C. Mitchell:

I. Trine Immersion is neccessary to carry out the great Commission.

II. The Washing of Feet is an ordinance commanded by Christ to be publicly observed until He comes.

In September, 1869, he held a discussion in Miami county, Ohio, with Elder McKinney, of the Christian Church, upon the subject of Freemasonry. This proposition was affirmed by Brother Quinter: *The Principles of Freemasonry are Inconsistent with the Principles of Christian Truth.*

He entered upon this work only at the urgent and repeated calls of his brethren; but, having once undertaken to defend the doctrines and principles he professed, he proved conclusively that sound scriptural truth formed the basis of these doctrines.

In 1867 he completed his compilation of a hymn book for the church. To this work he brought all the strength of his devotional nature, and it is a constant memento of his deep religious feeling.

His own preface is the best description of the work:

" Singing the praises of God may justly be regarded as an important part of the worship we offer to him, and it was enjoined by divine authority upon both Jews and Christians. The relation that the Hymn Book stands in to singing in the Church, is such, that gives it a place next in importance to the Bible, among Christians. And as the Hymn Book is an important auxiliary in promoting Christian worship and edification, the propriety of having one scriptural in its character, convenient in its arrangement, and varied and full in the hymns it contains, will be apparent to all. It has been the object of the compiler to make such a book. How far he has succeeded, those who make themselves acquainted with it, can best judge.

There has existed an impression among us for years, that our Hymn Book should be revised and improved; and this impression has grown with the growth of the Brotherhood. To meet the want of the Church in this respect, the annual meeting held in Tennessee, in 1861, appointed a committee to compile a new Hymn Book. That committee consisted of the following brethren: James Quinter, of Ohio; Samuel Garver, of Illinois; John Metzger, of Indiana; John Kline, of Virginia, and John H. Umstad, of Pennsylvania. But the members of the committee, living so far from each other, found it very inconvenient to co-operate together to accomplish the work committed to them, and confided it to the undersigned. We felt the responsibility great when we commenced the work, but had we anticipated that responsibility as we afterward felt it, and the difficulties attending the undertaking, we would have declined it, could it have been done in accordance with a sense of duty. It has given us a considerable amount of perplexing labor. But the thought that in our humble labors we were serving the Church, and through it the glorious Head of the Church, our Heavenly Master mingled some pleasure with our anxiety. The compiler regrets that remoteness of residence did not permit the other members of the committee to render more assistance in the important work, thinking that could their experience and judgment have been brought to bear upon it, greater satisfaction might have been given to the Brotherhood. But he assures his brethren that he has spared no labor, or pains, or expense that his circumstances made available, to compile a Hymn Book that in his humble judgment would best meet the wants of the Church. In collecting materials for the work, his library of works on Hymnology grew to nearly one hundred volumes. The most of these afforded some hymns. The books, however, hitherto in use among the brethren, have formed the basis of the new book, and a large proportion of the hymns in those books has been retained. The compiler is aware that upon the idea as to the number of hymns a Hymn Book should contain, a difference of opinion obtains. Some, in looking at a Hymn Book, as being designed especially for public worship, and finding that the number of hymns used on occasions of that kind is somewhat limited, think a large number of hymns is objectionable. *But when it is remembered that the Bible and Hymn Book constitute the library of some Christians; that the latter is the only book of sacred poetry they possess; that it is not only used as a book to sing from, but is also read and studied with pleasure and profit, the propriety of having some hymns beside those that are popular in the congregation, will be acknowledged. Some Christians who sing but little, and indeed some, who sing none at all, enjoy themselves very much in reading their Hymn Book, and regard it as an excellent companion in retirement.* Hymns are lyrical discourses generally addressed to the feelings; and though usually used to EXPRESS feelings, they may also PRODUCE them, and this may be done by reading them as well as by singing them, though not in the same degree. The Hymn Book now offered to the Brotherhood is in size, a medium between the two prevailing extremes.

Had the compiler consulted his own taste alone, there would have been hymns inserted which have been omitted, and some omitted which have been inserted. He has tried to keep before his mind the consideration that he was compiling a Hymn Book for the use of the Brotherhood and not for a few individuals only.

The doctrinal character of the hymns has not been disregarded, and it is hoped that nothing will be found in the book that will materially conflict with the teachings of the Gospel.

In the arrangement of the hymns, those of the same general character are brought together. This is more natural and more convenient than the arrangement that is founded upon the letters of the alphabet with which they commence. And a proper acquaintance with the arrangement adopted, and the help of the Alphabetical Index of Subjects, any one wishing to select a hymn adapted to any occasion, can readily do so. The Scriptural Index will also be found useful in selecting hymns.

The compiler thankfully acknowledges the suggestions, counsel, and selections with which he has been favored by the brethren, and though, as he is well aware, his work is not perfect, he hopes it will give general satisfaction to the Brotherhood. As the result of much anxious and prayerful labor, it now goes to the churches with his prayer to God that he may bless it, and make it minister to the promotion of the spirit of Christian devotion in all the departments of worship, and thereby exert a holy influence upon the churches, and through them upon the world, and thus contribute in some degree to advance the cause and kingdom of Christ. JAMES QUINTER.

COVINGTON, Miami Co., O., March 28, 1867."

In 1886 he published his work on *Trine Immersion*. This work is a careful compilation of all the evidence—both Sreiptural and historical—in favor of what he believed to be the only Gospel baptism. He was early in his life impressed with the necessity for a work of the kind and during the first years of his ministry he began to collect material for it and to make it a subject of special study and investigation. When asked how long he had been preparing for and writing his work, he replied: ".My lifetime."

He was ordained to the eldership in the summer of 1856, in the Mahoning Church, Ohio, by Elds. Henry Kurtz and Joseph Showalter. His manifest wisdom and prudent disposition, his strong affection for the Church and his deep concern for her welfare soon brought him into prominence among the leaders in the Church councils. Eld. H. B. Brumbaugh has given the following: "In the annual conferences of the Church he always felt a deep interest, and generally took an active part in all its deliberations. When he felt it his duty to take a position he did it with great zeal and positiveness; but, if the final decision was made against his views, he submitted with Christian meekness, feeling that he had done his duty in advocating that which his own conscience dictated as being right. A submissive spirit was one of the remarkable traits of his character."

"In these meetings, he, at different times, filled all the prominent positions and was for many years the writing clerk of both the standing committee and the conference sessions."

"On committees he had more calls than any other elder in the Church. To this work he seemed to be especially adapted, and when it was possible to do so, he seldom failed to have difficulties satisfactorily adjusted. His appeals to the erring members were so strong and imbued with so much Christian tenderness that few could withstand them. Though he was unyielding in his convictions of right, his sympathies were so easily touched, that, if err he did, it was always on the side of mercy. No man ever felt more deeply than he that, 'To err is human; to forgive, divine.'"

Upon the death of his mother in 1881, he thus writes:

"We received a telegram informing us of the illness of our mother. We hastened to her home in Mount Union, Ohio; but she died before we reached it. She died on the evening of the seventh of November. Her death was caused by no particular disease. Her constitution broke down under the infirmities of age. There was no written record of her age, but, according to her own statement, confirmed by several circumstantial testimonies, she was, at the time of her death, in her ninety-eighth year."

"She possessed a remarkably good constitution, was never much afflicted, and remained very active until about two years before her death, when she got a fall from which she never afterward recovered. She retained her senses and her mental faculties to the last. She was a member of our fraternity for nearly fifty years. She connected herself with the Church soon after we did. And she was a widow over fifty years. She was a kind and loving mother to her children. And among the many blessings we feel we are indebted to her for, under God, is a good constitution. Living to the age she did, she experienced a considerable share of the troubles of life. But her religion sustained her, and afforded her much comfort. The evidences she has left us of her faithfulness to God afford us much comfort. One of the earliest things we remember of our dear mother is that of seeing her on her knees at prayer. This was before either she or we made a profession of religion. And, though we preceded her in making the good confession, her prayers may have helped in bringing us to the Lord. As her end approached, and her infirmities multiplied, she became anxious to depart and expressed herself happy in the prospect of death."

"The religious services were performed by Brother J. A. Clement, assisted by Brother L. Glass, of the Georgetown congregation. She was buried in the Brethren's graveyard, at Freeburg."

"Our sister performed her part faithfully in taking care of mother, and, having been so long with her, and under many trying circumstances, the attachment to each other was unusually strong, and the separation was very sorrowful to sister."

"How full of comfort is the thought that, though a separation must take place, that separation is only for a time, and that Christian friends will meet again, and meet too, where their affections will be forever united, and where death and adversity will afflict them no more nor disturb their heavenly felicity. Such was our comfort when we looked for the last time upon our aged and Christian mother, and we thank God for such a never-failing source of comfort. We felt our blessed Christianity to be more precious than ever in the hour of affliction."

On the death of Brother Thomas Major, in April, 1888, he thus writes: "Brother Major and ourself entered the ministry about the same time, and we were together considerably in the early years of our ministry. A warm, brotherly feeling existed between us from our first acquaintance as Christian brethren. When we moved to New Vienna, Ohio, and started our school there, we were in the Fall Creek Church with him and our associations there were very pleasant, after a separation from one another for some years. . . . . In the death of Brother Major, there is another of our aged brethren taken from us. This class of brethren is passing away and there is a sadness felt by us when they leave us. But there is comfort, too, connected with the idea of their departure. 'They rest from their labors.' They meet one another beyond the river on the celestial shore. Blessed spirits! your brethren in the flesh are coming to join your happy band." How soon were these words fulfilled in his own life!

His educational interest grew out of his deep concern for

the welfare of the Church and his desire to see the youth of the Church, the ardent defenders of pure Gospel Christianity. His editorial work was accepted as affording him broader opportunities for Christian usefulness. But his deepest interest was reserved for his public ministry. He felt that this was his life-work and he loved it. He remarked at one time toward the close of his life that he did not enjoy a Sabbath spent without preaching, as he did not feel that he had fulfilled his work. Rarely, if ever, was a Sabbath so spent. In his preaching he was instructive and impressive. He was a man of intense convictions and what he strongly felt he expressed forcibly. Although he was a man of strong sympathies and deep emotional feeling, yet, the chief power in his preaching was in his Scriptural reasoning. His sermons were addressed to the intelligence. Conversion to him meant more than a change of feeling—it was a change of mind and judgment followed by a change of life and conduct. He was careful and thorough in the preparation of his sermons, and, though at times he used notes, he generally preached without them. His sermons were thoroughly systematized and elaborated. He was a life-long student and the Book of books was the subject of his most earnest study.

As all his writings gave evidence of careful study and reflection, his opinion and advice on questions of Church doctrine and Scriptural exposition were often sought. His replies to these requests formed a considerable portion of his editorial work. As a writer he was characterized as "mild, gentle and instructive." All his writings breathe the spirit of pure Christian love. His letters were precious messages from a heart filled with tenderest affection and deepest sympathy.

He had collected a library of about 1,300 volumes, consisting almost entirely of theological works. In his boyhood he conceived the desire to possess a library, and he has said that many times he deprived himself of a meal to save a few pennies to purchase a coveted volume. His early call to the ministry led to his selection of his library. His books were collected for personal use and study and are all works of interest. Except when his ministry called him elsewhere, he spent his time among his books in study and meditation. Here he did his writing, and here he prepared his sermons. His highest enjoyment was found in the hours so spent. The result of his thought and study, whether it developed new truths or emphasized principles, was always utilized in his writings or his ministry. His work was all directed to the help of his fellow-men, and he never spared himself to promote the cause for which he so earnestly labored. He spent much time during his ministry traveling and preaching among the churches. He gave his labor willingly and freely to the cause he loved so well, and fully realized in his life the truth of the promise, "They that seek the Lord shall not want any good thing." He never took a tour for pleasure; his traveling was for the good of the Church. There are few churches in the Brotherhood that have not been strengthened and helped by his influence. He loved the Church, and earnestly desired that peace, brotherly love and charity should be her strong characteristics. His love of peace was a marked element of his character, and nothing gave him deeper grief than to see the love and union which should exist in the Church broken by differences and dissensions. These words from one of his editorials may be said to embody the spirit of his life: "Let us cultivate brotherly kindness and charity, and labor in harmony to promote the glory of the Lord, the peace and edification of the Church, and the spiritual improvement of the world."

His life was eminently a prayerful life. His habits of prayer and devotion formed a very important part of his daily life. Each day was opened with a season of private devotion at his bedside, followed by Bible-reading and prayer with his family; he also closed the day with prayer at his bedside. His prayers with his family have left a hallowed memory. Beside these fixed times he spent many hours in meditation and silent communion. In a letter to Brother C. H. Balsbaugh he expressed himself as being in more profound sympathy with the absolute ideal of Christian character than he had the power to express.

He was a strong advocate of the cause of abolition in the days when zeal in that cause was often the price of sad experiences. He was also an earnest advocate of temperance, both in theory and practice. His habits of life were exceedingly simple, and he generally enjoyed remarkably good health.

He was deeply interested in the mission work of the Church, and for a number of years was Treasurer of the General Mission Board.

As a man he was modest and retiring in disposition, rather reserved, yet universally kind and courteous in his manner. His gentle, courteous manner won for him the respect and esteem of all that knew him. No one could come in contact with him without feeling the influence of his pure Christian character, and receiving higher views of life. His humility, his sincerity, and the purity of his life drew to him the love and esteem of all. " A well-known doctor of Huntingdon once said: ' Elder Quinter of the Brethren Church is the purest man I ever saw. His very presence is an inspiration.' "

In all the churches where he lived and labored, the personal attachment between himself and his people was a strong bond of sympathy, whose severing was always painful. Yet it was always evident that the changes of his life were not made for personal gain but for the good of the Church.

During the fifty years of his ministry he rarely, if ever, missed the annual Conference of the Church. He was always more prayerful and thoughtful during his preparation for this work. He felt so strongly the great responsibility resting upon those who directed the work. He made his customary preparation to attend the Conference of 1888, at North Manchester, Ind., and intended to leave home on Thursday, May 17th, but on Wednesday morning he rose very unwell. However, nothing serious seemed to be threatened, and as he had in a great measure recovered on Thursday, he decided to go on Friday. As he left home on Friday morning it was with the hope that he might return benefited from his journey. The following account is quoted from Brother D. L. Millers' editorial in the *Gospel Messenger.*

"We come now in our notes to describe a scene of peculiar and touching sadness, one that time will not soon efface from our memory; an occurence that has cast a deep gloom and heart-felt sorrow over the entire meeting. We refer to the death of our dear aged brother, Elder James Quinter. He reached the meeting-grounds about noon on Saturday, and greeted a number of those he loved so well, for all who knew him loved him, and this general feeling of love and respect shown him was fully reciprocated in his great sympathetic heart. He expressed himself as not feeling so well, and it was generally observed that he did not seem as strong as usual. In his last conversation with us he said he was glad to meet the Brethren in Annual Conference once more."

"At 3 P. M. Brother Daniel Vaniman preached in the Tabernacle, and Brother Quinter left the *Messenger* office, saying he would go and hear the sermon. It was to be the last he would hear in this world. He closed the meeting, using the 810th hymn, which he read in a most feeling and touching manner. After singing the hymn he spoke a few fitting words upon the sermon to which he had just listened, and then kneeling in prayer he thanked God that he was once more permitted to meet with those of like precious faith. It was noticed by those near him that his voice trembled, but the words were clear and coherent, and as he said, "We are glad to meet again," his voice ceased, never more to be heard is this world. Those who were kneeling by his side noticed that he grew very pale. Saving arms held him from falling to the floor, and he was tenderly and gently raised from his knees and laid on the table. He gasped a few times, and then, surrounded by a weeping congregation, his spirit took its homeward flight. And so passed away one of our great and good men, not great as the world counts greatness, but great in all the noble qualities of true Christian manhood. He was a man of strong mental power, an eloquent preacher, full of love and zeal for the cause of the Master. His courteous manner, his marked piety, his honesty and integrity of purpose, his great love for the Church, of which he was an honored member, gained for him the love and reverence of all who came to know him. He filled a place in the hearts of our people second to no one in our Brotherhood. His life was full of labor for the Church of his choice, and his name will long be held in sacred memory by his co-laborers and by a great Brotherhood of loving hearts."

"The manner of his death was a fitting close to a long life spent in labor for the good of humanity and for the Church he loved so well. He came up to the Conference, as he had done so many times before, to labor for the Church, and was to have preached in the Tabernacle on Sunday morning. Kneeling with the great congregation in prayer, surrounded by his co-laborers and those he loved as brethren and sisters in Christ, amid the tears and heart-felt grief of those who loved and reverenced him as a father in Israel, his pure spirit took its flight to the Land of Rest. " We are glad to meet again," were his last words, and as he uttered them his voice was hushed in death. Were these words spoken of us, or were they spoken to those on the other shore who were watching and waiting for the coming of our dear brother? God only knows. As death came to him on his knees in earnest prayer, with his face turned Zionward, he may have had a glimpse of the host beyond the river, and his last words on earth may have been his first greeting on the other shore."

" After it was known that Brother Quinter was dead, the Standing Committee adjourned its session and proceeded in a body to the Tabernacle, where his body was lying. Brother Enoch Eby made a few appropriate and touching remarks to the weeping congregation. A prayer was then offered and the remains were taken away and prepared to be taken to his former home in Huntingdon, Pa."

"For some years we have been very closely connected in our work. In all his advice and counsel to us his chief concern was for the good of the Church. In our private correspondence this one feature marked all his letters, showing how near to his heart was the prosperity of the Church. In our last conversation, an hour before his death, he expressed an earnest desire that the best interest of the cause might be promoted at this meeting. His life has been a blessing to the Church and a benediction to humanity. May we who are left behind labor, as did our dear brother, for the cause for which he fell with his armor on."

Such was a life whose energies were consecrated to a holy work, whose years were filled with arduous toil. Truly he lived in the spirit of these words taken from one of his letters : "We enjoy rest the more if our work has been arduous, and we have become weary in performing it. Where there is no labor and life is all rest, or rather idleness, there is no real rest. And so it is in regard to our Christian work. If there is no true Christian work there can be no true Christian labor. And the more we labor, and the more weary we become with the work we are engaged in, and with the cares and perplexities of life, the more sweet and enjoyable will our heavenly rest be. Our reward in the coming age will not only be according to our works but also to some degree to the suffering we shall have endured in performing our work." Thus has ended his life; but, though dead, "he yet speaketh," and the memory of his holy life is a sacred inheritance to all who shall come after him.

"His work in the Church militant has ceased and his work in the Church triumphant begun. He was not for God took him."

"Like the morning star's, his spirit's course was steadily upward, still glowing with its own peculiar effulgence, till lost in the glories of the opening day. In the fullness of his activities, with body, mind and heart all occupied in the Lord's work, without protracted sickness, feebleness, or suffering, he laid him down to die. The Master said: 'It is enough' and he passed at once from labor to recompense."

"God's finger touched him and he slept," yet around this sleep shines as a halo the brightest star in Christianity's diadem—the hope of the resurrection and the joys of the hereafter.

MEMORIAL SKETCHES.

OUR LOSS.

There are losses that we can feel, but can not describe. Such is the character of the loss which we have sustained in the sudden and unexpected death of our much esteemed elder, James Quinter. Our knowledge of him as a man, our association with him in business, and especially our relation with him in the Church, demands from us a tribute which we do not have words to express.

Of Brother Quinter's moral and religious character we have had some knowledge for a number of years, and it was on account of the very favorable opinion we formed of him that led to our business relations with him. While we, as publishers of Church literature, were endeavoring to labor for the promotion of the cause that was always dear to us, we felt that an association with him would add greatly to our possibilities for accomplishing good; and to this end we strongly favored the consolidation of our papers, as we were then publishing them, the *Pilgrim* and the *Primitive Christian*. This consolidation was affected in the fall of 1876, and on October 31st of the same year he, with his family, moved to this place.

At the time he came among us we had already succeeded in gathering a small band of members, and had prepared a chapel for worship in a room on the first floor of the building in which the *Pilgrim* had been printed, and in which the consolidated paper continued to be printed. The Normal School, founded by Brother J. M. Zook and some friends of education, was also commenced in this same building and rooms, in the spring prior to his coming in the fall. This we name because we feel that it had something to do in his making this place his home, as he always was a friend of education, and was interested in having schools founded where the brethren's children might be educated without being surrounded with influences antagonistic to the humble principles of the Truth and the Church.

To both the Church and the school his being with us proved a great blessing, as he was, in many ways, a father to both, and by each the loss is equally felt. In almost the beginning of the school he was elected president, and though he was not directly connected with it as a member of the faculty, yet the influence he exerted over it was a power for good. This influence was given in his presence at the morning religious exercises, in the joint meetings of the faculty and trustees, in trustee meetings, the prayer meetings, and in his public ministrations from the rostrum. Indeed, wherever and whenever he came in contact with either teachers or students, he was a living model of uprightness and Christian propriety, and there are hundreds to-day who will gladly stand up and testify that their lives have been made better to the extent of their association with this goodly man. It was impossible for any one to be under his influence without receiving higher views of life. His words of counsel were always given in a most kind spirit, and seldom failed to impress the person addressed that they were unselfish and intended for their good. Although firm in his convictions of right, he was a Christ in his readiness to forgive on the least appearance of repentance on the part of the offender, no matter how grave the offense. As a disciplinarian, he was tender and forgiving, almost to a fault, and it could be truly said of him: The mistakes he made in such cases were always on the side of mercy.

In the Church he was a father, and, we are sorry to say, in some cases to ungrateful and unappreciative children. How earnest was the preaching, how tender the exhortations and how pathetic were the appeals that he made to his children in Christ! Often were we made to weep under them and wonder how hearts less hard than flint could remain untouched. Although he was a man having sympathies easily touched, and of deep emotional feeling, yet he was not considered an emotional preacher. His power was in sound scriptural reasoning. He reached men and women through their intelligence rather than through their emotional feelings; and conversion, under his preaching, meant more than a simple change of feeling,—it was a change of mind, a change of judgment, to be followed by a change of life and actions. Anything short of this, he could not recognize as true conversion. There are but few Churches in the Brotherhood, throughout the United States, but what have some in their communion whose souls have been thrilled by his eloquence and zeal in preaching the unsearchable riches of Christ. In a letter before me, a brother says: "To Brother Quinter I owe much, if not all, the inspiration which prompted me to leave the service of sin and unite with the people of God. He will never be forgotten by me; for, though I am but a weak vessel in God's service, yet I know that I was benefited by taking the steps he urged me to take." Had hundreds of others the opportunity, they would say the same thing. Surely he will come up to the throne rejoicing, bringing his sheaves with him.

We will miss him not only on the chapel rostrum, but in our prayer meetings and church councils there will be a vacant seat and an ever-welcome voice unheard. To ourself and Brother Swigart he was a strong post against whom we leaned with great assurance. He was a bishop, indeed, who loved his co-laborers and his flock as only a truly regenerated and Christian heart could love. He ruled as a loving father, and expected in return the respect and regard that should be given by loving children, and we believe that there was not a single member in the Church that did not entertain for him the highest esteem and respect.

During his residence of twelve years with us, our associations as ministers were most pleasant. Indeed, they could not well have been otherwise, as, with his greatness as a Christian and a minister, he was as meek and as humble as a child. With him it was, "Not my will, but thine be done." Though deserving of the highest positions and first preferments, he was always willing to take the lowest. We do not say this in a spirit of flattery, or as a dead eulogy, because we always said the same thing of him while he was yet living, and we said it because we felt that he was worthy of all the esteem and respect that we were able to give him. And to-day we feel that we have sustained a loss such as we never felt before.

Though he had passed his three-score years and ten, little did we realize that our bereavement was so near at hand. On Wednesday before his death he was unwell, and when we went to see him about going to Annual Meeting he was undecided, so much that he instructed Brother Swigart, without my knowledge of it, to have me, on Wednesday evening, appointed as an alternate delegate, should he not go. He, however, got considerably better by Thursday morning, and when we called at his house before starting he said that he would start on Friday morning, if his health continued to improve. And it was with feelings of more than ordinary joy that we saw him coming towards our office on the Annual Meeting-grounds on Saturday noon. And there were many others that were, no doubt, as glad to see him as we were. As he walked towards the office through the grounds we heard, in every direction, brethren and sisters say, "There comes Brother Quinter." Yes, he was known and loved by all. But had all these loving brethren and sisters known that in only a few short hours Brother Quinter would take his final leave and go over to the other side, how different would have been the meetings and greetings! He seemed to be especially anxious to attend 2 o'clock P. M. services. He said: "Brother Vaniman will preach and I want to hear him." As our office was near enough to the tent to enable us to hear the preaching, we remained there during the services until a message was sent us that Brother Quinter had fainted. We at once went to his side, only to see life ebbing out,—twice he gasped for breath, and he ceased to live.

The scene of his death, there in the midst of the loved and the loving, we shall not attempt to describe. It was sad—so sad, and yet glorious—so glorious! It was a death so near not being a death, that it seemed befitting to say, "Brother Quinter is not dead—God has taken him."

The scene of his death we shall never forget. It was a congregation of weepers. And many a weeping Mary pressed forward to lay her hands tenderly on his face and say, "How blessed such a death! How glad I would be thus to die!" It was a blessed death—yes, it was. Thus to fall asleep in Jesus was an honor that the Lord was pleased to confer upon his servant, our Brother Quinter, and to the decree let all bleeding hearts say, Amen.

Preparations for the removing of the lifeless body to his home were now to be made, and the sad duty fell to our lot, self and brother. He died at 4 o'clock, and by 9 o'clock we had the body removed to the undertaker, carefully examined, placed in a metallic coffin, and put on the cars, ready to start for home. All this we could not have done had not duty impelled us, and the sadness of the work did not come to us until we were on our way homeward. How great the change! We went to the meeting with light hearts, rejoicing; we returned weeping, bearing with us the tenantless body of the one whom we had learned to so dearly love as a friend and Christian father.

Our homeward journey was such an one as we never

before experienced, and if it is the good Lord's will, we wish never to repeat. The scene that transpired on our arrival we shall sacredly cover over with the mantle of love and sympathy. It was a case for angels to look into, and for the husband of widows to temper. While there was deep grief there was also heart-felt sympathy and helping hands to administer, as the needs of the bereaved and stricken family required.

Preparations for the funeral were made for Wednesday at 2:30 P. M. It was the urgent request of the family that we, self and Brother Swigart, should lead in the services,— not because they felt that we could do it better than our surrounding ministering brethren, but because of our intimate and pleasant associations with the deceased, and the family, believing that we, on this account, could more fully enter into their feelings of loss and bereavement, and give the sympathy and comfort so much needed. Both of us felt much more like taking our seats with the mourners, and would gladly have done so had not duty directed otherwise. Our hearts were greatly comforted to see the large number of our ministering brethren and others, who came to mourn and weep with us in our time of bereavement and great loss. The funeral was very largely attended, and some seventeen ministers present, the larger part of whom took some part in the exercises.

H. B. BRUMBAUGH.

Huntingdon, Pa., June 5, 1888.

FUNERAL SERVICES OF ELDER JAMES QUINTER

Who Died in the Annual Meeting Tent at North Manchester,
Indiana, While on his Knees in Prayer, on the 19th of
May, 1888, and was Buried from his Home in
Huntingdon, Pa., on the 23rd.

At the request of the friends of the deceased and on account of the relation he sustained to this paper and the publishers, we here give a somewhat lengthy account of the funeral, with the sermons preached, as nearly as they could be reproduced, hoping that they will be read with pleasure and remembered with profit.

FUNERAL SERVICES.

The first services were held at 2 o'clock P. M., in the home of the deceased. Part of the 5th chapter of Second Corinthians was read by Eld. J. Z. Replogle; prayer by Eld. James R. Lane.

From here the body was taken to the Norman Chapel, where the services were opened by Eld. J. E. Garber reading the 598th hymn:

> "Asleep in Jesus! blessed sleep
> From which none ever wake to weep."

Presiding Elder M. K. Foster, of the M. E. Church, read the 90th Psalm; prayer by Eld. J. W. Wilt.

The following sermon was then preached by H. B. Brumbaugh:

HOPE THROUGH THE RESURRECTION.

"For if we believe that Jesus died and rose again, even so them also which sleep in Jesus will God bring with him."—Thess. 4 : 14.

Paul, with his co-laborers, Silvanus and Timotheus, it is thought, had labored in the Gospel for a considerable time in the city of Thessalonica, and their labors were attended with encouraging success, so that a large Church was established.

After having thus established and organized the Church they went to other fields of labor.

During their absence the newly established Church not only met with persecution, but several of the chief men among them were removed by death. Paul, hearing of their affliction, and wishing to show his sympathy for them and afford them such comfort as he could give, wrote them several letters. Part of the second of these letters we have read and use as a text on the present sad and impressive occasion.

Death has always had its terrors, yet surrounding circumstances may greatly modify our feelings in regard to it. To throw around it these modifying circumstances was the object of Paul in writing his letters to the brethren. And to present it in its most comforting and consoling light, he compares it to a sleep, "Them which sleep in Jesus." The figure is frequently used in the Scriptures. The martyr Stephen, after having prayed for his persecutors and committed himself to God in whom he trusted, it is said, "fell asleep." The Master, speaking of the death of Lazarus, says, "He is sleeping, but I go that I may awake him out of sleep." Ever since then the mission of Christ has been to awaken out of sleep—to awaken sinners out of the sleep of sin, and after awhile to awaken us all out of the sleep of death.

Paul speaks of death as a short slumber of the body,— the body to sleep in the dust, while the spirit returns to the paradise of God, there to await the resurrection of the body— when the trumpet shall sound and the body shall come forth, not in the habiliments of mortality and corruption, but to be fashioned after the glorious body of Christ. He has crowned his whole letter by the beautiful and inspired utterance that has been said in the midst of the weeping, and in tears, so often in the house of the bereaved and the mourning ones: "For if we *believe* that Jesus died and rose again, even so them also which sleep in Jesus will God bring with him."

This morning, as the daughter stood viewing the body of her dear, departed father, she said: "It seems to me papa is not dead, that he is only sleeping; after while he will get awake." How true were the words! and beautifully are demonstrated the truths of our text in the death of Father Quinter. He fell asleep. His body, as we see it lying before us, is only sleeping—awaiting the sound of the trump, when he will awaken and God will bring him with him. Asleep in Jesus! Oh, how comforting the words! No other three words are so often seen in our cemeteries and on the tombstones of our departed ones.

Death is only a temporary suspension of bodily activities. The body falls asleep and the door of mortal vision is closed and the spirit ceases to live in the earthly tabernacle—it awaits for the redemption of the body, when it shall come forth in its immortal and glorified form. Paul was filled with this great truth when he said he was willing to be absent from the body that he might be present with the Lord. The body had become aged and decrepit. In it he had fought a good fight. On it were the marks of the stripes and scars which he had received in the contests, and he was now willing that it should be laid away, to sleep, that it might rest and in God's own time be reinvigorated and brought forth to a reunion with the spirit for an enjoyment of an eternal life. "For they that sleep in Jesus will God bring with him."

In contemplating the death of our loved ones, there is no truth that falls so consolingly upon our hearts as the resurrection. In this truth our yearning hearts want to be established—want to be satisfied. Believe this and death has lost its sting, and the grave its victory. And if we believe that Jesus died and rose again, we have the hope, the comforting hope, that reaches beyond the grave—"Them which sleep in Jesus will God bring with him." In this life of labor, of trials, disappointments, afflictions and deaths, we need comfort and encouragement; something to enable us to endure and remain faithful until death. The Scriptures are filled with these divine assurances, and Paul concludes the chapter with these very encouraging words: "Wherefore comfort one another with these words." There is nothing else that can afford so much comfort to you who have been bereft of a husband—of a father. Only a few years at the longest, and the ties that through death have been riven will be again united, not again to be severed by the relentless hand of death, but a union that will be continued forever in the paradise of God. Then be comforted in this blessed hope, and try to feel that what the Lord hath done is well done.

A few words in regard to the deceased. Our acquaintance with Brother Quinter has been for a considerable length of time, but our more intimate relations date from the time of his coming among us. Early in his youthful days he gave his heart to God, and from that time forward he lived a most exemplary life. At the age of twenty-two he was elected to the ministry, since then he has been an able and faithful defender of the Truth and always loyal to the Church of his choice. Our business relations together have been most agreeable and satisfactory, and in the Church he has not only been a brother, an elder, but he has been a father to us all, and we are glad to say that his humble and exemplary life has done more towards building us up and establishing us in the faith than any other living man. He was great in goodness and a child in humbleness, and we yet fail to realize the loss that we have sustained, or that Brother Quinter is really dead. We can not tell how glad we felt on last Saturday, as we saw him come towards our office on the Convention ground, and how little did we think that so soon it would be our sad lot to return home, bearing with us the lifeless body of one that was so dear to us!

But in the time and place of his death we are all comforted. It was God's time, and the choice of our dear brother and elder, at the Annual Meeting with his people, on his knees pleading with God. And as the precious thought loomed up in his soul, and he said, "O Lord, I thank thee that we are permitted to meet again," the Lord said it was enough, and took his servant home. "Even so, them also which sleep in Jesus will God bring with him."

REMARKS BY W. J. SWIGART.

Many are the Scriptural texts that suggest themselves on an occasion such as the present. Were I to base my remarks on any particular text, I should refer you to the 24th verse of the 5th chapter of Genesis: "And Enoch walked with God; and he was not; for God took him."

If, in looking at humanity as it is, and as it has been, any man should grow skeptical at the spectacle; if the wickedness of men, and the weakness of human nature should weaken his confidence in his race, he should call up before him the fact that the world has furnished *some good men*.

In taking a retrospective view of man's history, there appear men who have been eminent in battle, eminent in politics, in personal prowess, and even in the perpetration of evil. But along with this is the satisfactory truth that God has always had a seed of righteousness in the world, and there has never been a time when there was not at least *some* person eminent for goodness and personal piety. Such was Enoch, and such was the subject of this funeral occasion.

Enoch walked with God. He lived at a time of great wickedness, yet his life was devoted and pious. While he was a fearless and truthful public preacher of righteousness, his private life was doubtless the representative life set forth here. It was here that "Enoch walked with God."

And how eminently fit is this thought in its application to the subject before us! Father Quinter was an eloquent and forcible preacher, a prolific writer, and a wise counselor, but his true greatness was in his holy walk and conversation, his integrity, his uprightness, his meekness, his devoutness, his piety. God seemed always to be with him, and how truly they walked together!

His present physical appearance, as he lies there in the coffin, is assuring testimony in itself. Who in looking at that face need be told that that body once enshrined a spirit embued with a high order of Christianity? I would have crossed the States just to look at that face. Oh, I loved him as a father, and my place were better filled to day could I sit yonder with the mourners, where "I could weep my spirit from mine eyes," rather than stand before you in the attempt to speak. On Sunday night, when his body was brought into the house and we could see it, I could have stood till the morning looking on that calm, meek, loving face—more calm, more meek, more loving, more sweet because seen in the embrace of everlasting silence and repose.

He was not. Just what the translation of Enoch was, I know not. Just how it was accomplished, I know not. In some way it was through the agency of faith. His people looked for him, but found him not. All their search was vain, *he was not.* Just how this *death* was accomplished I know not. "How wonderful is death" in any form! but this—in the twinkling of an eye, without a pain, without a struggle; one moment here, the next *there*—how doubly wonderful is it!

Enoch's body was translated, changed and adapted to the new realm by some other process than through ordinary death. Father Quinter's body was left for us to gather around, weep over, and directly carry away. This is probably the main difference, for it seems almost a "translation." Said one, who witnessed it, to me, "I think it was the nearest *not* death that it is possible to be."

For God took him. Enoch was safe with his God. He had "walked" with God on the earth, and now they walk together the streets of the Golden City. Oh, it is so of our brother. He delighted in the companionship of God when in the body. God has taken him to a higher appreciation of that companionship in the spirit. He is happy; aye, infinitely happy, and yet we mourn for him. How unwilling we are to give up our friends! How unwilling we are even to think it likely that they will leave us. We *must* give them up, and yet how unready we are! It is because we love them so, I suppose. The more useful and active they have been, the less ready we are to assent to their removal. However strong God's claim on them may be, we are still unwilling to release our own. How often has it been said to me by those away from here: "Brother Quinter is getting old, too," implying by word and tone that death at any time would not be any great improbability. I always evaded the force of the remark and answered by a reference to his good health and exceedingly temperate life (unless it *was* in the matter of hard work).

He was more than seventy-two years in this world, and if the amount of labor performed be accounted for, it was more than a hundred years of ordinary men's lives (for men's lives can not be measured exclusively by the number of years intervening their birth and their death), and yet we unwillingly received the message of his death as an utterly unexpected thing; nay, almost as an *unnatural* thing. I had thoughts of his death recently, but I had hoped to hear him preach after he was four-score years. Very recently, when indulging in this hope, it occurred to me that his fourth score year is only eight years thitherward, and the possibility that began to throw its threatening gloom even at that distance made me blanch. And now this is our last glance at his earthly form. When the word came, the most common explanation was, "*Can* it be true?" And more than once, since this audience began to gather to-day, have I heard through voices breaking with emotion, "I thought it could not possibly be." This is hardly because we thought the man of a different kind of flesh and blood, but because we loved him much, and felt his presence could not be spared. How unwilling we are to give up our friends!

Of the extent of this loss to the friends, and of the extent of the loss to the Church, I have no heart to speak to-day. Could the spirit of our loved elder look backward and take cognizance of affairs transacting here; nay, could his spirit communicate to ears of flesh and blood, what would be the import of the words we would hear?—" Grieve not for me. I was long time with you. I taught you often. I was with you much, but God took me. My little family—wife, children, sister, grieve not your lives away. I can not go to you, but by and by you come to me. Little flock in Huntingdon, mourn not for me. My work is done, all danger is past, the crown is won. *Be ye faithful,* earnestly contend for the faith once delivered unto the saints. Remember the words I spake unto you. Cleanse yourselves from all unrighteousness, double your diligence; by and by, your time, like mine, will come. In the last sermon I preached on earth, from the words, 'Whoso looketh into the perfect law of liberty and continueth therein, he being not a forgetful hearer, but a doer of the work, this man shall be blessed in his deed,' in speaking on the clause, 'shall be blessed in his deed,' I told you I felt good. I was happy in the contemplation of God and his law. But here I am more happy. Oh this glorious abode! Spend not your time in grieving there because I have come here, but prepare to come to live in this Land of the Leal, the home of the soul."

I can not close these remarks without some reference to the manner, place and attitude of his death.

The manner. It was sudden—oh, *so* sudden. Yet sudden deaths are often very merciful deaths. 'Tis true, you would like to have had some word to you or for you. But his last words were to God. His expiring breath was vocalized in thanks to God.

He died at his post,—blessed death! I think it was after he preached his last sermon that I thought of his decease. Would he die some time at his post in one of his bursts of enthusiasm, while preaching? Will he die in the possession of all his powers and faculties, or will some stroke disable him, and he languish for years, his body disabled, the powers of his great mind broken and impaired, and tardy death bring at last a glad relief? But how sadly soon was the queerly-born problem solved, and how truly did he die at his post! "He walked with God, and he is not, for God took him." Let it comfort our rebellious hearts!

The place. Over and over again you have thought, "Oh, if he could only have died at home." I do not wonder at this. And yet, when my mind has been abstracted from your personal grief, I have thanked my God and his, that, if his death had to be now, it happened just as it did. In an eminent degree he was the Church's. The Church claimed him and he yielded to the claim. I look on his still and silent form, and think, when, until to-day, was that body in a religious assembly, surrounded by a platform full of ministers, that his voice was not heard? He spoke and we gladly listened. He was our spokesman. To-day his lips are closed and his voice is hushed in the silence of death, and we try to speak in the presence of his body. No more will he come in and go out here; no more will he move over this rostrum; no more will the church hear his fatherly counsel; no more will hearts move under the persuasion of his eloquence. And while I grant that you have a place of sorrow that none other can feel or probably fully appreciate, yet it is the Church's sorrow. Oh, it is our *great grief*, it is our *great loss*. His mourners to-day are not all here at this service. They may be found from the Atlantic to the Pacific, wherever the Brethren Church has members. A few hundred are gathered here. In middle Indiana to-day are ten thousand bowed heads in one assembly, all mourning the loss of a Church father. Scores who have been converted; thousands whose hearts have moved and whose faith has been strengthened under his preaching, all over this land, will rise up and call him blessed. Old men, old women — fathers and mothers in Israel,— tremblingly waiting on the brink of Death's river, will remember that they heard him preach when he was almost a boy; and as they lean on their canes, or tremble and wait in their rooms, they will drop a tear and wonder why God took *him* and left *them*.

Is there not, then, an eminent appropriateness in the place of his death? True, he might have died in his pleasant home, surrounded by his faithful wife and daughters, but he might have died alone in his study where there was no arm to stay his fall, or sunk down in his yard or garden. He might have died on the cars, or fallen down on the unconsecrated planks of some strange depot, and been picked up by wondering and curious strangers. He might have sunk down here on this rostrum, in the presence of his flock—and who that has ever sat under his ministry, when in one of his flights of eloquence, has not been forced to think of the possibility of such a thing? *But no*, God had something else. His life had been given to the Church, and God gave him the Tabernacle for his death-chamber, and hundreds of his brethren of the ministry for a death-watch. In the national assembly, amid representatives of the Church, his death-bed was the public rostrum, and his dying words a public ministration.

His attitude. How eminently appropriate! Kneeling in devotion—always a delightful posture with him—removed only that his last breath might be expired while his body lay on the sacred stand, amid the bibles and hymns and papers of the meeting, in the presence and sight of thousands of his brethren.

He began his prayer amidst three thousand of his brethren of the militant Church on earth; and who doubts that he finished it amidst ten thousand times ten thousand, and thousands of thousands of his brethren of the Church triumphant in Heaven, and that the burden of his prayer was still for the militant Church which he loved and for which he gave his life.

His spirit broke away from earth amid a clamor of groans and wails. It entered the courts above amid a burst of welcoming joy which made the corridors of Heaven ring and reverberate. "We thank thee that we have met." His soul was happy in the thought. "We thank thee that we have met," *not on earth and in the body.* Did he repeat it in Heaven? As his earthly brethren, whose lips he had just kissed in fraternal greeting, rushed about his body to support it—and as they vanished from his physical recognition, and his spirit arose from this scene, came there rushing around it the spirits of just men made perfect—of those of his early brethren who had gone before, and of Paul, and of John, and of Abraham, and of Enoch? And as the glory scene flashed on his spiritual recognition, were the ears of the God of Sabaoth again greeted with the thanksgiving strain, "Oh, Lord, we thank thee that we have met—*and in heaven*—AND NEVER TO PART AGAIN?"

Of the value and influence of his life and example I shall not attempt to speak to-day. They will be strong and far-reaching. We thank the Lord for his life; we thank the Lord for his record; we thank the Lord that we have known him and lived under his ministry.

Certainly his real greatness was in his sincerity, humility, meekness and purity of life. After all, what a great thing it is to be able to say of any one, "He is good." As we linger to-day to look at the finished volume of his closed life, let us, who are left, emulate, above all, this glorious quality in the life of him who has passed away. World, take your greatness, take your power, your pomp, your honors, and your laurels. Let there be bound about our brow the chaplet insignia of a greater, though humbler, attainment—the consecration of self and the love of goodness for its own sake and the sake of God its author. Thus dead, he shall still live; silent, he shall still speak, and in example live. For, like Peter, his teaching seemed to say, "Moreover, I will endeavor that ye may be able after my decease, to have these things always in remembrance." Surely, he might say, "I am now ready to be offered, and the time of my departure is at hand. I have fought a good fight, I have finished my course, I have kept the faith, henceforth, there is laid up for me a crown of righteousness which the Lord the righteous judge shall give me in that day." And the Lord will say, "Well done, good and faithful servant, enter into the joy of thy Lord." And we may say, "Let me die the death of the righteous, that my last end may be like his." "Blessed are the dead which die in the Lord. Yea, saith the Spirit, that they may rest from their labors, and their works do follow them." Amen and Amen!

Brother Swigart was followed by Rev. Prideau, an aged Presbyterian minister, who spoke feelingly and touchingly of Brother Quinter as a Christian minister, and his associations with him. As a Christian eulogy it was expressive, touching, fitting and highly appreciated by all present.

Rev. J. B. Kidder, of the Baptist Church, who has

passed his four-score years, with bowed head, tendered heart and trembling accents, gave a few words of comfort and cheer, both for the church and bereaved ones.

Elder Geo. Brumbaugh, of James Creek, followed with a few remarks, but as the services were already quite lengthy, he did not feel like lengthening the time to give expression to the much that he felt like saying.

The 582d hymn was then read by Rev. Smith, of the M. E. Church, after which the body was borne to the town cemetery, accompanied by a large concourse of friends and citizens, where the funeral services were concluded by Elder Seth Myers and others.

The peace of God abide with the body of our dear elder that now lies sleeping in Riverview Cemetery. And may the same peace abide with the little flock that he left.

PART II.

SERMONS

—OF—

ELDER JAMES QUINTER.

SERMONS OF ELDER JAMES QUINTER.

I.

THE BROAD LAW OF GOD.

TEXT:—"Thy commandment is exceeding broad."—Ps. 119 : 96.

By commandment in the text we understand law. The idea of law is frequently contained in the word commandment. By the word commandment in the following passage law is probably meant: "The commandment of the Lord is pure, enlightening the eyes." Ps. 19 : 8. And in Rom. 7th. ch. Commandment probably means law generally where it is used. Then the passage may be read, The law of the Lord is exceeding broad. And by *law* we understand the divine rule of conduct contained in the Scriptures. This rule is exceeding broad, extending to all human beings that have access to it, and that have reached a sufficient maturity of age to have an understanding of it.

I will first notice the breadth or extent of the divine law, and then draw some inference from it. And as we must have a starting point, I remark, 1, That children are the subjects of the divine law, or that in the broad folds which it spreads out in its great breadth, it covers our childhood or takes hold of us in early life. The fifth commandment of the decalogue reads as follows: "Honor thy father and mother that thy days may be long upon the land which the Lord thy God giveth thee." Ex. 20 : 12. And the apostle admonishes the young, thus: "Children obey your parents in the Lord; for this is right. Honor thy father and mother; which is the first commandment with promise;

that it may be well with thee, and thou mayst live long on the earth." Eph. 6 : 1–3.

It began with us, my adult hearers, men and women, in our childhood; and it has never withdrawn its authority. Some of us are tolerably old, some not so old, and some are younger still, but that law commenced then, and its obligations are upon us this morning with all their divine weight and authority; and to that law you and I ever have been and ever will be while we live, responsible. The broad law of God begins with us in our childhood, as soon as we become accountable—just then. But we can not tell the precise time, when children become accountable. We depend upon the development of their mental and moral powers. When these become sufficiently developed to enable children to understand good from evil, and right from wrong, they become responsible. I feel of later years much impressed with the thought that we do not recognize the accountability of our children, as a general thing, at a sufficiently early age. We let them go too long without feeling a concern for them, and think that they are safe, though our little boys and girls may tell lies, and sometimes swear, and even steal, yet we may think they are pretty good. I am speaking of people in general, and yet when these little liars and thieves, and profane boys die, we do not feel much concerned about them, because we take it for granted that it is well with them, as they were too young to be held accountable. I am glad, however, to know that the circumstances under which we are placed in the present age, with our Sabbath-schools, and teaching of the importance of moral education in all our schools, that this state of things unquestionably is changing, and we are beginning to feel more and more, that children may be accountable. I am glad to know that this feeling is increasing, and God grant it may increase. And I think that we, as Sabbath-school teachers and parents, should look at this matter more carefully and see whether we have not been remiss in our duty in regard to the matter, and feel the necessity of the conversion of children at an earlier age than we have been doing. I draw out these thoughts from the broad law of God. You have heard me read that law—"Children, obey your parents." That is the divine law, and if that commandment is violated by children old enough to know that they ought not to do so, are they not, in some degree, guilty of a transgression of God's law?

I come, now, to the young men and women of our country, of our town, and of our families. "Remember thy Creator in the days of thy youth." Here is a precept of the broad law of God. It particularizes children as I have used it in the application. It passes on to the youth, and it does not only require of the young to obey their parents, but it also requires of them to remember their Creator. And the command to remember him, implies that they are to remember their duty to him, and with faithfulness perform that duty. Though our young men and young women are thoughtless about God, and indifferent to his claims upon them for their love and obedience, and think more about gratifying themselves than about glorifying him, nevertheless, he thinks of them, and among the aged men and women God selects the young as feeling a special interest in their welfare and has appropriated a part of his Word to them—pointed them out and directly calls and encourages them. God has honored you, young women and men, in especially calling you, and we need not wonder at it. It is not a mysterious problem why it should be so, when we think of the strength and vigor of the young, when we think of your capacity for usefulness, as the apostle John said when he wrote, "I have written to you, young men, because you are strong." 1 John, 2 : 14.

2. In passing on with this broad law, as it begins with

the child, and applies to our youth, I remark that it comes to the older, to the parents as well as to the children. Parents are thus admonished : " And, ye fathers, provoke not your children to wrath; but bring them up in the nurture and admonition of the Lord." Eph. 6 : 4.

We are all pointed out, parents and children, as subjects of the broad law of God, and according to that law there are duties connected with all the relations in which we stand to one another. And while our children should honor us, we should honor them. What do I mean by honoring them? I mean we should treat them not simply as our offspring, but as the offspring of God, and recognize in them a spiritual nature, and deathless spirits, which are to be cultivated, and which will, if cultivated, enjoy a glorious immortality; but if left uncultivated, they will be lost to themselves, lost to God, and lost to their Christian parents. So we should look upon our children. So God looks upon them, and hence the obligations that we are under according to the requirements of the divine and broad law, to train them for him and for immortality.

3. The broad law of God contains rules for the government of husbands and wives in their relations in which they stand to one another. " Wives, submit yourselves unto your own husbands, as unto the Lord. For the husband is the head of the wife, even as Christ is the head of the church: and he is the Savior of the body. Therefore as the church is subject unto Christ so let the wives be to their own husbands in everything. Husbands, love your wives, even as Christ also loved the church, and gave himself for it." Eph. 5 : 22–24. It may be laid down as a general rule, that a multiplication of relations in life, multiplies our duties. The more positions in life we fill, the greater will be our obligations that we shall have to meet. While an increase of business usually is attended with an increase of care, it is also

attended with an increase of obligations. And if we multiply our callings and obligations, we then shall need more divine grace to enable us to meet those obligations. And while we should not shun relations if they are lawful and right because they increase our obligations, we should enter upon them knowing that our obligations are increased by so doing.

The apostle says, "marriage is honorable in all." It is then sanctioned by Heaven, and like all other divine appointments, it is designed for good and benevolent purposes. But let the young man know, and let the young woman know, that when they enter into the marriage state, their responsibilities increase. Our young friends here this morning, both young men and young women, have duties to meet and obligations to bear in your single state. But when you pledge yourselves to each other at the hymeneal altar, and become husband and wife, you increase your responsibilities, obligations and duties. Moral responsibility is not felt as it ought to be. If it were more properly appreciated, we would look at the married state often in a different light to what we look upon it now. We would associate with it responsibilities and obligations that we now too often fail to do. As I have before remarked, when we enter into that state then our obligations increase; then we stand in a new relation, one which we never occupied before, and its duties we must meet. Then, when we are made parents, and, when we assume the relation of parents, there is another increase of responsibility. Then we must meet the duties of the parent; then the broad law of God comes to us and we are responsible to that law for the discharge of our parental duties.

4. I proceed to refer to our relation to one another as neighbors. We are to love 'our neighbor as ourselves. Matt. 19 : 19. It was asked in ancient times, "who is my

neighbor," and our blessed Lord, in his wisdom presented us with one of the most touching and valuable parables in his teachings to illustrate who the neighbor is. I mean the parable of the good Samaritan, Luke 10 : 25 – 36. We often may think our neighbor is the individual that lives next door to us or in the house close by. That may be so, but I want to tell you that your neighbors are in this school. Here in your school, you are all neighbors together, in the Scriptural sense of the word. As students you are neighbors; the professors are neighbors to each other and neighbors to the students, and the students are neighbors to the professors. The Scripture idea of a neighbor is one *that needs our help*, one over whom we can exert an influence. That is the idea of neighborship in the meaning of the broad and perfect law of a living God. Do not forget that. Let us all remember that we are neighbors and that the Lord requires us to love one another. It would help greatly to promote harmony and love and happiness and peace and success amongst us, in our church, and school and everywhere else.

5. We here stand related, children to parents, husbands to wives, wives to husbands, and we are neighbors related to neighbors, but we also bear a relationship to God. Would we sunder all our connections with God, and take a position that we are independent of him, and that we can live without him? Surely we will not take such a position. "For in him we live and move and have our being." Acts 17 : 28. Then will we recognize no obligations that we are under to Him? I have the satisfaction of believing this morning that there is not one here that would maintain that position. Young man, irreligious as you may be, I feel that you are not willing to say that you are independent of God; that you do not care for him. Then what is the true state of the case? We are the subjects of his government, and

we owe him our obedience. God once said to his people, and that appeal is as applicable this morning to us as to those to whom the appeal was made, "If I am a father, where is my honor? If I am a master, where is my fear?" Mal. 1:6. If his providence has sustained us, and benevolence and goodness have given us the comforts and enjoyments we experience, must we not acknowledge that we are under many obligations to him? We are all, both young and old, related to God. We are his servants, his creatures, his children, and God requires of us our service, our love, and in the folds of this broad law I find the commandment, "Thou shalt love the Lord thy God with all thy heart, and with all thy soul, and with all thy mind, and with all thy strength." Mark 12:30. I find that in this law, and that is what arises from the relation of dependence which we sustain to God. Here is the commandment of God growing out of that relation, and that command continues, and requires us to love him. It will stand and stand forever; and it will stand with increased weight and plainness when the volume of inspiration is opened at the judgment day, and when you and I shall stand before the bar of God, and be judged out of the broad law. That command will stand, and if we have not observed it then I need not tell you what the consequences will be.

6. There is another view of the divine law of God given in the Scriptures, and which is another evidence to prove that it is indeed a *broad law*. It is a law that takes cognizance of our very thoughts. Human law does not generally take notice of the thoughts of its subjects, and only looks at guilt generally when thoughts are put into actions. And it is proper that this should be the case, since neither the administrators of human law, nor the witnesses called upon to give testimony can see into the heart of the criminal. In the administration of human law, actions are necessary to

prove character, or to prove guilt. But in the administration of the divine or broad law of God, cognizance is taken even of human thoughts before they are formed into actions. So broad is the divine law, that in its unfolding applications, it covers our very thoughts. The tenth commandment of the decalogue reads as follows: "Thou shalt not covet thy neighbor's house, thou shalt not covet thy neighbor's wife, nor his man-servant, nor his maid-servant, nor his ox, nor his ass, nor anything that is thy neighbor's." Ex. 20: 17. Among the precepts of the divine law requiring equity between man and man, there is this one which strikes at the very root of injustice from man to man, by forbidding the corrupt desires and concupiscence of the heart. In accordance with the principle of the tenth commandment, Paul says, "I had not known lust, except the law had said, thou shalt not covet." Rom. 7: 7. Our Lord declares in reference to the spirit of this commandment, "Whosoever looketh on a woman to lust after her hath committed adultery with her already in his heart." Matt. 5: 28. And the apostle John declares, "Whosoever hateth his brother is a murderer." 1 John 3: 15.

Men often think that they are free from any sin that endangers their salvation if their life outwardly has been free from any gross sin. But would such look within themselves, into the evil thoughts of their hearts, and then apply to themselves the broad law of God which condemns impure thoughts as well as impure actions, they would form a different view of themselves. Such then is the broad law of God. I shall now proceed to draw some inferences from this extensive application of the divine law.

1. How liable we are to sin since we have so many duties to perform, growing out of our various and numerous relations which we fill in life. And every time we fail to perform our duty in any of our relations, we commit sin. We

commence to sin in our youth, if we fail to keep the divine law, for it makes its demands upon us in our youth as I have already shown. How have we met its requirements? Have we not all violated that law, at least in some of its parts, in some of the relations in which that law comes to us? May I not go back to our childhood and ask where are the persons that have always rendered honor and respect to their parents? My father died and left me an orphan when I was only thirteen years old. I was converted to God when I was in my seventeenth year, and hence I was unconverted for several years after the death of my father. Among the things that impressed my mind when I felt my responsibility, and saw the error of my ways, and felt the importance of doing right, was my unkindness to my father. But he was then dead, and I wished he was living, if for no other purpose, that I could go to him and tell him that I wanted him to forgive me. I was not particularly unkind to my father, but he was particularly kind to me, and a kind parent deserves special kindness from a child. And if I had not been converted, and my guilt blotted out, my sin as a disobedient boy would have met me in the judgment. And so it may be with others among us. If you did wrong under these circumstances, and have never obtained forgiveness, these wrongs will stand until they are washed away by the blood of Christ. Then as husbands and wives, as parents and children, and neighbors, how have we lived? How have we performed our duties to our associates and companions? And lastly, how have we performed them to God? Oh there is guilt, upon those living under a law so pure, and holy, and perfect as the broad law of God is if they have not been pardoned.

2. Then if all are guilty, how much need have we of a Saviour, and just such a Saviour as we need, God has provided for us in our Lord Jesus Christ. Through him the sins of

youth, of our maturer years, and the sins of our old age may all be pardoned. Through him we may be born again, and be made new creatures. This is a glorious truth—glad tidings. Sin has abounded extensively, but grace may much more abound. And whatever may be the number, or the character of our sins, they all may be forgiven. How necessary then is Christ for us all, as we have all sinned. And to him we should all go, on him we all should believe, and into fellowship with him, and his suffering, merits, and righteousness we all should be brought, for he is a needful, sufficient and only Savior.

3. While we need pardon for the transgressions of the broad law of God which we have already committed, we shall, if we keep that law in all its holy requirements and diversified applications, need divine help to enable us to do so. And that help we may obtain. The Saviour of the Gospel does not only pardon sin, but he also protects us from sin, and enables us to do right. "I can do all things" said Paul, "through Christ which strengtheneth me." Phil. 4 : 13. And he says to Timothy "God hath not given us the spirit of fear; but of power, and of love, and of a sound mind." 2 Tim. 1 : 7. By a diligent use of the means of grace, grace sufficient for every emergency may be obtained.

Finally, the broad law of God is a law of benevolence, and its great object is to promote the welfare and happiness of men. And the more fully it is carried out in all our relations of life, and lived up to in all our doings and dealing, the happier we shall be, while here in this state of being, and there is no hope of heaven without being right and doing right. "Blessed are they that do his commandments, that they may have right to the tree of life, and may enter in through the gates into the city." Rev. 22 : 14.

II.

THE GREAT END AND AIM OF THE CHRISTIAN.

TEXT:—"Herein do I exercise myself, to have always a conscience void of offense toward God, and toward men." Acts 24:16.

This is part of Paul's defense that he made when he was brought before the governor Felix. He was called to account for a number of charges which were made against him. These charges were made by the man that is here called Tertullus. It is probable that as Paul was to be tried under Roman law that the judges employed this Tertullus as a barrister or lawyer. The judges employed this lawyer Tertullus who was, as his name implies, a Roman, that he might the better present the case according to the Roman law. This was not done to favor Paul, for the Jews were bound upon his condemnation; but it was probably for the purpose of aiding them to secure his condemnation that Tertullus was employed. This man Tertullus, then, was their spokesman. He was the orator—the man who was to do the talking. His part, therefore, was to give the charges which they made against Paul. These charges were three in number. The first charge was that of sedition; the second, the crime of heresy; and the third was that of sacrilege. The charge of sedition is the crime of disturbing the peace of the community, or of awakening a disturbance among the people, either against one another or against the government. It is a crime somewhat similar to rebellion, though of a less degree. There are three crimes of this nature. These are sedition, insurrection and rebellion. Sedition is the mildest form of this kind of crime. Rebellion usually begins with sedition, and is the highest crime of this nature. It is upon the charge of sedition that Paul is brought before Felix. They accused Paul of being active in stirring up the people and disturbing the peace of the community. Another charge was that of heresy. They accused him of trying to lead the people from the faith of the fathers. The charge came through Tertullus who was a Roman, but it was heresy according to the Jewish law with which he was charged, that is, a departure from the Jewish mode of worship. The third charge was that of sacrilege. As it is said, he profaned the temple. Sacrilege is a violation of sacred things. It is the taking of things designed for sacred uses, and applying them to secular uses. The charge is here made that he profaned the Jewish temple; that he had not manifested a sufficient amount of respect toward the temple. The charge was, that he had been seen with certain Greeks in the temple. As the feet of a Greek profaned the temple, according to the Jewish ideas, Paul was accused of heresy because, they said he took these Greeks into the temple There is no evidence of this. The Jews, in their bitter hostility to Paul, were ready to adopt any subterfuge, to use any falsehood, or do anything else of this kind that would render the charges more certain which they made against Paul. After these charges were presented, Paul was permitted to reply. He did reply. He employed no lawyer, however. He did it without any help—human help, I mean. He had no human help. He had no Tertullus to plead for him. He had no Roman lawyer. His only help was that of God. "Herein do I exercise myself, to have always a conscience void of offense toward God, and toward man." He was conscious of his innocency, of his integrity and of the justice of his cause. He defended himself from the charges which were made against him. This defense was made very justly, very boldly, very clearly, and I think, very successfully. In this defense he used the language of our text: "Herein do I exercise myself, to have always a conscience void of offense toward God, and toward men." They had charged him with sacrilege—with profaning the temple. He now says, "Herein do I exercise myself, to have a conscience void of offense toward God, and toward men." This means, I would not, under any circumstances or for any consideration, profane the temple of God, or defile his service, or treat him with irreverence, or profane anything of a divine character, or any divine law, or disobey his government, or profane anything which pertains to God."

He was charged with disturbing the peace of the community. His language also replies to this: "Herein do I exercise myself, to have a conscience void of offense toward God, and toward men." He here signifies that he has corrupted no man, that he would not give any just occasion for disturbing the peace of the community, or lead any away from the path of duty. Instead of doing anything of that kind, he says, or rather implies it, that it has been one of his great purposes in life to discharge his duty toward men, and live with a conscience void of offense toward men, as well as toward God. That is what his language implies. In using this language, we will look at it under three heads, which seem properly to be contained in the subject.

The first is the grand end and aim of the Christian. And this is to live with a "conscience void of offense toward God, and toward men." Secondly, the great work of the Christian, which is to maintain the state referred to in the text. Thirdly, the motives which prompt the Christian man and woman to live with a "conscience void of offense toward God, and toward men."

The first point is the grand design of the Christian. And this is to "live with a conscience void of offense toward God, and toward men." This should be our object. It is the object of all sincere and intelligent Christians. You may not think of your object as Christians in the very thoughts that I present it in, but in substance it must be your thought, my brother and sister, if you are living with a proper end in view. Then your end will not be lower or any less in grandeur and excellency than was the end and aim of Paul, when he said before his persecutors, "Herein do I exercise myself, to have always a conscience void of offense toward God, and toward men." This is the substance of our purpose, and the real essence of our design. The subject does not necessarily require an explanation of conscience, and I have no explanation to offer upon it. Suffice it to say, it is a very important part of our being. It is one of the most striking characteristics that separate man from the lower animals of creation. The lowest type of human reason, and the highest order of brute instinct, come near together in some instances. There is not the wide gulf between man and the lower animals in regard to his intellectuality simply, that there is in some other respects, especially in the respect to which I have just referred you. There is no moral sense or conscience in the brute creation. There is no sense of right or wrong. There is, however, in man. There is a feeling of approval present when we know that we have been doing that which is right, and when we do that which is wrong, there is a feeling of remorse. This feeling is produced by conscience and is found in every man in which his moral nature has not been destroyed or swallowed up by sin. There is no such feeling as this in the brute creation. This conscience, this moral nature, this moral sense, is that which elevates us above the brute creation, and makes the difference, and forms one of the most striking lines of division between man and the lower animals. Looking at man from his moral standpoint, we find one of the most remarkable elements of his wonderful character. This element is conscience—something that, as we have stated, makes us feel happy when we have been doing right, and makes us feel the pangs of remorse when we have been doing wrong. This is manifested at an early age in our children. As we have moral and religious instruction that feeling becomes more and more developed. When we are converted to God, then we have a good conscience. When we have this we feel badly when wrong is done, and we feel good when the action is right. All men, however, who are not extremely depraved, have more or less of conscience, and feel unhappy when they have been doing wrong, and feel comparatively good when they have been doing right. Paul wanted to have a conscience void of offense. He wanted his conscience free from condemnation toward God. He wanted to be able to meet God with a conscience void of offense, for he knew that he must meet him, as we all must do. Paul wanted to feel that he could look upon God without any condemnation, without any remorse, without any awakening of painful feelings. He wanted to think of eternity with calmness. When he was brought before Governor Felix, and King Agrippa, he wanted there to have a conscience void of offense. He wanted also to meet his fellow-men and to be able to look them in the face without any condemnation. He wanted to discharge his duty so faithfully to his fellow-men that when he should meet them at the bar of God in judgment, they could justly charge him with no wrong to them. Such a conscience was the grand object of Paul's life, and to the attainment of such a state was his life devoted. These were his thoughts. His greatest efforts and all his labors were applied to that end, to the attainment of that state of having a "conscience void of offense toward God, and toward men."

Further, in regard to this conscience, three things are necessary. First, we must have a rule that we look upon as right, a rule of right by which we must govern our lives; secondly, there must be an impartial application of that rule to our conduct in order to find out that our conduct has been in harmony with our rule, and thirdly, we must feel assured that our conduct is strictly in harmony with our rule of right. In order that you may understand this point, I might, perhaps, say again, that we must have some rule of right. Perhaps you are aware that no individual, or body of men, is altogether without some rule of right. It will be impossible to accomplish any enterprise in which several persons are engaged, without some general rule of right for their government. Even robbers who have united together to accomplish the worst of objects, accept of some rule, or law for their government. We may, therefore, say that every man has some rule of right and wrong. Every man has this moral nature in him.

To have a conscience strictly void of offense towards God, and toward men, we must have a rule of right. This rule must be the word of God. To live with a conscience void of offense toward God, and toward men, it is plain to us all, that we must do right according to the law of God. Job. said, "I will say unto God, do not condemn me.—Job x, 2. Now, if we would not have God to condemn us, we must do what he requires of us, or we must make satisfaction to him by repentance. And so, if we would not have men to condemn us, we must do right to them.

In the last day we must stand before his majestic throne, with the open volumes before us, and have God judge us. To have a conscience, then and there, void of offense, we must previously have lived according to the Gospel rule of right. In regard to our living with a conscience void of offense toward men, by what rule must we live in order that they will not condemn us? By the same Gospel rule. This is to govern us in our conduct toward God and toward men. Though we do right to men, they may still condemn us. But if we do our duty to them, there will be no just ground for their condemnation, and God will acquit us in the day of judgment. The Saviour, himself, did not escape the condemnation of men. In one of his discourses were given some words, which contained a reproof of the Pharisees. The disciples came to him and said, "Knowest thou that the Pharisees were offended, after they heard this saying?" —Matt. xv. 12. The reproof was contained in these words, "Do not ye yet understand, that whatsoever entereth in at the mouth goeth into the belly, and is cast out into the draught? But those things which proceed out of the mouth come forth from the heart; and they defile the man." This was said when he was exposing a mistake of the Pharisees in following only an outside form in worship. They thought they could not eat a little meat without being unclean. If they drank a few drops of water out of a Gentile cup they thought it would defile them. Their misconception of right led Christ to rebuke them. "Do ye not understand," said he, "that it is not that which entereth in at the mouth, but that which proceedeth out of the mouth, that defiles a man?" He told them that they must be clean within, that it is not that which goes into the mouth that defileth a man, but that which comes out of his heart. It is our vulgarity and profanity and evil talking which comes out of the mouth that defile us.

We are to live with a conscience void of offense toward men. It is not necessary to have a conscience void of offense for us to live so that men will not abuse us or feel offended at us, because men of this world were offended at Christ. We are to live so that they may not have any just reason to be offended at us. That is the way we should live. We should so live that they will not justly have any reason to feel that we have done the many injury. The Saviour was right when he gave that rebuke. It was a grand lesson—a beautiful lesson. It was right that he did it. They took offense without any just ground for it. When I preach the truth to you, and I am in the right spirit, and try with all kindness and love to deliver the message to you; when I reprove and rebuke those who are out of the way, and they take offense at my preaching, it is not my fault. Are we, the teacher, the preacher, the neighbor, the friend who kindly reprove sin, in fault, if people become offended? No. If in my preaching the Gospel, from time to time, I give offense, when I meet these people at the bar of God, will my conscience condemn me? When I go out of the church sometimes, and go home, some one says to me, "Brother Quinter, you are too plain in your application, too close in your criticism, and the people were offended." Does my conscience condemn me? I think first about it, because we are sometimes impulsive. We say things, sometimes, which are not wrong in themselves, but the spirit may be. I ask my friend, what is the matter? To what truths were exceptions taken? When I find that it was not my manner, but the subject of my remarks, and the truth which I was trying to present, my conscience is easy.

"If God be for us, who can be against us?" asks the apostle.—Rom. viii. 31. So if we do right to men and to God, and we know that God is for us, it matters not what men may say about us. If our conscience is right and it does not condemn us, we will have the rejoicing of our conscience (2 Cor. i. 12), let men say and do whatever they may. And here is one of the great sources of enjoyment to the Christian. The assurance that he is right, is a great source of enjoyment to him. Men are offended at the truth because they do not understand it. If they understood it, they would not be offended at it. It is because men are in love with sin that they do not want to have their sins condemned. When they see the evil of sin, as they will sometime see it, then they will not be offended at hearing their sins reproved. Persons sometimes become so much offended at preachers that they will not go to hear them. Now if it is the truth at which they become offended, it is wrong. And they will see the wrong when they understand the truth. The time is coming when truth and error, and right and wrong will be distinguished the one from the other. And when that time comes, those who have loved darkness rather than light because their deeds are evil, will approve the right and condemn the wrong, though it may be condemning themselves. And if we love the truth, and are born of the truth, and have a conscience in harmony with the truth, and live with a conscience void of offense toward God and toward man, there will be no condemnation. And it is the great object of the Christian to have a good conscience, and to so live that his conscience does not condemn him.

But there are duties to be performed to God as well as man. Some people's religion (if I may call it religion—some people's morality) is to do right to their fellow-men. We may be charitably inclined, and we may be honest, and with this may be satisfied and feel no condemnation. But when the word of God will be fully opened, then you will find that you will owe duties to God as well as to your fellow-men. Then your conscience will realize that it is wrong. It will arise in its might, in its divinity, in all its power, and then you will feel it. Felix trembled before Paul when he preached, and if he never repented he will tremble worse in judgment. "I exercise myself, to have always a conscience void of offense toward God, and toward men." This is as much as to say, "I want to tell Tertullus, I want to tell Felix, that my Christianity is a Christianity that responds to all the just claims upon me, whether they come from heaven or from men." Paul says, "I must deny the charges. I deny that I wanted to spread sedition. My soul shudders at it. My Christianity is different from that.

It is the purpose of my life, most noble Felix, to do right to everybody; to accept of right in its purest sense; to accept of right as heaven has measured it, and as it has been implanted in my Christian conscience." This is the Christian code of right. Our grand aim in life is to do right to God and man. I call attention to the fact that the Scripture has presented duty to us in a two-fold aspect. In the Decalogue, the first four commands have reference to man's duty to God, and the remaining six have reference to his duty to men. We are to love God. We are not to worship any graven image. "Thou shalt not take the name of the Lord in vain—remember the Sabbath day to keep it holy." These have reference to man's duty to God. The rest of the commands have reference to his duties to men. "Honor thy father and mother; thou shalt not kill; thou shalt not commit adultery; thou shalt not steal; thou shalt not bear false witness; thou shalt not covet." Thus all through the Scripture is the fact recognized that we owe duties to God and to men. When the Savior was asked what is the first great commandment, he said, "Love thy God with all thy heart, with all thy soul, with all thy mind, and with all thy strength." The second is, "Love thy neighbor as thyself. Upon these two commandments hang all the law and the prophets." Here all religion concentrates—upon our love and duty to God, and upon our love and duty to man. Paul recognized it. We will find it running through the whole system of divine truth—doing right to God and to our fellow-men. To have a conscience void of offense, we must worship God; we must honor him; we must obey him; we must not take his name in vain; we must reverence him; we must demean ourselves to him, as he desires we should. As far as our duties to men are concerned, we should never harm anybody, nor defraud anybody, nor slander anybody, nor wound or grieve the feelings of anybody, nor do anything to encourage any one to do wrong. And, further, we are not only to avoid doing wrong to others, but we are to do good to them. In their endeavors to get rich, we sometimes see persons do unjust acts. How wrong it is! Whenever we do any one injustice, we should make restoration. When Zaccheus, who climbed a tree to see the Savior pass, came down and talked to the Savior, he said, "If I have taken anything from any man by false accusation, I restore him four-fold." That is what we should all do. That is justice, that is right. If we have done wrong, we must make amends for it. We read in 1 Samuel, xii. 4, that when Samuel was about to die, he met his people, and said unto them, "Whose ox have I taken? or whose ass have I taken? or whom have I defrauded? whom have I oppressed? or of whose hand have I received any bribe to blind my eyes therewith? and I will restore it. The Lord is witness against you, and his anointed this day, that ye have not found aught in my hand. And they answered and said, He is witness." Death must come to us all, as it did to Samuel, to preachers, to teachers, young and old, men and women. We shall have to leave our charges and our schools. Let us try, then, to live with a conscience void of offense towards men, that we can feel as Samuel felt towards his people. This is the meaning of the apostle.

Secondly. The great work of a Christian life. "Herein do I *exercise* myself, always to have a conscience void of offense toward God, and toward men." This holy and desirable state can not be attained without great and constant labor. It is to be attained by *exercise*, by practice. Such is the meaning of the apostle, when he says, "herein do I *exercise* myself." It means that he applied himself to this work of righteousness with great care and diligence. He did as Solomon admonishes when he says, "Whatsoever thy hand findeth to do, do it with thy might."—Eccles. ix. 10.

And if we would attain to that state of faithfulness and holy living in which we will have a conscience void of offense toward God and man, we must be careful to understand our duty. And to do this we must diligently, prayerfully, and candidly search the Scriptures. This is one way we are to exercise. We are to exercise our judgments in discriminating between truth and error, and guard against calling *good evil and evil good*. The name *disciple*, applied to us, implies we should be learners, scholars in the school of Christ, and learning of him our duty as he has taught it. And when we have learned our duty we must be true and honest to ourselves and to our convictions, and carefully perform it. All this requires exercise and work. And we must make this our great and principle work if we would succeed in attaining unto a life of Christian faithfulness, which implies faithfulness to men and faithfulness to God.

In the last place, I will notice the considerations which prompt Christians to labor to live such a life as they are aiming for, and which they are endeavoring to reach. The first and best reason there is to justify and require such a course of faithful living, is the simple reason that it is right, or in accordance with the will of God, and that he requires such a life of us. This ought to be a powerful reason, a sufficient reason, a controlling and influential reason. But, as another reason why we should exercise ourselves to live with a *conscience void of offense*, we should consider what the result will be, first, if we do not so live, and, secondly, what the result will be if we do. And, first, if we do not possess a conscience void of offense, we shall possess one that will condemn us. A conscience we have, and sooner or later, we shall feel its power in approving or condemning. And a condemning conscience is a most dreadful companion to have always with us. This is the worm that never dies, and the fire that is never quenched. It is a spring of sorrow, pain and suffering, opened in the most sensitive and tender part of our nature, from which the tears of anguish will flow. We have many instances of the terrible workings of a guilty conscience. Felix and Belshazzar trembled even here. What will they do if those guilty consciences go with them into eternity?

But if we succeed, and nothing can hinder if we make the proper efforts, in securing a *conscience void of offense*, we secure to ourselves a source of never-failing enjoyment. We carry in our own bosoms a spring, which is supplied from the heavenly hills with the purest joys, and which will always and forever refresh us with its healthy and life-giving waters.

Now I have set before you the high aim of the Christian. My Christian hearers, remember this is the aim of your profession, to live, "always with a conscience void of offense toward God, and toward men." Let this be your aim, and may you reach it. And my unconverted hearers, what do you think of our aim and end? You can not but approve of them. Then unite yourselves to the people who are pursuing these commendable objects.

III.

THE FAMILY OF CHRIST.

"While he yet talked to the people, behold his mother and his brethren stood without, desiring to speak with him.

"Then one said unto him, Behold, thy mother and thy brethren stand without, desiring to speak with thee. But he answered and said unto him that told him, Who is my mother? and who are my brethren? And he stretched forth his hand toward his disciples, and said, behold my mother and my brethren? For whosoever shall do the will of my Father which is in heaven, the same is my brother, and sister, and mother."—Matt. xii. 46-50.

The family of Christ.—The family of which he is the head, the proper representative, the father. In the ninth chapter of Isaiah there is a beautiful prophecy, in regard to Christ. In this prophecy are the following words: "For unto us a child is born; unto us a son is given; and the government shall be upon his shoulder; and his name shall be called Wonderful, Counsellor, the mighty God, the everlasting Father, the Prince of Peace." This prophecy which refers to Christ, has, among other terms, that of the "Everlasting Father." Some of our translations of this passage read it, "The Father of the everlasting age." By "everlasting age" is understood to mean the age of the Gospel. Of this he may with propriety be said to be the father. The apostle Paul calls him "the author and finisher of our faith." —Heb. xii. 2. The marginal reading has "beginner" instead of author. We may comprise in the family of Christ, the faithful of all ages. He sustains various relations to his family. He sustains the relation of a father to his disciples, and he feels toward them all the tender feelings, and affection, that the kindest father feels toward his children. "Children," said he, addressing them on one occasion, "have ye any meat?"—John xxi. 5. On another occasion he said to them, "Little children yet a little while I am with you." —John xiii. 33. He is likewise the "first born" and "elder brother" in the great family of the faithful.

The family of Christ is a divine family.—It is a divine family notwithstanding the fact that it is principally made up of human beings. We may call it a divine family because the divine element predominates in the characters of its members when they become proper subjects for membership. The human element enters into their character, but the divine element predominates. This family may be called a divine family, because the members of it have been born of God. They have experienced a second birth. The Saviour said to Nicodemus, "Except a man be born again, he can not see the kingdom of God," or, as we have it in the marginal reading, "Except a man be born from above, he can not see the kingdom of God." In order to make this truth more plain when he perceived that Nicodemus did not understand it, for it was very important that he should understand it, as he was deeply and personally interested in it, he said, "Except a man be born of water and of the Spirit, he can not enter into the kingdom of God;" he can not enter into the family of Christ; he can not be a member of the Church of Christ.

In the first chapter of John, we have this language: "He came unto his own, but his own received him not. But as many as received him, to them gave he power to become the sons of God, even to them that believe on his name, which were born, not of blood, nor of the will of the flesh, nor of the will of man, but of God." Notice these words, "To them gave he power to become the sons of God." In these words and the following ones, is presented to us the divine birth of all the members of the divine family of Christ.

Of the same import is the passage in 1 Peter, i. 23. Peter is speaking of believers, and says in reference to their new birth, "Being born again, not of corruptible seed, but of incorruptible, by the word of God, which liveth and abideth forever." Here we have believers born of the word of God. Our Lord taught Nicodemus that he must be "born of water and of the Spirit." Being "born of the word of the Lord," and being "born of water and of the Spirit," are different ways of stating the same great truth. The word of the Lord, or the Gospel, requires the sinner to be baptized in water, and be born of the Spirit, in order to become right. And when the Gospel is received and believed as the word of God, and prompts the sinner to repent and to be baptized, and to live a new life, he may be said to be born " by the word of God." And this is equivalent to being " born of the water and of the Spirit." To be born of the water, no doubt embraces in it the idea of baptism, though something more than the immersion itself is meant.

And when we are " born from above," or " born of the water and of the Spirit," or " born by the word of God," then according to 2 Peter i. 4, we are made "partakers of the divine nature," or of the divine character, which is one of the distinguishing features of the family of Christ. And being partakers of the divine nature, we will act in harmony with the divine nature. Hence the language of Christ in the text, " Whosoever shall do the will of my Father which is in heaven, the same is my brother, and sister, and mother." Or as we have our Lord's language as given by St. Luke: "And he answered and said unto them, my mother and brethren are these which hear the word of God, and do it." The meaning of these passages is the same. According to St. Matthew, our Lord makes the doing of his Father's will a test of membership in his family. While, according to St. Luke, he makes that test the hearing and doing of the word of God. But as the word of God is the expression of his will, the import of the two passages is the same.

There seems to me to be no greater absurdity than to suppose that we can truly be born of God, and yet not be anxious and willing to do his will. Such a thing can not be. If we are born of God, born from above, and born of the word of God, that word will be dear to us. We will have a reverence and a regard for it which will prompt us to obey it.

The family of Christ is a royal family.—" Ye are a chosen generation, a royal priesthood," says St. Peter, when addressing the family of Christ. 1 Peter ii. 9. "Unto him that loved us," exclaims St. John the divine, "and washed us from our sins in his own blood, and hath made us kings and priests unto God, and his Father; to him be glory and dominion for ever and ever."—Rev. i. 5, 6. John is one of the royal family of Christ, and speaks not of himself only, but of the honor which all the saints have, and declares they are made "kings and priests unto God." And he appreciates the glory and blessedness of the exalted calling, and his indebtedness to the Redeemer for conferring such honor, and in the gratefulness of his exulting heart, exclaims, " To him be glory and dominion forever and ever. Amen." Christians then are of a royal line, and belong to the royal house of the King of kings, and in due time we shall receive "a crown of glory that fadeth not away."— 1 Peter v. 4.

Alexander Pope says, " An honest man's the noblest work of God." I do not know whether he meant by an honest man, one who is strictly honest in all his dealings with his fellow-man. This perhaps is what he meant. But if his idea of honesty went no farther than that principle of justice which leads men to be just to one another, then such a man is not the "noblest work of God." However noble such a man may be, he has his superior in the Christian. For he is not only honest to his fellow-men, but he is also honest to his God. When the Pharisees were trying to find a cause by which they might prejudice the government against the Lord, he asked for a government coin. And when it was brought, " he saith unto them, whose is this image and superscription? They say unto him, Cæsar's. Then saith he unto them, Render therefore unto Cæsar the things which are Cæsar's; and unto God the things that are God's."—Matt. xxii. 20, 21. Here is honesty of the highest type inculcated, and it is enjoined upon the members of the family of Christ. And by the sincere and consistent members of this family it is carried out, and when carried out it produces the noblest of characters — the Christian character. And "a Christian is the highest type of a man," and a Christian character the perfection of man's character.

Young students, you may be successful in your studies. You may succeed in receiving high titles, you may have the title of A. M., LL.D., or D. D., offered to you. These are all honorable and high titles, and may add worldly honor to you, but, my young brethren and sisters, if you are worthy members of the family of Christ, if you are worthy of the name Christian, you will find that there is more in that name than there is in all the honorable titles which the world can heap upon you. Nothing can be compared to the title of Christian — one like Christ, one born from above, born of God; a holy man, kind, true, and just in all his principles, and faithful in all his duties.

The family of Christ is a numerous family. It is true, since man's apostasy, the majority in every age of the world have been strangers to God, and not members of the divine family. Our Lord said: "Enter ye in at the strait gate: for wide is the gate, and broad is the way, that leadeth to destruction, and many there be which go in thereat: because strait is the gate and narrow is the way which leadeth unto life, and few there be that find it."— Matt. vii. 13, 14. This is a representation of our race that is by no means honorable to it. Still when all the good, and true, and faithful of all ages and of all countries are brought together around the throne of God, they will constitute a numerous family. St. John says, "I beheld, and, lo, a great multitude, which no man could number, of all nations, and kindreds, and people, and tongues, stood before the throne, and before the Lamb, clothed with white robes, and palms in their hands, and cried with a loud voice, saying, Salvation to our God which sitteth upon the throne, and unto the Lamb."—Rev. vii. 9, 10. This multitude belonged to the family of Christ. While many refuse salvation, many accept of it. This is a great company. It is pleasant to think that so many will have been faithful, and will in due time be manifest as the result of the redeeming work of him that "gave his life a ransom for many."

The family of Christ is a rich family. In the eyes of the world many of them may be poor. Many of the members of this family may have been among the poorer ones of this world. Nevertheless they are wealthy. Paul, in his first epistle to the Corinthians, iii. 21-23, says, "Therefore let no man glory in men; for all things are yours; Whether Paul, or Apollos, or Cephas, or the world, or life, or death, or things present, or things to come; all are yours; And ye are Christ's; and Christ is God's."

Let us look at the expression, "Whether Paul, or Apollos, or Cephas." These men were all preachers. They are part of the family of Christ, and members of the Church. We have them in their lives and in their ministry. We have the Bible. We have the services of the sanctuary. We have our pleasant meetings together, and the world, and life, and death, and things present, and things to come. We have the use and enjoyment of all these to a degree and in a sense, which the wicked have not. Christians make the world their servant and not their god, and hence they enjoy it as far as there is enjoyment in it. May I not then say that we are a rich family?

The prince of darkness is represented to be reigning over this world. The world has been taken away from God and his people by wicked princes, wicked men, and devils. The time is coming when this world will be taken away from Satan and be given to us. Hence, the language of Jesus,

"Blessed are the meek, for they shall inherit the earth." We have within the last few weeks heard of the Springer law suit in regard to the city of Wilmington, Delaware. Baron Springer received a grant for a large body of land in Delaware. He did not occupy it in any way and others got possession of it. His heirs are now trying to recover it. The property may be theirs, and it may not. If it is recovered, it will be a great disappointment to many, though it may please those who get it. Property is often held by those who are not the proper owners. So it is in regard to the world. "The earth is the Lord's and the fullness thereof: the world, and they that dwell therein." Ps. xxiv. 1. "And all these possessions have been given to Christ."—John xiii. 3. His claims then are strictly lawful, and in due time he will assert his right. "And the seventh angel sounded; and there were great voices in heaven, saying, the kingdoms of this world are becoming the kingdoms of our Lord, and of his Christ; and he shall reign forever and ever."—Rev. xi. 15. And as all the members of Christ's family are joint heirs with him (Rom. viii. 7), they too shall possess the earth and reign with him.

The family of Christ is a loving family. Love is the badge of membership in this family. "By this," said Jesus, "shall all men know ye are my disciples, if ye have love one to another."—John xiii. 35. And John says, "We know that we have passed from death unto life, because we love the brethren. He that loveth not his brother abideth in death."—1 John iii. 14. And the love with which we are to love one another, is to be fervent love. St. Peter says, "Seeing ye have purified your souls in obeying the truth through the Spirit unto unfeigned love of the brethren, see that ye love one another with a pure heart fervently."—1 Peter i. 22. As love is such a prominent element in Christian life and character, we have its manifestation in many Christian practices. The Christian form of salutation is a symbol of love. "Greet ye one another with a kiss of charity."—1 Peter v. 14. Here is a manifestation of affection. The "feast of charity," Jude 12th verse, the Christian family meal that Christians eat together in brotherly love, also manifest their love as the name of the feast indicates. And as it is said of the Saviour, by St. John, when he was about washing the feet of his disciples, that, "having loved his own which were in the world, he loved them unto the end." —John xiii. 1. It is evident that what he did, when he stooped to wash the feet of his disciples was both the result and manifestation of the love which he had to his disciples. So when they wash one another's feet they show their love to one another.

Such being the love that Christians are to feel to one another, and such being the love that they have to one another, how inconsistent it is for Christians to strive with one another, to go to law with one another, and to kill one another! The apostle Paul, when he reproved the Corinthian brethren for going to law with one another, says, "Now therefore there is a fault among you, because ye go to law one with another. Why do ye not rather take wrong?"—1 Cor. vi. 7. And how strange it is that with all that is said about brotherly love in the Gospel, that any who profess to believe and practice the Gospel, should believe that Christians may without sin kill one another, and yet there are those who believe it! Those who believe that Christians may go to war, believe also that Christians may kill one another, for in wars in which nations professing Christianity are engaged, professing Christians are brought into conflict with one another, and, consequently, may kill one another. But surely in such cases there must be a want of genuine Christian love.

The family of Christ is a scattered family. The apostle

Paul, when speaking of the name of the family of Christ, says: "For this cause I bow my knees unto the Father of our Lord Jesus Christ, of whom the whole family in heaven and on earth is named."—Eph. iii. 14, 15. Here one part of the family is represented to be in heaven, while the other part is on earth. For it is only one family, yet it is both in heaven and on earth. Those on earth at this time who do the will of God, are members of Christ's family. But many of the same class who once lived on earth, live here no more. They are now in heaven. But they still belong to Christ's family. We sometimes mourn for our pious dead that have left us. But we should remember that they are "not lost but only gone before;" that the ties which bound us together are not broken, but still exist; that we are still members of the same family, and only separated by death; that when death is destroyed, the saints of all ages and all places will again meet.

There will be a final gathering of all the members of the family of Christ. The apostle Paul, in the same epistle in which he represents the family of Christ to be scattered, also refers to a time when there will be a glorious gathering together of all the scattered members of this great family. In speaking of what God has done for his people, he says: "Having made known unto us the mystery of his will, according to his good pleasure which he hath purposed in himself: that in the dispensation of the fulness of times he might gather together in one all things in Christ, both which are in heaven, and which are in earth; even in him."—Eph. i. 9, 10. Then all are to be gathered together. The thought is full of comfort, and the prospect is animating. Our sainted fathers, mothers, brothers, sisters, children and friends that have passed over, will meet us and greet us on the other shore. Then will our joy be full, and uninterrupted and perpetual as well as full.

Dear Christian brethren, let us not forget the royal character of the family to which we belong. Let us honor our family. And my unconverted friends, what do you think of the family of Christ? Do you not think it is an interesting family, and a very happy family? It surely is. Would you not like to become a member of it? You may by receiving Christ.

IV.

OUR CONTINUAL NEED OF CHRIST.

"As ye have therefore received Christ Jesus the Lord, so walk ye in him.

"Rooted and built up in him, and stablished in the faith, as ye have been taught, abounding therein with thanksgiving."—Col. ii. 6, 7.

The apostle opens this chapter with this expressive and peculiar language: "For I would that ye knew what great conflict I have for you, and for them at Laodicea, and for as many as have not seen my face in the flesh." What great conflict does Paul refer to? It was a conflict of mind and a distress of feelings. From what source did it arise? It was because he was afraid that the brethren to whom he referred, might not continue faithful in the good work which they had commenced. The same feeling causes trouble and concern on the part of many ministers and servants of God. We have an interest in the spiritual welfare of our fellow-men. We are trying to bring all those, over whom we can exert an influence, to Christ. Our first concern is to get them converted, reformed, and made ready for a better world—to get them to abandon their errors and receive the truth, to quit the work of sin, and engage in the service of God. Is the mind of the preacher relieved of all anxiety and care when the sinner is converted? Ah! there is concern still! From the fact that we are in a world of tempation, in a world of pride, in a world of error, in a world where the Prince of darkness holds sway—there must be concern. We are sorry to be compelled to acknowledge it, but it is true, that this is a world in which error and darkness have control, rather than heavenly truth and heavenly principle. Such is the fact and we can never lose our feeling of concern for our friends as long as they remain in the world. When their course of life is finished and we bear them to the grave, although we feel great sorrow and our hearts are sad, yet if we can believe that they died in Christ, our concern is over, and we are relieved. We know that they have gone to a world where there will be no temptation. The preacher feels for his people while they are in this world. The Christian father cares and watches over his children to protect them from temptation. We feel for one another. That was Paul's conflict. That is the conflict of all preachers. I might say to you, "I would that ye knew the great conflict I have for you. I would that ye knew the trouble and anxiety which I have lest ye do wrong and wander away from Christ in ways of wickedness. Such was Paul's concern; and with such feeling he used the words of my text, "As ye have received Christ Jesus the Lord, so walk ye in him." They had received Christ, and he was anxious that they should continue to walk in him. This confirms what I have just stated in regard to our concern.

I will present what I have to say under two leading thoughts and make the application as best I can. The thoughts are these—First, *Our need of Christ*. And, secondly, *The continuation of that need*.

First, *Our need of Christ*. Our text says, "As ye have

therefore received Christ Jesus the Lord." This would imply that these brethren at Colosse had received Jesus Christ. They received him because they knew they had need of him. They received him because they knew that they could not be saved in any other way. From these remarks I make the observation that we all have need of Christ. Religion is not the development and growth of some innate and natural principle within us. The smallest child in the room, the little babe in the mother's arms, has within it the elements of manhood or womanhood. It is true, that it may need nourishment to develop the man or woman, but it has the elements within it. But, we want some additional element which we have not to enable us to form the true Christian character. None of us who are Christians had all the elements of Christianity within us before we became Christians.

I say to the unconverted man and woman, you do not have all the elements of a Christian character within. No matter from what family you may have sprung, no matter what your natural temperament may have been, no matter what may have been your surroundings, no matter how pure your life has been from wicked desires, no matter how excellent your moral character, to form a genuine Christian character there must be an additional element. You must have Christ in you before such a character can be found. The Christian character consists in two things: First, in removal of sin, and secondly, the presence of a divine principle within us. The removal of the wrong is necessary. I am afraid that right here we are apt to fall into the error of giving our Christianity a negative character only. Many are too apt to look at it only as the absence of evil. I want to disabuse your minds of that error. I tell you, my Christian friends, and brethren, that Christianity does not consist alone in a negative character, that is, in an absence of wrong. There is a positive side to Christianity as well as a negative one. While it is our duty and a part of the Christian life to abstain from even "the appearance of evil," while it is our duty to deny ourselves of all "ungodliness and worldly lusts," it is no less our duty to "live soberly, righteously and godly." We must not only "cease to do evil," but we must also "learn to do well."

These Colossian brethren had received Christ, as many of us have done. Jesus is the Saviour that we need. He pardons our sins, takes away the wrongs that we have done. However numerous these wrongs have been, however heinous in their character, he takes them all away. Our lives are made free from guilt, and we enjoy the happiness of the Christian. This is the condition of the heart that has been washed in the blood of Jesus. The heart is now clean, pure and white. The heart now becomes the tablet upon which the divine commandments are written according to the language of Solomon: "Keep my commandments and live; and my law as the apple of thine eye. Bind them upon thy fingers, write them upon the table of thine heart."—Prov. vii. 2, 3. We are living under the circumstances alluded to by the Apostle Paul, when he says, referring to what God will do for his people, "I will put my laws into their mind, and write them in their hearts, and I will be to them a God, and they shall be to me a people."—Heb. viii. 10. The carrying out of these laws constitute the positive character of the Christian. Our hearts which were once evil, are emptied of evil and filled up with what is good. Our members which were servants of unrighteousness and wickedness, now become servants of holiness. We leave the service of Satan and enter the service of God. We are dedicated and consecrated to God.

I come now to the next point that is implied in the language of the text: "As ye have therefore received Christ

Jesus the Lord, so walk ye in him: Rooted and built up in him, and stablished in the faith as ye have been taught, abounding therein with thanksgiving." Paul here uses three metaphors. I have already spoken of the anxiety which he felt for his brethren. He therefore uses figure after figure to impress his meaning more firmly upon their minds. He uses metaphors here to present the life of the Christian after Christ has been received into the heart.

First, walk is used, "walk in him." Second, the figure of growth is used, "rooted in him." Third, the figure of a building is used, "built up in him." The meaning of these figures is plain. From the first we learn there must be action and progress, for such "walk" implies. The second indicates life and growth. The third implies stability. Various principles enter into and form the Christian life.

We receive Christ. He bears our sins away. We then become as little children. The work that we are now to do is to form a Christian character. This is to be the work after we have received Christ, received him in the pardon of our sins, received him in the incipient stages of the work to be done. We are then to walk in him, grow in him, build in him.

These truths lead us to the next thought, *that we are to continue in Christ.* It is not enough that the sinner seeks him, and then feels because his sins are forgiven that Christ is not needed any more.

This meaning of the text is that we are never done with Christ. We must walk in him, be rooted and built up in him. The roots or fibers of our life must sink deep into Christ. These fibers are to multiply and become stronger; the branches are to spread out and bear fruit abundantly to the glory and honor of God. The tree consists of two parts, the part below, and the part above ground. So one part of our Christian character must bring the nourishment from

Christ, and the other show the fruits to the world. Lay the foundation of this noble structure which we are building, deep in Christ. Let it go on to maturity. "Add to your faith virtue; and to virtue, knowledge; and to knowledge, temperance; and to temperance, patience; and to patience, godliness; and to godliness, brotherly kindness; and to brotherly kindness, charity."—2 Peter i. 5–7.

"As ye have therefore received Christ Jesus the Lord, so walk ye in him." Do not wander out of the way. If you walk in him there is no danger. Do not feel, however, that because you have received him, you do not need him any more. Do not feel because you have your name registered among the members of some Christian church, that you are safe. "As ye have received Christ Jesus the Lord, so walk ye in him."

I have been nearly half a century in the service of God. But I feel that I need Christ quite as much now as I did when I entered into the holy covenant with him. We can never do without him. Let our circumstances be what they may, let our locations be where they may, yet we must have the support of Christ. While our circumstances here in Huntingdon may not be the best in the world, yet we think that they are favorable. But do not, my brother and sister, allow the thought to enter your minds, that because you are thus surrounded by Christian associations and companions, that you do not need the help of the Saviour. Although you have friends around you to help you, and brethren to pray for you, yet you need Christ. As you have received Christ in holy baptism when you entered into the holy life, so walk in him. Whether you are here in Huntingdon, or anywhere else, you must have Christ. Remember that you must seek him daily. Avail yourselves of the means of grace which he has provided. As you have need of Christ, so walk in him. This walking in Christ refers to action and conduct.

Walking in Christ means walking after Christ's example, walking as Christ walked, walking in sympathy with Christ. Walking in Christ implies an identification with Christ's ends, principles and purposes. It means walking in the path which he has marked out for us. "And whosoever doth not take up his cross, and come after me, can not be my disciple." Luke xiv. 27. Then we are to walk in Christ, bearing the cross.

"Rooted in Christ." What does that mean? It means planted in Christ, Paul, in the sixth chapter of his Epistle to the Romans, says: "For if we have been planted together in the likeness of his death, we shall also be in the likeness of his resurrection." Paul is alluding to the subject of baptism, and speaks about being buried with Christ, and then makes use of the expression quoted. This has reference to Christians who have received Christ. That is the planting. We are regarded as trees having our roots in Christ, or as branches grafted into Christ. This passage stands in close connection with another which I will quote: "Know ye not, that so many of us as were baptized into Jesus Christ were baptized into his death?"—Rom. vi. 3. What does this mean, "baptized into his death?" I understand that by being baptized into his death, we are baptized into the fruits of that death, into the merits of that death. I quote a similar passage that is a little more expressive in its meaning: "For as many of you as have been baptized into Christ have put on Christ."— Gal. iii. 27. The passage in Romans says, "into his death." We may regard the other as explaining this, making it mean into Christ. I think that the meaning of the two passages is this: Paul is talking about planting. In our profession of Christianity, we become planted in Christ. Baptism in connection with repentance and faith, brings us into Christ. We are then *planted* in him, or *rooted* in him. The plant is tender and must be protected and nourished. Spring is now coming, when we transplant trees and shrubbery. Some of the plants may have very small fibres; many of these may be injured in transplanting, but as long as there is life, the plant may grow if planted in good soil. The fibers will draw nourishment from the earth. It will become larger and larger; its branches will become more and more fruitful. So we are planted in Christ. The soil is not wanting in fertility. Our spiritual soil is rich and will sustain us if we but send our roots abroad. You can not grow unless you are planted in that soil. Take the most excellent plant that you can find in our nurseries, plant it upon some of these pine ridges. Will it bring forth fruit? No; it must be planted in soil that will develop it. So it is with human nature. It will never bring forth any good fruit until it is planted in Christ. If it is planted there, it will bring forth godly manhood and womanhood.

In order to become good, you must receive Christ. You can not become good in any other way. "There is none other name under heaven given among men whereby we must be saved."—Acts iv. 12. I urge you to receive him. He will be your helper and your Saviour. No matter how far you have wandered away from him, he will lead you back.

In the second place, let us all be careful to walk in Christ. It should be a joy to us to know that we can walk in him. While we are walking in him, we are walking safely. Christian brother and sister, we have received Christ, are we walking in him? So the apostle in our text admonishes us to do.

V.
BLESSINGS LOST IF NOT IMPROVED.

"Take heed therefore how ye hear: for whosoever hath, to him shall be given; and whosoever hath not, from him shall be taken even that which he seemeth to have."—Luke viii. 18.

The difficulty often presents itself to thoughtful men and women, how can that which he has not be taken away from him? Can anything be taken away from a man which he has not in his possession? This can not be done. It is an impossibility. You can not take from a person that which he has not, but he may have other things which may be taken away from him

I will call your attention to the different kinds of the blessings of God. We may divide these blessings into two classes; those of a universal character, and those of a special or limited character. First, the blessings of God of a common or universal character. The Saviour in his sermon upon the mountain, you will remember, said to his disciples: "Your Father maketh his sun to rise on the evil and on the good, and sendeth rain on the just and the unjust." This blessing of rain, and the blessing of sunshine are very general, and common blessings. They are not confined to any class of characters. They are not confined to the good, but are conferred upon the evil as well as the good. What the Saviour said of the rain and the sunlight may be said of a good many other things. Many other things may be included in the catalogue of the common or universal blessings which the bountiful hand of heaven showers upon us irrespective of character. The first that I will notice will be the blessings of Divine revelation—as we have it in the sacred Scriptures. This embraces a knowledge of God and of our duty.

While God has left the principles of science to be searched out, discovered and applied by men, he has not done so with moral science, and with the principles of religious truth. Science is of God. The origin of many of our sciences is with God. Sir Isaac Newton, Kepler, or any other astronomer did not originate astronomy. God originated it. Astronomy is coeval with the formation of the earth and the heavenly bodies. By the exercise of the philosophic and searching minds of such men, the principles of astronomy were discovered. These principles have been reduced to the science which some of you have been studying. God did not disclose these principles. He left that for men to do. God established, and men discovered. God connected these principles with the heavenly bodies at the time when they were formed, and men have discovered these, and reduced them to a system. Euclid, the great geometrician, did not make the laws of geometry. They are coeval with the existence of matter itself. Euclid systematized these principles, brought them down to the form which they now have in geometry. He reduced these principles to a system, but the principles themselves existed long before Euclid.

But how was it with the religous truths in which you and I, as moral men and women, are most deeply and universally concerned? God did not leave these to be discovered by men. In my sermon last week, I told you about the dreams and errors of men. Had God left men to discover these laws, what confusion, contradiction, and darkness would have been the result! We would have very conflicting views in regard to our moral duty. But God himself has given us the religious truths which it is important that we should know. He has brought these principles out and written them in his word. This is a free gift that God has placed within the reach of all. Divine revelation is as free as the sunshine; it is as free as the refreshing showers that fall; it is as free as the atmosphere that we breathe. It is given to all, without money and without price.

Another blessing of God, closely connected with the gift of revelation, is the gift of the Christian ministry. Paul, in the 4th chapter of Ephesians, in speaking of the gift of Christ and of the gifts which were thus secured for us, says: "And he gave some apostles; and some, prophets; and some, evangelists; and some, pastors and teachers." Now notice the reason, "for the perfecting of the saints, for the work of the ministry, for the edifying of the body of Christ." What a blessed thought that these are designed for the edification of the body of Christ. The Saviour gave certain official characters to do the work of the ministry. What is the work of the ministry? The work of the ministry is to preach the Gospel, explaining and applying it to the various wants of the people; to administer the ordinances of the Gospel as the people may require them. It is the duty of the minister of Christ to teach the religion of Christ, to make it plain, clear, and at the same time attractive, and to give it that form which will present Christ as the Saviour to sinners. Who have the benefits of the work of the ministry? All classes of people can receive the benefits of its work. You are all welcome, my unconverted friends, you are as welcome to this place as the members of our Christian community. We welcome you all. We like to see you with us.

And as the Gospel is free, and its offers of mercy and salvation are made to all, if men and women who live where the Gospel is preached are not instructed and saved, the fault is theirs. If men prefer the saloon and other places of carnal enjoyment, to the sanctuary, and remain ignorant and guilty, they must blame themselves for it. The sanctuary is open for them, and they have access to the benefits of the ministry.

The Christian Sabbath, I prefer to call it the Lord's day, is a gift of God. Some of you may doubt the propriety of my applying to the Lord's day what God said of the Jewish Sabbath when he spoke by his prophet Ezekiel. "I have given them my Sabbath."—Ez. xx. 12. It was a blessed gift. God gave it to man that men and brutes might rest from labor. It was also given to men for their religious and spiritual improvement. God said: "I have given them my Sabbath." I think we may apply the language to our Sabbath, as it was used with reference to the ancient Sabbath. God has given us the Christian Sabbath. If it has not been given to us with all the formality that surrounded the gift of the ancient Sabbath, yet it was unquestionably given to us. The early practice of the Church as given in the New Testament, and the practice since that time, gives us every reason to believe that the change from the seventh to the first day of the week meets God's approbation. We are only carrying out his laws when we set apart one day out of seven for our moral and spiritual improvement. I regard the Christian Sabbath as a gift of God. When Saturday evening comes, we give up our labor, fix up our houses, and prepare for the Christian Sabbath, the day on which we come together as we did this morning to sing and pray, to teach and to be taught, and to gather up the crumbs of truth, that we may be better prepared to go out and meet the difficulties and trials of the week. Value the Lord's day. It is God's blessing given unto us.

God has given us time and opportunity to prepare to meet him, time and opportunity to work out our salvation. That is a blessing which is given to all. If we had a census of our country to-day, we would find in the statistics of our people that God has, as a general thing, given as long life to the ungodly as to the godly. There are a good many old men and women who are out of Christ, and who are living out of the Church. Many of them are fifty, sixty, or seventy years old. Where did they get that time? God gave unto them. They had time and opportunity to repent and make their peace with God. If any unconverted man or woman should be called to-day to the judgment bar of Christ, could he or she say, "I did not have time to prepare"? This could not be said. God is giving all time to come to Christ. The sinner has as long a time to live as the Christian. Life is theirs to enjoy. God permits them to live. What has been the point? God's universal, or common blessings which are bestowed, irrespective of character and moral condition. Among these we have referred to revelation, the Lord's day, the ministry, and time and opportunity. God has given these to all. He has given us these that we may use them so that we may serve him. My unconverted friend, he has given these to you as well as to any one of us who are trying to be Christians.

Some of God's blessings are limited to a number. What are some of these blessings? I remark that repentance is one of God's gifts which is limited. I refer to repentance as a gift because it is so spoken of in the Scriptures: "Him hath God exalted with his right hand to be a Prince and a Saviour, for to give repentance to Israel, and the forgiveness of sins."—Acts v. 31. In the 11th chapter of the Acts, 18th verse, Peter is preaching to the Gentiles at the house of Cornelius. The following words are found: "When they heard these things, they held their peace, and glorified God, saying, Then hath God also to the Gentiles granted repentance." Repentance is here spoken of as a gift. This is a gift in a certain sense.

Now we begin to make a distinction between persons in regard to these gifts. I have been speaking to you all. Now I must make a distinction.

This gift of repentance is limited to a certain number. I will now read the text as I think the sense requires it to be read. It is one of those texts in which there is a good deal more implied than there is expressed. "Take heed, therefore, how ye hear: for whosoever hath Divine revelation, the Christian ministry, the Lord's day, and the necessary time to work out his salvation, and improve these blessings, shall have given to him, repentance, pardon, salvation and heaven. The receiving of the special or limited blessings does not depend upon God's fore-ordination, but upon man's improvement of what we have called God's general or common blessings. These blessings, duly improved, lead to salvation. Hence, Paul's language, "the goodness of God leadeth thee to repentance."—Rom. ii. 4. "But whosoever hath not, from him shall be taken even that which he seemeth to have." That is, whosoever hath not properly used and duly improved God's common blessings, even these shall be taken from him. Such, unquestionably, is the meaning of the Saviour, in his words we are using as our text.

The limited or special blessings are properly gifts of God. They grow out of the blessings which he gives to all. Repentance is an indirect gift of God. It grows out of God's gifts. Belief implies knowledge. You can not believe unless you have something to believe. You must believe that Christ is the Son of God, that God is the ruler of the universe; that we exist in a guilty and lost condition; that salvation is obtained only from Christ. You can receive this knowledge only through Divine revelation. Dwelling seriously, thoughtfully, prayerfully upon these thoughts, the mind will be roused to a state of conviction, and if this conviction is properly followed up, it will lead to conversion. And thus it is that to him that hath more shall be given. And even after a man becomes converted and becomes a Christian he shall still receive more, if he is faithful and improves his talents. Christians will never be done receiving. Neither will what they now have be taken from them. They will continue to enjoy them in a certain sense. The ministry will not be taken from us. It will be given to us under better circumstances. We will listen in holy rapture to the explanation of the purposes and plans of God. We will sit at the feet of those whom we regard as our instructors. The Sabbath rest will not be taken from us. We now have one day out of seven; then, all our days will be days of rest. Our time will be taken away, but it will be swallowed up in eternity—an eternity of enjoyment. We may not have the blessed Bible in heaven; we will not need it there; we will have its laws and principles written upon the hearts and minds of those who will be there. We will dwell in rapture upon the knowledge and information we will receive.

But, my unconverted friends, neglect salvation, neglect religion, and you will go where the Bible is not. You will be cast into outer darkness, where there will be none of God's blessings. You will go where there is no Lord's day. "There is no rest, saith my God, for the wicked." It will be one uninterrupted scene of confusion and distress. Life will be taken from you. Opportunity to become better will be taken away from you. You will not be able to attend church any more. "Take heed, therefore, how ye hear; for whosoever hath, to him shall be given; and whosoever hath not, from him shall be taken even that which he hath." Improve the present, or else these blessings which God has given you will be taken away and you will live in utter destitution of all those comforts which you now have. The condition of the lost is one of extreme want. The rich man in hell could not get a drop of water. The condition of the righteous is one of fullness. "Blessed are they which do hunger and thirst after righteousness; for they shall be filled."

VI.
A TEST OF DISCIPLESHIP.

"And there went great multitudes with him; and he turned and said unto them:

"If any man come to me, and hate not his father, and mother, and wife, and children, and brethren and sisters, yea, and his own life also, he can not be my disciple."—Luke xiv. 25, 26.

Every passage of Scripture must be so explained as to not contradict any other passage. Every passage of Scripture must be explained in harmony with the general tenor of divine truth as we have it in the Bible. Looking at this text, according to these principles, we must get the meaning of hate as it was used at the time in which the passage was written. This text is an idiom of the Hebrew language. By this we mean a peculiarity of the language. This idiom is a peculiarity, not only of the Hebrew, but of every Eastern language, more or less. That idiom is this: When two things are compared between which there is a great difference, the less one is regarded as nothing. In the 40th chapter of Isaiah, 17th verse, you will find a confirmation of this view. God himself is there compared to nations, or to things of a worldly character. It is said in the passage, "All nations before him are as nothing; and they are counted to him less than nothing and vanity." Here is a wonderful contrast. The infinitude of God, the grandeur of his attributes and character are so much more highly exalted and lifted above all mundane or worldly and secular things, that the greatness of man is said to be nothing, or less than nothing. The same principle is involved in my text. I shall explain my text upon this principle.

The love of the Christian heart to Christ, the Son of God, who bled and died for us, must be so much greater than the love of country, companions, associates, and even our own lives, that our love for one another will appear as hate, when compared to the love which we should have for Christ. Our love to Christ must be so great that the other will be as hate. The Saviour uses the figure to which I have referred in another passage.

It is this: "No man can serve two masters: for either he will hate the one and love the other, or else he will hold to the one and despise the other." "Ye can not serve God and mammon."—Matt. vi. 24. He does not say, because ye must necessarily love one more than the other, but according to the figure of speech, Jesus says, "Either he will hate the one and love the other." The meaning is, that when he loves with a less love, it will be as hate. Instead of calling a less love by that name, he calls it hate. This is the way that we are to understand hate in the text.

We have a very striking representation of this in the 29th chapter of Genesis, 30, 31 verses. The passage has reference to the love of Jacob for his wives, Leah and Rachel. In the 30th verse we read, "And he loved also Rachel more than Leah." He loved Leah, but he loved Rachel more than he did Leah. In the 31st verse, we find the following words: "When the Lord saw that Leah was hated." The historian does not say that Leah was loved less, but that Rachel was loved more. On this account, his love for Leah was compared to hate. Here we have two things compared, and because there is considerable difference between them, one is not only represented as less, but as being of the opposite character.

We may look at Proverbs xiii. 24 with profit. "He that spareth his rod hateth his son, but he that loveth him chasteneth him betimes." You have often heard this text quoted, but may not have looked at it as I am now doing. You conceive of two men who have unruly boys. These children are to be corrected. Solomon had punishment by the use of the rod before his mind. We think that the rod should be avoided as much as possible, but correction should not be avoided. Solomon has these fathers before him. One spared the rod and the other used it. The one that spares the rod is said to hate his boy. This is an entirely new doctrine. We usually suppose that the one that spares the rod loves the child. The doctrine commonly held is that love spares the rod. We love our children so much that we can not correct them. Instead of love, Solomon calls it hate. It is not the right kind of love. The love that will withhold correction, and allow the boy to begin to drink, smoke, swear, and begin habits that after a while will cause the ruin of his body and soul, such love is really hatred. It is injustice to the boy; it is injustice to the girl. When we try to correct, using such means as may be best suited to promote the proper end of discipline, it is not hate, but love that prompts us. Sparing the child is hatred. When one allows his child to grow up without correction, Solomon thinks it shows the want of proper affection, and therefore calls it hate.

Upon such principles as the preceding, our text is to be explained. It sometimes makes us wonder when we read passages like the one quoted by Paul in Romans ix. 13. "As it is written, Jacob have I loved, but Esau have I hated." Can such a merciful God hate one of his creatures? But applying the principle we have been considering, the meaning is, God loved Jacob more than he did Esau. He loves his good children more than he does the bad ones. God loves the most ungodly, sinful young man in the world. He loves the giddy, foolish young woman. He does not, however, love them as he loves those who obey and serve him. If you come to him, he will take you to his heart, he will encircle you with his loving arms. If you go on in the way of sin and folly, he will finally condemn you to eternal punishment.

It sometimes seems a stumbling block to us that God would hate. But love exists in different degrees. And you will find, if you consult Webster, that his second meaning of hate is *to love less.*

I will now read this passage as found in a translation of the Bible by Charles Thompson, once secretary of the American Congress. "As a great multitude were traveling with him, he turned to them and said, If any come to me, and doth not comparatively hate father and mother, and wife, and children, and brothers and sisters, and even himself also, he can not be my disciple." That is the idea which is embodied in the text.

I regard the text as equivalent to a corresponding expression of the Saviour found in Matt. x. 37. It is an equivalent of that passage: "He that loveth father and mother more than me is not worthy of me; and he that loveth son or daughter more than me is not worthy of me." Here we have the same idea presented in this passage that we have in the text.

These principles should be used in the interpretation and application of various passages of Scripture, as they will give the proper meaning to many doubtful passages.

The doctrine contained in the text is this: *The discipleship of a true disciple of Christ is conditioned upon our supreme affection to him.* This doctrine is plainly and positively taught in the text. Where our love to Christ is not supreme, there can be no true discipleship. This is the condition of our entering the state of true discipleship. The occasion upon which the Saviour used the language should not be overlooked. There was a great multitude with him. This is one of the passages addressed to the multitude. A great many passages are addressed to the disciples. They, however, have their application to the outside world as well. This passage was addressed to a great multitude. It was then as it is now. There were a great many people who could not get work, or who did not want work. Owing to some cause, there was a scarcity of the comforts of life. This want on the part of the multitude aroused the benevolent feelings of Christ. The love that caused him to leave heaven and come down to earth to save man, could not resist the distress of those who followed him; he exercised his power and performed miracles. Out of a few loaves and fishes he produced plenty. All that sat down were satisfied. The people were charmed with his appearance and kindness. They were poor. The priests, and aristocracy, and the wicked of the world did not see the charms of Jesus. To them he was a root out of dry ground, but the poor loved him. He was a friend to them.

I have often thought that when the little children were brought to him to be blessed, there must have been something in the mien and appearance of Jesus that was attractive to them. Purity love and holiness must have shone from his countenance. The people loved him and many followed him from place to place. From various motives a multitude collected around him. He then turned to them when he saw them following. They may have began to think that they were his disciples, because they followed him in his journey, and that they were to be counted among his disciples. This may be the way with some of us in the church, especially in churches which practice infant baptism. They may begin to think that they are disciples of Christ because they have been in the church a long time and have associated with Christians. But it is not the length of time we have been in the church, or our associations with Christians that make us the disciples of Christ. And the Saviour would disabuse the minds of any who received it, of that error, and so he turns to the multitude and said in substance. "I do not want you to be mistaken. I know that you have been following me. I know that you regard me as your friend. I notice that you listened to my discourses with interest. However, I want to tell you candidly that when the crisis comes, if you love anything more than you do me you can not be my disciples. I want you to remember that. It is not only following me in person, but you must understand that you must adhere to the truth when persecution and the time of trial comes. You must hold up the doctrine when slander and reproach are heaped upon you. You must maintain it through love to me. If you can not do this, I can not recognize you as my disciple. You must hate father and mother, and wife and children, and brethren and sisters, and your own life also."

The discipleship of Christ's disciples depends upon the love which we manifest in our lives for Christ. Hence, the passage which is often quoted in which the Savior is representing those who knock, saying, "Lord, Lord, open unto us." Jesus says, "I never knew you." That is, I never knew you as my disciple. I never found you ready to sus- in my doctrine. I never found you in my household of faith. I never found you in my devoted family, among my cross-bearing brethren. I do not know you as members of the kingdom of God. The love of Christ must be supreme. This is the doctrine that we maintain. It is involved in the text. It is the doctrine which Jesus plainly taught.

The claims which Christ has upon our love are just. A father's claims upon our love are strong, so are the mother's. A wife has a strong claim upon her husband; a husband has strong claims upon his wife. The love of children to one another ought to be strong. Playing together in our childhood, born of the same parents, living under the same roof, should strengthen the ties of domestic love. The love springing from all these domestic relations is not only justifiable, but it is right and proper. When we contrast these claims with those which Christ, the Son of God, has upon us, we find that his claims are stronger than all. Ought we not to love him with our best love? Our parents have been kind to us. When they die, they leave us legacies. Has not Christ done more? Heaven is his gift. That is to be bestowed upon his disciples. He has given us the priceless legacy of his blood. He has supreme claims upon us, and it is just that he should demand our supreme love.

It is possible to love him in the way in which he wants us to do. It has been done. You have read of the martyrs. You have read of the martyr Polycarp. He was brought before the Roman authority and asked to renounce the Christian faith and blaspheme the Son of God. He was asked to swear by Cæsar. The danger of being thrown to the wild beasts was held out to him. The fire was spoken of as the result of his refusal. He said, "Eighty and six years have I served Christ, and he never has done me any wrong, I can not deny him." He met his fate as a martyr. He hated his own life. Life was pleasant to him, but when it came in comparison to his love to Christ, he hated his own life. It is possible to have such love, and it must be had.

We should allow nothing to interfere with our religious duties. I have heard of a young man who fell by allowing things to come between him and Christ. You may take the hint. He was a member of a church. He was prayerful and devoted. He married a giddy, irreligious young woman. She drew his affection away from Christ. He neglected his church, prayer and other religious duties. Sickness came upon him. Eternity loomed up before him. Judgment was felt to be near at hand. He turned to his wife, to whose influence he attributed his destruction, and said, "Rebecca, Rebecca, you are the cause of my eternal damnation." He was drawn away by her influence. Instead of loving Christ with a supreme love, he gave his love to her.

He saw his terrible mistake amid the solemnities of a sick-chamber and in a dying hour. Young people, be careful, and we older ones should also watch. Let not the love of money, or anything else, draw us away from Christ. Remember, that true discipleship depends upon our supreme love for Christ. You must love Christ more than anything else. If you do this, you are his disciples; if you do not, you can not be. Let the application be made by those who are members of the church, as well as by others. Remember that Christ's test of discipleship is supreme love to him.

VII.
THE JUSTIFICATION OF CHRIST.

"And without controversy, great is the mystery of godliness: God was manifest in the flesh, justified in the Spirit, seen of angels, preached unto the Gentiles, believed on in the world, received up into glory."—1 Tim. iii. 16.

This is Whit-Sunday or White-Sunday, the festival of the Christian Church observed in commemoration of the descent of the Holy Spirit on the day of Pentecost. It is called Whit-Sunday, or, to give it the full name, White-Sunday, because it was one of the times in the ancient Church on which baptism was performed. And as a symbol of spiritual purity which baptism expressed, the candidates for the sacred rite were clothed in white garments, hence the day was called White-Sunday. The feast of Pentecost was seven weeks after the feast of the Passover, and the descent of the Spirit occurring at the feast of Pentecost, Whit-Sunday comes seven weeks after Easter. The descent of the Holy Spirit is a memorable event in the history of the Church, and its anniversaries may be observed with profit.

I have selected my text as an appropriate one for the occasion, as it refers in part at least to the day of Pentecost, of which this Lord's day is the anniversary.

My subject is the justification of Christ. The justification of the sinner is a precious Gospel doctrine. To know that the sinner, though his crimes have been great and many, can be justified, is a part of what Paul calls "the excellency of the knowledge of Christ."—Phil. iii. 8. He further says, "Being justified by faith, we have peace with God, through our Lord Jesus Christ: by whom also we have access by faith into this grace wherein we stand, and rejoice in hope of the glory of God. And not only so, but we glory in tribulations also, knowing that tribulation worketh patience; and patience, experience; and experience, hope; and hope maketh not ashamed; because the love of God is shed abroad in our hearts by the Holy Ghost which is given unto us."—Rom. v. 1-5. Here is the precious fruit of justification. And justification, the source of so many blessings, is obtained through Christ, as Paul taught when he said in speaking of Christ, "by him all that believe are justified from all things, from which ye could not be justified by the law of Moses."—Acts xiii. 39. But before sinners could be justified by Christ, it was necessary that he himself should be justified. His justification is the ground of ours. As we have already seen, we are justified by believing in Christ. But to believe in him we must have confidence in his authority, in divinity, in his atonement, and in everything pertaining to him. Hence, the necessity of his justification or approval. He was "justified in the Spirit."

In presenting my subject, the *Justification of Christ*, I will first notice his *Condemnation*, and then his Justification.

First, his Condemnation. It is said, Mark xiv. 64, "And they all condemned him to be guilty of death." What cruelty, ignorance, and gross wickedness! The holy Son of God, condemned "to be guilty of death!" How much had our blessed Lord to endure and bear for us! And he did it without a murmur, though he was innocent. " Who did no sin, neither was guile found in his mouth : who, when he was reviled, reviled not again ; when he suffered, he threatened not; but committed himself to him that judgeth righteously: who his ownself bore our sins in his own body on the tree, that we, being dead to sins, should live unto righteousness: by whose stripes ye were healed."--1 Peter ii. 22-24.

He was condemned, for sedition. "He stirreth up the people," said his accusers. Luke xxiii. 5. And because he claimed to be a king, his accusers construed that claim interfering with Cæsar's honor and right. They said, "whosoever maketh himself a king speaketh against Cæsar." —John xix. 12. But this charge was altogether was false. He sought not Cæsar's honor nor his throne. This was proved by the answer he gave to them that tempted him, and sought to prejudice the Roman authority against him. When they brought him "a penny," and he found that it had Cæsar's superscription upon it, he said, " Render, therefore, unto Cæsar the things which are Cæsar's."—Matt. xxii. 21. He sought not Cæsar's kingdom, for the kingdom that he came to establish was not of this world.—John xviii. 36. He came to establish a kingdom of regenerated subjects. Hence he taught, " Except a man be born again, he can not see the kingdom of God " (John iii. 3), and " Except a man be born of water, and of the Spirit, he cannot enter into the kingdom of God. "—John iii. 5. Such are the nature and spirituality, of the honors, privileges, and enjoyments of the kingdom of God, or of that kingdom which Christ came to set up, that the natural or unrenewed mind of man can not appreciate or enjoy them. " The natural man receiveth not the things of the Spirit of God: for they are foolishness unto him; neither can he know them, because they are spirtually discerned."—1 Cor. ii. 14.

He was condemned, second, for blasphemy. It was blasphemy in the sense of arrogating or taking to himself power that did not belong to him. When the man sick of the palsy was brought to him, he said, "Son, thy sins be forgiven thee."—Mark ii. 5. Our Lord in this case did not examine the sick man as physicians examine their patients to know where the disease was located, or the nature of the disease; he directed his attention to the root of the trouble, and this was sin. Hence he said, "Son, thy sins be forgiven thee." But the scribes said, "Why doth this man speak blasphemies? who can forgive sins but God only?" The scribes knew enough to know that as sin is committed against God, and his law and government, no authority less than his can pardon it. But they failed to know, though they had evidence enough to prove it to them, that Christ acted by the authority of God, and hence he could forgive sin. He arrogated no power to himself but what was given to him by God, and therefore was no blasphemer, though he pardoned the sinner.

Other charges were made against him, and he was looked upon by many of the Jews as a malefactor (John xviii. 30), and consequently was crucified between two criminals. It is not a little strange that the human mind can become so perverted and prejudiced by sin, that truth and argument lose their influence upon it, and then it commits the most terrible blunders and errors. The Jews, under their bitter prejudices, looked upon the Saviour as a root out of dry ground, having no form and comeliness, and condemned him to death. And the Gentiles united with the Jews in the unjust condemnation.

But God is just, and justice and right must have their

dues.—The sentence of condemnation and death was executed upon the innocent Son of God to its full extent, and he was crucified upon the cross. From this he was taken down and buried. But the grave could not contain him, and the third day he rose again, having conquered death and the grave. In his resurrection he was vindicated and justified by God, as is declared by Peter in his sermon on the day of Pentecost, saying, when speaking of Christ, "Whom God hath raised up having loosed the pains of death: because it was not possible that he should be holden of it." Acts ii. 24.

But there was to be another vindication and justification by the Spirit. It is true, the Spirit had justified the Saviour at his baptism when it came upon him in the form of a dove. "And John bare record, saying, I saw the Spirit descending from heaven like a dove, and it abode upon him. And I knew him not; but he that sent me to baptize with water, the same said unto me, upon whom thou shalt see the Spirit descending, and remaining on him, the same is he which baptizeth with the Holy Ghost. And I saw, and bare record that this is the Son of God." John i. 32-34. This was a justification of his character as the Son of God. But his work, his doctrine, and his disciples must be justified as well as his character. And these were all most gloriously justified and vindicated by the Spirit on the day of Pentecost.

The Lord, knowing the greatness of the work his disciples were to perform, and their insufficiency to perform it without divine aid, said to them after he had given them their commission, "Behold, I send the promise of my Father upon you; but tarry ye in the city of Jerusalem, until ye be endued with power from on high." Luke xxiv. 49. In obedience to his command, they did tarry at Jerusalem, in "an upper room," "the number of names together being about a hundred and twenty." "These all continued with one accord in prayer and supplication." Acts 1. To the disciples and infant church this was a time of solemnity and interest. The whole number of disciples was engaged in prayer. Perhaps the character of the blessing for which they prayed was not very definite to them. But they knew they would receive a blessing with power, which would prepare them for their work. They prayed and waited. The anxiously-looked-for period at length came, and with it the divine Spirit. "And when the day of Pentecost was fully come, they were all with one accord at one place. And suddenly there came a sound from heaven as of a rushing mighty wind, and it filled all the house where they were sitting. And there appeared unto them cloven tongues like as of fire, and it sat upon each of them. And they were all filled with the Holy Ghost, and began to speak with other tongues as the Spirit gave them utterance." Acts ii. 1–4. This was the baptism with the Holy Ghost. As in the baptism in water the subject is overwhelmed and entirely immersed, so when the apostles were baptized in the Holy Ghost their entire being was brought under the influence of the divine Spirit.

And how was the Saviour justified in the Spirit when it came upon the apostles as it did on the day of Pentecost? In coming with its gifts and comforts, and power, upon the waiting disciples of Christ, it showed its approbation of them, and its preference to them. And as they were the disciples of Christ, and believed and practiced his doctrine, and imitated his life, its descent upon the followers or disciples of Christ was a virtual and manifest vindication and justification of Christ and his doctrine. And though he had been condemned as a criminal by the world, he was justified by heaven as a divine messenger. Although the Jews thought they did God's service in condemning the Lord, the Holy Spirit did not come upon the members of the Jewish Sanhedrim to testify of its approval of their conduct, neither did it come upon the Jews in general who desired the condemnation of our Lord, neither did it come upon the Gentiles who united with the Jews in condemning him. The Spirit in directing its course from heaven, made its way to the upper room in Jerusalem, in which was assembled the infant church of Christ, and there it diffused its light, its life, its liberty and power, showing that the imitators of Christ were the ones which heaven delighted to honor.

I draw two inferences from the justification of Christ in the Spirit.—First, as the system of Christian truth has been justified by the Holy Spirit as well as by God himself, how strong are its claims upon all men for their belief in it. And how reliable are all its facts, doctrines and teaching. Secondly, to my Christian friends I would say, hold fast the apostolical faith, since it has been justified in the Spirit. It is sometimes more than intimated that it is not necessary to be so particular in adhering so strictly to apostolic precepts and practices. Now as no form of Christianity has ever received the justification that the apostolic form has, it is wisdom, in respect to a matter involving interests so great as that of our salvation, to risk our hope of heaven and immortality upon nothing that has not been justified in the Spirit, and approved of by heaven. Apostolic Christianity has thus been justified and approved of, and consequently it is " worthy of all acceptance " (1 Tim. i. 15), and "Israel shall be saved in the Lord with an everlasting salvation ; ye shall not be ashamed nor confounded, world without end."

VIII.
THE EXCELLENCY OF GOSPEL POWER.

"But we have this treasure in earthen vessels, that the excellency of the power may be of God, and not of us."— 2. Cor. 4:7.

The first thought is the character of the Gospel presented to us in the figure of a treasure. And you all know that a treasure implies value, or something that is valuable. And especially do we know this to be the case when allusion is made to worldy treasure. It may be in the form of wealth, or any valuable commodity, or any valuable article.

The value of the Gospel is seen in its utility. Whatever is useful is valuable. That we lay down as an axiom. The value of a thing is in direct proportion to the utility, or the usefulness of it. And a thing that is really of no use, is really of no intrinsic value; consequently, worthy of little labor, sacrifice or exertion to secure it; while that which is useful is worthy of our attention, and deserving of sacrifice and exertion. The value of the Gospel and its utility is seen in the thought further presented in our text, in the following language. "That the excellency of the power may be of God and not of us." The value of the Gospel then, is seen in the excellency of its power. There is power in the Gospel. It is true, there is power in a good many others things, but it is often destructive, damaging and ruinous power; but the power of the Gospel is excellent power—valuable power. In this particular the value of the Gospel is seen. This thought is in harmony with the well known declaration of the apostle when he says, "The Gospel is the power of God unto salvation." Herein is the excellency of the power of the Gospel seen. It is a power that saves. We are in our unregenerated condition, represented to be "under sin."—Gal. 3:22; "under the curse," verse 10; "captives under Satan," 2 Tim. 2:26.

Now the Gospel has come to our deliverance. Hence the language of the apostle, "Who hath delivered us from the power of darkness, and hath translated us into the kingdom of his dear Son." Col. 1:13. And our Lord in speaking of his mission, says: "The Spirit of the Lord is upon me, because he hath anointed me to preach the Gospel to the poor; he hath sent me to heal the broken-hearted, to preach deliverance to the captives, and recovering of the sight to the blind, to set at liberty them that are bruised." Luke 4:18. All the effects attributed to the coming of our Lord, are accomplished through the power of the Gospel. And these effects are glorious indeed, and hence the power that produces them is an *excellent* power.

There is a great deal of power necessary to save us. Such is the power of sin over the young; upon human nature, upon our moral nature, that it has produced a condition that is not easily rectified; a condition out of which it is impossible for us to deliver ourselves. A divine power, a power from God is necessary, and if that power is not brought to bear upon us, and we are not rescued from sin, we are *lost*, forever *lost*. No arm but the arm of God can save us; and how unwise to venture on in sin and folly, when we can at any time be converted. Let us not go on in sin and sin away our healthful days, our best years, the most vigorous and active part of our lives, and think we can do better then and repent on a dying bed.

No doubt many of the supposed conversions that have taken place on the death-bed have been delusions. Oh! it is not to shed a few tears; it is not to express a few regrets for our misspent life, or to have prayers made by the faithful ones that saves. No; this is often a delusion. When we think of the treachery of the human heart, and its wickedness, we ought to avail ourselves of the times and opportunities of having the application of the divine power of God made to us, by which we may be assured that we are saved, by having a proper test of character. What do I mean by a proper test of character? Why, come out on the side of the Lord, and let the devil and earth and hell assail the soul and tempt it, and try to draw it away, and when these powers have been brought to bear against us, and we call upon Christ to resist these powers, and when we feel that our love for Christ and the church is sufficient to deliver us from these powers, then we may hope that we are right and our conversion not a deception.

Sometimes we are insulted. The young are tried. Not long since, a very painful fact was communicated to me. In a certain place, where there had been a revival of religion, a number of souls, among them a number of young persons, were gathered into the church. To-day several of them are out of the church. Had those young people on the sick-bed manifested a penitency or a religious interest, and had they died then, it would have been thought that they had gone to heaven; but is it so? They manifested some concern, but from some cause it was very evident that there was not a genuine conversion. And when they were tempted by the world, they yielded to the temptation, and did that which separated them from the church.

We ought to embrace religion under circumstances under which our religion can be tried, like many of you have done, and like others have done. Our Christian life is a struggle. It may be said of you that Satan desires to have you to sift you as wheat. He desires to have every brother and sister. He desires our ruin. He is trying to get us. Here is the conflict and here we can test our fidelity to Christ; our religious feelings, our safety. But we can do nothing of that kind when we turn to God on a dying bed. If we don't know much about temptation, we may fall into terrible delusion, and deception in regard to our spiritual state.

We want somthing great; we want the Gospel—the Gospel means of salvation. We want that. There is excellent power in it. Moral power, power to change our guilty hearts, power to change our moral natures.

It is said that the heart is deceitful above all things, and desperately wicked. It is so; but God's power is calculated to change the heart. It is valuable and calculated to save us, calculated to convert us, build us up, comfort us, help us, and finally to cap the climax of our salvation, in enabling us to overcome death and the grave, and secure immortality.

Another thought implied by the term "treasure" is something that is lasting. In the Gospel there is something that is durable. What is really useful is durable. This is another quality of usefulness—something that is lasting. Such is the value of the Gospel. There is something in it lasting. Peter said, "all flesh is as the grass, and the glory of man as the flower of the grass. The grass withereth and the flower thereof fadeth away, but the word of the Lord endureth forever." Did we ever look at the connection and get the real idea of the above passage?

"All flesh is as grass, and the glory of man, that is the glory of fame, glory of the world, glory of human applause, the glory of these things is like the flower of the grass which soon fades away. You all know, young men and women especially those of you who have studied botany, how delicate is the little flower. You can hardly analyze it and discover its class, genus and character before it withers in your hands. When we first looked at it, it was a pretty little flower, and we admired it, but how soon it withers! Young men and women, this is an illustration of your own glory, of your own carnal enjoyments, of your own worldly honor. Let the little flower preach to you. The grass withers and the flower fades, and soon all pass away. Until we had the late showers, the grass withered and its verdure disappeared. In this there is a lesson for us. So it is with man. As the grass will wither, and as the grass will die, and all things of a worldly character will fade, so will we pass away, but the word of the Lord endureth forever. In it there is perennial verdure, undying growth, unfading greenness, eternal life, eternal freshness and eternal comforts. The character of the word of the Lord endureth forever. Its enjoyments are durable. They do not soon wear out. Some of you have not been so long in the service of the Lord, but I hope your religion is not wearing out. I hope instead of that you are feeling more interested in it. I have enjoyed the comforts and consolation of religion for nearly half a century, and many living monuments of God's mercy have enjoyed them longer than this, but has it worn out? No; it is as precious to us as ever. I love to be with you. Some of us have enjoyed communion seasons a great while ago, but that latest communion season was quite as good, and better than many that we enjoyed forty or fifty years ago. What is the point? The durability of the Gospel, of its comforts, and its consolations. They will never get old. They will always be fresh, always enjoyable. If we live to be old and retain our mental powers, we can enjoy them to the latest hour in life. And is that all? No; we can enjoy them to the latest hour in life, and then be translated to heaven, there to resume our enjoyments, and have them perpetuated forever and forever. There they will never wear out. There they will always be new.

"We have this treasure in earthen vessels, that the excellency of the power may be of God and not of us." What are these earthen vessels? Men. Paul classes himself with the earthen vessels, and says that God did not commit this treasure to wooden, silver, or golden vessels, but to earthen vessels. If the Gospel had been committed to a holy order, of celestial beings, divine beings, with their powerful intellects, their great capacity and inventive genius, then it might have been thought that the power was inherent in them, originated in them, and that would have taken the glory from God and Christ.

God is a jealous God, and he will not give his glory to another; and let us, in our enjoyments, successes and labors, recognize God. Keep self out of the way and try to get under the influence of the divine Spirit, and when we succeed, give God the glory. Hence in order that the excellency of the power of the Gospel could not be attributed to the vessel or instrument by which it is preached, God committed the Gospel to men—to earthen vessels.

How frail is the human body! How frail is the human intellect! And how degraded is our moral character; and there can but little good come out of ourselves, consequently, the excellency of the power of the Gospel can not be attributed to men; because man has so little power in him, so little genius in him, we mean in regard to spiritual subjects, that he could not devise or originate anything like we have in the Gospel. Remember the thought. He committed the Gospel to earthen vessels.

We are earthen. We must remember our capacities as preachers and teachers; do not forget that we are earthy and imperfect, consequently can not expect much good to grow out of ourselves.

From the fact that the Gospel has been preached by imperfect men, a divine character of the Gospel is evident. I mean this: Look at the Gospel, and look at the doctrine contained in it; look at the standard of holiness inculcated in the Gospel; look at the grace and mercy and kindness, and all these things enjoined in the Gospel, all right in opposition to the human heart. Could man have originated them? Could man have originated a system of doctrines like that which we have in the Gospel? Could earthen vessels do this? Even Paul himself, with his mighty intellect and profound education, could not have devised a scheme like that which we have in the Gospel. Could he have originated doctrines so dignified, grave and sublime as the doctrines of the Gospel are? Could they have originated in a soil like the soil of the human heart or human character? They never could. Consequently these doctrines must be divine. The preachers that preach them did not start them. They are too holy, too peculiar, for man to have originated them; consequently we must acknowledge the divine character of these doctrines, because they did not originate with us. Men have their systems. I might get up something. Men have got up systems, but what are they? They are not worthy to be compared with the system contained in the Gospel; they bear no comparison to the excellency of the system of divine truth that we have in the Scriptures. The genius of men might originate a great many things, but they can not come up to the Gospel.

What is the example of the moral and spiritual character presented for our imitation? What is the example of life that we have presented to us in the Gospel? Think a moment. This is an important question. Without dwelling, it may be you will all answer me just as you understand the matter. Christ is the example, and what kind of a character is Christ? Could man devise that character, so pure, so perfect, so free from sin, so separate from everything that is unholy, containing everything that is true and good and pure, could men have devised a character of that kind? Can an artist communicate anything to the canvas but what he has in his own mind? He originates the ideas and he then places them on the canvas. That is what the artist must do; and could man ever have drawn such a character as

Christ, in writings, unless he had originated that character in his own mind? And could men have originated a character so kind and grand? It never could have been done. Hence the divinity of the Gospel. God's example is faultless. Think of that! I feel that it is worthy of consideration.

There are a great many evidences going to prove the divine authority of the Bible and Christianity, but one of the most plain and satisfactory evidences is the internal evidence of the Gospel. It is that pure life which it originates and inculcates. Man never would have devised a system condemning his own faults. One thing we may be assured of, and that is: "We have this treasure in earthen vessels that the excellency of the power may be of God, and not of us." What has the Gospel done? Has it not done more than any human system ever did before? What has the world done? Some of you students know something about philosophy; you will know something more about it hereafter perhaps. There were eight or ten systems of philosophy among the Greeks, but what did they do to make the world better? They did but little.

Socrates, it is said, after he delivered his lectures, complained to some of his friends that he did not know how it was that his system had not done more in reforming his countrymen, and in improving their characters. His doctrines were good, his efforts were strong, he was sincere, but he was at a loss to know why there was not any greater impression made; why the efforts of his labor were not more manifest. That was his concern; it was his discouragement. But when Christianity came, the world became better. Heathen temples were forsaken, heathen idolatry was abandoned. Paul in writing to the same church says: "Be not deceived; neither fornicators, nor idolaters, nor adulterers, nor effeminate, nor abusers of themselves with mankind, nor thieves, nor covetous, nor extortioners, shall inherit the kingdom of God. And such were some of you, but ye are washed, but ye are justified in the name of the Lord Jesus, and by the Spirit of our God." See the change that was produced in them! That the excellency of the power might be of God and not of us. The point is, the success of the Gospel, and the reforming power of the Gospel.

Brethren and sisters, try to show to the world the power of the Gospel by letting it reflect in your tempers and lives the holy principles and dispositions which it inculcates. Let the world see the influence of the Gospel in you. It is a pleasant sight to see the young man that was wild, wicked, and foolish, turn and become devoted to God, and faithful in his service, and the young woman who has been giddy and fashionable, to see her converted. She takes her place at the feet of Jesus. Oh! these conversions are the evidences that go to prove the divine power of the Gospel of our Lord Jesus Christ. Though all our conversions do not show the power as we would like them to, yet we have many glorious changes, so manifest, so striking, that there is sufficient evidence proving that there was a supernatural power there to change the bad man, and the bad woman, proving that the excellency of the power is of God and not of the preacher.

Seek this invaluable treasure. It is both useful and enduring. The young will find it very useful. Its excellent power will enable them to form good habits and good characters. It is useful to people in every age and condition of life. And its blessings and enjoyments will endure while the soul lives to need them. Fail not to secure this treasure. With the Gospel character and hope, though we may have nothing else, we are rich. Without them, whatever else we may have, we are poor.

IX.

THE PREPARATION FOR SERVING GOD.

"For if the blood of bulls and of goats, the ashes of a heifer sprinkling the unclean, sanctifieth to the purifying of the flesh: How much more shall the blood of Christ, who through the eternal Spirit offered himself without spot to God, purge your consciences from dead works to serve the living God."—Heb. ix. 13, 14.

The Mosaic law was elementary, typical and introductory. In the sense that our elementary school books are introductory to higher works in the respective sciences, where the subject is carried to the fullest extent, so the Mosaic law contained the elements of the Christian truth which is developed in the New Testament. The Mosaic dispensation was introductory to the Gospel dispensation. Reference is made in our text to certain ceremonies under the old law. If a Jew touched any dead body, he was unclean and was excluded from the worship which was then performed, until he was cleansed.

There was, in the ceremony of cleansing, the water of purification, in the making of which was used the ashes of the heifer. The heifer was burned and the ashes were taken to the priest. In the Old Testament we have a minute description of the manner in which this water of purification was prepared. Then we have the blood of bulls and goats which was used in other ceremonies connected with the Mosaic ritual.

Now Paul's meaning is, that if the water of purification made out of the ashes of a burnt heifer, and the blood of bulls and goats, "sanctified to the purification of the flesh," how much more certain will be the effect, how much more powerful will be the blood of Christ in cleansing the conscience from dead works to serve the living God. The apostle leads us from the means provided under the Mosaic law for the purifying of the flesh, to the means provided by God under the Christian dispensation for the cleansing of the conscience.

You have heard me read the 9th verse: "Which was a figure for the time then present, in which was offered both gifts and sacrifices, that could not make him that did the service perfect as pertaining to the conscience." The ceremonies of the old law failed to reach the conscience because they were not intended to do so. They failed to bring about the entire reformation and regeneration of the human character. They were not intended to do so. They were elementary and introductory. Now we have another dispensation. Under this the elements of divine power are given, and by a proper application of these, the conscience of fallen man is reached. The central part of the whole human being is reached. The very fountain of life is purified. Our consciences may now be cleansed from dead works, and be purified from the defilement of sin. That seems to be the meaning of the apostle. We have means provided which not only cleanse the body, but also the consciences of men. If conscience is cleansed, our whole nature is purified. Conscience is a part of our moral nature, but it is here unquestionably used to denote the whole of our moral nature, the whole heart with all its diversified faculties.

The Christian doctrine and view of God.—What is the Christian doctrine and view of God? It is that God is a *living* God. This is the view of God which is presented all the way through the Gospel. There are several occasions on which similar language was used. The Savior, alluding to God, does not call him the living God, but uses the very expressive language, *the living Father.* John vi. 57. It is not uncommon for the Jews under the old dispensation to speak of God as the *living* God, or to say "as the Lord liveth." The Lord himself uses the expression, "as I live, saith the Lord." This was done whenever he wanted to make his announcements especially expressive, or when he wanted to call their attention to what he said. The Christian view of God is, then, that he is a *living* God.

And the Christian view of God is in striking contrast with the heathen view of God. The gods of heathenism are dead gods. They do not live. They have eyes, but they see not; they have ears, but they hear not. Ps. cxxxv, 16. There is no life in them. I say there is a remarkable contrast between the living, personal God whom we worship, and the dumb, inanimate objects which the poor, deluded heathen worship as God. This view of God as a living God is in striking contrast with the secular view of God. The view of the secular and worldly philosopher and the view of worldly wisdom differ from the Christian view. Most men in our country have some view of God. Many, however, have a different view from the one which is taught in the Bible. In writing upon scientific subjects, many of our writers view God as a mere abstraction. They have some idea of the power of God, but they look upon him as a mere controlling force in the universe. They do not entertain the idea of a "living God," of a living personality, of a "living Father." They do not look upon him as a being possessing an intelligence which is informed of man's doings, as a being possessing passions and who is capable of sympathizing with his people. Such ideas do not enter into their philosophy. They look upon God as a mere idea, a mere notion of the mind. We have many other views of God with which the Christian view is in contrast. I might notice the Pantheistic view of God. The Pantheist holds that God and the universe are one. This view destroys the personality of God. I regard the Pantheistic view as but little better than the view of the idolator which looks upon God as an inanimate being. The Christian has another view of God. He regards him as a living being possessing intelligence, passions and sympathies. To such a God we can go in our sorrows and troubles, and feel that he will sympathize with us, and that he will help us.

David says: "My soul thirsteth after the living God." That is as much as to say, nothing but the living God will satisfy me; nothing but the living God can be to my mind what I want. Compared with the other views of God, we see how superior the Christian view is.

We can say with Job: "I know that my Redeemer liveth."—Job xix, 25. I know that he reigns; that he exercises power, and that when I need his help and sympathy I will have them.

He is the living God because he is the source of all life. Paul said, in his masterly sermon at Athens, to the people: "He giveth to all life, and breath and all things; and hath made of one blood all the nations of men for to dwell on all the face of the earth, and has determined the times before appointed, and the bounds of their habitation." He then gives several points further, and says: "In him we live, and move, and have our being."—Acts xvii, 26-28. He is, consequently, the cause of all existence from the least species of animalculæ to the highest form of animated existence; from the smallest herb to the largest tree; from the smallest spire of grass to the grand and mighty cedars of Lebanon. God is the cause of the vegetable life as well as of the animal. This, believers in Christian truth, is our doctrine. This is what we hold and what we believe. It is the Christian creed that God gives life to all.

If, by general reading and observation, we come to the conclusion that God is a living God, and that he is the cause of all life, and that he gives us breath, life, and everything;

from these considerations, it follows according to Christian law, and Christian truth, that it is our duty to love and serve him. This follows logically, and properly. In view of the relation which we sustain to God, in view of the relation to him as dependent creatures, we owe him our service. The Bible doctrine is, that we must love and reverence him. This Bible which we accept as true, requires this of us all. When you accept the Bible as true, and I hope that none of you do anything else, then you should serve God according to the teaching of the Bible. You sometimes look upon us Christians as not being consistent. You say that we do not walk with that consistency of life in our goings forth that our holy principles require. I acknowledge it. As a representative of the body of Christian believers, I acknowledge it. Many of us feel and mourn over our delinquency. If you could see us in secret, you would find us grieving over our misconduct. But we are trying to do right. We are preaching and praying and singing, and making use of all the heaven-appointed means that we may become better. We are striving by the use of all the means in our power to approach nearer to the divine character of him whose disciples we profess to be, and whom we call Master. We are professing to follow Christ and lead others to him; but even if we fail, are we not, my unconverted friends, more consistent than you are? You accept the Bible as true. You admit the binding and obligatory force of these principles upon all men who are brought in contact with them, yet you are not professing to follow them. Do you see the inconsistency? We see our failings, and we want you to see yours. There is inconsistency on the part of all those who read and respect the Bible, but do not try to practice its teachings. In our lecture rooms, in many of our societies, the Bible is read, but there is great indifference manifested in regard to its teachings. While many men respect and believe the Bible, they are not governed by its teachings in their daily life. Let us try to do better. Come along, my friends, we will try to aid you. In union there is strength. You ought to be trying to serve God, as we all live by him and in him.

In the third place, men in their unconverted condition are disqualified to serve God. The conscience is polluted by sin. Conscience is here used to denote the whole moral nature. And the moral nature or heart being defiled we are disqualified to serve God. Sin unfits us for the service of God. Hence, you must cleanse your hearts. The text tells us how: "For if the blood of bulls and of goats, and the ashes of a heifer sprinkling the unclean, sanctifieth to the purifying of the flesh; how much more shall the blood of Christ, who, through the eternal spirit, offered himself without spot to God, purge your conscience from dead works to serve the living God." Why did Jesus, on the wings of love, speed to earth? Prompted by mercy, why did he leave heaven and come to earth? Why did he assume a human body? Why did he become identified with our humanity? Why did he offer himself a sacrifice for sin? He suffered all these things so that he might be able to cleanse our hearts from dead works, so that we might be able to serve the living God. Without having the obstructions taken away, we could not serve God. Jesus came to help us by giving us a means to remove the obstacles. His life and his atoning merits are offered as a sacrifice for us. We can not serve God, nor enjoy him while defiled by sin. We must be made spiritually clean.

The infirmities of nature are often held as an excuse for not coming to Christ. Can you present this excuse in the presence of God? Will he accept it? I point you to Christ as a helper, a Saviour and a Mediator. How can we offer such an excuse when we have such ample provisions as we have in Christ, to meet all our wants? The man in the parable who did not have a wedding garment was asked, "How camest thou hither not having a wedding garment?" It is said he was speechless. So you, who have been brought up in a Christian land and under Christian influence, will have no excuse to offer. Paul says, "Thou art inexcusable, O man, whosoever thou art."

There are two considerations in the service that we are to render to God that must not be overlooked. First, we must serve him from a right motive, and with a right feeling. And secondly, we must serve him according to his word and will. We must serve him with a willing heart, and a ready and cheerful mind. We must not go about the service of God with an air of reluctance. We should enjoy it as our most pleasant work. Many persons pursue the service of God with an indifference which seems to indicate but little pleasure in it. This should not be. God has given us our part to do. We should therefore do it. In the language of the apostle Paul, "Let us have grace, whereby we may serve God acceptably with reverence and godly fear." —Heb. xii. 28. Let us have grace: it is free. We may serve him, yet not acceptably. A large class of persons are represented by the following language: "Many will say to me in that day, Lord, Lord, have we not prophesied in thy name? and in thy name have cast out devils? and in thy name have done many wonderful works? And then will I profess unto them, I never knew you: depart from me, ye that work iniquity."—Matt. vii. 22. Jesus will not recognize us among his followers unless we serve him acceptably. Serve God with profound reverence and godly fear. Let these principles be prominently before us—let them be stamped upon our minds, for upon them depends the proper method of serving God.

Let me illustrate this: I, as an employer, may employ some one to do some work for me. I contract to pay him by the month or year as the case may be. He does my work. If I am a farmer, he goes out into my field to work. He does not, however, want to do anything, but what he is absolutely compelled to do by the contract. When he has done that he will do no more. He may be altogether indifferent to my interests, and feel no concern about saving my property, but will see it wasted and will not try to save it. At the end of the period for which he was engaged the wages are demanded, and I must pay him, if he has completed the term, though he has been very selfish, and looked only at his own interests. The law requires me to pay him if he has done the work, whatever the motive may have been that has prompted him to do it. But in serving God, it is not enough that we do what he has required of us, but we must also do it in the right spirit. As we have already said, there are two things that must be kept in mind by Christians, if they would serve God acceptably. First, there must be a right spirit of feeling. We must do what we do to the honor and glory of God. Secondly, we must serve him according to the directions and rules which he has given us. It is too often thought that so we are sincere in what we do, it does not matter so much in regard to the manner or form in which we serve him. But this is a mistake. We should not only be sincere, but we should be strictly obedient to God's commandments. He is a very kind master, but his directions must be observed, or we shall not receive our reward. Provision has been made to supply us with all the means necessary to prepare us to perform our duty, and therefore God will not excuse us. He is the Judge before whom we must come. He knows our every act; he knows the motive which lies at the bottom of the service which we are giving him; he knows how much of the heart is enlisted in his cause. In the great day of final settlement, if the purest motives and best feelings have not been enlisted in his service, the reward will be withheld. The reason of this is that Jesus came to provide and make an atonement for the sins of the world, that all the obstructions might be taken out of the way. As Paul says, "The carnal mind is enmity against God: for it is not subject to the law of God, neither indeed can be." The carnal mind is to be taken out of the way. As a substitute for the carnal mind, the Christian mind is to be substituted. Conscience is to be purged from dead works. The heart is to be cleansed of evil, and filled with right principles and thoughts. As a natural result, if the heart is pure, holy principles and conduct will be produced in place of evil principles and wicked conduct. The Christian theory in regard to the matter is the mediatorship of Christ. He came into the world to cleanse us. As is remarked in the text he is to cleanse us of dead works.

My subject last night was, "Why tarriest thou? arise and be baptized, and wash away thy sins, calling upon the name of the Lord." One of the ideas brought out was, that Christ was to aid us in removing our sins. Christ is the power by which this may be done. There are many things to be done in applying this power. I offered some considerations to show that Christian baptism is a part of worship; that it is a part of the duty required by Christian law. Prayer is also a part of the worship. These are means to help us to purge our consciences. The text which we are presenting tells us where the whole power lies. The power lies in the blood of Christ. It is by faith, by prayer, by repentance, by baptism that this power is made available. The power must come to our hearts. These means are alluded to in the Bible. I want to present the Gospel. God forbid that I should preach anything but Christ as the power by which sin may be removed from our consciences. When this is done, then we can serve God acceptably. We will love the service of God. We will be born of God when we become Christians. He loves everything that is pure, holy and right. So will we. God hates everything that is impure and unholy, and so do we. We will therefore love the service of God. To a Christian, " his commandments are not grievous."—1 John v. 3.

We must serve God from proper motives. The less thought of self that we have in God's service, the better it will be for us. The Bible doctrine of self-denial grows out of these facts. If we make God our object in life, we will have grand principles actuating and moving us. Everything that we do, we should do with but one object in view, the glory of God. Die to self and live to God. Do all for him. In the great end it will be best for us. The holier the service, the greater the reward will be. Let us take an illustration. We will take the Christian grace of benevolence. Here is a rich man. He is a professor of religion. He has a large amount of wealth. He gives but little. When he is called upon to give to any charitable object, he replies, " I can not give, because I must take care of what I have for my children." He then gives his small contribution with great reluctance. He goes through the form of giving, but he does not have the spirit. It is said by the Saviour, "That the rich man also died." Rich men as well as poor men must die. You remember the beautiful illustration of the Saviour of the day of final judgment, when he says of the righteous, "For I was hungered and ye gave me meat; I was thirsty and ye gave me drink; I was a stranger and ye took me in," etc. Then shall the righteous answer him, saying, "Lord, when saw we thee a-hungered and fed thee, thirsty and gave thee drink," etc. Then the King shall answer and say unto them, "Verily, I say unto you, Inasmuch as ye have done it unto one of the least of these my brethren, ye have done it unto me." That is the spirit that must prompt and move us. The welfare of humanity should ever be before our minds. Whatever is done to Christ's church is done to him. Those who give will receive that which they have given. Those who have given nothing will die, and their wealth will be lost and they with it. Serve God and you will serve yourselves. Serve God honestly, and faithfully, and you will reap a larger reward.

It is one of the grand truths of Christianity that Christ can take everything out of the way that hinders us from serving God. Remember that our most pleasant service should be that of doing God's will. The better we perform this duty, the more it will redound to our glory and happiness in the end.

My Christian friends, try to do your duty to God cheerfully and faithfully. And you who have not yet engaged in the service of God, seek the removal of the obstacles that are in the way, and that are hindering you; and enter into his vineyard and labor, and you will receive with all the faithful, an "exceeding great reward."

X.

MAN'S WANTS, AND HIS SUPPLIES.

"He that spared not his own Son, but delivered him up for us all, how shall he not with him also freely give us all things?"—Rom. 8: 32.

Man's wants are evidently presented to us here in a very clear and impressive manner. "He that spared not his own Son." Who spared not his own Son? God spared not his own Son, but gave him up for us, and when that was done, that was not all. "He that spared not his Son, but delivered him up for us all, how shall he not with him also freely give us all things?" Not only did he give his Son, but he will give us all things! This idea suggests our wants, and our supplies. "Delivered up his Son." Necessity required it, and he was ready and willing to give us not only his Son, but even more. Our wants are deep and numerous, but our supplies are ample. Look upon the little child, the human babe. It is one of the most helpless of beings that we can behold. Look at the child in its mother's arms, and in its mother's lap, and when we see the parents taking such great care of it, we are impressed with the helplessness of the babe. And the thought is sometimes entertained, and language to this effect is used, that when it grows up and can run about and play, it will be more free from the parent's charge, more independent of father and mother; that it will not have so many wants. But it is right the reverse of this. There is never a time in our being, from our infancy to the most distant point in our future existence that the imagination can reach, that we are less dependent than in infancy. For as the babe grows up to childhood, and as childhood passes into youth, and as the intellect begins to develop, education is necessary to meet the wants of that intellect, which were not to be met when the child was in its infancy. And after awhile not only will its intellectual wants need to be met, but there will be a development of moral feelings, and these will require attention and cultivation. And so we go on, and our wants in some degree multiply as our years multiply, and there never will be a time in our existence that we will not want much; there is never a time coming in which we as men and women will be independent. There is no being that God has made, from the highest archangel, that approaches in its great moral character Jehovah himself, down to the lowest created being that is independent of God. We all have wants, and as our years multiply our wants increase and multiply.

If we, my Christian friends, have been renewed in the spirit of our minds; if we have been converted from the error of our ways, we have need of divine grace to help us. And if you, my unconverted friends, are yet in the "gall of bitterness and bonds of iniquity," guilty, unpardoned, and your souls away from God, O the depth of your needs! O the multiplicity of your wants! They are such that no other being can supply them but God. To no other place can we go to have our wants supplied but God's throne of grace.

We are guilty, if never pardoned; guilty, if never converted. We need pardon. We need forgiveness. We need to be renewed in the spirit of our minds. We need to be regenerated in our moral natures; for a change not less than regeneration, a change not less than passing from death to life, will fit or prepare us for heaven and immortality.

O friends, it is not a few years in the Christian Church; it is not a few penitential tears that are dropped; it is not a few formal prayers that are offered up to God; it is not a mere formal observance of the rites of the Christian Church that train the soul for heaven and fit it to rest in the bosom of God and enjoy the blessed influence of his divine presence. If any of us have fallen into such a sad mistake, may God remove the delusion from our hearts and show us, instead of such a course, the necessity of holiness of heart and consecration of life if we would see God.

We must be born again. We must be renewed in the very spirit of our minds. We must be made anew in Christ. Old things must pass away. Is that your feeling? Is that your idea and Christian creed? Are we acting on these principles? Do they enter into the daily meditations of our hearts? Do they lead us into a candid self-examination of heart? And if these principles are accepted by us, we can not fail to give a serious consideration to them. We need forgiveness; but O, my brethren and sisters, we need also sanctification. We need holiness of heart; we need holiness of life; for "without holiness no man shall see God." We need the restoration of the lost image of God to our moral natures. We need to resemble Christ. We need the spirit of adoption, that we may call the eternal God our Father. These are our wants. These are but imperfect statements of our wants; these are but mere sketches of our wants, and yet there are souls living, dying men and women, gliding along the stream of life, cheerful, prayerless, giddy and gay, without once thinking of what a great change they must undergo or be lost forever. They must experience this. These wants must be met. The subject must be pardoned. Forgiveness, justification, sanctification—these must be procured preparatory to our final glorification.

Numerous as our wants are, God can supply them all. And he alone can supply them. Our wants are not only many, but they are great, and there is something peculiar about them. The little babe, as I said awhile ago, lies in its mother's lap, its wants can be attended to by her. The mother, standing related to that child as she does, can meet the wants of that child. She can nurse and clothe it. Wants of this kind can be met. But when the child gets to that stage to which I alluded awhile ago, it demands more than the father and mother can give. The parents may educate that child. They may not only teach it the rudiments of education. But after awhile the child gets to the stage when its moral nature becomes developed and expands, and this requires attention. When it expands into a guilty life, and becomes polluted with vice and wickedness, its mother can not supply its wants. With all her maternal kindness, and with all her tender heart of love, and with all the warm and gushing affections of the father's heart, all combined together, can not reach the moral wants of that child. In the language of David, in the 49th Psalm, "None can by any means redeem his brother, nor give to God a ransom for him." No man can do it. But while no man can give the ransom even of a child, God has given a ransom for all of us. Here our wants become peculiar, and so peculiar that no source can supply these wants but God. He alone can do it, through Christ the mediator. Our wants become so peculiar that none but Jesus can help us as sinners.

Some time ago I read of a poor, dark, and guilty Hottentot of Africa, that became impressed with his guilt. He was a man given to very bad habits, and he became concerned. He went about among his friends, talking in regard to his condition, and wishing to know where to obtain relief. Finally he heard Christ preached as the ransom for all sin. He came to the missionary and said he wanted to become acquainted with Christ. He was led to Christ and there found what he longed for. Others pointed him to witchcraft, and other superstitious remedies, but all was insufficient, until he applied to Christ, and there he found all that he needed to supply his deep religious wants. Peculiar wants, yes, but in God, through our Lord Jesus Christ, they can be supplied. Don't forget that, don't stand still, don't live indifferently, and then think that anywhere, or at any time, or in any way we can, when disease approaches, and when the approach of death is apparent, become converted. The soul is too valuable to be lost. Heaven is too desirable for us to run the risk of losing it. Look at the value of the soul, and desirability of heaven as our final home.

God is amply able to supply. Look at the text again. "He that spared not his own Son; but delivered him for us, how shall he not with him also freely give us all things?" Has God given his own Son? What a thought! Delivered him up? To whom? To his friends that embraced him, that treated him kindly; delivered him up to them? *No;* delivered him up to his enemies—to wicked men. From the height of his exaltation, excellency and glory, God looked down upon that locality in Palestine, where our salvation was worked out, and saw the shameful, ignominious and terrible treatment that the Saviour met at the hands of his persecutors. He knew before the Saviour was born in the world, that such would be the treatment that he would receive from men. Notwithstanding all this he gave him up. Our wants were so pressing. The necessity was so apparent. It was the ruin of our race or the sacrifice of Christ. No other alternative; and when God comprehended the true condition of things, he gave his Son. Lived a life of suffering, and died as you know the ignominious death of the cross. Delivered up his own Son; permitted him to become the sin-offering for us. Is that all God will do? Oh, no! "He that delivered up his Son.........will freely give us all things." What a thought of God! Paul's language was encouraging; my subject is an encouraging one, and I want to encourage you, my friends. When we have confidence in God's goodness, and when we see what he has already done for us, we are encouraged.

Suppose that one of us in our financial affairs were to become troubled and embarrassed, and would be at the point of losing everything we have, and be reduced, perhaps, from plenty down to the extremity of want; but we have got some friend whom we know can render the assistance that the case calls for. We go to that friend and present our case and tell him our sad story. The rehearsal of our troubles has the desired effect, and it reaches his heart, moves his sympathy towards us, and he promises to help us, but it requires on his part the sacrifice of things that are most dear to him. However, he gives us the desired help.

Trouble passes away, and the sunshine of peace beams upon our hearts to the awakening of joy and pleasure in our minds. But suppose again, that, a few months after this, we are again thrown into the same trouble. Would we feel like going to that friend again for help? Oh, I should think we would do almost like Dr. Tanner in New York, who is trying to fast for certain purposes. We would almost try to fast for weeks and work along the best way we could, because it would be so unpleasant for us to go to that friend again for help. We would never go unless we were driven by sheer necessity, after receiving such a gift and blessing from our kind friend.

Our race went to God and appealed to him in their lost condition for help, and he gave his only beloved Son, his only begotten Son—Christ—the best of all gifts. He gave him to become a sin-offering for us. But now he gives us further whatever we want. This is the God that ungrateful men and women are sinning against; this is the God that they will not serve. That Saviour that died for us is the Saviour that we will not follow. Oh, what guilt! Oh, who would take that measure of guilt upon him? The simple guilt of ingratitude, is enough to damn the soul forever. Oh, what must be the future of the sinner who persists in sin, and never tries to serve God!

But more directly to the point, the encouragement of our text. "He that spared not his own Son, but delivered him up for us all, how shall he not with him also freely give us all things." There is a grand principle contained in this. *If God gave the greater, he will give the less.* And as he gave the great gift of his Son, he will give whatever else is needed. We need not be afraid to go to God.

The apostle James says, "If any man lacks·wisdom, let him ask of God, that giveth to all men liberally and upbraideth not." He will not say to us, are you here again?

Are you begging again? Are you at my throne of grace, begging and pleading again? Oh, no. God beckons us to come. If we are empty, God says, "Come;" and he will pour out his Spirit. "He that spared not his own Son, but delivered him up for us all, how shall he not with him also freely give us all things?" Don't overlook that word *freely*. He delights to give. No money is required but he will give it freely without money and without price, if we humble ourselves under his mighty hand, and if we appropriate his blessings to his glory and service.

XI.

SOME OF THE CHARACTERISTICS OF THE BIBLE.

"In whom ye also trusted, after that ye heard the word of truth, the gospel of your salvation: in whom also, after that ye believed, ye were sealed with that Holy Spirit of promise, which is the earnest of our inheritance until the redemption of the purchased possession, unto the praise of His glory."—Eph. 1: 13, 14.

Our subject will be some of the characteristics of the Gospel, with some of its effects as here represented. The first characteristic of it is said to be the word of truth: "In whom ye also trusted, after that ye heard the word of truth." This is one of the characteristics of the Gospel, and it is a distinguishing one. It is the word of truth, or, if you please, it is *the* truth ; the expression of truth, the representation of truth, or, to drop everything else, it is *the* truth.

There are many things false in the world. Solomon said, in drawing upon his vast resources of human experience and human knowledge, "all is vanity." He looked over the world in all stages of society, in all the forms that he had humanity presented to him in, and there saw so much emptiness; there saw so much falsehood, and so little that was dignified and grand among the race that he said "all is vanity." We are not to conclude that there was *no* good in his age; we are not to conclude that he had lost all confidence in humanity. But when he used the phrase "all is vanity," we must conclude that the predominating tendency of things was to vanity, emptiness and evil. There is so much error and falsehood in the world, that we should be careful when we lay down the novel, or newspaper of the day, or even a volume of history, with some doubts of the truthfulness of all their statements, and take up the Bible, that we do not feel the same hesitancy in accepting the statements of the latter that we do in receiving those of the former. We should be very careful when we turn to the holy book of inspiration, lest we open its pages with the same hesitation, and with the same want of belief in the authenticity of its contents, as we often do in reading the productions to which I have alluded. Open the Bible, the gospel of the Lord Jesus Christ, young men and maidens, children and parents, saints and sinners, with the deep and strong conviction that whatever falsehood there is outside of that book, in it there is truth, and the whole truth. It is the word of God and can he *lie?* It is the word of holy inspiration, and that can not err; consequently the Gospel is the word of truth. All it contains is true. Every delineation of human character is true. Every charge He makes to us as sinners is true. Every fact that it states is true. Every prophecy that is to be fulfilled in the future is true. Every historic fact is true; consequently all is true. Its great, weighty and important statements are all true. It is a truth that there is a solemn future for us all, and it is an eternal truth that there is a day of retribution coming. It is true that the "wicked shall be turned into hell, and all the nations that forget God"; and it is a truth that the righteous shall go away into everlasting life. The Word, then, is true. Remember these truths, and in remembering them let that remembrance elicit from you the attention that you ought to give it.

The next characteristic of the Gospel, as we have it stated in our text, is "the gospel of your salvation." "In whom ye also trusted, after that ye heard the word of truth, the gospel of your salvation." Whose salvation? Is it the gospel of salvation to fallen and guilty angels, who have departed from the path of rectitude and fallen under the displeasure of the Almighty? No; it is the gospel of our salvation. The Son of God took not upon Himself the nature of angels to make atonement for them, but he took upon Himself *our* nature to make atonement for our guilt; and in becoming our Saviour He has given us a gospel of the salvation He has provided us with; and in the text the gospel is called the gospel of *your* salvation; I want that emphasized. Paul used it when talking to his brethren at Ephesus—*your* salvation—perhaps intending to make a distinction there between the Jews and Gentiles. The church at Ephesus was mostly made up of converts from the Gentile world. The Jews at that time endeavored to monopolize all the blessings of the gospel, in the mistaken idea that it was for them alone that salvation was provided. Paul, to encourage his Gentile brethren, says it is *your* salvation. But I tell you to-day that the gospel we preach is the gospel of your salvation as well as the Jews. It is to offer salvation to you, to the Gentile world, as well as to the Jews. And I say with emphasis this morning, in direct personal application to the congregation assembled here, that *this is the gospel of your salvation*. You may well assemble in our chapel here on the Lord's day morning to hear the gospel; you may well resort to such places. And why? Because you are interested in listening to the gospel preached, and you are concerned in its announcement, for it is the gospel of your salvation. It is man's salvation, the salvation of our race, of our community, and of individuals. In what sense is it the gospel of our salvation? I embrace myself with those to whom the thought comes addressed. It is the gospel of our salvation because, if its instructions are heeded, if its lessons are studied, it will teach us all that we need salvation. This is one reason, and it is a good one. If we regard the teaching of the gospel we will discover that we need salvation. How did we learn that we needed salvation? It was by reading God's word, and because we were born in a land of Bibles. If we had been born away out among the heathens of our Territories, would we be the Christian members of the Church that we are? Would we be happy in Christ and in the enjoyment of the Christian's peace? No. Our minds would be as void and as blank of the doctrine of Christian truth as the minds of the wild men of the West are. It was by the instruction that we received from the gospel that we learned we were bad boys and girls, and were impressed with a sense of our gilt. It has made us feel the need of salvation? How does it do that? It does it in various ways. I can not tell you all, but will mention one, and that is this: The gospel holds out for us a proper standard of right and wrong. It shows what is to be done and what is not to be done. It presents unto us the will of God as the standard of right. Well, what has that to do with showing us the way of salvation? It presents us with the standard of right, and shows us how to compare our lives with that standard of right. Do our conduct and our principles correspond with the will of God? If they do not we are guilty of a departure from that law, and if there is a discrepancy between our lives and conduct and the divine law, that discrepancy proves our guilt. It must prove either our guilt on the one side, or the falsity of the standard of right on the other. But that can not be. The will of God is the standard of right, and in proportion to our departure from that will we are guilty. That's the idea. It is the gospel of our salvation. It shows how far we are wrong, where we are wrong, and that we are guilty.

The gospel does not only show us our guilt, or prove our guilt, but it offers us pardon, too. It offers us salvation. It does not only show us our guilt and sins, but it shows that God has provided a ransom for our sins. It shows the remedy. While it shows the wound it provides a cure. While it shows the wound that sin has produced it provides a cure in the Balm of Gilead. The old Prophet Jeremiah, in looking at the moral diseases of his nation, exclaimed, "Oh, that my head were waters, and mine eyes a fountain of tears, that I might weep day and night for the slain of the daughter of my people!" So he spoke when surveying the deplorable condition of his race. And on another occasion he said, "Is there no balm in Gilead; is there no physician there? Why then is not the health of the daughter of my people recovered?" Ah! he knew there was power in the Messiah. He knew all this, and he wondered why men and women could be so indifferent to their highest interests and so careless of their moral conduct as to go on in sin, subject to the terrible moral diseases of sin, and destined to meet the sinner's eternal doom. The gospel of salvation contains the remedy; it contains Christ. It is the gospel that holds him up. Do you remember that interesting account in the 16th chapter of Acts, where Paul and Silas dispossessed the damsel of the evil Spirit? Bad Spirits have a good deal of knowledge. Devils don't always lie. They sometimes tell the truth though terribly mixed with error. That young woman, though under the influence of a demon, said, referring to Paul and Silas, "These men are the servants of the Most High God, which shew unto us the way of salvation." You will probably remember it, but perhaps it never struck you with such deep force. Oh, that is the grand character of every minister and of every reformer who labors to raise the standard of the world's moral excellency higher. "These men are the servants of the Most High God, which shew unto us the way of salvation." A very pretty thought. This way of salvation must be showed to us. Suppose some of us were traveling away from home this morning, or were in pursuit of some person with whom we had business, and we knew not the way to the place of our destination or where to find the person for whom we were seeking. We would have to inquire, and somebody would have to tell us. Just so in regard to this salvation. Somebody must teach us the *way* of salvation. Why, you all know that had we had no teacher in our childhood to teach us the sciences and the different branches of literature, we would have, in all probablity, grown up in ignorance. It is true, we might have learned a little ourselves, but how much we needed a teacher you all know. We all get them for our children, in order that they might not grow up in ignorance. I want to get the truth plainly before you. "The gospel of your salvation." It comes to us and teaches us religion. It answers the same purpose in religion that our school-books do in our public schools. I want you to revere the Bible more. I want you to feel that it is the book that you are interested in, because it contains the way of salvation. "These men are the servants of the Most High God," because they show unto us the way of salvation. Well, what did that show? I will connect my subject with the case of the jailor to illustrate my point. This occurred in Philippi.

Now what about the Philippian jailor? He felt guilty. And what did he say? He said to these men, "Sirs, what must I do to be saved?" Here are these men sent by God to the Philippian jailor, and he cries, "Sirs, what must I do to be saved?" Did they answer? Yes, they did. They knew their business, and I would to God we all knew it; and to the question, "Sirs, what must I do to be saved?" they answered, "Believe on the Lord Jesus Christ and thou shalt be saved and thy house." There they made known unto him the way of salvation. The jailor was lost and guilty, corrupt and in heathen darkness. He saw no rays of light or prospect of pardon, and overwhelmed with the sense of his lost condition, from the depths of his distressed heart he cried, "Sirs, what must I do to be saved?" and they replied, "Believe on the Lord Jesus Christ." That was the doctrine in general. Why did I say in general? because a doctrine stated in a general way may be well enough in its general character, but we must not always be satisfied to accept truth on its generality. The truth is too often left in its generalized form. You may go into any religious sanctuary or house of worship, and hear the minister preach, and you will be very likely to hear him recommend the Bible. As a general truth we all accept the Bible, but when it comes down to the details of the Bible, you will find a division of sentiment. The truth in its generalization, the Bible as a general truth, will be accepted by all. But it is not enough that we preach truth in its general character, but we must come down to details. And we have reason to believe Paul did so in preaching to the jailor, for when he said, "believe on the Lord Jesus Christ," what followed? It is said that "in the same hour of the night the jailor was baptized, rejoicing in God with all his house." I want to know how the jailor knew anything about baptism. I will tell you what led him to baptism. Paul condescended to preach the truth in its minute details, for he had a heathen audience before him. He had individuals before him that needed much instruction, and, as a master teacher in making known the way of salvation, he came down to details and specifications. He preached Christian baptism as a part of the way of salvation. But I must drop the thought.

In the next place I wish to notice the use we can make of the gospel. "In whom ye also trusted, after that ye heard the word of truth." We should first *hear* the word of truth. Give the Bible a respectable hearing. Whenever you are brought into contact with Christian truths, give them a proper hearing. Hear the Word of the Lord. Why hear it? Hear it because it is the gospel of your salvation. That's the idea. Some people sometimes go to meeting and don't seem to go to hear, and they don't hear. They seem to be indifferent, and sometimes stupid, apparently unconcerned. That of course is wrong and very improper. Last night there was a political meeting down town, a democratic meeting. It was known to be a political meeting and a tolerably large crowd gathered, and for what purpose? Why, to hear something about politics, and to be encouraged in carrying out their political creed. And, I presume, they were interested. They were democrats; and if it had been a republican meeting, republicans would have been there. Now, my friends, I address you not as republicans, nor as democrats, but as dying men and women, and I bear a message that ought to interest you more than any political speech. It contains truths identified with your highest interests, and in which your highest interests are involved. And can you be unconcerned? It is the gospel of our salvation, and there is something in it which concerns us. Hear it because it is the gospel of your salvation, and because there is something in it which greatly concerns you. Hear the gospel because it comes to you personally and because it concerns you individually, and then believe it because it is the word of truth. How plain it is! How rational and philosophical! Oh! my hearers, if we turn away from the truth, if we turn away from God's word, so plain and clear, what will save us from the ruin that must inevitably follow? "I can not believe," says one. That's the way people talk. But *what* are we to believe? We are to believe the truth—the Word of God. Can we not believe the truth?

The third step in the use we are to make of the gospel is that of trust. "In whom ye also trusted." First hear, then believe, and then trust. Now, why trust? First hear, because we are concerned; believe, because it is the truth; and trust, because it is the gospel of your salvation. Trust; it is the mighty power of God. Trust; it is the Son of God inviting us to come. Trust; because the almighty power, unerring wisdom, the unmeasured depths of mercy, and the compassion and benevolence of God are concerned in the matter. Trust what? Simply trust God. Trust Christ. Take your guilty hearts and lay them at the foot of the cross on which the Saviour died. Trust; put yourselves in his hands. Trust; let him come into your hearts. For he says, "Behold, I stand at the door, and knock: if any man hear my voice, and open the door, I will come in to him, and will sup with him, and he with me." Can you trust the Saviour? Ought you not to trust him? *Must* you not trust him or be guilty of the greatest irreverence towards him? Now that's just what's to be done on our part. First hear, then believe, and then trust. That's just what the jailor did. When Paul preached Christ to the jailor, and said, "believe on the Lord Jesus Christ," he enlarged, pressed upon him the subject grandly and encouragingly. He brought before the jailor and his house the Lord Jesus Christ in his divinity, in his humanity, in his pre-existent state, and in his future glory. These things were all brought before the jailor as connected with Christ. And he trusted him for salvation. The jailor's trust was a trust of the simplest form. It was a trust in its practical character, and just so we ought to trust him. Why can not we all trust him? My unconverted friends, why can not you trust in Christ? Why can not you trust him and be saved? Trust, and then we feel that we are safe. Look at the little child trusting its parents. So when we get men and women to thus trust Christ and follow him in his precepts and example, we know they are safe, and they can justly feel that they are safe.

Another point yet remains to be noticed. What will be the consequences of a popular adherence to the word of the Lord? I have given you some of the characteristics of the word of God and our reception of it, and the next point would be the consequences. I will read the text again: "In whom ye also trusted, after that ye heard the word of truth; the gospel of your salvation; in whom also after that ye believed, ye were sealed with that Holy Spirit of promise, which is the earnest of our inheritance until the redemption of the purchased possession, unto the praise of his glory." "In whom ye were sealed." That's after you hear, after you believe and after you trust in Christ. Then you are sealed with the Holy Spirit of promise, which is the earnest of our inheritance. The reception of the Holy Spirit follows trust in Christ. Hence the teaching on the day of Pentecost, when the inquiry was made, "Men and brethren, what shall we do?" The answer was, "Repent and be baptized every one of you in the name of Jesus Christ for the remission of your sins, and you shall receive the gift of the Holy Ghost;" and in our text "ye were sealed with the Holy Spirit of promise." Then we are sealed with it. When the penitent and broken-hearted receive

Christ they become new creatures. You all know what a seal is. When the seal is applied to wax or clay, it makes its impression. The word of God must be applied to the heart by the Holy Spirit when the impression of the Christian character will be delineated in that heart. The impression must be made upon our lives. We must be sealed. Our country has its seal, and when its actions through the officers are authentic, the seal is used. It is the comfort of the Spirit that we first get. This is the earnest of the Spirit. What does that mean? I have a definition here from Webster which I will read as the meaning of the word *earnest:* "A pledge or payment given as an assurance of earnest or serious purpose to discharge an engagement or fulfill a promise; a token of what is to come." It is a pledge of God to us, of all that we will enjoy at the end. When we enter into holy covenant with God and promise to be his forever, he says, "I am going to pay you a certain amount down, and I am going to give you my Holy Spirit and this will be an earnest, a pledge, that in due time I will pay the last installment that is due you." That's the earnest of the Spirit that we get when we enter the service of God. I want to read you a sentiment from one of the ancient fathers, Jerome. When he looked upon the enjoyment the Christian experiences in the world, he said, "If the earnest is so great, how great must the possession be!" That's a beautiful thought. If our present joy that we experience is so great, what must the full possession be! that is, when we come to enjoy what God has promised us. That's the idea, and it is a pretty one. Then let us trust Christ that we may receive the Spirit, his installment now, and may God keep us forever to enjoy the final installment in the great day of Eternity.

XII.
THE PICTURE OF A HAPPY PEOPLE.

"Rid me, and deliver me from the hand of strange children, whose mouth speaketh vanity, and their right hand is a right-hand of falsehood: that our sons may be as plants grown up in their youth; that our daughters may be as corner-stones, polished after the similitude of a palace; that our garners may be full, affording all manner of store; that our sheep may bring forth thousands and ten thousands in our streets; that our oxen may be strong to labor; that there be no breaking in, nor going out; that there be no complaining in our streets. Happy is that people, that is in such a case; yea, happy is that people, whose God is the Lord."—Ps. 144: 11–15.

Reference is not made to an individual, but to a body of people. "Happy is that people, etc." And it will apply to a family, to a community, or to the entire body constituting God's peculiar people. There is a propriety in referring to a body of people, when their highest enjoyment is described, rather than to an individual. Man to be perfectly happy, or to attain unto the highest enjoyment he is capable of, must be in society. It is true, he can be very happy alone. If a believer has Christ in his heart, and is surrounded by the presence of God, he may be very happy. But nevertheless, we think our position is true, that to attain to his highest enjoyment, man must be in society. And we conclude this from the fact, that he is a social being, and designed for society. He was originally created with a want of society, and an adaptation to society.

In noticing the different groups which constitute the picture of a happy people, we will first notice the youth in the picture as a very prominent place is given to them in it. "That our sons may be as plants grown up in their youth; that our daughters may be as corner-stones, polished after the similitude of a palace." Our youth can not be neglected or overlooked if we would have a happy community or nation. "Our sons" are first referred to. It is desired and prayed by the patriot, King, and father, that 'our sons may be as plants grown up in their youth." And what is meant by this? It is not desired that they grow up as fops in pride, in idleness, and extravagance. But it is desired and prayed that they grow up in manliness, and that there be a full development of their manhood; that they grow as the plant grows; that there be life, and growth, and fruitfulness, that those around them may be refreshed and blessed by them. And in attaining to the full development of their manhood, there must be a healthy culture of their physical nature that it may be fully developed and matured, and also a cultivation and development of their intellectual nature. The mind must by no means be neglected, as it is a very important element in our manhood. If we look at the American Indian in his uncivilized state, we see in many instances a fine physical body. But the higher departments of his nature are not developed, and hence in his wild or uncivilized state he is far from being a perfect specimen of humanity, though there is a fine physical development. And our sons to grow up into perfect manhood, must also give attention to the culture of their moral or spiritual nature. There is surely such a nature in man, and to develop it properly it needs if possible still greater attention and cultivation than it does to cultivate our physical and intellectual nature. There can be no doubt but that David in desiring and praying for the sons and daughters of his people included in the accomplishments he desired for them those of a religious or spiritual character. These constitute too large a part of real manhood and womanhood to be left out. The character of any man or of any woman is very imperfect that does not embrace the religious element in it.

That the religious element is recognized in the picture of a happy people as drawn here by David, is very evident from the conclusion of the subject: "Happy is that people, whose God is the Lord." The religious character of the happy people will be referred to again, but we refer to it here to show that it was a part of the beautiful accomplishments desired for the youth of the Jewish commonwealth, and must form a part of the young everywhere and at all times, or there will be but a very imperfect development of their character.

There is another idea in reference to "our sons" in the subject that has struck our mind very forcibly. The desire is that "our sons may be as plants grown up in their youth." What is remarkable is that they should be desired to grow up in their youth. The way we commonly look at the young, we consider they have passed out of their youth when they have reached their majority, or when they are grown up. But David's language would seem to imply that in a certain sense they may be grown up while in their youth. And there is a sense in which our boys and girls may be men and women while yet in their youth. Boys and girls sometimes show a discretion, a maturity of judgment and steadiness of conduct much beyond their age. And we say of such that they are manly and womanly in their behavior. There seems to be an illustration of this in the case of Timothy. Paul, in addressing him, I. Tim. 4: 12, says, "Let no man despise thy youth; but be thou an example of the believers in word, in conversation, in charity, in spirit, in faith, in purity." Here Timothy is spoken to as a youth. But in another part of the same epistle when the apostle is admonishing him to guard against certain temptations to which he was exposed, he uses the following language: "But thou, O man of God, flee these things, and follow after righteousness, godliness, faith, love, patience, meekness."—I. Tim. 6: 11.

So he was both a "youth" and a "man of God." He was a youth in years, but a man in character and conduct. And you, dear youth, may be men and women in noble character and discreet behavior while you are yet young. This is very desirable; and to this we admonish you, and for this we pray. It was this manly and womanly behavior that David desired to see developed in the youth of his people, and hence the language of our text.

"That our daughters may be as corner-stones, polished after the similitude of a palace." Dr. Conant gives the meaning of the original thus: "Our daughters as corner pillars, sculptured after the structure of a palace." And Perowne, another Hebrew scholar, translates the original thus: "Our daughters as corner pillars, sculptured to grace a palace." Here we have in figurative and poetical language "our daughters" compared to corner-stones and beautiful pillars; and the two leading ideas are strength and beauty, and we wonder why "our sons" are compared to plants that are young and tender, while "our daughters" are compared to corner-stones and pillars. We might think that the figures should be reversed, and "our sons" be compared to the corner-stones and pillars and "our daughters" to plants. But we presume the spirit of God knew what it was doing when it dictated the figures and applied them as it did. There is great strength in female character. Oh, how much power is there in the gentleness and affection of a woman's pure heart! The strength of their affection has often been severely tried, and in the trial manifested great endurance and power. While a father's stern command, and mother's entreaty has failed to keep the young man from some haunt of vice, a sister's arms in warm affection thrown around his neck, with her tender appeals has accomplished it. Oh if the powerful influence of our young women was sanctified by the grace of God, and consecrated to his noble cause, what wonders would it accomplish, and what a powerful factor for doing good it would become! In the martyrology of the early church we have noble cases of female endurance in suffering for Christ's sake. Tender girls when brought to the severe trial of either renouncing their Christian principles or of meeting death in its most terrible form, chose the latter.

And then the idea of beauty is associated with our daughters as we have them presented in our text. Perowne's reading is, "Our daughters as corner pillars, sculptured to grace a palace." But it is not the beauty that so many of "our daughters" cultivate, and which is admired by the carnally-minded—a beauty which consists in a beautiful form of the body, or in the adornments of jewelry, silk and velvet that is here desired and prayed for "our daughters." Grace and modesty beautify female character. Gentleness of disposition, tenderness of feelings, purity of mind, sympathy with the suffering, and a desire to be useful in promoting the happiness of all classes, are adornments more to be admired, and highly valued, and sought after, than the richest attire and the most valuable pearls and costly jewels, that the fashionable ladies of the world wear. The polish and adornment that should beautify "our daughters," and our mothers too, is that referred to by the apostle, when he says in speaking to Christian females, "whose adorning, let it not be that outward adorning of plaiting the hair, and of wearing of gold, or of putting on of apparel, but let it be the hidden man of the heart, in that which is not corruptible, even the ornament of a meek and quiet spirit, which is in the sight of God of great price."—I. Peter 3: 3, 4. There is a sad mistake committed by young women when they seek the admiration of the other sex by attractions which appeal to their carnal feelings. The sensuous may be attracted by such attractions. But when the hand of a young woman is sought by a young man, because of her wealth or her exterior attractions, if the wealth is not what it was expected to be, or the attractions do not last, his attention, for love he had not, becomes cold, and she is neglected and perhaps dies broken-hearted.

We were present not long since when a conversation took place about a young lady of whom we had some knowledge. She had some wealth, and some personal attractions. The question was asked why she never married. The reply was, "She was not agreeable in her manners and disposition." It is true, these are not always a barrier to marriage. But they are to the discreet and observing. Prof. Upham, an author well known, says, "I have come to the conclusion, if man, or woman either, wishes to realize the full power of personal beauty, it must be by cherishing noble hopes and purposes; by having something to do, and something to live for, which is worthy of humanity, and which, by expanding the capacities of the soul, gives expansion and symmetry to the body which contains it."

We pass from the young to the old in our *picture of the happy people.* While the young, trained to holiness and usefulness, form an important element in the picture of the happy people before us, given us by the psalmist, the old are not left out. Their presence is plainly discovered. The old are characterized by a very strong solicitude for the young. Who was it that desired and prayed that our sons and daughters might be all that is implied in the high attainment that is desired for them? It was one of the parents in the body of happy people. And this is the characteristic of the aged saint. "Fathers, provoke not your children to wrath: but bring them up in the nurture and admonition of the Lord."—Eph. 6: 4. Such is the duty enjoined upon parents. The duty enjoined, they labor to perform. And it is very natural to suppose that while the parents and the aged labor to promote the piety of the young, that they will not neglect to cultivate holiness in themselves. And so it is a characteristic of all in a truly happy people, to labor to do right and to be holy. And it is their success in such labors that makes them the happy people they are.

The next thing we notice in the *picture of the happy people* is their secular prosperity. "That our garners may be full, affording all manner of store; that our sheep may bring forth thousands and ten thousands in our streets; that our oxen may be strong to labor; that there be no breaking in, nor going out; that there be no complaining in our streets." Secular prosperity has considerable to do with our happiness. We have bodies to provide for and our bodies are earthy, and through them we are related to the earth, and in a measure dependent on it. And our higher natures of intellect and spirit are closely connected with our physical nature, and more or less influenced by it. Hence a healthy state of the body is very desirable and important. And while it is true that a Christian may be happy in poverty and want, it is happiness enjoyed under disadvantages and amid temptation. Poverty and want are not crimes when they do not result from our improvidence or neglect. But they are very inconvenient, and often a great barrier to our usefulness and charity. The inconvenience of want, and its interference with happiness, are known at this time by our brethren and others in Kansas. If they could at this time experience the secular prosperity contained in the picture of the happy people of our text, it, no doubt, would add greatly to their enjoyment. To secular things too much attention and labor are given by some. While others are too dilatory and neglectful in their secular business. It is desirable that we have a pleasant home and enough of this world's goods to keep us from want and to enable us to give something to such as may be in want. And if we do our duty in all things, we may hope for a sufficiency if not abundance. "Seek ye first the kingdom of God, and his righteousness; and all these things shall be added unto you."—Matt. 6: 33. The things referred to here are secular things which are necessary for our comfort.

Another idea in connection with our secular prosperity is peace, or freedom from war. "That there be no breaking in, nor going out; that there be no complaining in our streets." Horne paraphrases these words, thus : "No irruption of aliens into the commonwealth, nor emigration of inhabitants to foreign countries, by captivity, or otherwise." Such blessings and such prosperity God promised to his people Israel upon condition that they kept his laws. "Wherefore it shall come to pass, if ye hearken to these judgments, and keep and do them, that the Lord thy God shall keep unto thee the covenant and the mercy which he sware unto thy fathers: and he will love thee, and bless thee, and multiply thee: he will also bless the fruit of thy womb, and the fruit of thy land, thy corn, and thy vine, and thine oil, the increase of thy kin and the flocks of thy sheep, in the land which he sware unto thy fathers to give thee." Deut. 7: 12, 13.

The last particular in *the picture of the happy people* contained in our text, is their religious character. "Happy is that people that is in such a case; yea, happy is that people whose God is the Lord." "Happy is that people that is in such a case." What case? The case of a people among whom the parents feel a proper solicitude for their sons and daughters growing up in holiness and usefulness; the case of a people enjoying in a high degree secular prosperity, the case of a people having the Lord Jehovah for their God. A people in such a case or condition is a happy people. Their religious character is plainly seen in the fact that they had a God. And the sufficiency and correctness of that religious character are assured from the fact that Jehovah was their God. No people can be a happy people without a God. The apostle in referring to the state of the Ephesian brethren, says, "at that time ye were without Christ, being aliens from the commonwealth of Israel, and strangers from the covenant of promise, having no hope, and without God in the world."—Eph. 2 : 12. According to this language, to be without God is to be without hope. But if we have God and Christ, we have a hope, and we are safe and happy. "Happy is that people, whose God is the Lord." There are "Gods many, and Lords many."—I. Cor. 8 : 5. "But to us," says Paul, continuing after the language we have last quoted, "There is but one God."—And this God is Jehovah, the true God, and the God that manifests himself in the three characters or persons, Father, Son, and Holy Spirit, into all of whom believers are baptized. And being baptized into all, they enjoy the power and offices of all, and consequently are a happy people.

The last truth we present from our text is this: The people who have the Lord for their God, and who serve him, and who are happy in his service, are in danger of being injured in their character and principles from the ungodly in the world to whose influence they are exposed. Therefore David prays, "Rid me, and deliver me from the hand of strange children, whose mouth speaketh vanity, and their right hand is a right hand of falsehood." These "strange children" are the children of the world as distinguished from the children of God. It is not to be confined to the young, but it refers to adults as well. Perowne translates it "sons of the alien." Their conversation was vain, and they were untruthful. Their promises were not reliable. The apostle Peter refers to the same persons and to their influence upon the good in the following language: "When they speak great swelling words of vanity, they allure through the lusts of the flesh, through much wantonness, those that were clean escaped from them who live in error. While they promise them liberty, they themselves are the servants of corruption."—2 Peter, 2: 18, 19. Christians, and especially young Christians, should be very careful what kind of companions they associate with. We are to "honor all men," and show kindness to the ungodly, and whenever we can do them a favor we should do it. We do not think that duty requires us to withdraw altogether from the society of the ungodly, but we should be very careful that we do not in our intercourse with them compromise our Christian principles, or permit our Christian character to become contaminated by theirs, since "evil communications corrupt good manners."

In conclusion we exhort you all to become like the happy people, whose pictures we have had before us, for "Happy is that people that is in such a case, yea, happy is that people whose God is the Lord."

XIII.
THE DANGER OF LOSING WHAT HAS BEEN DONE FOR OUR SALVATION.

"Look to yourselves, that we lose not the things which we have wrought, but that we receive a full reward."—2 John, 8th verse.

As the text reads, it conveys the idea that the apostle was anxious that the brethren might look to themselves and thereby continue faithful, that he and his fellow-laborers who had been the means of their conversion, might receive a full reward. Though the minister will not lose his reward, if he faithfully discharges his duty, even if those he has gathered into the church should not be faithful, and should be found wanting in the day of judgment. But his reward will be much greater, as his joy will be much greater, if those he has ministered for are accepted by the Lord. It appears from Paul's language, 2 Cor. 11: 2, "For I am jealous over you with Godly jealousy: for I have espoused you to one husband, that I may present you as a chaste virgin to Christ," that the minister at the proper time, will present his people to the Lord. Then according to the text, if we who minister to you here, would have our reward full, you, to whom we minister, must be faithful. And if you are not, our reward or joy will be diminished. This idea seems confirmed by 1 Thess. 2: 19, "For what is our hope, or joy, or crown of rejoicing? Are not even ye in the presence of Christ at his coming? For ye are our glory and joy." According to this language, the more the minister is the means of training for heaven, the brighter will be his crown. Hence the apostle's concern as expressed in the text, "that we receive a full reward." But there is another reading which we perfer, which seems to be more correct, and which makes the "full reward," refer not only to the ministers, but to all the members of the church as well. The *Vulgate*, a very ancient Latin version of the Scriptures, and the one which the Roman Catholic Church uses, reads our text thus: "Look to yourselves, that ye lose not the things which you have wrought; but that you may receive a full reward." Macnight says, five of Steven's manuscripts, the Alexandrian and other manuscripts, the second Syriac, and the Ethiopic read it as does the Vulgate. According to this reading then, *a full reward* is held out to all Christians to induce them to persevere in well doing. "Look to yourselves, that you lose not the things which you have wrought: but that you may receive a full reward." It is a suggestive, and it should be an awakening, and an alarming thought, that all that has been done may, through our indifference and neglect, be lost, and profit us nothing. "We then," says Paul, "as workers together with him, beseech you also that ye receive not the grace of God in vain." 2 Cor. 6: 1. Paul saw the same danger that John saw, namely, that of losing the personal and saving benefits of all that has been done to save us.

While the text, as we perfer to read it, has special reference to the loss of the labors that the Christian believers themselves had already done in the work of salvation, we will expand or enlarge the thought, and embrace within the scope of its application, all that has been done by all the agents concerned in the work of our salvation. These agents are three; 1, the divine; 2, the ministerial; 3, the individual.

1. By the divine, we mean the work of salvation in its objective character, that is the work of salvation in itself, independent altogether of man, and external to the mind of man. Salvation in its subjective character, is salvation in us, and thus realized and verified by our consciousness. This distinction is frequetly met with in theological writings, and is useful in expressing the different relations in which salvation stands to us. Salvation, then, in its objective or general relation, was wrought for us before we had a being and independent of anything that we did. Our heavenly Father, foreseeing the wants of our ruined race, before our race had a beginning, in the exercise of his love, mercy, and wisdom, devised a means by which he could pardon the guilty without in anywise sanctioning or encouraging sin. And what the Father devised or originated, in the fullness of time, the Son executed, and thus became "the author and finisher of our faith." Heb. 12: 2. The Holy Spirit also fills his office in the great work of human redemption. Now,

notwithstanding salvation is provided for all men, it will be lost to all that do not believe. And, further, men may believe and do works meet for repentance (Matt. 3 : 8) and realize some of the advantages of this great salvation, but if they do not then look to themselves, and hold out faithful to the end, they will lose all that has been done for them by what we have called the divine agents, and also all that they will have done for themselves. It is true, God has said in regard to his word, "It shall not return unto me void, but shall accomplish that which I please, and it shall prosper in the thing whereto I sent it." Isa. 55: 11. Surely what God has done will not be without important results in the purposes of his government in vindicating the righteousness and justice of all his proceedings with men; but while the Christian redemption will vindicate God, and be a witness for him, it will profit such only among men that believe, and hold fast their faith.

2. By the ministerial agents, we mean the ministers of the divine word. In the conversion of the most of people, the work of the minister is an important agent. "Faith cometh by hearing, and hearing by the word of God." Rom. 10: 17. "And how shall they hear without a preacher?" The agency of the ministry, both in the conversion of sinners, and in the culture and growth of Christian character, has much to do. And the faithful minister appreciating this will feel that a great responsibility rests upon him. It is his duty to feed the flock of God, the lambs with the sincere milk of the word, and the sheep with stronger meat as they are able to bear it, and as their wants require. John, the aged apostle, and servant of God, in the deep yearnings of his affectionate heart, for the prosperity and salvation of his brethren and spiritual children, says in his short epistle to "the well beloved Gaius," "Beloved, I wish above all things that thou mayst prosper

and be in health, even as thy soul prospereth. For I rejoice greatly, when the brethren came and testified of the truth that is in thee, even as thou walkest in the truth. I have no greater joy than to hear that my children walk in truth." 3 John, verses 2–4. Paul said to his Galatian brethren, "My little children, of whom I travail in birth again until Christ be formed in you." Gal. 4: 19. Such is the concern that faithful ministers feel for the salvation of the people to whom they minister, and with such a concern they spare no pains or labor in their endeavors to bring sinners to Christ, and to keep them faithful, after their conversion to the truth, and their consecration to God. And entertaining such feelings, it is not surprising that the apostle John expressed himself as he did in our text, showing that he "desired above all things," that his brethren for whom he labored, and he and his fellow laborers also, "might receive a full reward."

3. Then a part of the work of salvation is done by the persons themselves in whom and for whom the work is done. "Work out your own salvation with fear and trembling." Phil. 2: 12. This plainly implies the necessity of our own agency in the work of our salvation. "Look to yourselves that you lose not the things which you have wrought." All who have come to Christ and obtained pardon for their sins, and the gift of the Holy Spirit, have experienced a great work. They "have passed from death unto life." 1 John 3: 14, and have been delivered from the power of darkness, and translated into the kingdom of Christ. Col. 1: 13. And all those who have experienced this great work, have co-operated with all the Divine persons, and with the ministerial agents, in accomplishing the work.

And when a soul leaves the world, and forsakes its sins, and takes a decided stand on the side of the Lord, an important step is taken, and in a certain sense, a considerable part of the work that it has to do in working out its salvation is done. We say in a certain sense much is then done. We Baptists, who believe that baptism has something to do with our salvation, and preach that people should be baptized as well as believe and repent, and also preach that immersion alone is baptism, are sometimes charged with putting all our trust in baptism, and with holding the idea that when a person is baptized the work is done. We disclaim holding any such sentiments, and in reply to such charges, say that we believe the work of salvation is just properly begun in a person when he is baptized. For when he is born into the kingdom of God by being born of the water and of the Spirit, John 3: 5, he is then only a babe, and then must be nursed and fed, and taken care of, that he may grow "unto a perfect man, unto the measure of the stature of the fullness of Christ."—Eph. 4: 13 But, though the work is just begun when a soul is converted to God, nevertheless, a good deal is done. For when a person has overcome his own indifference, the pride of his heart, and his carnal mind which is "enmity against God," and sundered the chords that bind him to the world, and to the followers of worldly pleasure and fashion, and freed himself from the grasp of Satan, and has passed through the sorrows and agony of the state of true penitency, such a person has done a good deal in the work of his salvation. It is true, it is but little of what he may have to do if he continues in the world a considerable time, and shall have to fight the good fight of faith with all the foes with which he shall have to contend. Still, when the "first works" of a religious life are looked at in themselves, they are not small nor unimportant.

Now, according to the doctrine of our text, all this work may be lost. "That we lose not those things which we have wrought." And because we are in danger of losing all that we have gained, we are admonished to look to ourselves. For surely it would be a terrible loss to lose all that we have gained in our struggle and labor to get into Christ. We therefore should look to ourselves, and hold fast what we have. For should we ever lose what we have "wrought" or gained, its recovery, if recovered, would require more labor, more suffering, a more terrible conflict with the opposing powers of darkness, than was required to accomplish our "first works" that brought us into Christ.

But Christians are not only in danger of losing what they have wrought, but if they lose what they themselves have wrought, and should they never recover it, but be "cast away," they will also lose all that has been done for them by all others who have taken an interest in their salvation, and worked to secure it. They will lose all that heaven has done, and all that faithful ministers and Christian parents have done for them. And what a pity it would be, what a misfortune, and what a criminal neglect will it be on the part of all whether saints or sinners to lose all that has been done to save them.

We urge the thought upon the consideration of sinners as well as upon the consideration of saints. A great dea has been done for you. There is a sense in which Christ has died for you, for he "tasted death for every man." Heb. 2: 9. You have also made some proficiency in acquiring a knowledge of the scriptures. You have enjoyed the privilege of attending Sabbath school and the Bible class. And many of you have had the advantages of a Christian home and of Christian parents. And you have enjoyed the advantages of the Christian ministry. You have heard many sermons and many exhortations. Much has been done for you, and much has been given to you. Now the thought that all this should be lost is a painful thought, and it should startle you to think, and to feel, and to act, lest you lose all that has been done for you. Should you sustain this loss, you will never cease to feel it and to regret it. Then we say to you all, to saints and sinners, "Look to yourselves that you lose not the things which you have wrought; but that you receive a full reward."

And what is implied in "looking to yourselves?" The apostle speaks about deceivers and antichrist in the context. Hence there is implied a danger of being deceived. We would therefore say, look to your principles, and see that they are according to the principles of the Gospel. Look to your hearts and see that your motives and feelings are right. Look to your actions and see that they are right. Look to yourselves—turn your thought upon yourselves. There is so much in the outside world to draw our attention, that we very much neglect to look at the world within us. Hence we are too little acquainted with ourselves. We are therefore admonished in our text to look to ourselves. The idea is, we are to know ourselves, and if we are not right, we are to get ourselves right.

And if we look to ourselves as Christians, and lose not what we have already wrought or gained, and persevere to the end, we shall then receive a "full reward." And if those who have not yet commenced to work for themselves, now begin, and avail themselves of what has already been done by others for them, then they too, will receive a full reward. And what is the "full reward?" A full reward is all that is promised in the Gospel, and that is the "promise of the life that now is, and of that which is to come."—1 Tim. 4: 8.

We offer two thoughts which contain much of the substance of the text. The first is the generosity of heaven. Heaven has offered us a "full reward." With God there is no scarcity. And as he is able to do so he will abundantly reward all who serve him. Secondly, God wishes us to have all that he has provided for us. He desires that we should attain unto the highest state of holiness, that we may thereby secure to ourselves the highest state of enjoyment. Then let us all "Look to ourselves, that we lose not those things which we have wrought; but that we receive a full reward."

XIV.
OUR CHRISTIAN DUTIES.

"Finally be ye all of one mind, having compassion one of another, love as brethren, be pitiful, be courteous, not rendering evil for evil, or railing for railing; but contrariwise blessing; knowing that ye are thereunto called, that ye should inherit a blessing."—I. Peter 3: 8-9.

The apostle commences the chapter by admonishing his brethren and sisters to an observance of duties of a very personal and rather of a domestic character. He continued in this strain of admonition of practical Christian duties, and as the word "finally" implies, closes his train of thought with the words of our text.

I present my subject under three heads. The duties of Christians to one another; their duties to men in general; and their duties to their enemies; with the reason following why we should perform these duties: First, the duties to one another. "Finally, be ye all of one mind. Having compassion one with another; love as brethren." Thus far we conceive that the apostle addressed more particularly the brethren in regard to duties with one another. They are admonished to be of one mind. You, that are to any considerable extent acquainted with Christianity as we have it in the Gospel, are aware that we as Christians are commanded to be united. It is not only commanded by Peter, but we find it in the writings of the apostle Paul, and we find it taught by the Saviour, and it constituted one of the prominent petitions in that prayer of his that he offered up just before he was betrayed and crucified—the prayer is found in the 17th chapter of John. In that prayer, one petition was especially for the union of his people, the union of his church: "That they may be one; as thou, Father, art in me, and I in thee, that they may also be one in us." That was the prayer of Christ, and as a model and pattern of that oneness, he gives as an example the union between himself and his Father. The union that exists between the Father and Son is the model or pattern that we should seek after as members of his church. "That we may be one." Now in what does this union consist? How far is it obligatory upon us to endeavor to attain to the union mentioned in our text, and to the union for which Christ prayed when he prayed that his disciples might be one! That union consists in an observance of the doctrine taught us in the New Testament Scripture. Such as there is but one God; that there is but one Mediator between God and man; but one Saviour.

"There is one body, and one Spirit, even as ye are called in one hope of your calling; one Lord, one faith, one baptism, one God and Father of all, who is above all, and through all, and in you all."—Eph. 4: 4-6. And when Christ sent out his disciples after his resurrection, he said, "Go ye therefore, and teach all nations, baptizing them in the name of the Father, and of the Son, and of the Holy Ghost: Teaching them to observe all things whatsoever I have commanded you: and, lo, I am with you alway, even unto the end of the world."—Matt. 28: 19-20. Now as all who were converted to Christianity, were to have all the commandments of Christ preached to them, it was evidently their duty to receive and practice those commandments. Hence they were to be of one mind in practicing all the commandments of Christ. And this refers to all believers in all ages of the Christian Church. The same doctrine was to be preached at Rome that was to be preached at Corinth and Ephesus. Hence Paul writing to the Ephesian brethren declares as we have seen, "There is one Lord, one faith and one baptism," etc. This church was probably made up of Jews and Gentiles. And some were not to believe one thing and some another, but they were to be of the same mind, and have the same faith, the same baptism, and be united to the same body, which was Christ or his church. And from such Scriptures as I have quoted, we may form a pretty correct view of the oneness to which Christians are to attain.

We are to be one in all the doctrines of the gospel, and in all the commandments of our Lord, and in all that is designed to promote our Christian edification. Why do we not say we are to be one in all that is essential to salvation? Surely this is to be understood. But I say in all that is promotive of Christian edification. We have Christians in the world who are very zealous, very strong in maintaining what they think essential to salvation. But anything beyond what is essential to salvation, they do not think is of much importance. Now we look at the matter in a different light. Whatever our Lord has commanded, is essential to something. He does nothing, nor requires us to do anything that is altogether useless. We will illustrate our idea here by a reference to feet-washing.

We don't think that feetwashing is essential to salvation, some will say. Very well. Suppose we can be saved without it, my brethren, bearing whatever denominational name you please. I want to call your attention to what Christ said: "If ye know these things, happy are ye if ye do them." What things? Feet-washing was one of them. The performance of every duty brings its accompanying pleasure. "*Happy* are ye if ye do them." Suppose we can be saved without washing feet, can we enjoy the blessing that is connected with it without doing it? Whatever happiness I enjoy in the public sanctuary, in holy devotion, whatever joy I may have experienced in my holy baptism, whatever happiness I may experience around the Lord's table, what enjoyment I may feel in all these places, I have because I do them. So I can not enjoy the happiness consequent upon the observance of the rite of feetwashing unless I do the thing. Therefore, whatever happiness I enjoy, in anything else I can not enjoy the happiness of feetwashing unless I do the thing. Then, though you may think feetwashing is not essential to salvation, it is essential to our enjoyment of the blessing consequent upon it. That's the point I call your attention to. I maintain it for the reason that it is a *duty*, and the performance of that duty will contribute to our spiritual edification and enjoyment. Is it not plain and reasonable? There ought to be a union among us. If anybody else has something that promotes their edification I do not have, I ought to have it. If we have something that promotes our Christian edification that others have not, they ought to be with us. For there should be a sameness of mind touching our edification and sanctification.

Another grand point is our sanctification. "Sanctify them through thy truth; thy word is truth." Look at that connection. I want to call your attention to this. "Sanctify them through thy truth." What truth? The word of God is truth. I mean that word in all its parts, and connections and requirements. By that word, in all its fullness and by an impartial compliance with it, we are to be sanctified. There is a good deal said about Christian sanctification. And it is an important doctrine, but sanctification without obedience is a delusion. We are to obey the word of God. We are to be sanctified by its truth. We are to be set apart from the sinful world by the truth of God. The word of God is to separate us. It's to be a partition wall that is to be built up between the church and the world; and every Christian rite and practice is an additional layer of stone, as it were, that enlarges that partition, and this is a wall that divides the two. And what is the breadth of that wall? It is as broad as the law of God. It is composed of duty, and it is composed of holy principles, and that man or woman that is farthest from the wickedness of the world, is the one most controlled by Christian truth, the most molded in the mold of Christian truth.

Everything that has a tendency to take sin away, and everything that has a tendency to stamp upon us the divine image we should be united in. There must be a oneness in that, and to this end we are to work.

In the apostolic church that was comprised of Jews and Gentiles, Paul said, "There is one faith, one Lord, one baptism." When the Jews were very tenacious about eating flesh, the Gentiles could not see the necessity in being so, and what did Paul teach them? He taught forbearance with one another. He says: "Let not him that eateth despise him that eateth not; and let not him which eateth not judge him that eateth; for God hath received him."—Rom. 14:3. One sits down to his table with no meat on it and he thanks God for his herbs; another sits down to his table with meat on it and thanks God for it. In regard to this matter we have nothing in the new dispensation, therefore things of that kind are to be left to our discretion and to our circumstances. We present this thought in connection with that passage in which Paul says, "Let every man be fully persuaded in his own mind." If one wants to eat meat, let him eat it. Let all things be done in moderation. If one wants to observe the Jewish festive days, two or three Sabbaths, let him do it. If he can afford to abstain two or three days from work, why let him do it. Don't condemn him for it.

These are matters, we have said, that must be left to one's judgment, and discretion. But when you come to Christian doctrines and the things that God has ordained in his law, don't quote that passage, "Let every man be persuaded in his own mind," for we should be persuaded in our own minds only to accept the truth in its fullness. One thought more and I drop this one of the objects, at least, that this union should be obtained for. Why all of the same mind? Paul don't give the reason here. In preaching in this way one text presupposes another text. Why should this oneness be sought after? Why should we all try to be united? Why should all denominational divisions be put away? And why should we all come down to one order, one body and one organization—one fold of Christ? The Saviour answers it in that prayer to which we have referred. You will find the answer in the 17th chapter of John. The Saviour says, "That they all may be one; as thou, Father, art in me, and I in thee, that they also may be one in us; that the world may believe that thou hast sent me." That oneness promotes our efficiency, and it promotes our power; as you have heard it said, "in union there is strength." If all the believers in Christ had this oneness of mind, and then would labor together, what good could be done! But you know, unfortunately the Christian world is divided. One denomination preaches one thing and another preaches that thing down, and in this way our power is divided, and it is not simply divided; it is a little like it would be in the army. Take two armies meeting in battle array, and about to enter into deadly conflict. The guns are all planted on the ramparts. They all have their direction. But suppose there are twenty or thirty guns directed against the party for whom they were designed to protect, then when the match is to be applied and the word given, to enter the conflict, only one-half of the power is exerted on the enemy. They are turned right around against the army of which they formed a part. How then? Then you see what a condition of things there would be. That seems to be a pretty hard illustration, but it is a description of the Christian world. Our guns are directed against ourselves. I mean by that, that we in the churches, instead of meeting the common enemy are having difficulties between ourselves. One thing here and another thing there. The different churches are engaged in that. Now that is very unpleasant. Take the Baptist Church and the subject of open communion. One class is in favor of close communion and another in favor of open communion. So there is a difficulty here. I might mention other churches. And we come down to our own churches and we are sorry there is not the union among us that there should be. We are turning our artillery against ourselves. We are divided among ourselves, and we are spending our strength in contending with one another when that strength should be spent in defending our principles and general order. Now the importance of this union. These churches ought not only to be united, but they ought properly be united *together*. I believe we will have to render a terrible account for the condition existing between the different denominations. Christ prayed for the oneness of his people. There is a wrong somewhere. We ought to be united *together*, instead of being so estranged as we are, and be an unbroken power against the world. Oh, what good would be done! Go back to the apostolic church. There was no general division in that church then. There were some few difficulties, it is true, but no general rupture, and look at the power of that church. Look at the churches springing up in Rome, the city of idolatry, heathenism and crimes; and why was that? Because they brought the united power of the church to bear against the world. And so it would be to-day. But we will give more time to this thought again; for we feel it is an important one. "Be of the same mind." How far? We have alluded to that. We don't think you can object to the position we have taken. Don't say this thing and that is not essential to salvation. Is it essential to anything else in the Christian life? Will it increase my power to honor God? Will it give me increased help in manifesting my devotion to the Lord? Will it make me a better man or woman? And for the oneness of all such things we should labor. The next point is, "Be of one mind, having compassion one with another." We refer this still to Christian duty. To dispose of this in a few words we apply this to feeling. Be of the same feeling—be of the same feeling one toward another; a feeling of anxiety for one another's welfare. "Have compassion one toward another." We are all likely to get into trouble. We all have our troubles. You have your troubles and difficulties, all of you. Then we all should feel for one another. There should be a sameness of feeling in this respect. We quote the marginal reading which is also a translation of the original, "Have sameness of feeling." Try to be the same in feeling as well as in mind. It is the same doctrine that Paul preached, when he admonished his brethren to "weep with them that weep, and rejoice with them that rejoice." That's the idea. Same feeling. Suppose I am in trouble. You sit down by my side and you are in trouble with me. That's compassion. You show by the look of your countenance and of your eye that you are in deep sympathy with me. That's the kind of feeling we should cultivate. Some it seems can not do it. There are some people that are calculated to make all around them unhappy.

They have such language and complaining tone of voice, that if you are not careful you will get into the same condition. "Weep with them that weep," etc. There is something in that worthy of our attention. You must enter into our feelings if we are in trouble. Try to catch the feeling. Oneness of feeling. That's the idea. Have compassion one for another—be of the same feeling. We now notice another duty inculcated in the text. "Love as brethren." Let true love be maintained in the church. "Love as brethren." That's the love. This opens up a wide field for application. We must not work against one another. There are a great many negative things we must not do. Some people go to law with one another. We should not do that. Christians can not go to law with one another. It is not right. Christians must not go to war. Brethren should not kill one another, and whenever we admit that war is right, we admit the propriety of Christians coming in conflict with one another. Christians of the same denomination sometimes come in conflict with one another. What was the condition during our war a few years ago? Why on the fields of Gettysburg and Antietam members of the same denomination met and fought with one another. It was the case also in the war between England and America; and whenever we admit the justice of war we must admit the propriety of members of the same denomination meeting in conflict. But we must refrain from these things. Instead of fighting and killing one another, we must be kind to one another, pitiful and courteous. This is the spirit that should characterize Christians. While as Christians we are to be one in heart, and love as brethren, we are to be pitiful and courteous to all men. What is pity? Pity is the distress produced in the mind at the wrong and danger of others; a distress produced on account of the suffering of others. We are to feel for every one that suffers. And how is it with the outside world? Oh! when we look at the sinner standing on slippery rocks with the fiery billows rolling beneath, what pity should melt our hearts! It is our duty to feel distressed, and pity is something we ought to cultivate. And then be courteous. What does this mean? It has reference to our conduct towards one another. It is especially associated with kindness or the disposition for to help.

There is a class of pretty thoughts connected with the subject of courtesy. What does the word "courtesy" come from? It comes from the honors of the courts—the courts of kings and emperors. There is a great deal of etiquette observed by that class that associate with the courts of kings. The word "courtesy" comes from the courts, as the word rustic comes from the manners of rural districts. But don't misunderstand us. The courtesy that we cultivate is not the courtesy observed around the courts of royal greatness. What court then? The court of heaven. For this courtesy does not consist in outward show, but it consists in kindness of heart, and respect to our superiors and inferiors. It is the observing of those dignified and holy principles that govern the intercourse between high and holy beings. Is this not a grand thought? Those are the manners that are characteristic of the divine family, the Son of God himself, and the angels around the throne of heaven. There was once a rich merchant of Liverpool, who, when asked how he succeeded so well in accumulating so large a fortune, replied, "By my civility to others." It is a grand characteristic. It is one of the best you can make use of. Respect and kindness to all, with whom you associate are Christian duties. Students—be courteous one to another, and to your teachers, husbands, wives, parents and children, be courteous. Observe the habits of the divine family and the divine character. I can say to you, being the oldest in the room, that I have been for forty years traveling more or less over our country, alone and in company, and I have never met with much insult or unkindness from those among whom I have been thrown. In my early youth I tried to learn these Christian manners, I tried to be civil. I say not this to boast, but for your encouragement, young people. And in a similar way, we recommend every element of our holy religion. Our Christianity leads to courtesy. And, my hearers, we want to tell you that instead of giving wrong for wrong, and evil for evil, you must on the other hand, give good for evil. You are called upon to bless those that curse you and despitefully use you as Christ did. Don't render evil for evil, but good for evil. We are called upon to do that by the Great Master, under whose laws we should live. We must be loving and courteous and kind, and return good for evil. We would like to dwell upon the importance of cultivating these feelings. The Spirit of God plants these feelings in our hearts at our conversion, and we must cultivate them. We come into the world little babes, with two hands, ears and eyes, but, you know, these members must be developed; those little arms must be made strong. We must develop those little forms and bring them to maturity. And so it is with the virtues planted in our hearts at our conversion. They must be cultivated and developed. Do we study Christianity in that way? We can not expect to have great strength unless we cultivate these elements of Christian character. Let us cultivate the feeling of brotherly love, courtesy and kindness. They are to be subjects of cultivation. Our attention is to be given to them and in that way we will become men and women in Christ and will greatly beautify our Christian character.

In conclusion notice the thought that if we would inherit a blessing, we must try to bless others: "Not rendering evil for evil, or railing for railing: but contrariwise blessing;

knowing that ye are thereunto called, that ye should inherit a blessing." Let us then try to make our lives a blessing, and we shall be blessed by the Lord with all that he has promised to the faithful.

XV.
THE SERVANT OF GOD IS THE SERVANT OF HIS AGE.

"David, after he had served his own generation by the will of God, fell on sleep."—Acts xiii. 36.

The words of our text were used in a discourse delivered by the Apostle Paul at Antioch. The apostle was permitted to speak to the people, and he addressed his Jewish brethren. He gave a general outline of God's dealings with his ancient people down to the time of the Messiah. And in his allusion to Christ, the apostle alluded to his resurrection. And it was upon the subject of Christ's resurrection that the words of our text were used. The apostle quoted a passage from the 16th Psalm, the words of David, "Thou shalt not suffer thine Holy One to see corruption." And as David saw corruption, it was evident that he did not allude to himself. The apostle applied it to Christ. The words of our text are an incidental allusion of David. And it is worthy of observation that a great many very expressive, instructive and encouraging texts of Scripture are of this kind—incidental allusions to some persons or things in pursuing an argument, or some train of thought. David is referred to as being a servant of his generation. And we use the text in a broader sense, and make it express by implication the truth that the servant of God is the servant of his generation or age. The word generation in the Scriptures frequently means age. And by age, we understand the people of our time, or the time to which the age refers. When it is said that David served his own generation, it means he served the people that lived in his age of the world. And by the age in which we live, and which we are to serve, we are to understand the people who now live upon the earth.

The servants of God, in every age of the world, are to serve their age, or the people of their age. And to serve our age effectually, or in the way we understand we are to serve it, it is necessary that we be the servants of God. We can not render that complete service to men that they need to promote their varied and highest interests unless we are the servants of God. God's best servants are men's best servants. All who do not serve God, can serve men but imperfectly. In serving men, we are not to serve them in doing their will, but serve them in doing them good. There is a sense in which we are not to serve men. "Ye are bought with a price; be not ye the servants of men."—1 Cor. vii. 23 There is also a sense in which we are to serve men: "For, brethren, we have been called unto liberty; only use not liberty for an occasion to the flesh, but by love serve one another."—Gal. v. 13. If a company of four or five of you young men or young women would plan some project for improper amusement, and would ask another to unite with you, and he would refuse, and you would urge him, and say to him you do not serve us right by declining to take part with us in our contemplated sport, the one who would decline, and tell you that you would all better abandon it than to prosecute it, would really serve his companions better by declining than by consenting. God's servants serve men as he serves them; he does not minister to their lusts and impure desires, neither do they.

I. How shall we serve our generation?

1. By laboring, to the extent of our ability, to remove every cause of evil which exists among us. There is a terrible weight of misery resting upon the people of our age, as there has been upon the people of every age, in the form of ignorance, superstition, pride, intemperance, and all the evils that have been caused by the introduction of sin into the world. From these evils men should be delivered. They need help, both human and divine. It is for us to give them the human help, as God may enable us to do so.

2. By laboring to establish right principles among those to whom our influence extends. Character is the embodiment of principle. Right principles, reduced to practice, will result in the formation of good character, while wrong principles, reduced to practice, will result in making bad character. The idea, entertained by many, that it does not matter what people believe, so their lives are right, is very true, but while this is so, it is equally true that if we would attain unto a right life we must not be indifferent to principles, since a right life can only result from right principles. The idea prevails extensively that if people are sincere in their belief, they will not be condemned by the Lord. This we believe is very unsafe ground to occupy. Sincerity is a very important element in Christian character, but it is only one of the many elements which form a Christian character. If sincerity constitutes a right character, then some of the lowest characters among the Catholics, Mormons, and other denominations would be right, for many such are very sincere. But, as already intimated, sincerity is but one element of Christian character, and as all the sounds of the English alphabet are necessary to form our language, so all the principles of Christianity are necessary to form a complete Christian character. Hence, those who would serve their generation to the best advantage should labor to promote sound doctrine and right principles.

3. But right principles to form right character must be not only heard and believed, but also obeyed, or practiced. So, to serve our generation we must not only labor to inculcate and establish good principles, but we must also labor to get people to practically accept Christian principles. One department in the Christian ministry is exhortation. This differs from teaching in this: That while simple teaching communicates knowledge, exhortation is designed to stir up the feeling and to move to action.

To serve our generation effectually, then, we must labor to make people good. And we must labor in our various callings in life to accomplish this. The minister must labor in his calling to serve his generation by making people Christians. To this he is especially called. The parents should labor for the same end, and their position is such that gives them great influence, and that influence should be judiciously directed to promote the welfare of all within their influence. Teachers in all our schools should serve their generation by laboring to improve not only the intellect of their scholars, but also their hearts. The Sabbath-school offers a very inviting field in which the generation of the young may be served. And you, young people, should endeavor to serve one another and all whom you can serve. You all can render service which will tend to lessen the cares and labors of others, and promote their peace and comfort. Whatever happiness any one is the means of promoting, is so much added to the stock of human enjoyment. And the least evil that is corrected, is so much taken from the load of human misery that is crushing so many.

II. Why should we serve our generation?

1. It is the will of God that we should do so. The text says that David "by the will of God served his generation." And is it not equally true that it is the will of God that we all should serve our generation? It has already been inti-

mated that God himself serves his creatures. Jesus said to the Jews, "My Father worketh hitherto, and I work."—John v. 17. And our Lord, in speaking of himself, said, "The Son of man came not to be ministered unto, but to minister, and to give his life a ransom for many."—Matt. xx. 28. And as the Father, Son and Holy Spirit are actively engaged in promoting the highest interest of mankind, their spiritual offspring will be engaged in the same noble work. As God's will is contained in his law, whatever is his law is also his will. The second commandment is "Thou shalt love thy neighbor as thyself."—Mark xii. 31. This commandment evidently puts us all under obligation to serve our age. It is then the will and law of God that we serve one another, and serve our generation. Disinterested benevolence is a distinguishing peculiarity of the divine nature, and it should also be of the Christian character. The servants of God cooperate with him in all his holy purposes, and as he is constantly laboring to promote the well being of his creatures, his servants will not be idle, but will labor for the same end for which he is laboring.

To serve our generation effectually, so that our service will have the greatest effect upon those for whom we labor, and at the same time be acceptable to God, it must be prompted by love. "God is love." Love is one of the divine attributes. Love will therefore be an element in every Christian character. And this love will be the basis of the service that we are to render to our generation. And love as the basis will not only prompt us to labor, but it will also make the service pleasant and self-sacrificing to those who perform it. To labor successfully in any department of Christian labor, we must love the labor we perform. God loves a cheerful giver. And the charities bestowed and the labors performed will be received with greatly increased enjoyment by their recipients, when they can feel that their benefactors loved to give.

2. We are under obligation to serve our own age as former ages have served us. The apostle asked his Corinthian brethren the following question: "What hast thou that thou didst not receive?"—1 Cor. iv. 7. We have but little that we ourselves are the authors of. And while we recognize God to be the author and giver of all good, it is through our own age and others before ours that God has given us his blessings. The books we read, our institutions intellectual and moral, the wholesome and beneficent laws under which we live, have come to us through human agency, or the agency of society. The accumulated and valuable treasures of former ages this age inherits. And if this is true in regard to temporal blessings, it is no less true in regard to spiritual blessings. Paul said to Timothy: "The things that thou hast heard of me among many witnesses, the same commit thou to faithful men, who shall be able to teach others also."—2 Tim. ii. 2. It is through the medium of human agents that "the glorious gospel of the blessed God," with all its records, ordinances and institutions, has come down to us. And for all we have and are to-day we are indebted to those of the present age, and to the ages of the past, under God. All our hopes and comforts that we as Christians enjoy, we are in some degree indebted to Christians for. A solemn sense, then, of our obligations to the age in which we live, should prompt us to serve it faithfully, and by so doing we will be serving God.

There is another thought, in this connection, that we should not overlook. The Christians of this age are the binding link that unites the past to the future. As the gospel, then, with its precious blessings, has come down to us as a rich legacy from the ages of the past, let us preserve the divine treasure in its integrity, and hand it down to the coming age as we have received it. In this way we may not only serve the present age, but the future also. How wide is the field of labor which opens before us, and how many are our opportunities for doing good! And as our opportunities for doing good are great, our responsibilities are correspondingly great.

3. Another consideration prompting to the duty of serving our generation is the peaceful end to which such a life of duty, faithfulness and service will lead. "For David, after he had served his generation by the will of God, fell on sleep." This suggests a period of rest after labor. How welcome to the man of labor is the night of rest! And no less welcome will be the night of death to the faithful Christian who has served his generation. Death to him will be a rest—a calm repose. There remains a rest for the people of God after their life of suffering, conflict and labor is over.

But the sleep of David, and of all God's faithful servants which they fall into when their labors are over, suggests also a re-awakening. David saw corruption, and so do all the faithful. But light shines from the gospel on the grave, and we hear Paul saying, "It is sown in corruption, it is raised in incorruption."—1 Cor. xv. 42. Blessed thought! What a delightful prospect! At death, while the body sleeps in the grave, the spirit rests with Jesus. In the glorious resurrection of the just, the body and spirit will be re-united, and eternal life will be completed.

Let us all serve our God and our generation, that the reward of the faithful servant may be ours.

XVI.
CHRIST'S SAYINGS DESIGNED TO PROMOTE OUR HAPPINESS.

"These things have I spoken unto you that my joy might remain in you and that your joy might be full."—John 15:11.

These words constitute a part of our Lord's farewell discourse to his disciples. And while the same design, namely, the happiness of his disciples, characterized all his discourses, the phrase, "these sayings," had, we presume, special reference to the discourse of which they are a part. We offer our remarks under two general heads. I. *The things spoken.* II. *The declared object for which he spoke them.*

I. *The things spoken.* And these may be justly classed under several heads, a few of which we shall notice. 1. We may notice some of the doctrines which are contained in his discourse. And among these may be mentioned (a) the doctrine of human helplessness. "Without me," said the Lord, "ye can do nothing." V. 5. He evidently meant they could do nothing good without him. In our fall we lost our moral strength. Sin renders its subjects feeble, as well as guilty and defiled. How weak is man often in resolving to reform and live a holy life, and he is often still more weak in carrying out his resolutions when he attempts to do so in his own strength. (b) The second doctrine we shall notice is that God has provided help to meet us in our helpless condition, and that help is afforded us in Christ. When our Lord affirmed, "Without me ye can do nothing," his language evidently implied that with him they could do something.

In the 89th Psalm there is a reference to the Saviour in the following words: "When thou spakest in vision to thy holy one, and saidst, I have laid help upon one that is mighty: I have exalted one chosen out of the people." V. 19. This vision of prophecy had reference to Christ, the son of David, as well as to David himself. He is represented to be the mighty Redeemer of his church. This is indeed an encouraging view of our Lord. We needed a mighty Saviour to save us for we were utterly lost and ruined. Here is comfort for the young and for the old. He is able to help the tender youth, and also those who are old and frail. He is a mighty Saviour. "All power," said he, "is given unto me in heaven and earth."—Math. 28: 18. And in view of the mighty power of our Redeemer, the apostle Paul had the utmost confidence in his sufficiency to render him all the help that he needed, and he declared, "I can do all things through Christ which strengtheneth me."—Phil. 4: 13. How beautifully does Paul's language fit up to that of our Lord's: "Without me ye can do nothing." "I can do all things through Christ strengthening me." We then have an all-sufficient Helper provided, and none, not even the weakest, need be discouraged, much less have any occasion to despair. While we are greatly humbled at our Lord's declaration that we can do nothing without him, we are also greatly honored in him, since we can do all things through him. The gospel system is both an humbling and an exalting system. It humbles the sinner and exalts the saint; it humbles man and exalts the Lord. So the doctrine of salvation through Christ alone has nothing in it that should render it repulsive to man.

(c) The third doctrine alluded to in "the things" of our text, and taught by our Lord in his discourse of which our text is a part, is the doctrine that we must be brought into fellowship with Christ, in order that we may avail ourselves of his saving power and merits. The connection that is to exist between him and his disciples is a very close connection. It is not a mechanical or an architectural connection, or such a connection as exists between the different parts of a machine or a building. These connections are often very close, so much so that you can scarcely perceive where the different parts are joined together. The connection between Christ and his genuine disciples is a connection of growth, a vital connection. It is illustrated in our Lord's discourse by the parable of the vine: "I am the vine, ye are the branches," said he to his disciples. Then a connection like that which exists between the branches and the vine, must exist between Christians and Christ. It must be a very close connection, one of growth. The branches grow on the vine, and Christians must grow on Christ. The divine and vital power must pass from Christ to Christians, as the sap passes from the vine to the branches. The marginal reading of the phrase, "Without me ye can do nothing," is, "severed from me ye can do nothing." So we must be in close fellowship with Christ to avail ourselves fully of his power and merits. "As the branch can not bear fruit of itself, except it abide in the vine; no more can ye, except ye abide in me." The branch does not only depend upon the vine for its fruitfulness, but it also depends upon it for its very life. As it is with the branches and the vine, so it is in regard to Christ and believers. The believer apart from Christ can neither live nor bear fruit. Christ lives in all the true members of his Church, as the spirit of man animates and rules every part of the human body. This vital and close connection between Christ and believers is very clearly and forcibly set forth by the apostle Paul in the following words: "We are members of his body, of his flesh, and of his bones."—Eph. 5:30. This is a very practical and comforting doctrine. The believer's connection with Christ secures to him the life and power, and merits and glory of Christ.

This close and vital connection between Christ and believers is not only taught us by the apostle Paul, but he likewise alludes to the manner in which it is brought about. To the Galatian brethren he says, "For as many of you as have been baptized into Christ have put on Christ."—Gal. 3:27. This is in perfect harmony with the formula for baptizing believers. "Go ye, therefore, and teach all nations, baptizing them in the name of the Father, and of the Son, and of the Holy Ghost."—Math. 28:19. Instead of the reading baptizing them *in* the name, our best scholars now read, baptizing them *into*, etc. So believers are not only brought by their acceptance of Christian truth, into connection with Christ, but also with the Father and with the Holy Spirit as well.

(d) Another important doctrine taught by our Lord in his farewell discourse to his disciples, and alluded to in our text, is the doctrine that the divine power and efficacy of Christ are communicated through the medium of the words of Christ. "Now ye are clean through the word which I have spoken unto you. V. 3. This embraces our Lord's whole teaching. By his teaching believers are cleansed. There is in his word believed and obeyed, a cleansing power. Hence the declaration of Paul, "For I am not ashamed of the gospel of Christ; for it is the power of God unto salvation to every one that believeth; to the Jew first, and also to the Greek."—Rom. 1:16. The gospel, then, is the power of God unto salvation. But what is the gospel of Christ? It is made up of facts, doctrines, ordinances, promises, etc. And all these become the channels through which the grace of Christ is imparted to believers. There is an error obtains with some persons in regard to Christian ordinances or Christian rites. Some seem to look upon them as mere forms. They are forms, but forms which contain spiritual and divine truths. The Bible itself containing God's recognized revelation of saving truth to man, has a form, but it is not only a form, but it is also a power, it contains the seed of living truth. And it is so with Christian ordinances as well as with other parts of the gospel. The whole system of Christian truth in all its parts contains divine power in it.

We have the following statement of some important truths by the apostle, which seems to confirm the view of the gospel which has been stated above: "Christ also loved the church, and gave himself for it; that he might sanctify and cleanse it with the washing of water by the word, that he might present himself a glorious church, not having spot, or wrinkle, or any such thing; but that it should be holy and without blemish." Eph. 5:25-27. In the above passage the apostle represents Christ as cleansing the church by the washing of water by the word. By "washing of water," baptism is meant. This is admitted by commentators. The ordinance, then, is accompanied with divine power when it is properly received. But it must be noticed that the washing must be by the *word*. It is the place that baptism has in the word of God or the gospel that gives it the power it has. Instances have occurred where persons have been present at baptismal scenes and have been made to feel, witnessing the performance of baptism, the power of conviction. Similar effects have been produced in witnessing the performance of the ordinance of feet-washing. There is a language in symbols as well as in words, and symbolic language, as well as written and spoken language, may convey truth to the mind. If we refer to one of the evangelists, and read his account of our Lord's death, that event is brought feelingly to the mind. When the same event is presented in the bread and wine, the emblems of our Lord's body and blood, it also feelingly impresses the serious and reflecting mind. The apostle says, in referring to the communion service: "For as often as you eat this bread, and drink this cup, ye do shew the Lord's death till he comes." 1 Cor. 11:26. Christian rites or ordinances, then, have a language, and through that language Christian truth is conveyed to the mind. Christian ordinances and rites, then, are not mere forms; but they are the vehicles of divine truth as the written word is.

2. The second class of things referred to in our text we shall call *instruction*. Much of our Lord's farewell discourse is of an instructive character. And in that part which stands in connection with our text there are some important lessons taught us. We are taught how we may glorify our heavenly Father. "Herein is my father glorified that ye bear much fruit; so shall ye be my disciples." V. 8. We see it is by bearing much fruit that we glorify God. We also learn that true discipleship is conditioned upon our bearing fruit, and not only so, but upon our bearing much fruit. These are important lessons. In the following words of our Lord's discourse, he tells his disciples that he loved them: "As the Father hath loved me, so have I loved you; continue ye in my love." V. 9. It is a sweet and encouraging thought to us to know that the Redeemer loves us. And it is very desirable that we are to continue in his love: "If ye keep my commandments, ye shall abide in my love; even as I have kept my Father's commandments, and abide in his love." V. 10. These instructions are plain and practical, and we should study them well, and act upon them.

3. The third class of things referred to in our text we shall call *admonitions*. There are admonitions as well as doctrines and instructions contained in our Lord's discourse from which our text is taken. To admonish is to warn. This is one of the meanings of admonition, and in this sense we here use it. And warning implies danger. The danger to which the disciples were exposed was that of

departing from their Lord, and by departing from him they would become unfruitful and withered branches, and thus be in danger of being burned. The following passage contains one of his solemn admonitions: "If a man abide not in me, he is cast forth as a branch, and is withered; and men gather them and cast them into the fire, and they are burned." V. 6. "He is cast forth." A terrible doom! The unfruitful member of the church is often separated from the church in this world because of his unfaithfulness. But he may evade the scrutiny of the church and remain in it until death. But none wanting the wedding garment will escape the scrutiny of the King who will examine the guests at the marriage supper. "He is cast forth," out of the church and out of the world, to perish with the ungodly Such a solemn warning should lead to watchfulness and prayer. It has been justly said that these words of our Lord "demand rather to be trembled at than need to be expounded."

II. In the second place, we shall notice the design for which the Saviour spoke as he did to his disciples: "That my joy might remain in you, and that your joy might be full." From this language it appears there was a mutual joy between our Lord and his disciples. He had joy in them. It is one of the distinguishing features of Christians that they "rejoice in Christ Jesus." Phil. 3:3. And it is also said by the Psalmist that "the Lord taketh pleasure in them that fear him, in those that hope in his mercy." Psa. 147:11. It is remarkable that our Lord should speak of his joy at the time he was speaking to his disciples. He was near Gethsemane and the Cross. And yet he was joyful! His joy arose from his consciousness that he was doing the will of his heavenly Father, and that his Father loved him. Hence, no outward circumstances, however distressing and painful they might be, could disturb his joy. And so it may be with us. If our joy is "in the Lord," no troubles and afflictions can rob us of it. The light of God's countenance cheered him in his darkest hours, and so will it cheer us. Hence he was anxious that his disciples might be faithful, so that their joy might continue and even be full. To love God and to be loved by him is to secure a fullness of joy. By Christian joy all the capacities of the soul are filled. Who then would not be a Christian? And who that is a Christian, and is connected with Christ, would lose that connection, and forfeit his joy and be cast forth and burned?

How strange that any should entertain the idea that Christianity tends to make us melancholy! It produces joy in heaven, and on earth, in the divine, and in the human heart! "That my joy may remain in you, and that your joy may be full."

XVII.
THE SERVICE OF LOVE.

"And if the servant shall plainly say, I love my master my wife and my children: I will not go out free. Then his master shall bring him unto the judges; he shall also bring him to the door, or unto the door-post; and his master shall bore his ear through with an awl; and he shall serve him forever."—Ex. 21: 5, 6.

There was a system of slavery admitted under the Mosaic economy. But it did not sanction modern slavery. The advocates of slavery in the Southern States used the slavery of the Hebrews to justify theirs. But the candid reader or inquirer will readily perceive in comparing the two that there is but little similarity between them. There is a spirit of benevolence in the divine revelation of God designed to bring about the emancipation of our race from all forms of oppression. In the modern system of slavery, man is made a mere chattel. But in the Hebrew form of servitude referred to in our text, the servant's manhood is recognized, and his sovereignty over himself showed by the circumstance that he was allowed the privilege of choosing whether to remain a servant, or to go out free at the close of six years.

The system of servitude alluded to in our text is a beautiful type of the service of love, which we are to render to God, our great and common Master. He only was to serve "for ever" who preferred to do so on account of the love he had to his master and to his wife and children. The service of love is a pleasant and delightful service. Of it the servant never becomes weary. This is the true Christian service rendered by Christians to God. Christians are not kept in the service of God against their will. Christian soldiers are not conscripts pressed into the army of the Lord against their will, but they are volunteers. Their language is "I love my Master, and will not go out free." Love as a principle of obedience renders it pleasant to him who performs the service, and also to him that requires the service.

In illustrating and applying the service of love, we shall look at it exemplified in the service rendered by our Saviour. He was a servant. He accepted the title and the work of a servant. He is called the Lord's servant. (Isaiah 42: 1.) And he should be regarded as our example in his character as a servant as well as an humble and devout worshiper. We should never forget that our blessed Redeemer is in all things our great pattern. And we should ever be found "looking unto Jesus." The great work that he came to accomplish was our redemption. Every joyful emotion and every spiritual comfort that we experience is the fruit of his labor. His labor was arduous, his life one of continual self-denial, and his death ignominious and painful in the extreme. Nevertheless, he prosecuted his work, not only with cheerfulness, but with delight. His great work was indeed a service of love. It was characterized by love to God and love to man. In the following expressions of our Lord, we see the spirit in which he prosecuted his redemptive work: "Sacrifice and offering thou didst not desire; mine ears hast thou opened; burnt-offering and sin-offering hast thou not required. Then said I, Lo, I come; in the volume of the book it is written of me, I delight to do thy will, O, my God; yea, thy law is within my heart." (Ps. 40: 6-8.) The apostle Paul quotes this passage and applies it to Christ. In the phrase, "Mine ears hast thou opened," in the marginal reading we have, "Mine ear hast thou digged." This is the same in the Hebrew as bored. And there is evidently an allusion to the idea in our text of the servant preferring to remain in his master's family, and submitting to the law for having his ear bored. And the language as our Lord used it, implies that he was wholly consecrated to the work which he came to perform, and that he would prosecute that work to the end, whatever sacrifices he would have to make, or whatever suffering he would have to endure. Loving obedience he pledged to his Father "forever," and as an expression of this, he is represented as having his ear bored, according to the law referred to in our text. "I delight to do thy will, O, my God. Yea, thy law is within my heart." Such was the interest and pleasure our Lord took in his work. "With desire have I desired to eat this passover with you before I suffer," said he to his disciples. (Luke 22: 15.) With the terrible sufferings that were to terminate His holy and blessed life in full view, he went forward deterred by no threatening, and discouraged by no trouble.

Now, as the same mind is to be in us that was in our Lord (Phil. 2:5), all who have faith in Him and sympathize with Him, and enjoy His divine presence, will with Him run in the ways of God's commandments, as He had enlarged their hearts. (Ps. 119:32.) To such the service of God will be a "service of love," and His ways will be ways of pleasantness, and his paths will be paths of peace. Such has been the experience of God's faithful people in all ages. There is a beautiful allusion to the devotedness of the patriarchs to God by the apostle Paul in his epistle to the Hebrews. In referring to the faith of the ancient saints, he says, "These all died in faith, not having received the promises, but having seen them afar off and were persuaded of them, and embraced them, and confessed that they were strangers and pilgrims on the earth. For they that say such things declare plainly that they seek a country. And truly, if they had been mindful of that country whence they came they might have had opportunity to have returned. But now they desire a better country, that is a heavenly; wherefore, God is not ashamed to be called their God, for he has prepared for them a city." (Heb. 11:13-16.) The thought in the passage quoted to which we call your special attention, is the thought that "had they been mindful of the country from which they came out, they might have had opportunity to have returned." That is, had they had their minds fixed on the country that they had left, like the unfaithful Israelites had their minds fixed on the land of Egypt, they could have returned to the country they had left. They had left Ur of Chaldea for the promised land of Canaan. They had not been driven out of Chaldea, and it is not probable that God would have so interfered as to prevent their return had they wished to return. But they had no desire whatever to return. When Abraham sent his servant to his fatherland for a wife for his son Isaac, the servant said, "Peradventure the woman will not be willing to follow me unto this land; must I needs bring thy son again unto the land from whence thou camest? And Abraham said unto him, beware thou that thou bring not my son thither again." (Gen. 24: 5-6.) God had called Abraham to leave his native land and friends, to go out, as Paul says, "into a place which he should after receive for an inheritance," and he "obeyed, and he went out, not knowing whither he went. By faith he sojourned in the land of promise, as in a strange country, dwelling in tabernacles with Isaac and Jacob, heirs with him of the same promise." (Heb .11: 8-9.)

Although those ancient fathers could have returned to the land they had been called to leave, they did not do so. The will of God had been revealed to them, and that will they loved to obey. They looked forward and not backward. The motto of the faithful is "Onward." And their course is upward. "We are not of them who draw back unto perdition; but of them that believe to the saving of the soul." (Heb. 10: 39.) So affirms Paul. It is noticed not to the honor, but to the disgrace of some of the early believers that they had left their first love. (Rev. 2: 4.) They had not their ear bored to live in their Heavenly Master's house forever. They apparently became weary in well doing. Their service to God was not the service of love, or they would have continued in it. It is strange, indeed, that any should, after they have seen the exceeding sinfulness of sin, and the terrible end of the sinner, and experienced the joy of pardon, and the gift of the Holy Spirit, go back to a sinful life. While we believe it is possible for a soul that is converted to fall away, we believe it is barely possible, and that it seldom occurs. A large proportion of those looked upon as backsliders were never converted. Those who are really converted, and who have enjoyed the divine comforts of the

Holy Spirit, and who have taken a place in God's house, and who have had their ears bored, and from the love they have felt to God have pledged themselves to serve Him forever, do not often go back, for they know to go back is to go back to destruction.

We will give you another case that illustrates the joyful feeling with which the service of God should be pursued; and when it is so pursued it will be a *service of love*. It is the Lord's address to Israel. "If thou turn away thy foot from the Sabbath, from doing thy pleasure on my holy day, and call the Sabbath a delight, the body of the Lord honorable, and shalt honor Him, not doing thine own ways, nor finding thine own pleasure, nor speaking thine own words; then shalt thou delight thyself in the Lord, and I will cause thee to ride upon the high places of the earth, and feed thee with the hermitage of Jacob, thy father, for the mouth of the Lord hath spoken it." (Isaiah 58 : 13, 14.) They were to call the Sabbath a "delight." They were to spend it in such a way as would make it a delight to them. It was intended by the Lord to be a delight to His people, as it was designed to be a blessing to them. But to make it a blessing, or to spend it as was necessary to obtain the blessings of God upon them, it was necessary that they should spend it to the honor of God, and not consult their own pleasure, or rather their carnal pleasure. For their own pleasure, and their highest pleasure, would have been promoted had they used it as God designed; for then it would have been a delight to them, and if a delight, of course a source of pleasure. But they did their own work on the Sabbath, and not the Lord's work. It appears that six days were not enough for them to have to do their own work; they wanted more time to work for themselves. This is too often the case; worldly and business men are not satisfied to work six days and let their animals and employes rest one day in the week. They occupy all the week, the seven days, in business and work of a worldly character, and thus rob God and themselves. But God admonishes his people to turn their feet from the Sabbath; that is, from doing their own work, and from seeking their own pleasure of a secular character, and to take delight in doing his work, and in spending the day as he had willed it to be spent. They were to call "the Sabbath a delight, the holy of the Lord." They probably called it a dull day when they had to use it for divine worship, because they realized no spiritual enjoyment in holy worship. The sanctuary of God is a prison to some, and the Sabbath confined to worship a burden. Some people do not apparently like God's arrangement in requiring us to spend one day in his worship and in cultivating our hearts in holiness. We suppose there may be some people so desperately wicked that that they would like to see the Sabbath abolished and meeting houses destroyed. They would then not be so much reproved, and they could indulge in their sinful ways without any restraint. But we hope that this is not the case with any of you in this congregation. You would not wish to see the Sabbath abolished or public worship discontinued. These are great promoters of the welfare of society. To remove all restraints from the wicked, and permit them without any restraint to indulge in their sinful desires and habits, would be to expose society to a most terrible affliction.

And who is there among you here to-day that would wish to see any part of the divine law stricken from the Bible? We hope there are none. It is all good and useful, and designed to promote the highest and best interests of men. Our corrupt nature may sometimes rebel against some of the requirements of the divine law, but when we consider its origin and its character, that it is from God, and that it is a "perfect law of liberty," our judgments must approve of it, however our fallen nature may rebel against it. We have said, we presume that none of you would want any thing taken from the divine law. Would it not strike us as a most wicked act to expunge any thing from God's law? And would we not think that the right hand should be "cut off" rather than commit such an act? Well, that is right. We should have the most profound respect and reverence for the law of God. But do you, my friends, perceive the predicament you are in? By entertaining the correct views of the divine law that we have attributed to you, and then fail to obey that law, you condemn yourselves. Consistency would require of you to obey, without hesitation or delay, a law so high in authority and so perfect in its character, as you admit the law of God to be.

But while the carnal mind is enmity against God and not subject to his law, those who have been renewed in the spirit of their minds can say with Paul, "I delight in the law of God after the inward man."—Rom. vii. 22. And when we thus delight in the law of God, we will find that "his commandments are not grievous."—1 John v. 3. Then will our service be *the service of love*—that service that is rendered to God by all holy beings. And while it will be acceptable to God, and in his sight of great price, it will be a pleasure to us to perform such service. It is to such servants of God as have, in spirit, had their ears bored according to the text, and who love their master, and who feel that they will never go out of his service, that the Saviour's yoke is easy and his burden light. The bearing of that yoke and that burden with pleasure and in love will make it easy and light.

Looking, then, at the service of God as a *service of love*, it unites pleasure with duty, and makes a holy life not a life of bondage, dread and gloom, but a life of freedom, joy and peace.

XVIII.

THE KNOWLEDGE OF BELIEVERS A PROTECTION FROM ERROR.

"But ye have an unction from the Holy One, and ye know all things."—I. John 2: 20.

The following disposition of the text may be made:
I. The Holy One from whom the unction is received.
II. The unction itself.
III. The knowledge obtained from the unction.

I. *The Holy One from whom the unction is received.* This is a very suggestive and honorable title given to our Redeemer, for it is to him that it is to be applied. It is true some commentators apply it to the Holy Spirit. But as it is *with* the Holy Spirit itself, we are represented as being anointed, when the same is referred to as it is here, and in the manner in which it is, the Holy One most likely refers to Christ. And while it is an expressive name applied to him, he is well deserving of all that is expressed in it. He is spoken of by Paul as follows. "For such a high priest became us, who is holy, harmless, undefiled, separate from sinners, and made higher than the heavens; who needeth not daily, as those high priests, to offer up sacrifice, first for his own sins, and then for the people's: for this he did once when he offered up himself."—Heb. 7: 26, 27. And the devil acknowledged his holiness when he said: "I know thee who thou art, the Holy One of God."—Mark 1: 24. He was holy in his nature and in all his conduct. He was closely watched, and that too by his enemies who entertained the strongest prejudice against him, and who sought eagerly some failure in his life-that they might find some excuse for their opposition to him, and something upon which they might condemn him. But from the fact that Pilate, after his enemies had done all they could to find some cause for his condemnation, declared "to the chief priests and to the people, I find no fault in this man," Luke 23: 4, it follows that his life had been a spotless one, or the contrary would have been proved, as his enemies were so anxious to find something against him. And the wretched Judas with his intimate acquaintance with Christ after he had sold him and betrayed him, "brought again the thirty pieces of silver to the chief priests and elders, saying, I have sinned in that I have betrayed the innocent blood."—Matt. 27: 3, 4. He was indeed the Holy One.

And the perfect holiness of our Lord is one of the attributes that fit him for the great work he came to accomplish. He came to call sinners to repentance. And as we sinners whom he came to save had no holiness in us, but "all our righteousnesses are as filthy rags" (Isaiah 64: 6), it was necessary that he who undertook our salvation should have no sin in him. A Holy Saviour is needed to save unholy men. Such a Saviour we have in Christ, who saves "his people from their sins."—Matt. 1: 21. And how unsuitable are unholy members to belong to a body which has such a holy head as the Holy One! And justly does the apostle Peter reason when he thus writes to his Christian brethren: "But as he which hath called you is holy, so be ye holy in all manner of conversation; because it is written, be ye holy; for I am holy!"—1. Peter 1: 15, 16.

II. *The unction itself.* Reference is here made to the practice of anointing with oil, or with the ointment used in the religious services of the Jews. Much use was made of ointment in the various ceremonies of the Jews. There was a special ointment prepared for religious purposes. The ingredients of which it was composed and the manner of preparing it were given to Moses by the Lord. This was the "holy anointing oil." The people were forbidden to make anything like it for common use. Exodus 30.

The more special use of anointing with oil is for the consecration or setting persons apart for some important or holy office. There were special offices for which the persons who entered into them were anointed: 1. The king was anointed when he entered upon his office. Samuel was sent by the Lord to anoint Saul king over Israel. I. Sam. 15:1. And Elijah was directed to anoint Elisha to be a prophet. I. Kings 19:16. And Moses was commanded to anoint Aaron and his sons for the priest's office. Ex. 28:41. Besides persons, things also that were used in the service of the Lord were anointed. Ex., 30th chapter. Now, as the anointing oil was used in setting apart persons and things for the holy service of God, and as Christians are kings and priests, and prophets too, as they are to understand and teach the ways of the Lord to others, so they are to be anointed. But the anointing or unction that is to be applied to Christians in setting them apart for the holy service that they are to perform in the house of God is not the anointing of the apothecary under the former or Jewish dispensation. That anointing with the other ceremonies of that dispensation was typical of the ceremonies and services of the Christian Church. The holy oil used in the anointing under the law of Moses was typical of the unction of the Holy Spirit with which Christians are anointed under the Christian dispensation. Christ, the head of the church, was himself anointed, not with oil, but with what the oil was a type of, namely, with the Holy Spirit. Peter, in his preaching to Cornelius, declared, "How God anointed Jesus of Nazareth with the Holy Ghost and with power; who went about doing good and healing all that were oppressed with the devil; for God was with him."—Acts 10:38. Here the Christian anointing is explained, and we learn that it is the Holy Spirit. Paul thus refers to it: "Now he which stablisheth us with you in Christ, and hath anointed us, is God;

who hath also sealed us and given the earnest of the spirit in our hearts."—II. Cor. 1 : 21, 22. This anointing is the unction referred to by John in our text. And it is said we have this "unction from the Holy One." We have seen that the "Holy One" from whom the unction comes, is Christ. And we have seen that Christ was anointed with the Holy Spirit. And while this anointing, which he received in his baptism, prepared him for the office of prophet, and of priest, and of king, which he was to fill, it does the same to all his members. And as "the precious ointment upon the head, that ran down upon the beard, even Aaron's beard: that went down to the skirts of his garment," Ps. 133 : 2, so does the unction from "the Holy One" flow down to all the members of his body, which is the Church, even to the least.

III. *The knowledge obtained from the unction:*

"And ye know all things." This implies a great deal—too much to be applied to human attainments in knowledge in this life, when even Paul, though the chief of apostles, and inspired, only knew " in part." I. Cor. 13 : 12. We must therefore by the help of other passages of Scripture explain this phrase 'all things," which at first reading would appear to embrace universal knowledge. We must remember in explaining Scripture, that it is to be taken as a whole, and that one part is to be explained by another.

1. Then instead of applying the phrase "all things" to all kinds of knowledge, we are to limit it more particularly to *religious things,* or to what Jesus meant when he said to his disciples, "And ye shall know the truth."—John 8 : 32. It is divine knowledge or a knowledge of divine or holy things, that knowledge that will make us " wise unto salvation," that we are most interested in, and that we should seek as we "seek for hidden treasure."

2. It is the things that are revealed that Christians

may know. The number and extent of things of a divine character are very great. "O the depth of the riches both of the wisdom and the knowledge of God! how unsearchable are his judgments, and his ways past finding out."—Rom. 11: 33. God has not yet revealed all his plans and purposes to man, as is plainly implied in the following language of Moses: "The secret things belong unto the Lord our God; but those things which are revealed belong unto us and to our children forever, that we may do all the words of this law."—Deut. 29: 29. Here we find that God has reserved some things to himself which he has not revealed. And when John the revelator was receiving revelations from God concerning his plans and purposes, he informs us that when an angel which he saw, "cried with a loud voice, seven thunders uttered their voices." And when he heard the seven thunders utter their voices, he was about to write the import of those voices, but he was directed to seal up what the thunders uttered.—Rev. 10: 3, 4. What those thunders uttered, we may have opportunity hereafter of knowing, but they are yet sealed up. And it is encouraging and cheering to us to know that there is so much of God and his works to be learned, that this life is too short for us to learn them, and that we shall learn in the future world as well as in this. And the more we learn of God, the more will we adore and admire him "for his wonderful works to the children of men."—Ps. 107: 8. In reference to the vastness and number of the themes presented to man for study in God's works of creation and redemption, Dr. Young has justly said,

> "Were man to live coeval with the Sun,
> The patriarch-pupil would be learning still,
> Yet, dying, leave his lesson half unlearn'd."

3. But while all things that are revealed may be known by diligent, persevering and humble study, with the unction from the Holy One which the Christian has, yet but few

Christians make the proficiency they might do in the study of divine things. And when it is said in our text, "Ye know all things," we may apply the words to what must be known to make us Christians, and to give us a saving interest in Christ. There are some things which all Christians must know, and which all Christians do know. All know that they were once sinners. All know that Christ died for sinners, and that he is the only Saviour. They all know that they must come to him and believe on him. They all know that whosoever would be his disciples, must take up their cross and follow him. All should be so familiar with Christ and his truth, that they can not be deceived by any that would deceive them. In the parable of the good shepherd, Jesus thus speaks of himself as the shepherd, and his disciples as the sheep: "And when he putteth forth his own sheep, he goeth before them, and the sheep follow him; for they know his voice. And a stranger will they not follow, but will flee from him; for they know not the voice of strangers."—John 10: 4, 5. This familiarity with Christ, and this experimental knowledge of his word, opened and applied by the unction from the Holy One, is what will prove the effectual protection from all the errors of antichrists. And it was this that the apostle wanted his brethren to understand, namely, that if they would avail themselves of the knowledge the unction from the Holy One afforded them, the antichrists, however many, and however hostile to Christ they might be, could not deceive nor injure them.

What a glorious thing it is to be a Christian, and to be spiritually anointed with the heavenly unction from the 'Holy One," and to know all things that is necessary to know to enable us to shun the errors and wicked ways of the world, and to secure an "inheritance among them that are sanctified." If we are anointed with the heavenly unction, or Holy Spirit, we will not only be wise to know, but we shall also be strong to suffer and do, "for God hath not given us the spirit of fear; but of power, and of love, and of a sound mind."—2 Tim. 1 : 7. Happy are those of whom it can be said, "Ye have an unction from the Holy One, and ye know all things."

XIX.
CHRIST OUR ADVOCATE.

"My little children, these things write I unto you, that ye sin not. And if any man sin, we have an advocate with the Father, Jesus Christ, the righteous; and he is the propitiation for our sins; and not for ours only, but for the sins of the whole world."—1 John 2: 1, 2.

What tender parental expressions we have here from this aged saint of God. "My little children." How strong was his affection for his brethren! And what a noble object prompted him to write: "These things write I unto you that ye sin not." But he would encouragingly say to them, "If any one among you sin after all that has been done to keep you from committing sin, I would not have you discouraged. We have an advocate with the Father, Jesus Christ, the righteous."

The word *advocate*, in its primary sense, means one who pleads the cause of another in our courts of civil law. But it is applied to one who pleads the cause of another before any tribunal. In American and English courts, *advocates* are the same as counselors or lawyers. In the scriptures, as in our text, Christ is called an advocate for his people. The term *advocate* is here used in the sense of a helper, though the idea of a pleader is contained in it. This character is frequently applied to Christ as in Heb. 7 : 25 : "Wherefore he is able also to save them to the uttermost that come unto God by him, seeing he ever liveth to make intercession for them." "And he bore the sins of many, and made intercession for the transgressors." (Isaiah 53: 12.)

According to the usages of the English law, every person tried for the violation of the law has the privilege of an advocate or counselor to advocate his cause, that justice may be done to him. Now the advocacy of Christ for us is not so much that justice may be done us, as that we may be justified, or that we may be lawfully acquitted as criminals or transgressors of the divine law.

1. Christ as our advocate or intercessor, differs from the ordinary pleading of lawyers or advocates for criminals. These try to have their clients acquitted on the ground that the charge against them is false; or if not altogether false, mitigated by circumstances, so that there is nothing very wrong in it. If some person in our country commits a crime, and he employs a lawyer to conduct his trial, and to defend him, he will summon witnesses and adduce testimony and plead before the court to show that his client is not guilty of the charge. Or, if the charge in the main is true, he will endeavor to show that there are extenuating circumstances connected with the case, which greatly diminish the guilt, if there is guilt, connected with the act.

But Christ, our advocate, who pleads for us when we commit our cases into his hand, makes no attempt to prove that we are innocent, or that our guilt is any less than what it appears to be. He accepts the case in its true condition and acknowledges his clients to be guilty of all that they are charged with in the divine law. But, nevertheless, he asks for their acquittal or justification, not on the ground of their innocence, or of any extenuating circumstances connected with the case, but on the grounds that he has suffered for penitent and believing sinners, and in their stead. "Surely he hath borne our griefs and carried our sorrows; yet we did esteem him stricken, smitten of God, and afflicted. But he was wounded for our transgressions; he was bruised for our iniquities. The chastisement of our peace was upon him, and with his stripes we are healed. All we like sheep have gone astray; we have turned every one to his own way; and the Lord hath laid on him the iniquity of us all." (Isaiah 53: 4-6.) "Christ was once offered to bear the sins of many." (Heb. 9: 28.) "Who his own self bore our own sins in his own body on the tree, that we, being dead to sin, should live unto righteousness: by whose stripes ye were healed." (I. Peter 2: 24.) Thus on the grounds of the atonement and satisfaction which our Advocate has made for us, does he obtain our freedom from the curse and the penalty of the divine law. And not only does he free us from the penalty of the law, but he makes us righteous by his righteousness, and thus are we justified. "Therefore, being justified by faith, we have peace with God, through our Lord Jesus Christ." (Roman 5: 1.) "Much more then, being now justified by his blood, we shall be saved from wrath through him." (Rom. 5:9.) "But of him are ye in Christ Jesus, who of God is made unto us wisdom and righteousness, and sanctification and redemption that, according as it is written, he that glorieth, let him glory in the Lord." (I. Cor. 1: 30, 31.) Then the believing sinner is justified and made righteous by our advocate himself. And our advocate pleads his own work as the grounds of the believer's acquittal. There is no occasion for one who has given himself into the hands of Christ to seek to cover, or to extenuate his guilt, for it matters not how great a sinner he has been, he will find pardon. "But if we walk in the light, as he is in the light, we have fellowship one with another, and the blood of Jesus Christ, his son, cleanseth us from all sin." (I John 1: 7.) Our high Priest, Intercessor, and Advocate, accepts the charge against his clients in all its fullness, or the bill that has been found against them with all its indictments in it. There is nothing left out, there is nothing extenuated. He answers for all the guilt that is found to rest upon his guilty clients, their sins having been borne by him, and his righteousness having been imparted to them.

As an illustration of the fact that no sinner has any occasion whatever to cover, deny, or extenuate his guilt, we refer to the case of the apostle Paul. He calls himself the chief of sinners. (I. Tim. 1: 15.) The greater the guilt the greater the pardon; and the greater the pardon the greater is the honor to which our Advocate or High Priest is entitled. "Where sin abounded, grace did much more abound." (Roman 5: 20.) This doctrine of the advocacy of Christ for sinners, and their full salvation through him, is a glorious doctrine, and replete with comfort to the guilty and penitent sinner. There is nothing to produce fear, and if possible, still less to produce despair, but much to produce faith and hope.

2. In view of what we have said in regard to the advocacy of Christ, we may now take a view of the relation that Christ's redemptive work stands in to the believer. It has sometimes been insinuated and pretty plainly declared that the gospel view of God's method of pardoning sinners is calculated to lessen the enormity of crime. It has been said that because the guilty sinner, upon his confession of his guilt, and application to God in the way the gospel directs, can obtain forgiveness in a very easy way, with but little or no punishment whatever for the crime or crimes which he had committed, that this method of dealing with sin detracts from its enormity, as he can repeat the crime and again obtain forgiveness in the same easy way. The idea is that because pardon can be so easily obtained, it en-

courages sin. It is implied in the language of those who made this objection to the gospel plan of pardoning sin, that if the sinner would have to suffer more punishment for his crimes, sin would become a greater terror to men. But as God will pardon sin in the way he does, it is thought, or at least insinuated, that his easy way of dealing with sinners is calculated to encourage sin under the system of government by which he governs the world.

It is argued by those who are in favor of capital punishment that the life of the murderer should be taken to make him an example to others to make them fear and to deter them from doing the like wicked deed; and if they are not thus severely dealt with, murder will not be looked at as so criminal, and therefore increase. And in the same way it is argued that other criminals must be kept in confinement to prevent them from injuring society. So it has been thought by some that God's method of pardoning sinners is calculated to lessen the enormity of sin because forgiveness is so freely offered by him and so easily obtained by the evil doer.

But if the principles of God's government in relation to the pardoning of sinners are properly understood, the foregoing objections will have but little weight and not much application to the subject to which they are designed to apply.
1. It should be remembered that according to the scripture Christ was made an offering for sin, and that he died for sinners. "For he hath made him to be sin for us, who knew no sin; that we might be made the righteousness of God in him." (II. Cor. 5: 21). In the foregoing words, where it is said Christ was made sin for us, the meaning is, he was made an offering for sin. Then, according to the principles of God's economy of grace for saving sinners, they could not be saved without an offering or sacrifice for sin was made to God. Such an offering was made by Christ when he offered himself to God, "a lamb without blemish and without spot."

(I. Peter 1: 19.) And this idea is contained in our text: "And he is the propitiation for our sins: and not for ours only, but also for the sins of the whole world." Propitiation here means the atonement or atoning sacrifice which removes the obstacle and prepares the way for man's salvation. And Christ is this propitiation.

We then perceive that God's method of pardoning and saving sinners as revealed in the gospel, does not make sin a small offense of such magnitude that no sacrifice less than that of the Son of God could atone for it. "Forasmuch as ye know that ye were not redeemed with corruptible things, as silver and gold, from your vain conversation received by tradition from your father; but with the precious blood of Christ." (I. Peter 1: 18.) God's plan of saving sinners, in which Christ's suffering and death constitute a prominent place, does not only exhibit in the plainest and most impressive manner before all the intelligences of the universe, his love and mercy, but it also shows the exceeding sinfulness of sin and God's abhorrence of it as well. The intense suffering of our Lord in Gethsemane, and his painful and excruciating death on the cross, all being endured by him in making an atonement for sin, show clearly that sin is the "abominable thing which God hates." And further, let it be remembered that the sinner in a true state of penitency, experiences a painful degree of remorse. And if after he has obtained pardon he returns to his sins again, his latter end is worse than was the beginning. (II. Peter 2: 20.) And consequently should he again repent, he will have to pass through a more severe and terrible state of remorse than he did at the first. Such being the way that God deals with sinners, and such being the conditions upon which he pardons sin, there is surely no encouragement whatever given to people to sin. But on the contrary, sin in the scripture being made offensive to God and injurious to men's present and future interests, does not only offer no encouragement to indulge in it ut has everything in it to deter men from committing it.

Finally, how completely does the gospel take away from sinners all excuses for sin. "We have an advocate with the Father, Jesus Christ, the righteous." And though the clients for whom he pleads are guilty, his own righteousness is freely offered them, and in that righteousness they will stand justified. He has, for his people, brought in an everlasting righteousness. (Dan. 9: 24.) Upon this ground he pleads that the sins of sinners may not be laid to their charge. And this plea of our Advocate will be accepted by the Judge, and because of our partaking of Christ's merits and righteousness we will be released. (2.) And while we have an advocate at the throne of heaven to plead for us with the Judge, we have also an advocate within us, according to the following language of the apostle: "Likewise the spirit also helpeth our infirmities; for we know not what we should pray for as we ought; but the spirit itself maketh intercession for us with groanings which can not be uttered." (Roman 8: 26.)

In view then of all that has been done for us, no sinner need be lost, none need despair. And, as God "will have all men to be saved and to come unto the knowledge of the truth" (I. Tim. 2: 4), he has made ample provision to save all. And while it is the will of God that all men may be saved, it is also his will that those who are saved shall be sanctified. "My little children, these things I write unto you, that ye sin not." "For this is the will of God, even your sanctification, that ye should abstain from fornication, that every one of you should know how to possess his vessel in sanctification and honor." (I. Thess. 4: 3, 4.) I would, in view of the foregoing encouragement, say: "Having, therefore, these promises, dearly beloved, let us cleanse ourselves from all filthiness of the flesh and spirit, perfecting holiness in the fear of God. (II. Cor. 7: 1.)

XX.
THE VALUE OF A TEACHABLE SPIRIT.

"As an ear ring of gold, and an ornament of fine gold, so is a wise reprover upon an obedient ear."—Prov. 25 : 12.

Gold and fine gold are highly valued by the people of the world. And they are very fond of ornaments made of gold. There is an ornament for the ear made of gold. The value of gold and of ornaments must be kept in mind in order to get the practical and spiritual truth contained in our text. Bearing the value of gold in mind, the comparison in the text will convey the idea that an ear that hearkens diligently to instruction and reproof, is ornamented with something more valuable than the finest gold, and with something that is more beautiful than any ornament with which the people of the world adorn themselves. For there are ornaments that in real value, and in the judgment of those most capable of judging, are of much more value, than are ornaments of gold, or of fine gold. The apostle Peter in admonishing Christian women, says: "whose adorning, let it not be that outward adorning of plaiting the hair, and of wearing of gold, or putting on of apparel; but let it be the hidden man of the heart, in that which is not corruptible, even the ornament of a meek and quiet spirit, which is in the sight of God of great price." According to the language of Peter, the inward adorning of the mind, with a meek and quiet spirit, adds more in the estimation of God to the real worth of persons, than do any external adornments of gold or costly apparel.

Our subject will be, *The value of a teachable spirit.* This seems to be the great moral truth taught in the text. Our text is thus paraphrased by Dr. Hall in his *Explanations of Hard Texts:* "A docile and pliable ear accounts a loving and discreet reproof of his friends, more precious than the richest ear ring of gold, or whatsoever more curious and costly ornament."

Under the following heads we shall present our subject:
I. The design of reproof.
II. The duty of reproving.
III. The manner of reproving.
IV. The result of wise reproof to the obedient ear.
I. The design of reproof.

1. When reproof is given, he that gives it must not do it to depreciate the character of him to whom it is given. We should ever be pained upon the discovery of faults in others, and not seek to expose them to darken their characters. If our own characters can not be sustained in the presence of others that are as good as we are, or that are better than we are, and we reprove to expose their faults, that ours may be extenuated, or altogether overlooked, we had better not reprove others, but direct our attention to the improving of ourselves. 2. The design of reproof should be to improve others. The object of reproving others for their faults should be to help them to see themselves, and their faults, that they may see the evil of their conduct, and be induced to reform and do better. If we possess the spirit of Christ, and of the true Christian, we will rejoice in the well-doing of others, and labor to help them to do well. We should all labor to increase the general stock of piety in the world and to diminish the amount of sin. We should be prompted to labor for this; first, to promote the enjoyment of others, and, secondly, to promote our own. All men are so related to each other that they are much like a joint stock company. In such a company, the more the interests of the whole company are promoted, the more the interests of each one are promoted. The more sin is diminished in the world, the more our temptations will be diminished; and the more the cause of Christianity prospers,

the more Christians will be likely to be brought into contact with it, and to receive of its divine power.

II. *The duty of reproving.* One of the commands under the law was as follows: "Thou shalt in any wise rebuke thy neighbor, and not suffer sin upon him." Lev. 19 : 17. And we have a Christian admonition in the following words: "Have no fellowship with the unfruitful works of darkness, but rather reprove them." Eph. 5 : 11. Paul said to Timothy, and we presume his language applies to all ministers: "Preach the word; be instant in season, and out of season; reprove, rebuke, exhort with all long suffering and doctrine." 2 Tim. 4 : 2. Reprove and rebuke are a good deal alike in their meaning; they both express disapprobation. A reproof may be given long after the offense is committed, and is designed to bring about a reformation of the offender. But a rebuke is commonly given at the time the offense is committed, and it has more of the idea of punishment in it than reproof.

From such passages of Scripture it appears plain that it is our duty to reprove sin. If then a brother or neighbor offend us, we must tell it to him face to face, and not let his sin remain upon him without making any attempt to get him to see it. If he does not see it he will not repent of it, and it may ruin him. If a sin is committed against us, we, as Christians, may feel like taking no notice of it; and if it has been done against us, we may think we should bear it. But we must remember that a sin committed against us is also a sin against him that committed it. And though we could very easily bear it, we should consider whether we are not unfaithful to him if we do not reprove him or tell him his fault.

Our Lord's direction to Christians, in Matt., 18th chapter, in regard to the manner in which they are to proceed when a trespass is committed by a brother, shows that it is the offender's welfare and salvation that are to prompt the offended brother, to reprove or tell the offender his fault. "If thy brother shall trespass against thee, go and tell him his fault between thee and him alone; if he shall hear thee, thou hast gained thy brother." If the offender is not told of his fault which he has committed, and if he does not see it, and feel it, and repent of it, he is lost, to the church and to himself. But if he is properly approached and reproved, and if he receives the reproof, and it has its desired effect, then he is gained or saved. But the idea that we want noticed is this: it is not the honor or gratification of the offended party, that is to prompt that party to seek satisfaction from the party that is the offender, but it is the welfare of the latter that is to be looked at.

III. The manner of reproving. "As an ear ring of gold, and an ornament of fine gold, so is a wise reprover upon an obedient ear." Notice that it is the *wise* reprover whose reproofs are so salutary upon the obedient ear. Success in administering reproof may depend much upon the manner in which it is done. Good preaching, good counsel, and good reproof, often fail of success, because of the manner in which they are done. The same thought of our text that we are now presenting, namely, the manner in which reproof is to be given, is beautifully, and forcibly presented in the verse preceding our text. It is thus presented: "A word fitly spoken is like apples of gold in pictures of silver." Here it is the word that is fitly spoken that is so highly commended. The manner then of administering reproof, and indeed the manner of doing whatever is done in the great work of reforming the erring, and in saving the lost, should receive the attention of all who are laborir in the work of reformation.

There is much wisdom in all our Lord's teaching, and

the way in which he always adapted his teaching and reproof to the persons for whose benefit they were given, clearly shows that he well understood the nature of men, and the best way to approach them to gain their confidence, and to benefit them. In his directions to his disciples, in which he teaches them how they shall proceed to deal with their offending brethren, a subject to which we have already referred, he directs the offended brother, or the one that would reprove and seek to gain the offender, to go first privately and labor with his brother. "Go and tell him his fault between thee and him alone," is our Lord's counsel.

1. Then let reproof be given at first privately. It may be very unpleasant and offensive to a person to have his fault made public, if it was of a private character. And even if it had been of a public character, still, the reproof will be more likely, as a general thing, to be successful if given in a private way. If it is done in the presence of others, it may lead the person reproved, to make a defense which he would not be so likely to make if he were approached privately. It is true, Paul gives the following direction to Timothy, but we presume he had an illusion to sins that were committed under circumstances that made it necessary for the church to take notice of it, and perhaps, to act upon it. And such would seem to call for a rebuke before the church. The words of Paul, referred to, are these: "Them that sin rebuke before all, that others also may fear." 1 Tim. 5 : 20.

2. Reproof should be administered with great discretion and judgment. Some people seem to boast that they are not afraid to speak to anybody, and to speak in any way, and they think it is a great commendation to them to be so free from fear. Well we all should have a sufficiency of courage, or, if you please, of boldness, to not be afraid to do our duty. But we should not

approach a person if we have occasion to reprove him, with the feeling that men approach each other with when they are preparing to fight one another. In the exercise of discretion, in reproving, we should ascertain, if possible, the disposition and temper of those we have occasion to reprove. A wise reprover, like a wise school teacher, will study the disposition of people. And according to their nature and disposition, the reproof should be given. And then the nature and magnitude of the crime should be taken into consideration. It has been very justly said, "To reprove small faults with undue vehemence, is as absurd as if a man should take a hammer because he saw a fly on his friend's forehead." And Cowper says, "No man was ever scolded out of his sins." And another writer has said, "To reprove in anger is like giving a sick person a medicine scalding hot."

3. Reproof should always be given affectionately and tenderly. Even if the case requires some severity, still let tenderness and affection appear in the reproof. Let a person know that you love him, and he will take a great deal from you without becoming offended. And then we ought to have our hearts full of love when we go to reprove, that the offender might imbibe some of it. For should we appear unkind, or as an enemy to the offender, his feelings will at once prompt him to assume an antagonistic position, and in such a position we shall not be likely to do him much good. Our looks and tone of voice when we reprove, should show love. And to show love, we should feel love. And that we may be the more likely to feel right, and act with the discretion that we should act with, we should remember, that the soul of the offender is in danger of being lost, and that if we succeed in restoring him, we "gain" a brother or a friend, and in either case we "save a soul from death."

IV. The result of wise reproof to the obedient ear. "As

an earring of gold, and an ornament of fine gold, so is a wise reprover upon an obedient ear." The obedient ear is put for an obedient heart. And the wise reprover upon an obedient ear, means, wise reproof upon an obedient heart. And we may give the words a form something like the following, to bring out the last idea we want to bring out: wise reproof, or divine truth, given to, and humbly, penitently, and obediently, received by an erring soul, will correct that soul of its errors, and impart a value and beauty to it somewhat like, but far superior to, an earring of gold, or an ornament of fine gold. We have already quoted Peter's language, in which he says, "the ornament of a meek and quiet spirit is in the sight of God of great price." 1 Peter 3:4. Now that ornament of a meek and quiet spirit, the soul that receives the reproof of God's word, is adorned with. The word of the Lord is purifying, correcting, and beautifying to an humble and obedient soul. "The law of the Lord is perfect, converting the soul." Ps. 19:7. And as the law of the Lord is perfect, it will, when believed and obeyed, form a perfect character—a character symmetrical in all its parts. And such a character will be beautiful in the estimation of all who can appreciate, and properly estimate spiritual worth and beauty. "He will beautify the meek with salvation." Ps. 149:4. "In that day shall the Lord of hosts be for a crown of glory, and for a diadem of beauty, unto the residue of his people." Isa. 28:5. As jewels are considered valuable and precious by the world, so the Lord compares his people, and their excellent and amiable characters to gold and jewels. "And they shall be mine, saith the Lord of hosts, in that day when I make up my jewels." Mal. 3:17. A Roman lady was showing and displaying her costly and beautiful jewels to a Roman mother, who had a couple of interesting little boys. She called them to her, and said to her friend that was showing her jewels, "These are my jewels." So the Lord regards his loving and faithful children as his jewels or treasure.

In conclusion, we would remark that the greatest sinners are not such that have sinned most, for many great sinners have received divine reproof, and have become saints. But the greatest sinners are those that will not receive reproof, but continue to persist in their evil ways. Beloved friends, let us gladly, and meekly, receive heaven's reproofs, from wise reprovers, the ministers of God, and all who kindly tell us of our faults, and we shall then become the Lord's jewels and treasure.

And permit us to say to you, young friends, who through want of experience, and frequently through want of consideration, are liable to err, do not forget that your "best friends are those that tell you your faults, and teach you how to correct them." Then turn not away from wise reproof, but carefully regard it, and obediently yield to it, and you will find it more valuable than "an earring of gold, and an ornament of fine gold."

XXI.
LIFE PROMOTED BY DEATH.

"And it came to pass, as they were burying a man, that, behold, they spied a band of men, and they cast the man into the sepulchre of Elisha; and when the man was let down, and touched the bones of Elisha, he revived, and stood upon his feet." (2 Kings, 13: 21.)

The occurrence related in our text is a remarkable one. It was a miracle. It was a very clear manifestation of divine power. At the time this strange occurrence happened, the people of Israel were afflicted in various ways on account of their unfaithfulness to God. They were oppressed by the Syrians, and they were also annoyed by roving bands of the Moabites. Elisha the prophet had died, and he was resting in his sepulchre. And some one else among the Israelites had also died. And as the people were bearing this man to the place where they designed to bury him, they were met by a band of Moabites, or, at least, they saw such a band, and, apparently, fearing they might fall into the hands of these, their enemies, they laid the corpse of the man they were carrying, in the sepulchre of Elisha, as they were near to that. And as the dead man touched the bones of the prophet of God, he revived "and stood upon his feet," and probably went home, to the joy as well as to the surprise of his friends.

However strange the occurrence may appear, it is no more strange than several of the miracles of the New Testament are. A ruler of the Jews appealed to our Lord to raise his daughter from the dead. He complied with the ruler's request, and went to the house of the ruler. And when he entered the house he took the daughter of the ruler by the hand, and she arose and lived. It was the touch of our Lord that was imparted to the dead maid. This, too, was certainly a wonderful occurrence. It was the same power that produced both effects, namely,—The Divine Power. In the case of the daughter of Jairus, the divine power operated through the living Saviour. In the case of the man that was thrown into the sepulchre of Elisha, the power was imparted to the dead man through the medium of Elisha's bones. The instrumentality was very feeble, and the excellency of the power manifested was of God, and not of the feeble instrument.

The following truths are suggested by the text:

I. *In God's government of the world, life is promoted by death.*

II. *The work of God survives the death of his servants.*

III. The influence of men upon the world, survives their natural lives.

I. In God's government of the world, life is promoted by death.

1. This is the case in the natural or physical world. As the vapors rising from the various bodies of water form the clouds, and these, in emptying themselves, replenish the bodies that supplied the clouds with water, so the productions of the earth of one age, when dead and decayed, furnish many of the fertilizing elements which form the productions of succeeding ages. The principle that life is promoted by death is clearly recognized and beautifully illustrated by our Lord's words: " Verily, verily, I say unto you, except a corn of wheat fall into the ground and die, it abideth alone: but if it die, it bringeth forth much fruit." John 12: 24. The principle stated by our Lord here is that in the vegetable kingdom, and especially in plants and seeds, life comes by death. The seed must be planted in the ground, and decay and die, if we would have it to produce fruit and yield a crop. If we keep our seed, and refuse to let it decay and die, we can not expect to gather a crop.

2. And especially do we see the principle that life is promoted by death, in God's spiritual Kingdom, or in the work of redemption. It was to teach and illustrate this principle in redemption that our Lord alluded to the fact that the corn of wheat must die, if it brings forth fruit. He designed to show the importance of his own death and the relation his death bears to the spiritual life of men in the great work of human redemption as completed by him. In the plan of salvation, or in the Gospel way by which God saves sinners, the death of Christ is made to occupy a very prominent place. " Great is the mystery of godliness," affirms Paul. And as this is the case, we can not

understand how certain causes produce the effects attributed to them. For us it is enough to know that God has made use of certain means to accomplish his purposes. We may feel assured that those means are right and that they are efficient, otherwise would God not have made use of them. We accept, then, the Scriptural fact that Christ died for our sins, and the Scriptural doctrine of the atonement built upon that fact, though we can not fully understand it.

That the death of Christ occupies an important place in the Gospel method of saving sinners is evident from the following Scriptures: "For I delivered unto you first of all that which I also received, how that Christ died for our sins according to the Scriptures." 1 Cor. 15:3. "For if, when we were enemies, we were reconciled to God by the death of his Son, much more being reconciled, we shall be saved by his life." Rom. 5:10. "And for this cause He is the mediator of the New Testament that by means of death, for the redemption of the transgressions that were under the first testament, they which are called might receive the promise of eternal inheritance." Heb. 9:15. But we need not multiply Scriptural testimonies to prove that the death of Christ has much to do with our salvation. This is a well known Scripture truth. We, however, would yet remark that such is the importance of the death of Christ that a commemorative ordinance, namely, that of the communion of the body and of the blood, has been made a standing ordinance in the church to commemorate his death. "For as often as ye eat this bread, and drink this cup," said Paul to the Corinthian brethren, "ye do shew the Lord's death till he comes." 1 Cor. 11:26.

The great Gospel truth that Christ died for sinners is very instructive. It plainly shows the value of the human soul, or of humanity, when its redemption was secured by a sacrifice no less than the life of the Son of God. "Forasmuch as ye know that ye were not redeemed with corruptible things, as silver and gold, from your vain conversation received by tradition from your fathers; but with the precious blood of Christ, as of a lamb without a blemish and without a spot." 1 Peter 1 : 18, 19. And what a remarkable manifestation of the love of Christ have we in his death? We may exclaim as the Jews did when they saw Christ weep at the grave of Lazarus, "Behold, how he loved him?" John 11 : 36.

> "O'erwhelm'd with this abyss of love,
> We stand astonish'd at the grace
> That brought the Saviour from above,
> To die for all the fallen race."

And as the dead man carried by his friends, and thrown by them into the sepulchre of Elisha, lived when he touched the bones of the holy man of God, so the penitent sinner, when his faith embraces Christ crucified, and he is brought into fellowship with him, lives, and stands on his feet an upright man before God. Or, in the expressive language, and apt illustration of Paul, "We are buried with him by baptism into death: that like as Christ was raised up from the dead by the glory of the Father, even so we also should walk in newness of life. For if we have been planted together in the likeness of his death, we shall be also in the likeness of his resurrection: knowing this that our old man is crucified with him, that the body of sin might be destroyed, that henceforth we should not serve sin." Rom. 6 : 4–6. The apostle's language, "we are buried with him by baptism, into death," seems to imply that in our baptism, and when we are put into the watery grave, we are brought into the possession of the merits of his death. The third verse of the sixth chapter of Romans seems to confirm this idea: "Know ye not that so many of us as were baptized into

Jesus Christ were baptized into his death?" And with the foregoing agrees the twenty-seventh verse of the third chapter of Galatians: "For as many of you as have been baptized into Christ, have put on Christ."

There is another thought brought out by the apostle in harmony with the truth we are sustaining, that life is promoted by death, in connection with his language above quoted. It is the sixth verse of the sixth chapter of Romans "Knowing this, that our old man is crucified with him, that the body of sin might be destroyed, that henceforth we should not serve sin." We are frequently admonished by the inspired writers to mortify, and crucify what they call the "old man," that is our sinful nature. And unless attention is given to this, and we, by self-denial and mortification, keep our body, our appetites and passions under control, we can not expect to experience improvement and growth in the divine or spiritual life. The more we die to sin, the more shall we live to righteousness. "For if ye live after the flesh, ye shall die: but if ye through the spirit do mortify the deeds of the body, ye shall live."—Rom. 8: 13.

II. The work of God survives the death of his servants. And this being the case, we see that God's work does not depend upon any one man or upon any body of men. We may sometimes wonder what will become of the church when certain faithful servants of God, that occupied a position of so much prominence in the church, that they almost seemed to be essential to the very existence of it, shall die. But we need not fear that the work of God will come to a close before his purposes are accomplished. His servants may die, and the most devoted and faithful of them, but that will not stop the work. Abraham, as the head of the Jewish nation, through which Christ was to come, was called to be the father of the faithful. He occupied a very prominent place in the holy nation of which he was the head. But after a life full of remarkable incidents, he was laid in his sepulchre.

Isaac succeeded him. He finished his course, and died. Jacob followed, and the following touching words describe his end: "And when Jacob had made an end of commanding his sons, he gathered up his feet into the bed, and yielded up the ghost, and was gathered unto his people."—Gen. 49: 33.

Thus, as death removed the servants of God, he filled their places with others. Elijah had preceded Elisha. And when Elijah died his mantle fell upon Elisha. And when the latter died, the work of the Lord still went on, and Elisha's bones were used as a medium through which divine power was exerted. The mantle of the workers of God in one age, when they ceased their work, fell upon the workers of the succeeding age, and thus the work of God was perpetuated.

The redemptive work of God having passed through the preparatory, or the Jewish age, finally reached the Christian period of redemption. John the Baptist introduced the Christian age. He finished his course honorably and successfully. But the current of his eventful life did not run smoothly. His faithfulness brought him to a premature, but a glorious end. He anticipated his end, and when he was about leaving his work and the world, he pointed to Christ, his successor in the great work of reformation or redemption, in the following expressive language, which showed his great humility, and the clearness of his views of Christ: "He must increase, but I must decrease."—John 3: 30. And so it proved. Though John "was a burning and shining light" (John 5: 35), yet his light was eclipsed by the light of Christ, as the stars are lost in the light of the sun.

Christ was the Alpha and the Omega in the work of redemption. He was the connecting link between the servants of God that came before him, and those that came after him, and he imparted to them all the power, wisdom and holiness that they possessed. And he could not continue his personal presence on earth with his church. He, too, died, but he rose again. And after his resurrection, he ascended to heaven, the success of his work requiring him there. His disciples feared the failure of their cause when he died. But his death gave new power to the redemptive work of God. And that work has advanced with marvelous rapidity since the glorification of Christ. He finished the work of redemption in its objective character. And he organized the Church to perpetuate the work of redemption. His disciples followed him. He said, in his prayer to his Father for his disciples, "I have given unto them the words which thou gavest to me." John 17 : 8.

Thus, we perceive, the work of God was to be perpetuated by the apostles. They stood in an important relation to that work. Nevertheless, the work of God did not die with them. It survived them. They were followed by others in the Lord's vineyard, and as one generation of the faithful was called from its work, another succeeded it, and thus the work of God has gone on from age to age, though death has been active in removing his servants. And we of the present generation must leave the work after a while, however much we may love it. And we may comfort ourselves in death with the pleasing thought that the work of God will survive us and still gather trophies of victory to the honor of our Lord.

III. The influence of men upon the world survives their natural lives.

That men have an influence upon the world while living is a truth that will be readily accepted by all. It is true, the influence of people differs very much. And the influence of some is very small. But there are few but that have some influence. The influence of Christians is recognized by our Lord in the words addressed to his disciples: "Ye are the light of the world." Matt. 5:14. And also in the following words: "Let your light so shine before men that they may see your good works and glorify your Father which is in heaven." Matt. 5:16. It is not only the good that leave an influence after them, but the unfaithful and disobedient do the same. It has been said, with much truth, that we are the pupils of the past and the teachers of the future. The coming generation will inherit much from the present. Children do not only inherit possessions, such as lands and property, from their parents, but, to a considerable degree, they also inherit their habits, their principles and their religious creeds. This being the case, there is a great responsibility resting on all of us of the present generation. The thought that we should entail evil upon posterity is a terrible thought. And we should carefully avoid the danger of doing so. We should so live that our influence, whatever it may be, may go down to posterity as a blessing and not as a curse. "The righteous shall be in everlasting remembrance." Ps. 112:6.

There are different ways in which we may influence posterity. 1. By impressing our principles upon the age in which we live, by our example and conversation, and in every way in which it can be done. And if we impress our principles upon the present age, our influence will reach posterity according to well established laws. 2. By committing our thoughts, views, and principles to writing. Books, if read, have an influence upon those that read them. And if we write what will have a tendency to promote Christianity, it may continue to operate for good, long after we have passed away from earth. 3. Another excellent way to do good after death, is to invest money, if we have it, in institutions that are calculated to do good. Money invested in the missionary work may, if judiciously expended, enable those who so invest it to exert an influence for good long after death. There is something very pleasant to those who appreciate the importance of doing good, and who love to do good, in the thought that they can continue to work for the Lord in the world after they will have gone to their heavenly home.

One of the thoughts to the dying Christian, that may give him some sorrow, is the thought that he must, in death, cease his labors for the Lord, for he feels that he can never do enough for the Lord, who has saved him, and prepared an everlasting mansion in heaven for him. And if he can feel in death, that he has so lived, and so labored that he will continue to exert an influence for good upon the world, and for the Lord, when he is dead, it will afford him much comfort.

Beloved friends, then let us all so live, that when we are remembered by those who come after us, they may associate our lives with noble actions, and holy principles. And if our graves or anything else remind them of us, how pleasant and profitable, if at the same time, they are reminded of our holy words and deeds, and are thereby strengthened and stimulated in the prosecution of their life's work in the holy service of God. Oh, how many considerations there are to urge us to holy consecration to God! Shall they have their influence? We hope so. May we all be raised up by the magnet of Christ's death, from our state of death in "trespasses and sins," to "walk in newness of life," and to exert an influence while living and after death, that will be a blessing to the world, and an honor to God.

XXII.
SECRET WORSHIP.

"My heart was hot within me; while I was musing the fire burned."—Ps. xxxix. 3.

The subject of secret worship or devotion is one that commends itself to all who would make their Christian life a source of enjoyment to themselves, and a means of usefulness to others. We therefore feel as if we should present it to your consideration. The subject we have selected for our consideration to-day is very practical. "My heart was hot within me; while I was musing the fire burned." This language expresses very strong feelings. And it is understood to express the feelings of devotion. Bishop Horne thus explains it: "The fire of divine charity, thus prevented from diffusing itself for the illumination and warmth of those around it, and, like other fire, rendered more intense by its confinement, presently ascended in the flame of devotion towards heaven; while it continued to be fed and preserved, in brightness and vigor, by meditation on the goodness of God, and the ingratitude of man; the transient miseries of time, and the durable glories of eternity."—*Horne on the Psalms.*

This intense religious feeling seems to have been that which the disciples felt when our Lord conversed with them on the way to Emmaus. "And they said one to another, did not our heart burn within us, while he talked with us by the way, and while he opened to us the Scriptures?" Jeremiah felt something of it when he said: "his word was in mine heart as a burning fire shut up in my bones, and I was weary with forbearing, and I could not stay." Jer. 20:9. Burn, according to Webster, means to be inflamed with passion or desire; as to burn with anger or love. In our text it means a strong feeling of devotion, the heart and desires going out after God.

1. *What is secret worship?* It is worship not manifested with those outward signs which usually distinguish public worship. Neither is it promoted nor produced by the external means by which public worship is promoted. Secret worship does not imply that we must always be in secret when we perform secret devotion. The devotion may be secret when we are not in secret. It means the worship of the heart in a peculiar way. It is true, our public worship must be the worship of the heart if it is acceptable to God. But in public worship there are external and visible forms which usually accompany it. Secret worship may, however, have some form too. In secret worship the worshiper may prefer to kneel down, and he may prefer to express his feelings in words. The general exercises or services which are performed in public worship are performed in secret worship; but those performed in secret are performed in the heart, and the worshiper worships alone. When our Lord said: "When thou prayest, enter into thy closet, and when thou hast shut thy door, pray to thy Father which is in secret; and thy Father which seeth in secret shall reward thee openly" (Matt. 6:6), he did not mean that to perform secret prayer it is absolutely necessary to go into a closet to pray. The idea is secret prayer, meaning by this that we should retire within ourselves and pray to God mentally. The idea of a literal closet is by no means excluded, and in performing secret worship it is desirable to retire from the world when it can be done; but when this can not be done, then we must retire within ourselves and separate ourselves as much as possible in thought and feeling from those around us, and make God and Divine things, in their relation to ourselves and to our spiritual interests, the subjects of meditation and musing. This may be done in company as well as when we are alone. It may be done when the company in which

we are placed is noisy and even profane. Our eyes may be closed so that we may see but little of what is around us, and to some degree we may close our ears, or, which is the same thing, withdraw our attention from the external world, and retire within ourselves. Then we are in one sense in the closet. This is secret worship or secret devotion.

2. *The advantages of secret worship.* (a) If we have learned to cultivate the spirit, and if we have formed the habit of secret worship, we can worship in any place in which our lot may be cast. We have the temple, the altar, the minister, and the choir with us, and with the disposition and desire, we can worship. It often happens that we can not get to public worship. Sometimes it happens that the distance is so great that we can not get to the place of public worship. It is the lot of many to live so far from the place of public worship that they can seldom enjoy the public means of grace. If, then, they have not learned to worship God in secret, their religious interest and enjoyment will decline. If we keep the fire of devotion always burning upon the altar, Lev. 6 : 13, as we may do, and as we should, we must feed it with worship, both private and public, if we have access to public worship. To secret worship we always have access. It often happens that affliction keeps us from public worship, but it need not keep us from secret worship.

(b) There may be great enjoyment experienced in secret worship, as is evident from our text. "My heart was hot within me; while I was musing the fire burned." The same pious author, in referring on another occasion to his secret devotions, says, "My soul shall be satisfied as with marrow and fatness; and my mouth shall praise thee with joyful lips: when I remember thee upon my bed, and meditate on thee in the night watches."—Ps. 63 : 5, 6. Such expressions indicate a very high degree of enjoyment. And under what circumstances was it that he experienced such a strong religious feeling? It was not when he was with a great multitude of his Jewish brethren at some of their great feasts at which the Jews enjoyed themselves so much, when thay sang the expressive psalms used on such occasions. Neither was it when David was enjoying himself with his music that the fire of devotion burned with such warmth and brightness. It was when he was musing, when he was meditating upon the great things taining to God, to man, and to eternity.

Many professing Christians do not seem to enjoy themselves unless they are in what they call lively meetings. There must be good preaching, and good singing, and everything must be just so. And sometimes the meeting is not sufficiently attractive to draw some to it, unless there is a strange preacher to preach. The home ministers, though they may preach the truth, can not make the meeting interesting enough for some. Such have not learned the importance of getting their own minds into a devotional frame if they would have profitable and happy meetings, and it is to be feared they have not learned the practice of secret worship as well as it should be learned and practiced. Those who appreciate and practice secret worship are not so entirely dependent upon preaching and other public means of grace for the promotion of their Christian edification, as those are who have not so much cultivated the spirit of secret worship.

(c) In regard to the advantages arising from secret worship, we may remark further, that while it has some advantages that public worship has not, as we have already showed, it has also the general advantages that public worship has. And the last of these advantages to which we shall allude is the spiritual strength which it imparts to the worshipers, preparing them for labor and duty. The promise our Lord gives in connection with his precept for secret prayer is both encouraging and suggestive. "Thy Father which seeth in secret shall reward thee openly." The sincere and humble worshiper will come forth from his closet and from the public sanctuary, with the blessing of God upon him, and if it does not show itself as plainly as did the glory which Moses obtained in his interview with God, when "the skin of his face shone" with the divine glory, it will be manifest that he was "with Jesus." The promise is, "they that wait upon the Lord shall renew their strength; they shall mount up with wings as eagles; they shall run and not be weary; and they shall walk and not faint."—Isai. 40: 31. This happy result will follow waiting upon the Lord in secret as well as in public.

3. *The examples of secret worship that we have in many of the saints of the Bible.* (a) Isaac is an example. It is said that "Isaac went out to meditate in the field at the eventide."—Gen. 24: 63. The marginal reading is, "he went out to pray." (b) That faithful mother in Israel, Hannah, the mother of Samuel, is a worthy example of secret worship. "She spake in her heart; only her lips moved, but her voice was not heard." I. Sam. 1: 13. The unfaithful Eli did not understand Hannah's spirit or exercises, and thought she was under the influence of wine. Did he mistake her devotions because he was unacquainted with secret worship? It seems he could not sympathize with her in her "bitterness of soul." (c) Daniel's practice shows that he had his secret worship. "Now when Daniel knew that the writing was signed, he went into his chamber; his windows being open in his chamber toward Jerusalem, he kneeled upon his knees three times a day, and prayed, and gave thanks before his God, as he did aforetime."—Dan. 6: 10. It will be remembered that the writing referred to was

the decree that whosoever would call upon any God or man for thirty days, except the king, was to be cast into a den of lions.

(d) The next example we shall refer to is that of Peter. He was called to Cescrea to preach the Gospel to Cornelius. His mission was an important one. Christ was to be preached to the Gentiles. Peter, in some degree, appreciated his work, and, as the company approached the city, "Peter went up upon the housetop to pray about the sixth hour." And it was when he was at his devotions that he saw the vision of the "great sheet knit at the four corners, and let down to the earth." God has often manifested himself to his people when they were at their secret devotions.

(e) The last example that we shall notice is that of Jesus. Matthew says: "And when he had sent the multitudes away, he went up into a mountain apart to pray: and when the evening was come, he was there alone." Matt. 14:23. Henry has the following just remarks upon this passage: "Though he had so much work to do with others, yet he chose sometimes to be alone, to set us an example. Those are not Christ's followers that do not care for being alone; that can not enjoy themselves in solitude when they have none else to converse with, none else to enjoy, but God and their own hearts."

4. *We shall next notice the manner in which secret worship is to be promoted.* "While I was musing the fire burned." The intense religious feeling which seems to have been experienced by David was produced by meditation. Musing means meditation or contemplation. It has been said, and probably with much truth, "Meditation, which is the mother of devotion, is the daughter of retirement." The humble believer, in retirement from the world, and engaged in pious meditation, will be likely to share in David's devout feelings. Meditation is an excellent pro-

moter of devotion. "While I was musing the fire burned." "Then spake I with my tongue," etc. And from what he spake we may form an idea what were the subjects upon which he was musing when the fire of devotion was kindled in his heart, which produced so much religious feeling.

(a) He thought upon himself. Alexander Pope justly remarks: "The proper study of mankind is man." And the inscription: "Know thyself," was written by some of the ancients upon their temple. It is in retirement, and by meditation, that we come to a knowledge of ourselves. This was the experience of the prodigal son. If we all would study ourselves more we would become better acquainted with ourselves, with our infirmities and imperfections. And such knowledge would lead to spiritual improvement. David thought upon his end. And, apparently, he wanted to have a feeling in regard to his end, as well as knowledge, and hence his prayer: "Lord, make me to know mine end, and the measure of my days, what it is; that I may know how frail I am." V. 4. When we realize that our mortal life shall end, and that our days on earth are but few, then we will be likely to feel the importance of improving our time and of doing whatever is to be done.

(b) The vanity of the world, or the vain pursuits of mankind, was also a subject of meditation. "Surely every man walketh in a vain show: surely they are disquieted in vain: he heapeth up riches, and knoweth not who shall gather them." V. 6. To look at the world when we have retired from it, and with a devotional feeling, we shall learn more of its true nature than when we are mingling with the crowd and sharing in its exciting scenes.

(c) God was also present to David's mind, and constituted an important subject in his meditations. And no subject of meditation is more impressive or profitable, and no subject will be so likely to awaken the spirit of devotion, as this. Alas! how little is God thought of, and as a consequence he is but little feared. David, in thinking of the goodness, the power and the truthfulness of God, apparently had a clearer view of his character, and, with this, increased confidence in him, and hence he said "my hope is in thee." V. 7. Our devotions, when proper, will confirm and brighten our hope. Oh, who can think of God, and of Christ, and of judgment, and of death, and of hell, and of heaven, without being humbler, wiser and holier?

5. *In view of the importance of secret worship, we should cultivate the spirit of it.* It takes some cultivation and attention. To have such a control of our minds as to be able to take them from surrounding objects, and to fix them on divine things, requires attention and practice. But it may be done. As students, you can so cultivate the habit of study, so as to pursue your studies when there may be company around you, and more or less noise. It is desirable to be free from all annoyance when you are studying, and it should be so as much as possible. Nevertheless, you may so learn to study as not to be easily interrupted. And so it is in our devotional exercises. We may, by cultivation and habit, learn to withdraw our minds from surrounding objects and to fix them on divine things, and thus promote the spirit of devotion.

The cultivation of the spirit of secret worship, and the formation of the habit of retiring within ourselves, and of making things that we have stored away in the mind, and other subjects of a proper character, the subjects of musing or meditation, will tend much to the promotion of our Christian edification and improvement. As we have already remarked, such as can worship in secret, or edify themselves by their devout meditations, are not so dependent upon others for spiritual edification as those are who have not cultivated the spirit of secret worship. It appears that some can only worship or be edified when they have outward helps. We sometimes see a congregation that has assembled for worship before the time for commencing, indulging freely in conversation, even to such a degree as to be heard distinctly over the house. This does not seem to be commendable in an assembly met for Christian worship. It may be altogether allowable to converse at times on such occasions, but to indulge in it to the degree it is oftentimes done does not agree with the solemnity or character of the occasion. Still more out of place does the practice appear which is sometimes indulged in, in places in the country, for people, especially for members of the church, to remain outside of the house, sitting about in companies, talking upon worldly matters, until the public exercises commence.

If the importance of secret worship is appreciated, and the spirit of secret devotion cultivated, the time before the public services commence may be well employed in secret devotion—in "musing." The fire of devotion may be thus kindled, and then, when the public services commence, there will be a much better preparation for these than there will be if the time has been spent in conversing on worldly subjects. A season of secret devotion before public services will add greatly to the profit of the latter.

We would, in view of the importance of our subject, recommend to you all the cultivation of the spirit and habit of secret worship. You need not expect to make any great advancement in the divine life without it. It can not be done. But by cultivating this spirit you can turn every place into a Christian temple, and find Christ there. "And thy Father which seeth in secret shall reward thee openly."

XXIII.

AN ADMONITION AGAINST NEGLECTING PUBLIC WORSHIP.—DEDICATORY SERMON.

"Not forsaking the assembling of ourselves together, as the manner of some is, but exhorting one another, and so much the more, as ye see the day approaching." Heb. 10 : 25.

The suitableness of the text to the occasion upon which we have assembled this morning, we presume will appear to you all. Christians are admonished not to forsake the assembling of themselves together. And while the admonition comes with peculiar propriety to Christians, it comes with much propriety to all men, for all men are under obligations to God. We recognize him to be the maker and supporter of all things, and the "fount of every blessing." And in requiring of us our worship and service he requires no more than what he is justly entitled to. And while God may be, and should be worshiped in secret, he should also be worshiped in public. There are very good reasons for public worship. Under the Jewish dispensation, very explicit commands were given for public worship, and for its promotion special places were to be provided: One of these places was the tabernacle. In the Lord's communication with Moses concerning this tabernacle, he said, "And let them make me a sanctuary, that I may dwell among them. According to all that I show thee, after the pattern of the tabernacle, and the pattern of all the instruments thereof, even so shall ye make it." Ex. 25: 8, 9. "And there will I meet with thee, and I will commune with thee from above the mercy seat, from between the two cherubims which are upon the ark of the testimony, of all things which I will give thee in commandment unto the children of Israel." Ex. 25 : 22.

In due time the temple was built, and it became the place to which the Israelites resorted to worship God. The following is Solomon's language in reference to it: "And, behold, I purpose to build a house unto the name of the Lord my God, as the Lord spoke unto David my father, saying, thy son, whom I will set upon thy throne in thy room, he shall build a house unto my name." 1 Kings 5 : 5. While there were special localities named in which suitable buildings were to be prepared as places for worship in the land of Israel among the Jews, it is not so among Christians. We have not the same minute detail of circumstances in regard to localities in which Christian meeting-houses are to be built, and the plan upon which they are to be built. These things are left to the wisdom, discretion and benevolence of Christians to decide. The Jewish religion was only intended for a time, and only for the Jews. It is true there were some proselytes to the Jewish religion from among other nations, but the number was comparatively small. The Jewish religion was never intended to be a universal religion. And because of the peculiar character of the Jews, of their country, and of their government, the regulations made for public worship among them are not adapted to the wants of the world in general. The Christian religion was designed for all nations, and for all time, until time ends.

But while we have not the same specific directions for building and preparing places for worship in the gospel of Christ that the Jews had in the law of Moses, still we have the principle of public worship clearly recognized, and plainly taught in the Gospel. In our text we are admonished not to forsake the assembling of ourselves together; and if we are to assemble ourselves together we must have places to assemble in, such as you have built here. The admonition to Christians in our text has suggested it as a suitable one for the present occasion. Our subject will be, *An admonition to Christians not to neglect public worship*. We shall present our thoughts under the three following heads:

I.   *An implied duty.*
II. *The danger against which Christians are admonished.*
III. *The motive upon which the admonition is given.*
We shall then notice:

I. *The implied duty.* When the apostle admonishes Christians not to forsake the assembling of themselves together, it is evidently implied in the admonition that it is the duty of Christians to meet together for public worship. The duty is also implied in our Lord's language, in which he makes the following promise: "For where two or three are gathered together in my name, there am I in the midst of them." Matt. 18:20. The propriety and utility of public worship are grounded upon principles that are found in our nature or organization. Christianity is eminently adapted to the wants of men. And the means designed to promote it are in perfect harmony with the principles of our organization. We are social beings. We love society, and men, women and children all find it to their advantage in promoting their interests and their pleasures to associate. People meet together to counsel and exhort one another in evil things as well as in good. "Iron sharpeneth iron; so a man sharpeneth the countenance of his friends." Prov. 27:17. Conversation and communication between men cheer their hearts, and when the heart or mind is cheered it will show itself in the countenance or looks. Good people's good properties are improved by associating with the good, and bad people are made worse by associating with wicked companions. It is no less true that good communications confirm and improve good manners, as well as evil communications corrupt good manners. There are three reasons why Christians should meet together for public worship. 1. They should meet together to promote their own comfort and edification. "Not forsaking the assembling of ourselves together, as the manner of some is; but exhorting one another: and so much the more as ye see the day approaching." The object here stated for which Christians were to assemble together is that they might exhort one another. And what does exhortation mean? It means, to use Webster's definition, *to use words or arguments to incite to good deeds.* In this sense it is probably to be understood when it is said of Peter, " With many other words did he testify and exhort, saying, save yourselves from this untoward generation." Acts 2:40. We have the word exhort in the following text and many others: "And Judas and Silas, being prophets also themselves, exhorted the brethren with many words and confirmed them." Acts 15:32. Exhortation is very much the same as prophesying, as Paul explains prophesying. He explains it thus: "He that prophesieth speaketh unto men to edification, and exhortation, and comfort. He that speaketh in an unknown tongue edifieth himself; but he that prophesieth edifieth the church." 1 Cor. 14:3, 4. And Paul to his Roman brethren writes as follows: "Having then gifts differing according to the grace that is given to us, whether prophecy, let us prophesy according to the proportion of faith; or ministry, let us wait on our ministering; or he that teacheth, on teaching; or he that exhorteth, on exhortation." Rom. 12:6, 8. Here exhortation is distinguished from ministering and teaching. As we have seen from the definition which Webster gives it, it means to incite to good deeds. That is, it means to stir up, to wake up, and to move to action. In teaching, the teacher imparts knowledge and instructs in gospel doctrine and duty. While in a state of sin or spiritual death, we are not only not doing anything that is good, but we are often very ignorant of what is good and of what is right. So we must be first instructed in what is right. Hence the commission of our Lord to his disciples, "teach all nations." But it too often happens that after people are taught their duty, and the ways of the Lord, that they are very slow to perform their duty and to enter upon a Christian life. This being the case, they need then to be stirred up from their spiritual drowsiness and inactivity, that they may run in the ways of God's commandments (Ps. 119 : 32) and enter into the Lord's vineyard to work. And to stir people up to duty, both before they enter upon a Christian life and likewise afterwards, seems to be a work more particularly for the exhorter. While people want to be enlightened, they must also be moved. While they need to have the understanding enlightened, they also need to have the feelings stirred up. And Christians need after their conversion helps to keep them faithful, and so they are to exhort one another. This kind of help they should all be able to render, and hence we are admonished to exhort one another. All this work of exhortation must not necessarily be performed by the preachers. All may lawfully engage in it, and all should engage in it according to the text.

Similar to the idea that we have in the word *exhort*, we have in the verse preceding our text in the word *provoke*. That verse reads thus: "And let us consider one another to provoke unto love and good works." And then follows our text with some ideas closely related to those in the above verse quoted, admonitory, and designed to stir men up to diligence in working out their salvation. We are to provoke one another, as well as exhort one another, "to love and good works." Notice the state into which we are to be brought, and in which we are to abide; it is "love and good works." Love here probably means the Christian grace of charity, that grace that is such an important element in, and which constitutes such a large part of, the Christian character. This love is to be connected with good works. The faith of the Gospel, and the faith that justifies and saves, is said to be a faith that works by love. Gal. 5 : 6. Faith works, and it works by love, and the result is, the good works, the prominent Christian characteristic of a true Christian life. The difference, perhaps, or one of the differences, between exhorting and provoking, is this: in exhorting we speak and use words to stir up persons to do what we look upon as their duty, and what is to their spiritual interests, as well as to the spiritual interests of others; while in provoking people to do their duty, we do it by our own example, or by setting before them the noble and powerful examples of the good. Sometimes some Christians may have grown somewhat cold and formal, and dilatory in their Christian life and experience. If then such do not forsake the assembling of themselves together with the Church, but assemble with their brethren, who have the "love of God shed abroad in their hearts by the Holy Ghost which is given unto them." Rom. 5 : 5. When the cold or lukewarm see and hear their brethren rejoicing in the Lord, and are brought into associations with them, they will be likely to be stirred up or provoked to such an exercise, or performance of duty, that will result in making them also joyful in the Lord. Christians that are blessed with "the joys of salvation" should provoke and exhort others to a like holy and happy state. And none should forsake the assembling of themselves together, as it is in the house of the Lord, and among the people of the Lord, in the holy exercise of Christian worship, that the declining branches may be revived, the lukewarm brought to do their first works over, the weak made strong, the babes in Christ made to grow, the seekers find Christ, and the ungodly be brought to feel the need of an interest in Christ.

2. The second reason we offer why Christians should assemble together and encourage and support public worship, is the moral effect it has upon the people of the world.

Many who are now Christians and members of the Church owe their conversion to the influence of public worship. And though many who attend public worship do not seem to profit by the opportunities thus afforded them, still there may be an influence exerted which will eventually bring some at least of these to Christ. And if the administration of the word does not reform many who have access to it in the sanctuary of the Lord, it has more or less a restraining influence upon them, which keeps them from many evils. If we had not the Lord's day every week to afford us time, and if we had not our churches and the ministration of the Gospel to afford us Christian instruction, we would certainly have a much worse state of society around us. However little many of our young people seem to profit by their attendance upon public worship, if we had no public worship for them to attend, and they would spend their Lord's days and all their leisure time at places and amusements altogether free from such influences as the sanctuary of the Lord affords, we would have a terrible state of morals around us.

The influence exerted by the ministry of the gospel, and by the general services comprised in public worship, is such, that its value can scarcely be estimated. Consequently Christians should not only by their attendance upon public worship encourage it, but they should also, to the extent of their ability, help to build meeting-houses for public worship, and help to promote it in every way they can. Brethren, you can not expend money, or invest it in any better way than to appropriate it to the promotion of the worship of God, considering the various and the great influence which the public worship of God has in enlightening the public mind, and in restraining the people from evil, and in furthering the cause of justice, truth and righteousness in every community in which the true worship of God with all its connections is regularly performed.

3. The third reason we offer for public worship is, that in this worship, when it is properly performed, God is honored and his name glorified. This is a consideration that is too much overlooked by us all. We do not generally see the advantages as clearly or as readily, growing out of the friendship of God, as we should. But when we consider our relation to God, and our dependence upon him, the importance of securing his favor and friendship must be very apparent. It is always greatly to our advantage to live at peace with all men. But as our happiness and well-being depends more upon God than it does upon men, it is of still greater advantage to us to live at peace with God, and to enjoy his friendship. It is said, "When a man's ways please the Lord, he maketh even his enemies to be at peace with him." Prov. 16 : 7. And if the Lord makes our enemies to be at peace with us, when we please him, he himself will surely be at peace with us. And if he is at peace with us, he will be our friend, protector and helper. And well might the apostle say, with holy confidence, "If God be for us, who can be against us." Rom. 8 : 31.

II. *The danger against which we are admonished.* "Not forsaking the assembling of ourselves together as the manner of some is." When we consider the advantages of assembling ourselves together in the sanctuary of the Lord, to ourselves, and to our neighbors, and when we know that we may honor the Lord by so doing, it may seem strange that Christians should forsake the holy assembly of worshipers. But they have done so, and are in danger of doing so, and hence the admonition of our text.

There are different reasons given by those who forsake the sanctuary of God and its holy service. I. We hear it said sometimes that the distance is too great to the meeting. Now this may sometimes be a sufficient reason for staying at home, but it is to be feared that it is often given as a mere excuse, when the distance might be traveled very readily by the time of meeting. But if the distance is really too great, if those who have the difficulty to contend with would take a greater interest in going to meeting this difficulty would be overcome. One way to overcome the difficulty would be to increase the number of meeting-houses. And the propriety of doing so should be duly considered by those who have so far to go to meeting as to prevent them from going. More Christian liberality would sometimes remove this obstacle. The most of people who have anything like a proper appreciation of the gospel, acknowledge that it is the duty of Christians to have the gospel preached that people may have the advantages of it. But it is a fact that should not be overlooked, that if the gospel is to be preached to the people, and if we are not to forsake "the assembling of ourselves together," we must have a place in which to assemble. This is plain. Hence the propriety of building meeting-houses in every community in which they are needed to promote the worship of God.

We have started a mission over in Denmark, and under God's blessing it seems to be prospering. Our brethren there, not being among the more wealthy classes, had but small houses, and hence no suitable places for worship, as they generally worshiped in private houses. And under such circumstances they found it especially inconvenient to hold their communion meetings. Brother Hope informed the brethren in America of the disadvantages the brethren in Denmark labored under in consequence of having no suitable place of their own to worship in, and last spring at our annual meeting, some of the brethren suggested the propriety of making an effort to collect funds there for building a meeting-house in Denmark. The effort was made, and made too very successfully. This was right.

We must have places to worship in. And now you people that live in this community, have a good house here to worship in, and do not forsake "the assembling of yourselves together as the manner of some is."

2. We have heard it said by some that they have not a comfortable place to meet in, and therefore they do not go to public worship. Years ago when our brethren worshiped generally in private houses, in some places their houses were not large, and the people knew that the accommodations were limited, and fearing they would interfere with the convenience of the members of the church, they would not go to meeting. We are glad that this reason no longer exists to any considerable degree. Our brethren are now wisely building commodious houses for worship. This is as it should be. We should build and prepare convenient and comfortable houses for the people to assemble for worship, and Christian edification. We are pleased to see that you have built such a house here. It is commodious and comfortable. There is nothing extravagant about it. You have it comfortably seated. This was formerly too much overlooked. We were, some time ago, in a large meeting house, in which the seats had no backs. Many people in collecting took seats back against the walls of the house, to have something to support them. Convenience and comfort should be consulted, while extravagance and display in Christian houses for worship should be avoided.

3. We can not enumerate all the reasons that people give for forsaking the assembling of themselves together. They are many. But all people, and especially Christians, should not forsake the public worship of God without a sufficient reason—a reason that they could give to God, if they had occasion to do so, and they may sometime have occasion to do so. We shall yet notice what is a very common cause for some Christians forsaking the assembling of them-

selves together for public meeting People sometimes do not feel like going to worship, and hence do not go. This is not right. It often happens that we may not feel like going to meeting, but when we get there we feel better. And this will generally be the case. If we do not just feel as we would like to feel, but go and fill our place in the house of the Lord, we will be very likely to feel better. To remain away, because we do not feel like going, is a dangerous course to pursue. If we stay at home one time because we do not feel like going to religious service, perhaps by the next time there is meeting we shall feel still less like going. The text makes it our duty to attend public worship, and it likewise contains an admonition against neglecting this duty. We therefore should not neglect it.

There is another idea we want to present to you in this connection, and that is the importance of avoiding bad example; "as the manner of some is." The manner of some was to forsake public worship. Paul would caution his brother from following the example of such. It is a fact that some people seem inclined to look at bad example rather than at the example of the good. Unconverted people will sometimes pass by the example of the good, and apparently see only the faults of certain members in the church who are not distinguished for their piety or consistency. It would seem strange that any of us would let the example of the lukewarm and indifferent influence us, and draw us into their way that will lead to ruin. The example of such should rather lead us to greater watchfulness and prayerfulness. When we consider what they are doing, how they are dishonoring their holy profession, and pursuing a course that must, if continued, bring them to sorrow and destruction, will we follow their evil course? It is very unwise to do so.

III. *The ground of the admonition.* "And so much the

more, as ye see the day approaching." As a motive to induce his brethren to observe the important admonitions given them, the apostle reminds them that a certain day is approaching. They no doubt knew what day he alluded to. It was the day that is called the day of the Lord. Paul says to the Thessalonians, "For yourselves know perfectly that the Lord so cometh as a thief in the night, for when they shall say, peace and safety; then sudden destruction cometh upon them, that as travail upon a woman with child; and they shall not escape." 1 Thess. 5 : 2, 3. The day referred to in our text is the day referred to by the apostle in his epistle to the Thessalonians that we quoted above. That day will surely come, and it will come as a thief. And when it comes there will be no time to prepare to meet the Lord.

We may also, in making a practical application of the subject, apply the day alluded to, to the day of death. This also will close all our opportunities for working out our salvation. Then in applying the term day to either the day of death, or to the day of the coming of the Lord, the practical meaning is, there is a day approaching, which will cut off further privileges for salvation. Notice it is approaching, and we who walk by faith see it approaching.

Then there is another thought. While that day closes the time of probation to man, it also closes the time of the saints' conflicts, troubles and sorrows. It is the day of the saints' redemption. Then let this powerful motive of the apostle have its desired effect in inciting us to faithfulness in our attendance upon our christian meetings for worship and edification, and to a practical improvement of the lessons and encouragements we receive there.

XXIV.
TRUE MANHOOD—BACCALAUREATE SERMON.

(Preached Sunday Evening, June 24, 1883, to the Graduating Class and the Students of the Huntingdon Normal College.)

"Run ye to and fro through the streets of Jerusalem and see now, and know and seek in the broad places thereof, if ye can find a man, if there be any that executeth judgment, that seeketh the truth; and I will pardon it."—Jer. 5:1:

This is a part of a prophecy of Jeremiah, delivered to the Jews at a time of great degeneracy or apostasy. And in consequence of their apostasy, they were threatened with terrible judgments by the Lord. We shall read a few verses in the closing part of the chapter, preceding that from which our text is taken, referring to the threatenings of the Lord: "For thus hath the Lord said, the whole land shall be desolate; yet will I not make a full end. For this shall the earth mourn, and the heavens above be black: because I have spoken, I have purposed it, and will not repent, neither will I turn back from it. The whole city shall flee for the noise of the horsemen and bowmen; they shall go into thickets, and climb up upon rocks: every city shall be forsaken, and not a man dwell therein. And when thou art spoiled, what wilt thou do? Though thou clothest thyself with crimson, though thou deckest thee with ornaments of gold, though thou rentest thy face with painting, in vain shalt thou make thyself fair: thy lovers will despise thee, they will seek thy life."

Our text contains the reason why the Lord purposed to inflict the punishment upon the people that he did. It was because of the universal prevalence of sin in Jerusalem— The state of the Jews at that time reminds us of the condition of the antediluvian world, in reference to which it is said, "And God looked upon the earth, and, behold, it was corrupt; for all flesh had corrupted his way upon the earth." Gen. 6:12.

According to our text, there was not a man in Jerusalem. The Lord could see none,—and yet there was a large population in Jerusalem. And no doubt, had some Jew answered the Lord, he would have said, "We have a great many men in Jerusalem." But according to the Lord's meaning he would have answered, "You have many men according to your idea of a man, but according to my idea of a man, you have none." This must have been startling to the Jews, to have it insinuated that there was not a man in Jerusalem with its great population! We are reminded of what is said of the Lord in connection with the selection of a king to fill the place of Saul. It is said, "The Lord seeth not as man seeth; for man looketh on the outward appearance, but the Lord looketh on the heart."—I. Sam. 16: 7. And it was when the Lord looked into the heart of the people of Jerusalem and saw not that inward state of thought and feeling that are necessary to constitute a real and true man, that he expressed himself as he did, in language that implies there was not a man in Jerusalem. "Run ye to and fro through the streets of Jerusalem, and see now, and know, and seek in the broad places thereof, if ye can find a man, if there be any that executeth judgment, that seeketh the truth: and I will pardon it."

Our subject will be, *True Manhood*. And we shall present our thoughts under the four following heads.

1. *God's idea of true men.*
2. *The scarcity of true men.*
3. *The value of true men.*
4. *The formation of true men.*

1. GOD'S IDEA OF TRUE MEN.

The prophet's language implies that there was not a man in Jerusalem. As we remarked above, according to human judgement, there no doubt would have been many men in Jerusalem. But God's judgment and men's differ in regard to many things. It surely is a very unfortunate circumstance for man that he finds his original nature so perverted and corrupted that his judgment is in conflict with that of God's. When God and man differ in their judgment, there should be, and we hope there will be, no hesitation in deciding who is right. God can not err. Hence the apostle's language, "Let God be true, but every man a liar."—Rom. 3:4. Let us not forget that God is always right. This great truth is the foundation of our faith in God. And however strange the idea may seem that there was not a man in Jerusalem with all its swarming population, it was correct. But God could not accept man's idea of a true man. God made man originally "upright" and "in his own image." But he has lost so much of his original character, that until he recovers what he has lost. God can not recognize him as a true or real man.

It has been said, and probably with much truth, that were an angel sent to find the most perfect man, he would probably not find him engaged in forming a body of divinity, but rather find him to be a cripple in a poor-house, whom the people of the parish wish dead. He would also be very humble before God, and perhaps have lower views of himself than others have of him. We may, perhaps, confirm and illustrate this idea by the rich man and Lazarus. Had it been left to a man of the world to decide which of the two was most of a man, no doubt the decision would have been given in favor of the rich man, who "was clothed in purple, and fine linen, and fared sumptuously every day." Wealth, and display, and power, are much more prominent elements in the world's ideal of true manhood, than purity, meekness, and poverty of spirit. The prophet Malachi, in reproving the people of his day for their errors in judgment, says, "And now we call the proud happy; yea, they that work wickedness we set up; yea, they that tempt God are delivered."—Mal. 3:15. It is the men of wealth and of show, that the world honors most, and elevates to positions of authority in government. We were in a community, some little time ago, and the character of public men was the subject of conversation. It was said that in an election in the past, there was a candidate for an office, whose competency was not questioned. But he was poor, and a cripple, and he was defeated. Such occurrences are not uncommon. True manhood passes with many at a discount, while wealth and display command a premium.

But what is true manhood in the estimation of God? And whatever it is in his estimation, it is in truth and reality. He is described as one that seeks the truth. We presume you will all agree with us that by truth in our text, we are to understand the holy law of God, as He has revealed it to us in His Word. "Sanctify them through thy truth: thy word is truth."—Jno. 17:17. So prayed the Saviour, and so honored He God's word and truth, in making it a means of purification in the system of redemption. In seeking the truth, there is implied a conscious need of the truth. Man, in his natural or sinful condition, is represented as being "dead." His spiritual nature is so stupid, unfeeling and debased, that he is represented as being dead. And while he is in that stupid and indifferent condition, in regard to his spiritual nature and his eternal interests, he has no desire for the truth of God, and of course will not seek it. He does not want it though he much needs it. His animal nature is alive, and he needs provision to meet its wants; his intellect is alive, and he craves knowledge and seeks knowledge, to satisfy his intellect, as he seeks food to satisfy his bodily wants. But while the spirit slumbers, or is dead, there is no felt want of spiritual food, or of the truth of God, and it is not sought. When, however, the spiritual nature in man is awakened, and begins to be quickened, then he begins to feel the need of some thing spiritual to meet his spiritual wants, and he begins to seek the truth. Or, in the language of our Lord, he begins to "hunger and thirst after righteousness." It was the deep and religious wants of David's spiritual nature, that prompted him to use the expressive language that he did when he exclaimed, "As the heart panteth after the waterbrooks, so panteth my soul after thee, O God. My soul thirsteth for God, for the living God." Ps. 42 : 2.

We have another plain illustration of the point we are upon, namely, the fact that when the higher nature in our manhood is quickened, there will be a turning to the truth of God for the obtaining of the necessary provision to satisfy our spiritual wants. The case we allude to is that of the Ethiopian eunuch.—Amid the religious influences that were in active operation at Jerusalem, the place to which he had been to worship, his mind being greatly awakened to the importance of religious things. He became a seeker. And from what source did he seek light and comfort? He sought the truth. He turned his attention to the Word of God and was reading the prophet Isaiah, when Philip joined himself to him. Here he sought effectually what he needed. The prophecy was opened, and Christ was found in it, and he was presented to the eunuch, and he believed in him, and he and Philip both went down into the water, and he was baptized by Philip, and then went on his way rejoicing, because his anxious, troubled and thirsty spirit was satisfied. He felt as David had felt, when he said, "My soul shall be satisfied as with marrow and fatness; and my mouth shall praise thee with joyful lips." Ps. 63 : 5.

But notice, the character that God recognizes as a man, must seek the truth. This implies labor, research and investigation.—God has given us His word, and He has given us the ministry, and other helps. Nevertheless, we must seek to know and understand. God's Word comes to us through human language, and we must get the meaning of God's mind and will, by fairly, justly, and properly interpreting the language through which God's Word comes to us. We are especially concerned to understand the English version of the Scriptures, as this is our language and the language through which God speaks to us.

Again; the truth has been misinterpreted, and there is much error in the world. And the author of error has mixed some truth with his errors to make them more effectual in deceiving. And the early education of us, perhaps, has not been altogether free from error. We have different churches, and we preachers of the different churches do not all preach alike or explain the Scriptures alike. We said awhile ago, that Philip and the eunuch went down into the water. Now some will tell you that they did not go down into the water. We differ in regard to Christian rites and Christian doctrine. Hence the necessity of all of us seeking. We should seek diligently. In the following premise our success is conditioned upon earnest effort: "If thou criest after knowledge, and liftest up thy voice for understanding; if thou seekest her as silver, and searchest for her as for hid treasure; then shalt thou understand the fear of the Lord, and find the knowledge of God." Prov. 2 : 3-5.

We should also seek the truth prayerfully and humbly. Our Lord thanked his heavenly Father that he had hidden divine truths "from the wise and prudent and revealed them unto babes." Our Heavenly Father does not, by any direct agency or power, hide the truth from any. But He has adapted it to the humble and simple mind; those that have such a mind will understand it, and receive it; while it is not adapted to a vain and self-conceited mind, and such will not appreciate its beauty nor receive it, and hence it is said to be hidden from them. Knowledge is hidden from the idle student, but revealed to the diligent, patient and persevering. Such are the results of the ordinary laws governing us in such things.

In the second place, a true man is described as one that *executeth judgment*. The word *judgment*, in the Scripture, frequently means law. Such seems to be its meaning in the following passages: "I will praise thee with uprightness of heart, when I shall have learned thy righteous judgments." Ps. 119:7. Bridges says, in his exposition of this verse, "*The righteous judgments of God!*" include the whole revelation of his Word—so-called—as the rule by which he judges our present state, and will pronouce our final sentence. Such also seems to be the meaning of the word *judgments* in the following passage: "My soul breaketh for the longing that it hath unto thy judgments at all times." Ps. 119:20.

A true man, then, executes judgment.—That is, he executes the law of God, he applies it as it is to be applied in all the affairs and business of life. This law is said to be "exceeding broad." Ps. 119:96. It covers all the duties that grow out of the relations we stand in to one another, as well as those we stand in to God. And a faithful and true man will execute the law of his God in all of its requirements and in all of its applications. As the head of a family, he will execute it in his family; as a pastor of a church, he will execute it in the church; in whatever position in life he is called to fill, he will use his utmost endeavors to execute the truth. And in his individual capacity he will do the same, whatever sacrifices he must make, or whatever self-denial he must endure. So will the true man—the man of God—the man recognized by God to be a man, execute judgment, and do justice and right to all.

II. THE SCARCITY OF GOOD MEN.

There was not found a true or good man, according to

the standard of true manhood, in Jerusalem! This is a humiliating truth to the pride of man. This is not the only passage of Scripture we have declaring the scarcity of good men. Ten good men could not be found in Sodom. It may be said, these are special cases. But we have Scripture testimony that makes this truth of a very general character. "Who can find a virtuous woman?" asks Solomon. Pv. 31:10.—Solomon has been thought by some to be pretty severe in his insinuation in regard to women. But it would seem from the following language, that he had no better opinion of his own sex. "A faithful man who can find?" Pv. 20:6. So, according to Solomon's language, faithful men were scarce, as well as virtuous women. And the great Christian Teacher declares, "Strait is the gate, and narrow is the way, which leadeth unto life, and few there be that find it." Matt. 7:14. Our Lord also teaches that there will be few true believers upon the earth when he comes again. He puts the suggestive truth He wished to present, in the form of a question, thus: "When the Son of man cometh, shall he find faith on the earth?" Luke 18:8. There is much profession at the present time in the world, but it is to be feared there is comparatively little true Christianity, little of that true manhood which in the estimation of God, constitutes true and good men. And so it appears it will be when our Lord comes. While there will probably be much that will be called "faith," there will be comparatively little true faith, little of that faith that accepts all the teachings of Christ as important, and as essential to the formation of perfect Christian character.

From the solemn truth taught in our text, and confirmed by numerous other texts of Scripture that there is a scarcity of good men in the world, we all should look well to ourselves, our principles, and our characters, to see whether we are right. And let us not forget that it is not according to the world's standard of manhood that we are to be judged, but according to God's standard. His Holy Word, and if we want to meet his approbation and enjoy His favor, we must execute judgment and seek the truth.

III. THE VALUE OF TRUE MEN.

One good man, according to God's estimation of a true or good man, would have saved Jerusalem. And ten righteous men would have saved Sodom. And, as Sodom was destroyed for the want of righteous men, and as Jerusalem was severely chastised for want of a true man, the fact that other places have not met the same fate, would seem to indicate that these places have been more favored with the holy influences of the good than were Sodom and Jerusalem.

The influence that good men have exerted in the world, is yet to be realized, for it never has been. "Ye are the salt of the earth," said Jesus to his disciples. The good have always been the salt of the earth. They have preserved the earth, and they have been the earth's benefactors by blessing it with their holy labors, and by bringing down the blessings from Heaven upon it by their prayers. And you, beloved hearers, we are fearful, do not appreciate your obligations to the good of the world for what you now are, and for what you are enjoying. Many of you have had good parents, and your ancestors before them were good. And had it not been so, your condition to-day, would, in all probability, be very different from what it is. It is to the good you are indebted for your greatest privileges and your richest blessings. How deeply are we impressed with the obligations we are under to the good Christian friends under whose good influences we were thrown, and thus saved! Among those gathered into the fold of Christ in our late revival, there was one, whose father we well knew, and whom we regarded as a good man, and an humble and faithful minister of Christ.

In thinking about the conversion of his son we were impressed with the thought that perhaps that father's holy influence is now bearing the fruit of his son's conversion. The influence of a good and holy life often continues after the death of the good. Let us say to you, honor and respect the good. They are your best friends and benefactors. Above all, honor and respect God, who has blessed us with the influence of the good.

IV. THE FORMATION OF TRUE MEN.

While the state of man, in his guilty and fallen condition, is sad to contemplate, we are glad to know that that condition may be improved. God has remembered us in our low estate, and laid hold upon one that is mighty. And by availing ourselves of the provision provided for us in Christ by our Heavenly Father, our lost manhood may be recovered. By "being born again, not of corruptible seed, but of incorruptible, by the Word of God, which liveth and abideth forever" (1 Pet. 1: 23), we are made partakers of the divine nature" (2 Pet. 1:4), and thus become men of God. There is, then, hope for man, Jesus has died, and man may live, and live forever. Paul, in addressing believers, says "Ye are God's husbandry, ye are God's building." (1 Cor. 3: 9.) Under the transforming power of God, the barren land becomes fruitful, and the temple in ruins is rebuilt.

And now, beloved hearers, will you not all seek to become true men, that you may enjoy the honor, glory, and value of true manhood? Surely you all should feel a deep interest in our subject, as it concerns you all. Young women and young men, let us say to you, seek the culture and development of your womanhood and manhood to the highest possible degree. And while, we would, from the great importance of our subject, press it upon you all, we would call the special attention of the graduating class to it. By no means let your education and culture stop short of true manhood. It is the cultivated and renewed mind that makes the man. Dr. Watts, the author of many of our hymns, was dignified in his conduct and manners, but below the common size of men in his stature. On one occasion when he was in company, it was said by one, "Is this the great Dr. Watts?" In good humor he turned round suddenly, and repeated the following stanza from one of his poems:

> "Were I so tall to reach the pole,
> Or grasp the ocean with a span,
> I must be measured by my soul;
> The mind's the standard of the man."

The company manifested silent admiration.

Let us then give less attention to the adornment and gratification of the body, and more to the mental and spiritual culture of the mind, as it is the mind that makes the man.

XXV.

THE RELATION OF CHRIST'S RESURRECTION TO THE CHRISTIAN'S HOPE.

EASTER SERMON.

"Blessed be the God and Father of our Lord Jesus Christ, which according to his abundant mercy hath begotten us again unto a lively hope by the resurrection of Jesus Christ from the dead, to an inheritance incorruptible, undefiled, and that fadeth not away, reserved in heaven for you."—1 Peter, 1: 3 4.

Among the ideas contained in the text is the idea that there is a relation between the resurrection of Christ, and the Christian's hope. And this will be a prominent point in our remarks, and the subject of our present discourse. We can bring out this evening but a few of the ideas contained in this suggestive text. We shall notice the following:

1. *The second, or the new birth.*
2. *Unto what Christians are said to be begotten.*
3. *Why Christians are said to be begotten by the resurrection of Christ.*

1. *The second, or the new birth.*

God, whom the apostle calls in our text, "The God and father of our Lord Jesus Christ," is said to have "begotten us again." Again means another time, or once more. And when God is said to have begotten us again, the language implies that he had begotten us before. And so he had, for he is the Father of us all by nature. The prophet asks, "Have we not all one Father? Hath not one God created us?" (Malachi 2: 10.) And the apostle Paul declared that God "hath made of one blood all nations of men for to dwell on all the face of the earth." (Acts 17: 26.) He is also said to be "the God of the spirits of all flesh." (Num. 16: 22.) But while all men are the children of God, they have, by following their own evil ways, became disobedient to him, and alienated from him. And the following language of complaint uttered by the Lord in reference to the Israelites, will express the moral or spiritual state of all men who have not been begotten again: "Hear, O heavens, and give ear, O earth: for the Lord hath spoken, I have nourished and brought up children, and they have rebelled against me. The ox knoweth his owner, and the ass his master's crib; but Israel doth not know, my people doth not consider. Ah, sinful nation, a people laden with iniquity, a seed of evil doers, children that are corrupters: they have forsaken the Lord, they have provoked the Holy One of Israel unto anger, they have gone away backward." (Isa. 1: 2–4.) What a sad picture of children who have such a kind father as God is! But it is a true picture. It is confirmed by the declaration of Paul, which seems to be applied to all persons who are not begotten again: "the carnal mind is enmity against God: for it is not subject to the law of God, neither indeed can be." (Rom. 8: 7.) Such being the condition of God's human family by nature, he can not take the pleasure in them, and admit them to that intimate friendship and familiarity with him, that he as a loving and kind father would like to do. He is pure and holy and can not take sinners into fellowship with him, though they be his own children. Hence the necessity of men and women in their natural condition being "begotten again." Our kind and merciful Father, instead of forever casting off or blotting out of existence his rebellious children, has made provision through Christ to have them "begotten again." Our heavenly Father has done for his rebellious children in reference to their spiritual state what earthly fathers often do for their sons in reference to financial affairs. Young men who start out in business through idleness, extravagance, intemperate habits, or mismanagement, sometimes fail in business and become bankrupt. Their fathers, when they can do so, and when they are inclined to do so, pay their debts and start them in business again, and put them where they were when they first started out in life. So when men, the children of God, had failed in life's great work, and had become involved in debt and spiritual bankruptcy, God made provision through Christ to pay men's debts, or, in other words, to forgive their sins and to start them in life again with every chance of success. All this, and more too, is implied in being "begotten again."

Though our text has a very plain and interesting allusion to the new birth, it does not state positively the necessity of being begotten again, but rather the result of such a change. It is, however, evidently implied that there is a necessity for being "begotten again." When the same subject was presented by Christ to Nicodemus, the absolute necessity of being "begotten again" was declared by Christ. "Verily, verily, I say unto thee," said our Lord, "except a man be born again, he can not see the kingdom of God." John 3: 3. And again: "Verily, verily, I say unto thee, except a man be born of water and of the spirit, he can not enter into the kingdom of God," verse 5. But as the necessity of being "begotten again" is not made a point in our text except by implication, we shall not dwell upon that aspect of the new birth further. We would remark that as we have the same subject presented in different places in the Scriptures, we have it presented sometimes under one aspect, and sometimes under another. This applies to all subjects.

The possibility that we may be "begotten again," and that "unto a lively hope," and thus have all our former life, with all its defects, with all its dark spots and crimes, blotted out, and be as free from sin as the new-born babe, and begin our spiritual career anew, is a most encouraging thought. And all persons should gladly avail themselves of the opportunity presented to them in the gospel of experiencing this new birth with all its advantages and enjoyments.

2. *Unto what Christians are said to be "begotten again."*

We are said to be "begotten again unto a lively hope." When a man is born again, or "begotten again," in the words of our text, and has experienced the change which the idea of a new birth implies, and has passed from a state of spiritual darkness, and ignorance, and death, to a state of marvelous light, wisdom and life, and walks by faith, and lives by faith, believing all that is contained in the Scriptures, whether it be in the form of doctrine, precepts, commandments, or promises, he has a great future before him. His faith scans the developing events and the successive steps of his endless career as far as the Scriptures reveal that career, and his present capacity for spiritual discernment will enable him to do so. Surely he is begotten "unto a lively hope," when his new birth into a spiritual life secures to him the hope of the Gospel, with the number, the magnitude, and the endless unfolding of new scenes in the happy eternity of the future.

How different is a birth into the world according to nature, in reference to the prospect before it, to what is a second or new birth—the birth by which we are begotten unto the lively hope of Christianity. When an infant is born into the world, could it behold and comprehend its future, should it reach maturity, and should its future extend to the final state or doom of the lost, what a terrible state would it be to behold and to contemplate! The very prospect of it would be most tormenting. But when a soul is "begotten again," and it takes a survey of its future—such a future as we have already alluded to—how glorious is the view. In our first or natural birth, "man is born unto trouble, as the sparks fly upward."—Job v. 7. But in our second or spiritual birth, we are begotten unto a "lively hope," and unto "an inheritance incorruptible and undefiled, and that fadeth not away."

But we are not only informed in our text that we are begotten unto a "lively hope," but we are also informed what that hope consists of. It is "an inheritance incorruptible and undefiled, that fadeth not away, reserved in heaven." We are begotten unto an inheritance—born to an estate. We become sons, and consequently heirs, of a rich father, the proprietor of heaven and earth. We call your attention to the fact that the Christian's hope, or what constitutes that hope, is called an "inheritance." An inheritance is something that is not purchased with money, or obtained as a reward of labor. Webster, in giving the meaning of inheritance in law, thus defines: "A perpetual or continuing right to an estate in a man and his heirs; an estate which a man has by descent as heir to another, or which he may transmit to another as his heir; an estate derived from an ancestor to an heir in course of law." So the inheritance of the children of God is given to them as a legacy from their divine Father. You will notice that it is said in our text that it is according to his "abundant mercy" that God has begotten us again. Mercy was the moving cause of man's redemption, or of God's work for redeeming man. Though we are created unto good works, as Paul says, "For we are his workmanship, created in Christ Jesus unto good works, which God hath before ordained that we should walk in them" (Eph. ii. 10); and though we are to wash the saints' feet, and "diligently follow every good work" (1 Tim. v. 10 still by grace we are saved.—Eph. ii. 8.

There is another interesting thought suggested by this inheritance. It is the security of the tenure by which it is held. It is well known that there is no right that it is more difficult to break, than the right to an inheritance. Indeed it can not be broken if it is legal. If the right of him that gives the property is good, and he makes a good title to him on whom it is conferred, the title of the latter is indisputable. This inheritance is "reserved in heaven," for those who are "begotten again to a lively hope." And those who are thus begotten, and continue faithful, "are kept by the power of God through faith." So we can make our "calling and election sure." 2 Pet. 1:10.

In the description we have of the inheritance, which constitutes the sum of the hope to which we are begotten, it is first declared to be "incorruptible." This means that it is incapable of decay or dissolution. Hence it is called "the everlasting kingdom." 2 Peter 1:11. The new heavens and the new earth that are to be formed, and which are to constitute at least a part of the inheritance of the saints, will not be susceptible of the change and decay that the present earth with its surroundings is. Our earth was once destroyed by water, and is now "reserved unto fire." 2 Peter 3 : 7. It is corruptible and subject to change and decay. But the inheritance of the saints shall be imperishable and unchangeable. It will forever retain all its freshness and beauty that it possesses in the beginning.

And, secondly, it is said to be unfading, or that it will not fade away. This allusion may be to fading flowers. How soon the most beautiful flowers wither and fade away! But in the inheritance of the saints, whatever beauty, and glory and vigor that are possessed at first, will continue forever.

"There everlasting spring abides,
And never withering flowers."

There is another idea suggested by the unfading nature of the beauty and glory of the inheritance of the good. And that is the idea that that beauty and glory will never lose their charms to the good, or never cloy upon their spiritual tastes. Here on earth, the things that are the most beautiful, and that give the most enjoyment, in time lose their effects in some measure, and we get tired of beholding them. Our great and long familiarity with them diminishes our joy in them. But this will not be the case with the unfading charms of the musical sounds, and of the beautiful sights that will greet our ears and eyes "in the sweet fields of Eden."

And, in the third place, this inheritance is declared to be undefiled. We have left this to the last, though we regard it as the most precious characteristic of the saints' inheritance. To a mind that is full of sympathy with holy beings and holy principles, among all the beautiful things said of heaven, nothing will commend heaven to it more highly, than the fact that it is undefiled. When we read the glowing description of the holy Jerusalem in the 21st chapter of Revelation, of its foundations "garnished with precious stones," of its pearly gates, and of the city being of pure gold, like unto clear glass, how precious does that city appear! But when we approach the close of the description, and read that "there shall in no wise enter into it anything that defileth, neither whatsoever worketh abomination, or maketh a lie," this is the climax of its excellency, and we are "lost in wonder, love and praise" to think that in that city into which no evil can ever enter, we may have an inheritance! Oh, sin is such a terrible thing! Whatever it touches, it defiles, and whatever it defiles it injures, and to the extent of the defilement it kills. Christian brethren and sisters, go back to your first love, to the time you were "begotten again." And in your great joy you can sing with the poet:

"I would not believe that I ever should grieve,
That I ever should suffer again."

But temptation came in some form, and not being on your guard, you yielded, and as soon as you did so, your peace was disturbed and your joy diminished. Often the family circle has been the home of peace and domestic joy, but the tempter found admission, and sin was introduced in some of its forms, and it is no longer the home of peace, love and prosperity, for the enemy, who is ever watching for an opportunity to do evil, found a place to sow discord, enmity, jealousy, or some other form of evil, and in the same manner is the peace of the church disturbed, and its usefulness diminished. Oh, how comforting the thought that we shall one day possess our inheritance, and be where sin can never defile us.

3. *Why Christians are said to be begotten by the resurrection of Christ.*

1. The resurrection of Christ proved the truth of his

mission and the justice of his claims to the Messiahship. He claimed to be the Messiah and the Son of God, and that God had sent him. One of the ways in which his claim was to be proved was by miracles. Hence he did many miracles. He raised the dead to life, and did many marvelous works. His faithful reproofs of sin in the various forms in which it existed, and his exposure of the cold formality of the religionists of his time, and his attempts to introduce a new order of things in the religious world, an order of things that would render justice to all, to the poor as well as to the rich, and to God as well as to man, offended the people. They laid plans for his death, and those plans finally succeeded. And the blessed Saviour, with his heart full of love to man, and with an unsurpassed disinterestedness, and with a self-denying spirit, that led him to seek the good of others rather than his own, was condemned to death, and met it in the form of the ignominious crucifixion. He was taken by his friends and buried in Joseph's tomb. You will remember what precautionary measures were taken by those in authority to guard this grave. But notwithstanding all the efforts made by his enemies to prevent his prophecy in regard to his resurrection from being fulfilled, he rose the third day.

His resurrection was then, and that, very properly and justly, made the ground of argument, and of unanswerable argument for the divine mission of Christ, and for the divine character and authority of his teaching. His resurrection was attributed to the interposition and power of God. This was done to prove that God vindicated and approved of Christ, and of all he said and did. It is true, the Saviour said in regard to his life which he gave as a ransom for sinners, "No man taketh it from me, but I lay it down of myself. I have power to lay it down, and I have power to take it again. This commandment have I received of my Father." (John 10: 18.) It will be seen from his language that while he claimed the power to take up his life, he acted under the authority in doing so. Then in doing what he did, he acted under the power and authority of his Father. Hence, as we have already remarked, his resurrection is attributed to the power of God. When Peter was vindicating the cause of Christ, in reference to the healing of the lame man that was laid at the gate of the temple, he said, "Be it known unto you all, and to all the people of Israel, that by the name of Jesus Christ of Nazareth, whom ye crucified, whom God raised from the dead, even by him doth this man stand here before you whole." (Acts 4: 10.)

In order that we may understand clearly the relation between Christ's resurrection and the Christian's hope, and new life, we must keep in mind the relation between faith and the Christian's hope and conversion. This relation or connection is plain, and frequently stated in the Scriptures. We have it in these words of John: "Whosoever believeth that Jesus is the Christ is born of God." (1 John 5: 1.) We then are to believe that Jesus is the Christ, the Son of God. But we must have testimony to believe any truth or fact. And what testimony have we that is sufficient to prove that Jesus is the Son of God? We have such testimony in the fact of Christ's resurrection. Hence the connecting link, or the relation between Christ's resurrection and the new birth of the Christian. This relation is seen in other ways, but we can only at this time present the great gospel fact of Christ's resurrection, as proper ground and conclusive argument for belief in him. And everything that promotes belief in Christ has an important relation to, and bearing upon, the new birth, Christian life and Christian hope.

In view of the important relation that Christ's resurrection has to the conversion and regeneration of sinners, his resurrection was made an important part in apostolic preaching. And when the apostles were consulting about filling the place of Judas, Peter said, "of these men which have companied with us all the time the Lord Jesus went in and out among us, beginning from the baptism of John, and that same day that he was taken up from us, must one be ordained to be a witness with us of his resurrection." (Acts 1: 21-22.) And Paul's language to the Corinthians shows what use was made of Christ's resurrection by the apostles in establishing Christianity, and in the conversion of sinners. He says, "I delivered unto you first of all that which I also received, how that Christ died for our sins according to the Scriptures; and that he was buried, and that he rose again the third day according to the Scriptures; and that he was seen of Cephas, then of the twelve," etc. (1 Cor. 15: 3-5.) The fact of Christ's resurrection was among the first things preached to people to win them to Christ. The relation of Christ's resurrection to Christian belief, is clearly seen in Paul's preaching at Athens. In referring to God, he declares, "he hath appointed a day, in the which he will judge the world in righteousness by that man whom he hath ordained; whereof he hath given assurance unto all men, in that he hath raised him from the dead." (Acts 17: 31.) Instead of the phrase, "he hath given assurance," the marginal reading is, "he hath offered faith." That is, God by raising Christ from the dead, has offered to men sufficient ground for belief in him.

We that are living in this age of the world, when Christianity is so well established, and among people who generally believe in its Divine character, seeing as they do so much that is good in it, and that is calculated to meet the wants of suffering and guilty humanity, can not appreciate the moral power of the great fact of Christ's resurrection, like those could who lived in the age of the world in which Christianity was planted. Let us imagine the apostle Peter preaching, and one of us as a hearer, and that that one of us was as ignorant of divine things as the people of the apostolic age generally were. That hearer becomes interested in the great, practical, and diversified subjects presented in the preaching of Peter. He approaches Peter, and says to him "I am interested in your preaching. If what you say is true, I am a lost man, and I ought to change my life. How do you know that the Christ you preach was a divine being and teacher?" Peter replies to him in language something like the following: "We knew him personally, and we knew him well. We, early in his ministry, became his disciples. We were with him about three years. We saw many of the marvelous and supernatural works that he did. We finally saw him crucified, and we know that he was dead. He was then buried. But he rose from the dead. And we associated with him after his death, and know, and are assured beyond a doubt, that he was restored to life, and we therefore must believe, and do believe that he was a divine teacher, and that all that he taught is true."

Under such circumstances the preaching of Christ's resurrection would have much to do in leading men to believe. And many would say in the language of our text, "Blessed be the God and Father of our Lord Jesus Christ, which, according to his abundant mercy, hath begotten us again unto a lively hope by the resurrection of Jesus Christ from the dead," etc.

And now, dear readers, as Christ is risen, Christianity is true. And because it is true, it commends itself to your belief, and because it will regenerate you, and give you a "lively hope" and a glorious "inheritance," it commends itself to your immediate acceptance.

XXVI.
SOME OF THE SPIRITUAL LESSONS TAUGHT BY SPRING.

"Thou renewest the face of the earth."—Ps. 104: 30.

The Psalmist, in the psalm from which our text is quoted, has said many interesting things in regard to the ample provision that God has made to meet the wants of his creatures, both of the lower and higher order. And in setting forth the sovereign power of God exercised over the entire dominion of being, the Psalmist in adoring the greatness and goodness of God, says, "Thou renewest the face of the earth." That Spring is referred to here, there can be no reasonable doubt. And the term used to express the change that takes place when the dominion of winter over the earth ceases, and when Spring follows with its peculiar effects upon the earth, is a term used to express the spiritual change that takes place in the conversion of sinners. This change is a renewing of the mind. "And be not conformed to this world; but be ye transformed by the renewing of your mind, that ye may prove what is that good, and acceptable, and perfect will of God." Rom. 12: 2.

The works of God are frequently referred to in the Scripture as teaching us things concerning his character or doings. The language of the nineteenth Psalm is familiar to you all. We refer to the following: "The heavens declare the glory of God; and the firmament sheweth his handiwork. Day unto day uttereth speech, and night unto night sheweth knowledge." But it is not only the heavens that declare the glory of God; the earth does the same. "Thou renewest the face of the earth." The annual return of Spring, with all the blessings which it introduces, and the diversity of seasons which contributes so materially to the enjoyment and welfare of man, these also declare the glory of God, or his goodness, for his glory is his goodness. The young Elihu, one of the characters of the book of Job, in his zeal to defend the character of God, gives us to understand that he endeavored to learn from the providence of God. His language is: "I said, days should speak, and multitude of years should teach wisdom." Job 32:7. And Job, in speaking to his friends rather reprovingly, admonished them thus: "Speak to the earth, and it shall teach thee; and the fishes of the sea shall declare unto thee. Who knoweth not in all these that the hand of the Lord hath wrought this?" Job 12:8, 9. The Spring, as well as nature in all its diversified forms, teaches us lessons of both the natural and the redemptive providence of God. By the redemptive providence of God we mean his goodness, wisdom and power as manifested in the works of redemption.

We shall look at Spring as a powerful confirmation of the Scriptural character of God. 1. It is a confirmation of his faithfulness or truthfulness. Soon after the flood, the Lord said: "While the earth remaineth, seedtime and harvest, and cold and heat, and summer and winter, and day and night shall not cease." Gen. 8:22. From this we learn that the course of nature shall continue while the earth continues. It seems to be intimated here that this earth is not to continue always. And this intimation agrees with the apostle Peter, who declares that "the earth also and the works that are therein shall be burned up." 2 Peter 3:10. Though the earth may not continue always, we are assured that while it does continue God will carefully preserve the regular succession of times and seasons. These seasons have never ceased, and they will never cease until the present general course of nature ceases. There is a wonderful change in things taking place continually around us, but the seasons continue, and have continued since this promise was made, and this was made some four thousand years ago. And the return of Spring every year for four thousand years has been a witness to the truthfulness of God's promise.

This promise of God that summer and winter, and day and night shall not cease, is called *God's covenant of the day and of the night,* Jer. 33: 20, and it is mentioned by the prophet to show that his covenant of grace is as sure as his covenant concerning day and night, and summer and winter. His promises to his *creatures* can not fail, and much less will his promises to *believers* fail. "He is faithful that promised." Heb. 10: 23. "All the promises of God in him are yea, and in him Amen, unto the glory of God by us." 2 Cor. 1: 20. With what trust and confidence, then, may we all believe in Christ. "He that believeth and is baptized shall be saved; but he that believeth not shall be damned." Mark 16: 16.

2. The annual return of Spring is not only a confirmation of the truthfulness of God, but it is also a confirmation of his power. The power of God is very clearly manifested in the creation. "Thou hast made the heaven and the earth by thy great power and stretched out arm, and there is nothing too hard for thee." Jer. 32: 17. When we consider the greatness and the number of the works of God, we are impressed with the greatness of his power by the exercise of which all things that exist are created. And were we to see new additions made to his works in the creation of new worlds, we would be deeply impressed with the power that would produce them. But is not the renewing of the face of the earth every year equivalent to a new creation? In the dreary and cold winter nature seems dead. But there is a secret power at work, a power proceeding from God, and that power in the seeds of the earth and in the various parts of the vegetable kingdom renews the face

of the earth, and a change follows which is almost like a new creation. And herein is manifested the power of God. And all the power of God that is exerted in the natural world to further his purposes in that department of his works is also exerted in the spiritual world to further his purposes in the work of redemption. And hence Abraham was "fully persuaded that what he had promised he was able also to perform." Rom. 4: 21. And having confidence in both the truthfulness and the power of God, as we may have, and as we should have, for he is a God of power and of truth, we may trust in him and feel perfectly safe in his hands. Hence Paul could say, and every believer can say the same, "I know whom I have believed, and am persuaded that he is able to keep that which I have committed to him against that day." 2 Tim. 1: 12.

3. The renewing of the face of the earth in the Spring by the Lord should teach us and impress upon our minds the great truth that he is the fountain of all life. Such he is justly declared to be. "With thee," said David, addressing the Lord, "is the fountain of life." Ps. 36: 9. Paul calls him the "living God." Heb. 9: 14. He is not only called the "living God" to distinguish him from the lifeless gods of the heathen, but because "he giveth to all life, and breath, and all things." Acts 17: 25. In the Spring of the year the face of the earth, being renewed by the Lord, shows signs of life everywhere. The very heart of nature seems to send out into all its departments, and especially into the vegetable kingdom, streams of vitality, and the face of the earth throbs with the tide of life. "The trees of the Lord are full of sap; the cedars of Lebanon which he hath planted." Ps. 104: 16. In view of the truth we are presenting, namely this, that God is the fountain of all life, Job exclaims, "who knoweth not in all these that the hand of the Lord hath wrought this? In whose hand is the soul

of every living thing, and the breath of all mankind." Job 12: 9, 10.

4. The renewal of the face of the earth is a beautiful and expressive symbol of spiritual renovation. The same term that is used to represent the change that takes place upon the face of the earth at the approach of Spring is also used to express the spiritual change that takes place in persons who experience a gospel reformation or transformation. Barren, dreary, and lifeless to a considerable degree is the aspect of the earth in winter. And so the unrenewed soul is barren, bearing no fruit of righteousness, and "dead in trespasses and in sins." Eph. 2: 1. Without the Spring-showers, and sunshine of the Divine Spirit, and the Gospel of the grace of God, there is no eternal life, and no fruit of righteousness in the human soul. But as the return of Spring renews the face of the earth and transforms the dreary and barren earth into a scene of beauty, life, animation, and increased enjoyment, so those who have been renewed in the spirit of their minds, and passed out of the cold, dreary, and barren state of sin, experience a new life, a new creation, and a new enjoyment. "If any man be in Christ, he is a new creature; old things are passed away; behold all things are become new." 2 Cor. 5: 17. There is as much difference in the lives of such before they became Christians and their lives as transformed by the gospel as there is between Winter and Spring. There is a great change. Their feelings, their enjoyments, their purposes, their fellowships, and their sympathies, are all different.

In the renewal of the mind, in a Christian sense, a new life is inaugurated. The germ of eternal life is planted in the renewed mind. And this eternal life is a divine life, the highest kind of life, and consequently it is a life that relates us to, and brings us into connection with Divine beings. The believer is planted into the death of Christ, Rom. 6: 5, and grafted into Christ, John 15: 1–7. And if he then abides in Christ, his life is sure, and will be productive of fruit, and will develop into that glorious and perfect life, to which the present life is introductory.

5. Spring is also a symbol of the resurrection. The consigning of the human body to the earth is compared by the apostle Paul to the planting of seed in the ground: "But some man will say, how are the dead raised up? and with what body do they come? Thou fool, that which thou sowest is not quickened, except it die: and that which thou sowest, thou sowest not that body that shall be, but bare grain, it may chance of wheat, or of some other grain: but God giveth it a body as it hath pleased him, and to every seed his own body. All flesh is not the same flesh: but there is one kind of flesh of men, another flesh of beasts, another of fishes, and another of birds. There are also celestial bodies, and bodies terrestrial: but the glory of the celestial is one, and the glory of the terrestrial is another. There is one glory of the sun, and another glory of the moon, and another glory of the stars; for one star differeth from another star in glory. So also is the resurrection of the dead. It is sown in corruption, it is raised in incorruption: it is sown in dishonor, it is raised in glory: it is sown in weakness, it is raised in power," etc. 1 Cor. 15: 35–43. Such was Paul's illustration of the resurrection. We say illustration. For his reference to the grain planted in the ground is rather an illustration than an argument. In part of this great discourse he argues the certainty of the resurrection. But in the passage we have quoted at some length, he illustrates it, or proves from the analogy of nature, there is nothing irrational in the Christian doctrine of the resurrection. Seeds die to rise again. Spring starts up to life after winter has passed, and its resurrection is welcomed. And why should it be thought incredible that

it shall be so with man? There is nothing incredible in the doctrine.

The doctrine of the resurrection is in harmony with what we see around us in nature. The heathen, with their obscure views of man's future existence, thought it somewhat strange that nature should show such tenacity to life, and that vegetation should be revived after being apparently dead, and that man should continue to sleep the sleep of death. They seemed almost to envy nature. The following is an epitaph written upon a heathen:

> "Alas! the tender herbs and flowery tribes,
> Though crushed by winter's unrelenting hand,
> Revive and rise when vernal zephyrs call.
> But we, the brave, the mighty and the wise,
> Bloom, flourish, fade and fall,—and then succeeds
> A long, long, silent, dark, oblivious sleep;
> A sleep which no propitious Pow'r dispels,
> Nor changing seasons, nor revolving years."

But very different to the above language is the language of Christian faith and hope: "But I would not have you to be ignorant, brethren, concerning them which are asleep, that ye sorrow not, even as others which have no hope. For if we believe that Jesus died and rose again, even so them also which sleep in Jesus will God bring with him. For this we say unto you by the word of the Lord, that we which are alive and remain unto the coming of the Lord shall not prevent them which are asleep. For the Lord himself shall descend from heaven with a shout, with the voice of the archangel, and with the trump of God: and the dead in Christ shall rise first: then we which are alive and remain shall be caught up together with them in the clouds, to meet the Lord in the air: and so shall we ever be with the Lord." 1 Thess. 4: 13–17. What a glorious future does the above language of the apostle open to the Christian! Well may he follow it with this application: "Wherefore comfort one another with these words."

The renewal of the face of the earth by the return of Spring, presents a beautiful sight. The idea of life, and growth, and fruitage in the natural world is very pleasant, and we contemplate it with much pleasure. But the idea of the renewal of our sinful natures, with the spiritual beauty, and the heavenly enjoyments, and the glorious future associated with that idea, is still a much grander subject for contemplation. And it is what we may all enjoy. We may all realize a resurrection or a resuscitation of our spirits from a state of death, unto a state of life, and beauty, and usefulness, and heavenly enjoyment. And he that renews the face of the earth every Spring, will renew us in the spirit of our minds, if we seek that renewal. As we have seen, he is a God of truth and of power, and as he has promised to save, he will save. And as it is the influence of the natural sun that produces Spring in nature, so it is the influence of Christ, who is the sun of the spiritual world, that renews the soul, and changes its winter into Spring, and raises it up from a state of gloom and death unto one of light and life. Christ is our life, and when he shall appear then shall we also appear with him in glory. Col. 3: 4.

XXVII.
HOSTILITY TO CHRIST.
CHRISTMAS SERMON.

"When Herod the king heard these things he was troubled, and all Jerusalem with him."—Matt. 2 : 3.

This is a time of general festivity and cheerfulness. Gifts have been freely distributed and the hearts of both young and old have been gladdened by them. This morning we heard of God's unspeakable gift to our lost and guilty world. But while this season of the year is a time of joy to many—a time of Christian joy to those who turn the occasion to their spiritual edification, and a time of carnal joy to such as know no higher joy, and who turn everything, and often things of a sacred character, into carnal pleasure—still, there are a great many amid all the rejoicing around them, who are unhappy and miserable. Such are the diversified conditions of the children of men, and such the extremes which obtain in the world.

Such was the condition of the people in Judea when our Lord was born, the event we commemorate at the Christmas festival. There was great joy; and there was abundance of cause for joy. "Unto you is born this day in the city of David a Saviour, which is Christ the Lord." Luke 2 : 11. Such was the announcement of the angel to the shepherds when watching their flocks by night. And surely an announcement that a Saviour was born, a Saviour to save our ruined race, was enough to awaken joy and gladness in the world. And the angel who bore the glad tidings to the shepherds was joined by "a multitude of the heavenly host praising God, and saying, glory to God in the highest, and on earth peace, good will toward men. And it came to pass as the angels were gone away from them into heaven, the shepherds said one to another, let us now go even unto Bethlehem and see this thing that has come to pass, which the Lord hath made known unto us." Luke 2 : 15. They accordingly went, and found the infant Saviour with his parents. And the manner in which the shepherds were affected by the sight of the infant Messiah is seen in what followed their discovery. It is said "the shepherds returned, glorifying and praising God for all the things that they had heard and seen, as it was told unto them." Luke 2 : 20. Thus we see that both men and angels rejoiced at the birth of our Lord. And as we have already remarked, the occasion justified all the joy that was manifested. For an event had occurred which was interesting to men and angels. And we are not surprised that there was joy, but we are surprised that there were any among our fallen race that did not share in the joy. But alas, for the blindness, the ignorance, the selfishness, and maliciousness of the human heart when sin has fully taken possession of it. While there was joy among the humble shepherds in their tents, in the palace of Herod there was trouble. You heard me read the following: "When Herod the King had heard these things, he was troubled, and all Jerusalem with him. v. 2. Here we find trouble. Kings are not always happy. Royalty does not always confer bliss. Purple robes and glittering palaces often cover a great deal of misery as well as crime. Herod was troubled. And what troubled him? A babe troubled him! With all his military power, and the nation to protect him, he was afraid of a babe! Poor man! He was himself his greatest enemy. He was not right before God, nor with his God.

Then we see all were not happy when the Saviour was born. And this thought has suggested the subject for our sermon and the train of thoughts that we will offer to you this evening. It is sometimes profitable and edifying to the mind to contrast things. We compare things when they have similar properties; we contrast them when they have different properties. And this is a difference between comparison and contrast. And while Christmas is associated with so much joy and gladness, it is also associated with trouble. And as it is connected with things so widely different in their nature, we have thought that a view of the trouble associated with the origin of the event we have just commemorated may be edifying, and make the joy more apparent. "Herod and all Jerusalem," as well as the angels and shepherds, should have welcomed the Saviour, and rejoiced at his birth, but they did not. They were angry, they murmured, they had no sympathy with his mission as a Saviour and reformer of the world. They took a position of hostility to him.

1. The intelligence of the birth of the long-looked-for king of the Jews, or the Messiah, at length reached the court of Herod. He was not altogether ignorant of the prophecies of the Old Testament, which pointed to the Messiah and his kingdom, and the limit of his coming according to Daniel's prophecy of the seventy weeks. Dan. 9:24. And as the character of a king was given to the Saviour, Herod seemed to look upon him with feelings of jealousy. A man of his character, having, apparently, little regard to the spiritual welfare of his people, and probably little regard to their welfare in any respect, and occupying his throne, and administering the government of his nation from selfish and ambitious motives, would be very likely to receive the news of the birth of the king of the Jews with just such feelings as were awakened in Herod's heart when he heard the tidings that reached him concerning the infant in Bethlehem whose birth was ominous of a character something more than that of an ordinary man. Hence he was troubled. The fulfilling of the Scriptures and the maturing of God's purposes, have nothing in them that gives promise of peace or comfort to the wicked.

It seems that Herod was not the only one that was troubled at the birth of the king of the Jews. All Jerusalem but the few that "waited for the consolation of Israel," Luke 2:25, was likewise troubled. The idea that all Jerusalem was hostile to Christ and troubled at his birth as soon as he was born, is suggestive of painful thoughts to such as fully appreciate the moral condition that such a course implies. How true it is that "the carnal mind is enmity against God. Rom. 8:7. And how strange it is that many of that class will persist in that course of enmity to their ruin! But the wicked are to be pitied as well as censured, for they are ignorant of the true character of their conduct and of their destiny.

The hostility that Herod felt to Christ culminated or terminated in a most aggravated crime. He first sought to accomplish his purpose by deception. He first gathered the chief priests and scribes together and inquired of them, where Christ should be born. Having learned this, he then called the wise men and inquired of them the time when the star appeared. He then "sent them to Bethlehem, and said, go and search diligently for the young child; and when ye have found him, bring me word again, that I may come and worship him also." He professed to want to know where Christ was, that he might go and worship him. What heaven-daring hypocrisy! And what terrible crimes have been committed under the cloak of religion. But Herod failed to obtain the desired information. And being disappointed and defeated in obtaining his end through a false pretence, he threw off the mask of religion by which he first sought to accomplish his purpose, and openly and plainly showed his hostility to Christ, by seeking his life. "Then Herod, when he saw that he was mocked of the wise men, was exceeding wroth, and sent forth, and slew all the children that were in Bethlehem, and in all the coasts thereof, from two years old and under, according to the time he had diligently inquired of the wise men." Matt. 2:16. In Herod we have a manifestation of the general character of persecution. When the design of persecutors can be reached in no other way, the most violent means are used. Herod hesitated not to commit the dreadful crime of murder, and the murder too of innocent infants, to accomplish his purpose, of removing Christ out of the way, that he might have no rival in him for the throne which he occupied, and no reprover of his sins. No doubt he hated the light and feared its exposition of his wrongs. He knew his course of life was wrong, his character faulty, and that the truth would condemn him, and therefore he sought to destroy it in its introduction into the world. The wicked world has always hated the truth because it condemns its spirit and course, and like Herod, has sought to destroy it.

2. The hostility showed by Herod and others to Christ and Christianity, subjected his friends to severe trials. The trials of Joseph and Mary were of a very painful character. Theirs were not only the feelings of true and deep parental affection toward their child, but they were much more. However, they might have failed to comprehend fully the character of their child, the circumstances that attended his birth, and the spiritual impressions that had been made upon their minds, were such as to lead them to look upon him as an unusual child, and as destined to become much more than a common man. It is said of the honored and pious mother of our Lord, in regard to the manner in which she looked at the strange occurrences that had taken place in her family, "But Mary kept all these things, and pondered them in her heart." Luke 2 : 19. Her study of the things referred to, no doubt, threw more or less light upon them, and made her and Joseph feel no common interest in the child that had been born unto them. And, as already remarked, they did not only feel the common feelings of parents to their children, but they felt that this child was to be the deliverer not only of the Jewish nation, but of the human race. Such an idea may not have been grasped by them in all its glory and in all its magnitude; nevertheless, that truth in its germinal character had been planted in their hearts, and it grew to maturity as their child grew to manhood. Now the thought that Herod's bloody decree should be executed on

such a child was an affliction of the most distressing character.

But still, great as were the trials of the parents of this wonderful child, and the devoted friends to the great system of divine truth, that he was born to establish, by his life and death, those trials were not without their useful and happy effects. The trials of the faithful often have had such effects upon their minds as to prepare them for more clear, impressive, and more full manifestations of divine things. The spiritually minded, under trials, become thoughtful, prayful, and observant of the divine teaching. And under such circumstances there will be an expansion of mind, a humiliation of spirit, an enlargement of Christian experience, which will lead to a more full development of Christian character. The danger that Joseph and Mary felt their child—a child that had more than human hold upon their feelings—was exposed to became a matter of the deepest concern to their minds. It became a subject of intense interest to them. It absorbed their thoughts by day and night. And it was at night, when Joseph's mind was dwelling with the greatest anxiety upon the subject, that revelations were made to him from the spirit world. Not knowing where to flee to protect the precious treasure, God's unspeakable gift to man, an angel appeared to him in a dream, and gave him warning, which enabled him to preserve the life of the child. Matt. 2:22. It is a precious principle in God's dealings with us, that the more intensely the soul is exercised within us in regard to divine things, the more susceptible we are of impressions from the spirit world.

When Hagar, in the wilderness, had given the last of the water she had to her child, and when she had laid the lad under a bush to protect him from the burning rays of the sun, and had retired to save her from the sorrow of seeing him die, and when "she lifted up her voice and wept," it was then that her feelings were stretched to their utmost tension of anxiety about her child, that "an angel of God called to Hagar out of heaven and said unto her, what aileth thee, Hagar? fear not; for God hath heard the voice of the lad, where he is. Arise, lift up the lad and hold him in thine hand; and I will make him a great nation. And God opened her eyes and she saw a well of water; and she went and filled the bottle with water and gave the lad drink." Gen. 21: 17-19. Hagar's trial was great, but in that trial she learned more of the divine supplies than she had ever known before. Cases of this kind could be greatly multiplied. The fact seems to be this: the more the spiritual within us is exercised and stirred up, the closer will the spiritual influences without us, and above us, come unto us, and the more thorough will be our acquaintance with them.

3. Though Christ and his cause have had enemies, hostile, formidable, and numerous, and though the friends of Christ have had trials, many and sore, Christ and Christianity yet live, and their friends, though often cast down, have never been forsaken; and often exposed to trials, those trials have been sanctified to their good. Christ escaped from Herod's power, and he escaped, too, from the power of death. And he now lives to die no more.

The cause of Christ has triumphed. It had hostile foes, but it had friends more powerful than were its enemies. It had friends human and divine. Joseph and Mary are types of the former. How anxious were they for the safety of the child Jesus. He was to be the incarnation of Christian truth, as well as the revealer of that truth. In their anxiety for the protection of the infant Messiah, two very important things were observable, and these should characterize the human friends and guardians of Christian truth in every age of the world. These were, (1) a warm and sincere affection. They loved the child that they sought so diligently to protect, with more than the common affection showed by parents to their children. And all the true friends of Christ and his cause must love him supremely. (2) They followed strictly the divine direction. Divine direction was given them through the ministry of angels. We have divine direction given us, to show us how we may honor Christ, and how we may be saved by him in the gospel of the kingdom which he preached when he entered upon his public ministry. We can do nothing better for the truth, nor anything that will the better protect it and promote it, than to strictly follow its directions. Though it may take us into "Egypt," or into circumstances of less liberty and comfort than we might sometimes desire, it will in due time bring us into the "land of Israel," and not only so, but into "the new Jerusalem."

Christianity has also divine protectors. This divine protection was very strikingly manifested in the deliverance of the infant Saviour from the cruel Herod. The divine power was interposed, and the wicked king was removed. And it would seem that heaven's displeasure was showed in his miserable death, for according to Josephus he died a terrible death. Heaven has often interposed its power in behalf of the cause of truth and righteousness, and hence we may confidently conclude they are of God. And as God has owned Christ to be his Son, and put his approval upon his ministry as well as upon his birth, we have no excuse for not believing in him.

In conclusion we would ask you, how does the truth of Christ effect you? Can you unite in the songs of praise sung by men and angels at the birth of Christian truth? Has that truth made you free—free from guilt and condemnation, and filled your hearts with holy peace and joy? Or, does Christ and his truth trouble you as they did Herod and others? If they do, you know why it is. It is because you are not following the divine direction. "There is, therefore, now no condemnation to them that are in Christ Jesus, who walk not after the flesh, but after the spirit." Rom. 8: 1.

XXVIII.
THE GRATEFUL REVIEW.

A SERMON FOR THE CLOSING YEAR.

"And Jacob said, O God of my father Abraham, and God of my father Isaac, the Lord which saidst unto me, return unto thy country, and to thy kindred, and I will deal well with thee; I am not worthy of the least of all the mercies, and of all the truth, which thou hast showed unto thy servant; for with my staff I passed over this Jordan; and now I am become two bands. Deliver me, I pray thee, from the hand of my brother, from the hand of Esau; for I fear him, lest he will come and smite me, and the mother with the children. And thou saidst, I will surely do thee good, and make thy seed as the sand of the sea, which can not be numbered for multitude."—Gen. xxxii. 9–12.

The paragraph read is a part of the Bible history of the eventful life of the patriarch Jacob. His life was subject to the general changes that human life is subject to in our world, in which good and evil are in conflict, both having their influence to some degree either directly or indirectly upon all men. In this part of his history we find him at prayer, and the language of our text is a part of his prayer. He was in great trouble. Domestic affairs in his father-in-law's family became seriously disturbed, and a proper regard to his peace and duty seems to have justified, and perhaps demanded, a separation. Jacob had served his father-in-law Laban twenty years, fourteen years for his two daughters, and six years for cattle. And notwithstanding he had served him so long, and so successfully, Laban's sons became jealous of their brother-in-law Jacob, and prejudiced their father against him. In the beginning of the chapter we have the following: "And he heard the words of Laban's sons, saying, Jacob hath taken away all that was our father's; and of that which was our father's hath he gotten all this glory. And Jacob beheld the coutenance of Laban, and, behold, it was not toward him as before. And the Lord said unto Jacob, return unto the land of thy fathers, and to thy kindred; and I will be with thee." We see from this that the sons of Laban, the brothers-in-law to Jacob, became envious toward him, as we remarked before, and no doubt made the home of Jacob and his family very unpleasant. The Lord, that had seen the afflictions of his people in Egypt when oppressed by Pharaoh (Ex. iii. 7), now saw the affliction of Jacob and directed him to return to the country of his father.

But in escaping from the troubles of his father-in-law, and returning to the home of his youth, another trouble awaited him. He had to meet his offended brother Esau. Thus we perceive that Jacob was in a strait. And in this dilemma he carried his trouble to the Lord in prayer. This is the way that good people—people who have learned to trust the Lord—do. So Peter admonishes, when he says, "Humble yourselves, therefore, under the mighty hand of God, that he may exalt you in due time; casting all your care upon him; for he careth for you."—1 Peter, v. 6, 7. Notice, we are to cast *all* our care upon God. He will bear it all for us. So did our father Jacob at the trying period of his life at which we are now considering him. And we have his beautiful and instructive prayer which we have read, and which we selected for our subject to-day. In it occur these words: "For with my staff I passed over this Jordan; and now I am become two bands." This suggests an important thought in the text, and gives the title of our subject, which will be, *A Grateful Review*. This day, the last day of the year 1882, has suggested the text and the subject. In looking at the prayer of Jacob offered in his perplexity and trouble, we shall notice some of the religious ideas contained in it.

1. *The manner in which he addressed God*, may be looked at with profit. "And Jacob said, O God of my father Abraham, and God of my father Isaac." He addresses himself to God as the God of his fathers. We read of strange gods among the people, and strange gods had even been introduced into Jacob's family, probably through Rachel his wife. But Jacob neither worshiped them, nor tolerated them in his family. Gen. 35: 2. He worshiped and prayed to the God of his fathers, the God whom he well knew, and of whom he learned much of his fathers. God himself testified to Abraham's faithfulness in his family, when he said concerning him, "I know him, that he will command his children and his household after him, and they shall keep the way of the Lord, to do justice and judgment; that the Lord may bring upon Abraham that which he hath spoken of him." Gen. 18: 19. The ancient patriarchs and saints were careful to instruct their children in the ways and of the wonders of the Lord, as is evident from the following words of the psalmist: "We have heard with our ears, O God, our fathers have told us, what work thou didst in their days, in the times of old. How thou didst drive out the heathen with they hand, and plantedst them; how thou didst afflict the people, and cast them out." Psalm 44: 1, 2. Thus it was that the children were taught to know God. And being taught of God as they were, and learning from

their parents the wonderful works of God, the impressions made upon the minds of the children were lasting and profitable.

. With God and his altar of worship, the children of the ancient fathers were familiar. And the love, reverence and devotion, which the parents showed to God, endeared him to their children, and thus the God of the parents became the God of their children. And hence Jacob's manner of addressing God, "O God of my father Abraham, and God of my father Isaac." And some of you, brethren and sisters, have got your first impressions of God through your parents. The customs among our brethren have been such that parents have taken the children with them to the common meetings for worship, and to our love feasts, and thus they have been brought into associations with the service of God, and seeing their parents happy there, and also happy in their religion at home, they have formed favorable ideas of God and his service, and have made their father's God their God. And let us all who have families and children now, or who may hereafter have, so worship and serve God, that he may so bless us, and so make his blessings manifest to us, that our children may become so favorably impressed with the character of our God, that they will choose him for their God and portion

2. *Jacob in his prayer, plead the promises of God to him.* He wisely and properly took advantage of God's promises to him, and the remembrance of them, no doubt, greatly encouraged and emboldened him to urge his case before the Lord. "And thou saidst, I will surely do thee good, and make thy seed as the sand of the sea, which can not be numbered for multitude." Thus did he remind God of his promise. Such a promise God had given him on a former occasion. Gen. 28: 14, 15. And he knew that that promise had not been fulfilled. And perhaps he knew, or had some idea

of the fact, that that promise did not only affect him as an individual, but also affected the purposes of God in regard to the Jewish nation. And it might have occurred to him, had his mind grasped the promise in some of its prophetic aspects, that should he fall a victim to the anger of his brother Esau, the purposes and plans of God would be interfered with. And hence it was, perhaps, that he plead the promise as he did.

Jacob's example in pleading the promise of God in prayer, commends itself to our consideration, and is worthy of our imitation. Though God does not now appear to us, and make the promises to us personally and individually as he did to the saints of old, we have many of his promises contained in both the Old and the New Testaments, and those promises to whomsoever they were made, or to whatever churches they were made, as far as they are applicable to us, and as we may need their fulfillment to promote our spirituality of life, our edification, or our welfare in any respect, belong to us, and are virtually made to us. If we belong to the family of believers, or to them that love and serve God, his promises are the common portion and blessing of them all. And further, there are promises also made unto sinners—penitent sinners. Whenever a person desires to turn from his evil ways, and to do right, and to live a new and divine life, such a person may "come boldly unto the throne of grace, that he may obtain mercy, and find grace to help in time of need."—Heb. 4 : 16. "To this man will I look," says God, "even to him that is poor and of a contrite spirit, and trembleth at my word."—Isa. 66 : 2.

To approach God acceptably, and to prevail with him in prayer, we must pray in faith. This is difficult for us to do sometimes. We are tempted to doubt. But we must not doubt, but believe. The condition upon which we may expect our prayers to be answered is thus stated by the apostle James: "But let him ask in faith, nothing wavering. For he that wavereth is like a wave of the sea driven with the wind and tossed. For let not that man think that he shall receive anything of the Lord."—James 1: 6, 7. But when we know that God has promised to give us what we pray for, and that he has invited us to come to him with our prayers, this will beget faith in us, and enable us to believe that we shall receive the things we pray for. It is very desirable and important that we keep in mind the promises of God when we go to him in prayer.

3. *Another consideration encouraged Jacob to pray to God for deliverance from the hand of Esau, and that was the thought that God had directed him to take the journey that he was then taking.* "And Jacob said, O God of my father Abraham, and God of my father Isaac, the Lord which saidst unto to me, return unto thy country, and to thy kindred, and I will deal well with thee." When the Lord saw that Jacob was not receiving the kind treatment from his father-in-law and brothers-in-law that he should receive, he directed him to return unto to the land of his fathers. And this Jacob reminded the Lord of as we have seen. When we ask the Lord for help to do some work, or to perform some duty to which he has called us, we may be encouraged to approach him with freedom, and to ask in faith. For surely if we need his help to do what he has called us to do, he will give us that help. And he will never ask us to do anything but what we can do with his help. If we are doing something that we know is wrong in the sight of God, and contrary to his holy law, we would not dare to ask him to help and bless us in such work. And if we would attempt to do something about the lawfulness of which we would have some doubts, we could not pray in much faith to God for his help, and of course we would not obtain his help. "Ye

ask and receive not," says James, "because ye ask amiss, that ye may consume it upon your lusts." James 4 : 3. We must not expect God's blessings when we would use them in gratifying our lusts. But when we are prosecuting the work of the Lord, or pursuing a course to which he has called us, we then can go with confidence to God in prayer, and look up to him without shame upon our countenance, or in our hearts. Then we can indeed come " boldly to the throne of grace."

4. *The self-abasement that he felt and showed in his prayer, was a commendable trait in Jacob's character, and especially when he was a suppliant before the throne of God.* When men with their entire dependence upon God, and all their infirmities, and unworthiness, come into his presence, who is all holiness and purity, and in whom " is no darkness at all," I John 1 : 5, humiliation and self-abasement well become them. This excellency of character with many others Jacob exhibited. "I am not worthy," said he in his prayer, "of the least of all the mercies, and of all the truth, which thou hast showed unto thy servant." Jacob was greatly humbled under the thought that God had dealt so graciously and liberally with him, notwithstanding he was entirely unworthy of the very least of all the favors he had received from him. This is an amiable feeling. Meekness is one of the characteristics of the Spirit that is in the sight of God of great price. 1 Peter 3 : 4. Hence we are admonished to be "clothed with humility," and the reason given is, that "God resisteth the proud, and giveth grace to the humble." 1 Peter 5 : 5. This feeling of humility or self-abasement is a characteristic of all the saints of God. Abraham possessed it. He said when pleading with God for Sodom, " Behold now, I have taken upon me to speak unto the Lord, which am but dust and ashes." Gen. 18 : 27. David possessed much of the feeling of humility. When God revealed

to him his gracious purpose in regard to his son Solomon, he was greatly affected, and said, "Who am I, O Lord God, and what is mine house, that thou hast brought me hitherto? And yet this was a small thing in thine eyes, O God; for thou hast also spoken of thy servant's house for a great while to come, and hast regarded me according to the estate of a man of high degree, O Lord God." 1 Chron. 17:16, 17. Though God treated David with great honor and respect, and as "a man of high degree," it did not make him proud or vain. Paul spoke of himself as "the least of all saints," Eph. 3:8. True humility consists in low opinions of ourselves as we see was the case with those holy men to whom we have referred. There is no element in the renewed mind upon which more depends for the progressive and full development of Christian character, than humility. Indeed a person that is vain and conceity, will not improve much in anything that is good. And while we would say to all, we say it with emphasis to you, young women and young men, "Be not wise in your conceit." Rom. 12:16. Self-conceit will never commend anybody to the wise and good. It is evidence of both a mental and spiritual defect.

5. *We also have in our subject, Jacob's grateful acknowledgment upon a review of God's gracious dealings with him in the past.* "With my staff I passed over the Jordan; and now I am become two bands." The true spirit of religious devotion is favorable to, and promotive of, ideas and reflections. It promotes the health and vigor of the mind. With the time which he had lived, full of instructive incidents, with the peculiar surroundings that then surrounded him, and with the anticipated future before him, his mind was active, and his thoughts were many. He reviewed the past. Former years with many of their occurrences passed in review before his anxious and devotional mind. He remembered that some twenty years before, he had passed over the

memorable stream of Jordan a lonely wanderer, with his pilgrim staff, comparatively young, inexperienced and poor. He compares his condition at that time with his condition as it now was some twenty years after. He finds the contrast was striking and great. As remarked already, when he passed this way twenty years before, he was comparatively young, lonely, inexperienced and poor. Now he is rich in the blessings of domestic happiness, rich in secular wealth, and he was also enriched by a more full and experimental knowledge of God, for God had been with him, protected him, and blessed his labors. To the depth and sincerity of his piety, his words and actions bear testimony. Upon the review of his life, he gratefully acknowledges God to be the author and giver "of all the mercies, and of all the truth, that had crowned his life and his labors.

And now, dear friends, let us review our lives from the point of time we occupy to-day, the last day of the year of our Lord, eighteen hundred and eighty-two. And upon such a review, what shall we find? In comparing our present life with the past, will we find an improvement? We trust many can. God has blessed some of us with temporal blessings, and though none of us may be wealthy, the pecuniary circumstances of some are more easy, and more free from embarrassment than they once were. The domestic joys of some have increased, and we have happy homes and families. None of us feel that we have much knowledge, but we have learned some things we once did not know, and we trust we are a little wiser than we once were. And last of all, and best of all, some of us feel that in reviewing our past lives, and in comparing our present spiritual state with what it once was, we find we are not "dead in trespasses and sins," as we once were, but "have passed from death unto life," and have made some progress in the divine life of the holy, and have laid up for ourselves some treasure in heaven. With Jacob, we can say, applying his language to our inner and spiritual life, "with my staff I passed over this Jordan; and now I am become two bands." And to God we ascribe the glory, for each will say, "I am not worthy of the least of all the mercies, and of all the truth, which thou hast shewed unto thy servant." Dear friends, God has been good to us all, and let his goodness lead us to repentance, and from henceforth let us all consecrate ourselves to his service.

6. *Finally, notice the success of Jacob's prayer.* The meeting between him and Esau occurred. But Esau did not come to meet Jacob as he feared he would as "an armed man" for battle. But he came as a brother with extended arms to embrace Jacob. "And Esau ran to meet him, and embraced him, and fell on his neck, and kissed him, and they wept." Gen. 33:4. Such was the meeting between Jacob and Esau! Esau's anger gave place to love, and the meeting was a meeting of loving brothers. Jacob's prayer was answered, and God's power was remarkably manifested. "A brother offended is harder to be won than a strong city." Prov. 18:19. But God's power can subdue even an offended brother. We have in the reconciliation of Jacob and Esau, a confirmation of the following promise: "When a man's ways please the Lord, he maketh even his enemies to be at peace with him." Prov. 16:7. May the God of Abraham, and of Isaac, and of Jacob, and of all the faithful, be our God.

XXIX.

THE RELIGIOUS CHARACTER OF COMMON BUSINESS IN THE LIFE OF CHRISTIANS.

"Servants, obey in all things your masters, according to the flesh; not with eye-service, as men pleasers; but in singleness of heart, fearing God; and whatsoever ye do, do it heartily, as to the Lord, and not unto men; knowing that of the Lord ye shall receive the reward of the inheritance; for ye serve the Lord Christ. But he that doeth wrong shall receive for the wrong which he hath done; and there is no respect of persons. Masters give unto your servants that which is just and equal; knowing that ye also have a Master in heaven."—Col. 3: 22-25; 4: 1.

We have read the first verse of the fourth chapter, as the apostle's admonition to the masters seems naturally to follow his admonition to the servants. Masters and servants are correlative terms, implying reciprocal duties to each other, as do the words fathers and children, and husbands and wives. And as these terms imply reciprocal duties to each other, there are obligations growing out of these relations resting upon each party. And the apostle is teaching, in this part of his epistle to the Colossians, the importance of meeting these obligations. We select on this occasion for our subject the apostle's admonition to servants, as this contains a grand truth, and one of very wide application, namely, this, *The religious character of common business in the lives of Christians.*

We shall present our ideas under the following heads:
I. Christ is our Master.
II. The service we are to render to him.
III. The reward of the service rendered to Christ.
IV. The impartiality of the Divine Master.

I. Christ is our Master. He said to his disciples in his interview with them when he washed their feet, "Ye call me

Master and Lord ; and ye say well ; for so I am."—John 13 : 13. *Master* here expresses the relation of the disciples to Christ as learners, and Lord, their relation to him as servants. There seems to be some difference in the relation of Christ to his disciples expressed by the words, Master and Lord. And the difference is probably something like that we have given. We are not to serve the Lord in ignorance, but we are to do it intelligently. Hence he teaches as well as commands. And as he teaches the truth, when we obey him, we may feel that we are doing reverence and obedience to the truth. As Master stands here in connection with Lord, Master is to be understood in the sense of Teacher. And in some translations we have the article added to Master and Lord, making the reading, *the* Master and *the* Lord, showing the supremacy of Christ over all others, in accordance with his teaching when he says, "For one is your Master, even Christ.—Matt. 23 : 8.

But to whom is Christ Master? Or, who are his servants? Does he require obedience and service of those only who have given themselves to him, and who are his professed disciples? His requirements are by no means confined to these. When the Father spake out of the cloud, and said in referring to the Saviour, "This is my beloved Son, in whom I am well pleased; hear ye Him" (Matt., 17 : 5), did the Father mean that his command to hear his Son was designed only for the disciples of Christ? We must not confine the command to them. He came to call the sinners to repentance, and they should hear the call. And if they do not hear, they are disobedient, and as such they will be dealt with in the great rewarding day. It is said in our text, "He that doeth wrong shall receive for the wrong which he hath done." Now, we can not confine the application of these words to the disciples, and understand from them that the disciples only shall receive for the wrong that they have done. According to such an explanation the wicked would go free, while only those among the disciples of Christ that do wrong will be punished. Such an explanation will not do. We must, therefore, come to the conclusion that Christ is our common Master, and that we all owe Him our service, whether we are serving Him or not. It is not only that which we have promised that we are under obligations to perform, but we are under obligations to do whatever Christ, our Master, commands us to do. "And the times of this ignorance God winked at; but now commandeth all men everywhere to repent, because he hath appointed a day, in the which he will judge the world in righteousness by that man whom he hath ordained; whereof he hath given assurance unto all men, in that he hath raised him from the dead."—Acts 17 : 30, 31. Here we see who are under obligations to God. He has commanded all men to repent or reform; and he has a perfect right to do so. And we are his servants, whether we are serving Him or not. But if we do not obey his commands, and reform and serve Him, we then do wrong, and we shall receive accordingly.

II. *The service we are to render to Him.*

"Servants, obey in all things your masters according to the flesh, not with eye-service as men-pleasers, but in singleness of heart, fearing God. And whatsoever ye do, do it heartily, as to the Lord, and not unto men." This language is somewhat remarkable. Or, perhaps, we should rather say, the idea contained in the language is remarkable. This language was addressed to servants, and perhaps some of these would come under the class of servants called slaves. Many of these servants, and especially the slaves, were required to do a great amount of labor, and often unpleasant and painful labor, and were exposed to sufferings of the most trying character—sufferings that could scarcely be endured. And, notwithstanding the hard and suffering condition of the servants in those ancient times in which the apostle wrote his epistle in which our text occurs, it seems that some embraced Christianity. And it was to instruct and encourage and comfort these that the apostle wrote as he did.

The universal terms used by the apostle in admonishing servants to faithfulness to their masters, at first thought might seem to convey the idea that the apostle would have them to obey their masters in spiritual as well as in secular things: "Servants, obey in all things your masters." But the words "*according to the flesh*," following the words "Servants, obey in all things your masters," modify these last words, and convey the idea that the relation between the masters and servants was only a temporary and worldly relation, and did not extend to spiritual things. Or, in other words, what seems to be a universal command, "Servants, obey in all things your masters," must be understood with the same limitation that applies to all the commands that enjoin relative duties. In all cases in which the commands of men conflict with the laws of God, we are to "obey God rather than men."—Acts v. 29.

But the words, "and whatsoever ye do, do it heartily, as to the Lord, and not unto men," set secular and even menial service before us in a manner that is calculated to elevate and dignify all lawful human labor. These expressive words of the apostle resolve all labor into a divine service, for it was not the civil magistrate who is declared to be "the minister of God" (Rom. xiii. 4), nor was it the learned professor in our college work in leading the minds of youth into the higher departments of science, nor the teacher in our common schools in his useful and responsible calling, nor was it any of the many laborers in the different offices in the Christian church, that the apostle addressed when he said, "Whatsoever ye do, do it heartily, as to the Lord, and not unto men." But his admonition of encouragement was given to servants, in their humble calling, and oftentimes in their hard and unappreciated and unrequited labors. And probably it was also designed for slaves whose manhood was sunk into chattels as far as slavery could so degrade them.

And what a soul-comforting, soul-inspiring, and soul-elevating thought was it to the poor laboring and oft oppressed servants, to learn from their Christian brother Paul, who was directly prompted by the Holy Spirit to speak to them and for them, that if their labors in their lawful calling were sanctified by the spirit of Christianity, which they had professed, those labors were done to the Lord, and that they would be remembered, and in due time be rewarded by him! This great truth is plainly taught by Paul in our text: "And whatsoever ye do, do it heartily, as to the Lord, and not unto men." This language was addressed directly to servants. And it is very evident that it had reference, not to spiritual service or devotional duties, but to secular labors. Constituted as human society is, and bearing the various relations to one another that we do, and our interests being so many, and so various, our duties become numerous and various, for it is by the faithful performance of our duties that we do our part in promoting the well-being of society. And as God has had the welfare of mankind in view in giving to all their positions and duties, whether according to the laws of nature or revelation, we are serving God when we are doing our lawful work, whether in the church or in the world.

A due regard to God, and a settled purpose of heart to co-operate with him in his benevolent designs to promote the entire interests of our race, are the governing principles in the life of Christians. And these principles should govern masters and servants, and parents and children, and all intelligent beings in all their relations to one another. And when these principles do govern us, and we possess that state of Christian experience and attainment implied in the apostle's language when he says, "Whether, therefore, ye eat, or drink, or whatsoever ye do, do all to the glory of God" (1 Cor. 10: 31), our secular or business duties, our domestic duties, our civil duties, and all our duties, partake of a religious character, and become a part of our religion. Christianity sanctifies the whole life of a truly faithful Christian. This grand truth is practically taught by the apostle in our text.

And as Christian servants were serving God as well as their worldly masters, they are admonished in our text to "do it heartily, as to the Lord, and not unto men." That is, they were not serving men only, or chiefly, but God also, and they are therefore admonished to do it heartily, or sincerely, for God will accept of no service but that which comes from the heart. This sincerity or heartiness in service alone distinguishes it from what the apostle calls, in our text, "eye-service."

Eye-service is service done under the eye of the master. Unfaithful and dishonest servants will labor very diligently, perhaps, while the master or overseer is watching them. But in the absence of the master, they will often neglect their work. The principle inculcated by the apostle, and which we have been considering, namely, that the Lord is the great Master to whom all our service should be mainly directed, is calculated, if practically carried out, to make all men honest in their service rendered to their masters. For while they are serving their worldly masters, they are also serving God, and though the eyes of the former may not be upon them, the eyes of God always are. Unfaithfulness in work is a sin, and God will see it, and mark it.

III. The reward of the service rendered to Christ.

It is not every servant that succeeds in life and makes a fortune. But the Christian servant does. "Ye shall receive the reward of the inheritance: for ye serve the Lord Christ." Truly, "Godliness is profitable unto all things, having promise of the lifé that now is, and of that which is to come." 1 Tim. 4: 8. Notice it is "the reward of the inheritance." The reward will be a glorious possession. "In my Father's house," said the heavenly Master, "are many mansions: if it were not so, I would have told you. I go to prepare a place for you. And if I go and prepare a place for you, I will come again, and receive you unto myself; that where I am, there ye may be also."—John 14: 2, 3. Such are the encouraging words of the divine Master to his servants. Equally encouraging and comforting are the following words of the Christian's Master: "If any man serve me, let him follow me; and where I am, there shall also my servant be: if any man serve me, him will my Father honor."—John 12: 26. How cheering is the prospect to the poor servant or slave, who is faithfully serving "the Lord Christ," as well as his worldly master, of the "glory, honor and immortality," that will reward his labors.

> "A home in heaven! what a joyful thought,
> As the poor man toils in his weary lot!
> His heart oppress'd, and with anguish driv'n
> From his home below to his home in heav'n."

But it is not only the consideration of the heavenly inheritance that should incite the Christian servant, and all Christians, to faithfulness in all their relative duties. They shall not only lose that reward if they are unfaithful and do wrong, but they "shall receive for the wrong" which they have done. This means they shall be punished for their wrong doing, for their idleness, their dishonesty, and for their hypocrisy and deceitfulness. Such considerations or incentives are well calculated to encourage us all to perform our duties and service faithfully, whatever troubles we may have to endure in the prosecution of our work.

IV. The impartiality of the Divine Master.

"And there is no respect of persons." This means there is no respect of persons with him who will be the final judge of both masters and servants. In the last verse of those we have read, and the first verse of the fourth chapter, we have these words: "Masters, give unto your servants that which is just and equal: knowing that ye also have a Master in heaven." As we said in the early part of our discourse, Christ is the common Master of us all. He is the Master of human masters as well as the Master of the servants of men. And he will also be the judge of masters as well as of servants. "And there is no respect of persons" with him. "He will judge the world in righteousness." And if the master has done wrong to the servant, or the servant to the master, he shall receive for the wrong. And so in regard to all the duties that have been incumbent upon us, in consideration of the relations we have sustained to one another, and to our heavenly Master.

Let us imagine, and the scene will be an impressive one when it occurs, and it will occur, the old Roman and Grecian masters with their servants and slaves standing before the judgment seat of Christ, having justice meted out to them all! And we may add to the scene, American masters with their slaves! Alas, for the cruel tyrant! But joyful will be the time to the truly faithful servant of Christ! And, dear friends, let us not forget that with those masters and servants we will all appear, to be judged according to our works, and our everlasting destiny will also be according to our works. How important then it is that we all should be diligent and faithful servants, serving "the Lord Christ," as he is the Master of us all. And if we do so, we shall receive "the reward of the inheritance."

XXX.
A TEST OF CHRISTIAN CHARACTER.

"And every man that hath this hope in him purifieth himself, even as he is pure."—I. John 3 : 3.

Our subject will be, *A Test of Christian Character.* There are many tests of Christian character presented unto us in the scriptures, and that which is contained in our text is one of them. In the verses preceding our text we have presented to us the hope of the Christian. And from the hope itself the apostle proceeds to notice the effects of that hope, and says in the verse we have read as our text, "And every man that hath this hope in him purifieth himself, even as he is pure." Hence, we have in our text, *A test of Christian Character.* Every person that is a sincere and true Christian, and possesses and enjoys the hope of the Christian, is represented in our text to be engaged in the work of purifying himself. And all persons who are not endeavoring to purify themselves whatever their pretentions may be to Christian character, and the enjoyment of the pleasures of Christian hope, have neither. And if they think they have, they are deceiving themselves. The accompaniment of Christian character and Christian hope is a desire and striving for purity.

In opening and applying our text, we shall notice,

I. *The hope to which allusion is made in the text.*

II. *The effects of that hope.*

Under these heads the leading ideas of the text may be presented.

I. *The hope to which allusion is made in the text.* The verse preceding our text reads thus: "Beloved, now we are the sons of God, and it doth not yet appear what we shall be: but we know that, when he shall appear, we shall be like him; for we shall see him as he is." Christians already in this life are made the sons of God. This sonship is not a subject of hope, but it is now possessed. It is possessed when the new birth of the Christian takes places, or when he is "born of water and of the spirit." John 3:5. Or "by the word of God." I Peter 1:23. But while Christians are made the sons of God at the time of their regeneration, and are put into possession of all the honor and blessedness that are implied in that relation, these do not constitute all that the saints are entitled to. There is more reserved for them, and this constitutes the hope of Christians while they are in this life. Hope covers or embraces all that is reserved for Christians in the life that is to come. They are to see and be like the Lord. And in presenting this form of the Christian hope as we have it in connection with our text, we may notice,

I. The seeing of the Lord, "We shall see him as he is." That is, as he is, or will be when he makes his appearance. We have the same idea presented to us in a passage in Paul's epistle to Titus. And it is there presented in a very impressive manner. Christians are represented as "Looking for that blessed hope, and the glorious appearing of the great God and our Saviour Jesus Christ."—Titus 2:13. Here, as in the verse preceding our text, the hope of the Christian is represented to be the witnessing of the "glorious appearing of the great God and our Saviour Jesus Christ." It is to be a glorious appearance. We have the representation of it, in some degree, in the transfiguration of our Saviour on the mountain, in the presence of three of the disciples, Peter, James and John. "And after six days Jesus taketh with him Peter and James and John, and leadeth them up into high mountain apart by themselves: and he was transfigured before them. And his raiment became shining exceeding white as snow; so as no fuller on earth can white them."—Mark 9:2. This indeed was a "glorious appearing of the great God and our Saviour Jesus Christ." And something like this will be the appearance of our Saviour when he comes the "second time without sin unto salvation," only his appearance at his second coming will, if possible, be still more glorious. For when he comes in the glory of his second advent, he will be accompanied by angels and by his saints. And this will greatly add to the grandeur and glory of the scene. The sight will be a glorious one, the face of our Lord shining as the sun, and his "raiment white as the light!" It is very difficult, and indeed impossible, for us to properly conceive the glory of the appearance of our Lord, at his second coming, though we have the transfiguration on the mountain to help us to form an idea of his glorious appearance at that time. And probably the transfiguration of our Lord while he was here on earth the first time was designed in part to assist us in forming a proper idea of his appearance at his second coming.

We would remind you that the glorious sight that constitutes in part the hope of the Christian is said to be the "appearing of the great God and our Saviour Jesus Christ." So Paul expresses it, John referring more particularly to the Father when he says, "We know that when he shall appear, we shall be like him, for we shall see him as he is," might seem to refer to the appearing of the Father. But as he had been speaking of the Son in the previous chapter, and as the idea of the Son pervades his writing more or less throughout, we may consider the Son as the character referred to. We, however, have the idea presented unto us in the scripture, that we shall see God as well as the Son of God, and, consequently, John, in the verse preceding our text, may have reference to the Father as well as to the Son. Christ was God manifested in the flesh. Hence he said to Philip, "he that hath seen me hath seen the Father."—John 14:9. And it is altogether likely, that when our Lord comes at his second advent, there will be a much clearer manifestation of God than there ever had been before. This is probably the reason why the glorious appearing at our Lord's second advent embraces the appearing of the Father as well as that of the Son. "The glorious appearing of the great God, and our Saviour Jesus Christ."

But let us look at the manner in which we shall see the Lord. There is a sense in which we see the Lord now, or in this life. But now, "we walk by faith and not by sight."— 2 Cor. 5:7. To our believing minds things present themselves as we have learned them, and as we have believed them. Last night while we were attending to the ordinances and services belonging to our meeting, many things were presented to our minds if we were properly engaged in the religious work of the occasion, and we saw them by faith. While we were engaged in washing one another's feet, in obedience to our Lord's command, had we not our Lord before us performing the same work that we were doing? No doubt we had. And in our mental visions we saw our blessed Redeemer bowing himself to wash his disciples' feet. So, when we were commemorating his death by the expressive symbols we used, did we not by faith see him nailed to the cross, and dying as a ransom to redeem us from the curse of the law? In that suffering condition we saw the Lord by faith.

But this is not the way in which we shall see him when he comes again to complete our redemption. It is not by faith that we shall then see him, but by the sense of sight, for it is said, "Behold, he cometh with clouds; and every eye shall see him."—Rev. 1:7. And the angels addressed the disciples as they were gazing into heaven when the Saviour ascended from them, as follows: "Ye men of Galilee, why stand ye gazing up into heaven? this same Jesus, which is taken up from you unto heaven, shall so come in like manner as ye have seen him go into heaven."—Acts 1:11. Another passage that shows that his coming will be a visible coming is the following: "And they shall say to you, see here; or, see there: go not after them, nor follow them. For as the lightning, that lighteneth out of the one part under heaven, shineth unto the other part under heaven; so shall also the Son of man be in his day."—Luke 17:23, 24. But the language of Job is very clear and expressive. It is this: "For I know that my Redeemer liveth, and that he shall stand at the latter day upon the earth: and though after my skin worms destroy this body, yet in my flesh shall I see God; whom I shall see for myself, and mine eyes shall behold, and not another."—Job 19:25-27. Job's views of the future were very definite and positive. "Yet in my flesh I shall see God." The mind has eyes with which we can see God by faith, as we have already remarked. But Job speaks of seeing God in the flesh, that is, his Redeemer and of beholding him with his eyes. It is, however, in the resurrection state that he and all the saints will behold the Redeemer. And this appearing of our glorified Lord to his saints is now their hope, and it will be to them an unspeakable enjoyment when they realize it. To see him face to face, and not through a glass darkly, will be a sight that will fill the soul with delight and rapture.

This language of Job implies a personal view of the Redeemer. "Whom I shall see for myself, and mine eyes shall behold, and not another." This language means that Job himself would see his Redeemer, and not another see him for him. In our present state, much of our knowledge comes through others. In our early Christian life, much that we learn of the dealings of God with his people, we learn through the experience of others. You young Christian believers have not yet learned what older ones have of the gracious dealings of the Lord with his people. That is, you have not learned it by experience, but you have learned it from others. In due time, if you are faithful, you will experience it yourselves. You will know it, not merely from the testimony of others, but by your own consciousness. Much that we know by faith, we shall hereafter know by our own consciousness, or by our own senses, we mean by the senses of our spiritual bodies, for we shall have spiritual bodies, 1 Cor. 15 : 44, and with the eyes of those spiritual bodies we shall behold "the glorious appearing of the Great God and our Saviour Jesus Christ." And we shall behold him ourselves, and obtain a knowledge of him from our own personal observation and experience. We now know something of the glory and character of our Lord's appearing. Peter, James and John saw him in his glorified state, and they have communicated unto us what they saw and felt when on the mount of transfiguration. And we read their account with interest and delight. But we now get the knowledge from others. After a while we shall see him for ourselves, and have all the holy pleasure and delight of seeing our blessed Lord in his glorified form, with his face shining as the sun, and his raiment white as the light. This is a part of the hope we have in us, and this hope will be fully realized in due time.

2. But however delightful the thought of seeing our Redeemer in his glorified form is to us, filling as it does the believing soul with holy rapture, this is not the climax or the full extent of the hope alluded to in our text. And we proceed to notice that we shall not only see our Redeemer when he comes in his glory, but we shall be like him. "We know that, when we shall appear, we shall be like him; for we shall see him as he is." This is still better. To see him as he will be when he comes, by his own people, those who love his appearance, and to enjoy his presence, and to be with him forever, expresses a degree of " joy that is unspeaka

ble and full of glory." And if so, what shall be the effect of the thought of being like him! This seems to be almost too much for the mind to grasp, or our faith to believe. But that is no more than what is promised, and for the enjoyment of it, God will prepare us. "Beloved, now are we the sons of God, and it doth not yet appear, what we shall be; but we know that, when he shall appear, we shall be like him; for we shall see him as he is." Yes, it is indeed so, "it doth not yet appear what we shall be." We only know that we shall be like our Lord, and that is enough to fill us with holy joy. "Our conversation is in heaven; from whence also we look for the Saviour, the Lord Jesus Christ; who shall change our vile body, that it may be fashioned like unto his glorious body, according to the working whereby he is able even to subdue all things unto himself." Phil. 3:20, 21. This is plain and positive. Our Lord's glorious body is the pattern, and the divine power that which is to conform us to that pattern. The hope itself is great, but the foundation which sustains it is amply able to do so.

II. We shall notice in the next place the effects of this hope. And every man that hath this hope in him purified himself even as Christ is pure. The fifth verse of the chapter from which our text is taken reads as follows: "And ye know that he was manifested to take away our sins; and in him is no sin." Then our Lord is not only pure in himself, but he came into the world to make men pure. And different considerations require that those who profess to be the disciples of Christ should purify themselves. (a) Consistency requires it. As Christ himself is pure, and as the heaven which he has promised to his people and for which he has prepared them is pure, it would seem to follow that they should be pure. If they love a pure Saviour, and desire to enjoy a pure heaven, they can not with any consistency take any pleasure in sin, or have any fellowship with it. It is altogether inconsistent with Christian character, Christian hope, and Christian principles.

(b.) The safety of Christians also requires their purity. Sin is destructive as well as corrupting in its tendency. It was because sin disqualifies men for the fellowship of God, and the enjoyment of heaven, that Christ came to save sinners. And if sinners can be saved in their sins, why did Christ come and suffer and die? But we can not go to heaven defiled by sin. Of the holy city, the new Jerusalem, the future home of the saints, it is said, "And there shall in no wise enter into it anything that defileth, neither whatsoever worketh abomination, or maketh a lie; but they which are written in the Lamb's book of life." Surely then every man that has the hope of becoming an inhabitant of that city must purify himself. And our Lord says, " Blessed are the pure in heart: for they shall see God." Matt. 5 : 8. It follows that the impure shall not see him.

Finally, let it be noticed that this work of purification is a work that every man must do for himself. "Every man that hath this hope in him purifieth himself." Another can not do this work for us. Each one of us must do it for himself. God through Christ has provided the means for purification, and we are to apply those means. These means are contained in the gospel of Christ, and by properly observing them, purification of heart, life and character will follow. Hence the following language of Peter: "Seeing ye have purified your souls in obeying the truth through the Spirit unto unfeigned love of the brethren, see that ye love one another with a pure heart fervently: being born again, not of corruptible seed, but of incorruptible, by the word of God, which liveth and abideth for ever." I. Peter 1 : 22, 23. It is then by obeying "the truth as it is in Jesus," that we purify ourselves.

In view of the glorious character of the Christian hope,

and of its great importance, let us become Christians as we all may do, and "cleanse ourselves from all filthiness of the flesh and spirit, perfecting holiness in the fear of the Lord." 2 Cor. 7:1. Then we shall see the Lord, be like him, and be for ever with him.

XXXI.
CHRISTIANITY A HID TREASURE.

"Again, the kingdom of heaven is like unto treasure hid in a field; the which when a man hath found, he hideth, and for joy thereof goeth and selleth all that he hath, and buyeth the field."—Matt. 13 : 44.

Our text is one of seven parables which our Lord here uses to illustrate "the kingdom of heaven" or Christianity for we may regard the phrase, "the kingdom of heaven" as here used equivalent to Christianity. And each of these parables present something peculiar to Christianity, or presents it under some aspect different to what the others do. And the great Christian teacher in using so many parables or metaphors to illustrate " the kingdom of heaven" under its various aspects shows the greatness and the richness of his subject, and his anxiety to have it fully understood by his hearers under all its various and numerous aspects. Our Lord in his teaching fully appreciated the ignorance of men concerning divine and heavenly things, and the difficulties the teachers who taught them spiritual things had to contend with, in communicating to them a knowledge of such things, and hence his frequent use of parables, and of parables, too, of the plainest kind. His teaching was characterized by great wisdom, discretion, earnestness, tenderness and persuasion; and it was not without the greatest propriety that it was said of Him, " Never man spake like this man."

The parable of our text is comprised in the single verse that we have read. It is short, but very expressive. "The kingdom of heaven is like unto treasure hid in a field; the which, when a man hath found, he hideth, and for joy thereof goeth and selleth all that he hath and buyeth that field." To understand the parable, and to see its beauty and fitness, we must bear in mind the state of things concerning the hiding of treasures as they exist in the East. In the parable there is represented as a treasure, money or something precious buried in the earth by the person who had owned it. This was done that it might be kept in safety. The people in the East had not the safes, and banks, and the various facilities for securing their money and jewels that we have. And yet the state of society, and the frequent changes of the governments under which the people lived, made it necessary for them to secure their money well, if they would not lose it. It is said that many rich men in the East divide their goods into three parts, thus: One part they employ in trade, or for their present support; one part they turn into jewels, which they can take with them should it be necessary for them to flee; while they bury the third part. Then should they go to war and be killed, or should they go away and not return, it would remain hid until by chance some lucky person, while walking over the field, or plowing or digging in the field, would find it. For the owner would not permit any person to know where he had buried his treasure. Where this practice obtains, persons very often in a very short time rise from poverty to great wealth by finding a hidden treasure. And when such a treasure would be found it would cause great joy to him who found it; and to a person thus finding a hid treasure, and experiencing great joy at the result, our Lord compares a person finding or obtaining the "kingdom of heaven," or Christianity.

This parable, with its practical instructions, we propose to call your attention to this evening. Our subject will be, *Christianity a hid treasure;* and several important lessons may be learned from the parable.

1. We observe that Christianity is a treasure, or something of great value. You all know that a treasure is something of great value. But there is one idea in a treasure that is not always noticed, and it agrees so well in its present application to Christianity, that we will give Webster's explanation, and in that we have the idea I have alluded to. He thus describes treasure: 1. "Wealth accumulated; especially, a stock or store of money in reserve. 2. A great quantity of anything collected for future use; abundance." You will notice that there is in Webster's definition of treasure an idea in reference to the future. This is the idea we alluded to when we said there is an idea in the meaning of treasure that is not always noticed. Webster brings out this idea. He makes it something in "reserve," something "for future use." How well this expresses the character of Christianity. It is indeed a treasure held in reserve, and for future use as well as for present use.

There are several rules by which the value of an object is to be estimated. We can but notice a couple of these for want of time. There are several points in the parable that we want to bring out. 1. The first rule that we shall notice is the decision of competent judges. Whatever object is declared valuable by persons whose judgments are considered good upon such subjects, will have for this reason a reputation for goodness. There is a pretty general inclination or readiness to give weight to the authority of those we think are competent to judge. Young people, though very often not as submissive to their parents as they should be, still they will pretty generally have respect to the judgment of their parents. We think it very likely that some of you students that are here at school, are here because your parents thought it would be well for you to come. Perhaps they told you that they experienced disadvantages from their want of a better education, and advised you to go to school, though your own inclination may not have been very strong in that direction.

Now let us apply the foregoing thoughts to Christianity. And we ask your attention to the fact, that we have in our text the judgment of the Son of God upon the value of Christianity. He declares it is like a treasure. You all will acknowledge His competency to judge. He knows, and knows well, what is most conducive to man's interests and happiness. And his counsel is, "Seek ye first the kingdom of God, and his righteousness." He is our friend. He, moved by love and pity, came to save us, and gave his life a ransom for us. Surely He would not deceive us. Then we have the weight of his divine judgment in favor of righteousness. This should have great influence upon us. And let us hear Paul's testimony: "What things were gain to me, those I counted loss to Christ. Yea, doubtless, and I count all things but loss, for the excellency of the knowledge of Christ Jesus my Lord, for whom I suffer the loss of all things, and do count them but dung, that I may win Christ." Phil. 3:7, 8. And what would be the testimony of departed saints could we get their judgment? We hear them exclaim as the stand upon the sea of glass, "Just and true are thy ways, thou king of saints. Who shall not fear thee, O Lord, and glorify thy name? for thou only are holy: for all nations shall come and worship before thee; for thy judgments are made manifest." Rev. 15:3, 4. And what is the verdict of the lost in regard to the value of Christianity? We have this given in a very impressive manner in the case of the rich man. "Then he said, I pray thee therefore, father, that thou wouldst send him to my father's house: for I have five brethren; that he may testify unto them, lest they also come into this place of torment." Luke 16:27, 28. And what is the judgment of men and women generally, in regard to the importance and value of Christianity? However indifferent people may be to the practice of Christianity, they will very generally acknowledge the necessity of it to prepare them for death and eternity.

2. In estimating the value of an object, its durability is taken into consideration. This principle is recognized and applied more or less in all the common affairs of life. Things that wear well, and will last a long time, are considered more valuable than those that are of but short duration. The gospel is an "everlasting gospel." Rev. 14:6. It is the "*incorruptible* seed," "the word of God, which *liveth and abideth forever.*" 1 Peter 1:23. And the character and joys produced by this "everlasting gospel" will endure forever. "In thy presence," said David, addressing the Lord, "is fullness of joy; at thy right hand there are pleasures forevermore." Ps. 16:11. Heavenly joys and pleasures are enduring. They will never cloy, never get old, and never wear out. How valuable they are! They are for future use as well as for present enjoyment according to the meaning of treasure, as already noticed.

II. We notice in the next place that "the kingdom of heaven," or Christianity is "hid." It is, to a certain degree, unknown to the great mass of people. While the gospel and church are in the world, and while the gospel is preached, and the church organized in many places, nevertheless, the real excellency, the true value, and the heavenly character of Christianity is but very imperfectly understood and known. The fact that there are so many that do not possess and enjoy it, is proof clear that they do not understand and appreciate its value. When this heavenly treasure is known, it will be accepted and possessed. While the multitude may see much in Christianity to admire, they but see its outward form; of its greatest beauties and charms and worth they are ignorant.

1. One cause of the prevailing ignorance of the real excellency and value of Christianity is the want of close attention to it on the part of many people. While they frequently hear it discoursed upon from the pulpit, and read about it in books, yet they do not examine it carefully and candidly, and as a subject in which they are deeply and personally concerned. Hence their views of it are vague and superficial.

2. Another reason why Christianity is in a considerable degree hidden from people is owing to the spirituality of its nature. The natural man does not discern spiritual things in their true light and importance. "The natural man receiveth not the things of the spirit of God: for they are foolishness unto Him: neither can he know them, because they are spiritually discerned." I Cor. 2 : 14. To appreciate both the excellency and importance of Christianity it is very desirable that there be some moral culture in people. To a heart so morally corrupt that it loves and takes pleasure only in what is evil, the pure principles and heavenly enjoyments of the Gospel will not have much attraction. We can but appreciate, understand and enjoy that to a very limited degree, with which we have no sympathy, and to which we have no resemblance." Hence Paul says in the language above quoted, that the natural man can not know things of the Spirit. There is so little sympathy and affiliation between the natural or sinful man and the pure and holy things of the Spirit, that the sinful man but very imperfectly appreciates them. And hence moral culture in people will prepare the way for the appreciation and reception of the Gospel.

There is an idea connected with the foregoing train of thought to which we would call the special attention of believers. It is this: The purer and holier we are the more will we appreciate, love and enjoy Gospel holiness, and the more anxiously will we cultivate and pursue it. Who is it that have the most and strongest asperations after heavenly enjoyments and heavenly feelings, and who sing with the spirit and the understanding the familiar and expressive words of the poet

"Nearer, my God, to thee,
Nearer to thee!
E'en though it be a cross
That raiseth me?"

And who is it that fill their places in the sanctuary the most punctually, and are found at the prayer meeting, and at the Bible class the most frequently? It is those who appreciate the most the "hid treasure," and who have experienced its sanctifying influence to the greatest degree, and who enjoy the divine comforts of the Gospel the most. In other words, it is those who are the most holy. They know more of the "hid treasure," because they are the more assimilated to it, and the more they know of it the more they want to know of it.

There is a class of professing Christians that seem to be "at ease in Zion" (Amos 6:1), and who seem to be perfectly satisfied with their present attainments in the divine life. If you were fully acquainted with their prayers and meditations it is to be feared you would never hear them bemoaning their errors and failings, or anxiously calling upon God for a deeper work of grace in them, and for a more heavenly frame of mind. The "hid treasure" remains in a great measure hidden to them, and they have not discovered its concealed beauties and excellencies sufficiently to appreciate its depths of joy and heights of bliss. And their hearts have never been aglow with the love of God shed abroad in them by the Holy Spirit.

Yes, brethren, the more we know of the hid treasure, the more we shall want to know of it, and the more shall we want to enjoy of it.

III. *We pass on to notice that when men are convinced of the value and importance of Christianity, they will be anxious to obtain it.*

According to the parable, the man found the treasure, apparently without being in search of it. In the next parable, namely, that of the merchantman seeking goodly pearls, the merchantman is represented as *seeking* for pearls. These two parables teach some things in common, but, each one has something peculiar to itself, especially in regard to the different ways in which the gospel is received in the beginning of a Christian life. The parable of the " hid treasure," represents the class of persons who find Christianity without making any special effort to do so.

Such persons, and oftentimes young people are among these, may go to the house of God with no special design or even desire to obtain salvation. But the truth reaches and effects the heart in a way that leads to conversion. The mind from some circumstance, and it may be because of the presence of the Spirit of God, is in a favorable state for the reception of the truth, and the truth enters with its enlightening and convicting power, and conversion followed. And it is not always under the preaching of the gospel that a religious feeling comes over the mind that leads to conversion. It may be under other circumstances; it may be when persons are alone, or are under some circumstances that bring divine subjects to the mind, and the mind becomes interested in them, and yields to their influence. The Samaritan woman is a representative of this class of persons. When she left her home, it was not to seek the Lord. She went to the well for water. But she came unexpectedly upon the treasure of truth there. In her interview with our Lord, her mind was enlightened and she recognized him to be the Messiah. See the circumstance in the 4th chapter of the gospel by John. When the truth thus comes to the heart, apparently unsought, as it does come to many persons, it should be accepted and that too with the eagerness with which the man secured the hid treasure when he discovered it. If it is not then accepted and secured, it may be that it will have to be sought for afterwards with much diligence and perseverance if it is found. It will have to be sought as the man sought the pearls in the other parable we have alluded to, the one following our text.

IV. *We notice in the next place the manner in which the treasure of saving grace is obtained.*

Often has the individual, so to speak, walked over the field of the gospel, and, though he may have admired much in it, he did not see the importance and value of Christ. But his attention is now arrested as it never was before. And he feels an interest in Christianity that he never felt before. And he determines to obtain it, and takes the necessary steps to do so. He "buyeth the field." And to do so, he gives up everything that is in his way, or that is contrary to the gospel. This is what is meant by buying the field. When the love of money, of ease, of fashion, of carnal pleasure and worldly honor are given up for Christ's sake, and the gospel's, then, in the spiritual or practical sense of the parable, we sell all we have and buy the field. We must give up our pride and self-righteousness, and become "poor in spirit." "Blessed are the poor in spirit: for theirs is the kingdom of heaven."

V. *We notice in the last place that the finding and securing the treasure of grace produces joy.*

This joy begins to some degree when the interest in our

personal salvation begins. Even in the cup of penitential sorrow there are drops of joy mixed. We feel glad that we see our danger and the need of salvation. And we are made glad to know that Christ can and will save us. The pentecostian sinners "gladly received the word" of instruction, and consequently had some joy before they were pardoned, and before they received the Holy Spirit. Joy accompanies the believer through all his life and its changes, and when he reaches the right hand of God he will have fullness of joy, and that forevermore. Psalm 16:11.

My unconverted hearers, if you have found the treasure of Christianity, that is, if you perceive its importance, accept it. Buy it at once, though you have to sell all you have. And you, my Christian brethren, appreciate the divine treasure you have secured. Do not lose it. Seek to increase it. Rejoice that you have found it.

XXXII.
CHRISTIAN CONSISTENCY.

"He that saith he abideth in Him, ought himself also so to walk, even as He walked." I John, 2:6.

Our subject will be, *Christian Consistency*. And to present this prominent idea of the text in the most satisfactory manner, there must be some other ideas presented with it. We therefore propose the following division of the subject:

I. What the Christian confession implies.

II. The necessity for this confession.

III. What consistency requires of those who make this confession.

I. We are to notice *what the Christian Confession*

implies. "He that saith he abideth in him," is equal to, he that confesseth him. It will be understood that the words "him" and "he" in the text refer to Christ. And the person referred to in the text is considered as saying, *he abideth in Christ.* But we can not abide in Christ except we first get into him. So the person referred to first got into Christ, and then he declared that he abode in him. All this is implied in an intelligent and sincere confession of Christ. All who have made such a confession of him say they abide in him. This is saying a good deal, but it is saying no more than what is true. Believers who have made the good confession, and made it properly, are in Christ. And this they declare to the world. They do not only declare it in word, or mainly declare it in that way. They declare it by their Christian profession; by the Christian name which they bear; and by their connection with the visible church of Christ.—"He that saith he abideth in him." The prolonged life of the Christian believer saith he abideth in Christ. All you, my friends, who have made a profession of Christianity, and all persons of every Christian community who have made such a profession, say that they abide in Christ. And this is saying a great deal. To profess to have got into Christ, and to abide in him, with all that such relation to him implies, is to profess a great deal — to make a very high profession. But it is what we all profess who have made the Christian profession. And whether or not we all realize this, we profess to do so, for it is implied in the Christian profession. And if we do not realize it, our profession is of no practical influence or of no saving power. Oh, let us all understand and remember what is implied in our Christian profession, and what we are continually declaring to the world, namely, that *we abide in Christ.* The apostle fully realized the responsibility of the Christian profession, and he would have all Christians to realize it, and to realize that that profession requires us to walk as Christ walked. "He that saith he abideth in him ought himself also so to walk even as he walked."

That those who embraced the faith or religion of Christ made a public confession of him, seems evident from a number of passages of Scripture. Paul says to Timothy, "Fight the good fight of faith, lay hold on eternal life, whereunto thou art also called and hast professed a good profession before many witnesses." 1 Tim. 6 : 12. From the fact that this confession or profession is connected with his call to eternal life, would seem to indicate that it was made when he entered upon a Christian life. And while Timothy made this good confession, it seems to have been a common thing among Christians, from the following language of Paul: "If thou shalt confess with thy mouth the Lord Jesus, and shalt believe in thy heart that God hath raised him from the dead, thou shalt be saved. For with the heart man believeth unto righteousness; and with the mouth confession is made unto salvation. For the Scripture saith, whosoever believeth on him shall not be ashamed." Rom. 10: 9–11. In harmony with the foregoing passages of Scripture is the confession of the Ethiopian eunuch, for he made the good confession. Having been taught baptism by Phillip, as he evidently had, or he would have known nothing about it, and being willing to do anything that was necessary to obtain the object he was in pursuit of, namely, salvation, the first opportunity that presented itself to him for receiving baptism he was anxious to embrace. "And as they went on their way, they came to a certain water; and the eunuch said, see, here is water, what doth hinder me to be baptised? And Phillip said, if thou believest with all thine heart, thou mayest. And he answered and said, I believe that Jesus Christ is the Son of God." Acts 8: 36, 37. Here was the confession made.

Then a gospel confession of Christ embraces a knowledge of him and an acceptance of him as our Saviour, that we may live a new and holy life by his grace, and after his example. And this is manifested in the ordinance of baptism, as by this we own and put on Christ, and pledge ourselves to a life of faithfulness to him. And to abide in Christ is to continue in the confession we have made in baptism, and after our baptism observe the precepts and commandments of our Lord, as he gave them to his disciples who were to complete the organization of the Church. Christians do not only say by their confession of Christ that they have entered into him, or commenced a new life, a life of faith, but they say also that they continue in him, or, in the language of the text, they say they *abide in him*. In harmony with this view of the Christian profession or confession, the apostle Paul thus exhorts Christians: "Seeing then that we have a great high priest, that is passed into the heavens, Jesus the Son of God, let us hold fast our profession. For we have not a high priest which can not be touched with the feeling of our infirmities; but was in all points tempted like as we are yet without sin. Let us therefore come boldly unto the throne of grace, that we may obtain mercy, and find grace to help in time of need." Heb. 4: 14, 16. In these words the apostle exhorts us to hold fast our profession. And this implies a faithful observance of the truths, doctrines and ordinance of the gospel. And as this can only be done by the grace of God, we are in the above exhortation admonished to come boldly to a throne of grace that we may find grace to help in time of need.

A genuine confession of Christ, then, implies a genuine conversion to Christianity by being brought into fellowship with Christ the author of Christianity, and by virtue of that fellowship divine life is communicated to all that make that confession intelligently and sincerely. To abide in Christ, then, and to make the good confession is to partake of his righteousness and to be like him.

II. In the next place we shall notice *The necessity for Confessing Christ.* A failure to confess Christ will be attended with a loss of all that is implied in such a confession, and we have seen that much is implied in it. Our Lord said, "Whosoever, therefore, shall confess me before men, him will I confess also before my Father which is in heaven." Matt. 10: 32, 33. To be denied by Christ when his relation to us as our judge is manifested to all, and when "the doom of eternity hangs on his word," will be an event at the thought of which we should tremble. To be rejected by him when there is no other source to go to for help and comfort will be a condition of wretchedness and hopelessness that we can not be too anxious, or do too much, or sacrifice too much, to avoid. To be condemned when there remains no further means for justification, and to awake up to a sense of our guilt when there is no hope of pardon, will be such a state of sorrow that it can only be realized when it is experienced.

The confession and denying of Christ, standing as they do in connection in the words of our Lord that we have quoted, and he having declared on another occasion, "He that is not with me is against me, and he that gathereth not with me scattereth abroad," Matt. 12: 30, we must come to the conclusion that all who do not confess Christ will be considered as denying him. Here is the absolute necessity of confessing Christ, if we would avoid the doom of his enemies, and enjoy the favor of his friends. While his rejection of us will be our ruin, his confession of us that we are his friends and disciples will be the highest honor, and the passport to everlasting bliss.

There being so much involved in our confessing Christ, we should confess him and thus make the good confession that leads to a good life, a peaceful death, and a glorious immortality beyond. On the one hand, the advantages of a Christian life can not be overrated; and on the other, the terrible consequences of neglecting such a life can not be justly estimated until they are epxerienced.

In regard to the Christian profession, that we may further understand the nature of it, and the importance of it, we have the following: "Beloved, believe not every spirit, but try the spirits, whether they are of God; because many false prophets are gone out into the world. Hereby know ye the spirit of God; every spirit that confesseth that Jesus Christ is come in the flesh is of God; and every spirit that confesseth not that Jesus Christ is come in the flesh is not of God; and this is that spirit of anti-Christ, whereof ye have heard that it should come; and even now already is it in the world." 1 John 4: 1–3. Here the confession that is alluded to is the public, sincere, experimental and practical confession we have already explained. The spirit that prompts and leads to such a confession shows that it is of God, and that they who possess such a spirit are of God.

III. We notice the last division of our subject which is: *What Consistency requires of those who make the Christian confession.* "He that saith he abideth in him ought himself also so to walk even as he walked." There are great and solemn obligations assumed by all who confess Christ, or who profess to abide in him. Our Lord asks the suggestive question: "Do men gather grapes of thorns, or figs of thistles?" Matt. 7: 16. And the question is easily answered. And all who make the Christian confession, and say that they abide in Christ, should "walk even as he walked." He is the vine, and his disciples, or those who confess him, are the branches, John 15: 5. Then as the branches are of the same nature as the vine, of whatever character the vine is, of that character will the branches be, and as a necessary consequence the fruit will be of the same kind as is the vine. And to profess to abide in Christ as Christians do, and then to walk as the Gentiles walk, or as the people of the world walk—for Gentiles here mean the world in distinction from Christians—is to be guilty of the grossest inconsistency. It is like the fig tree bearing thistles, or the grape-vine, thorns. It is an anomaly, or a deviation from the common course of things. "He that saith he abideth in him, ought himself also so to walk, even as he walked." He *ought*, this shows the obligation he is under to do so. And while he is, from the confession he has made, under obligations to live a life like Christ lived, propriety and consistency should impel him to the same course of holy living. A man in Christ, as every Christian professes to be, is one of Christ's holy brethren, having holy fellowship with Christ,— and having the spirit of Christ, and the same mind in him that was in Christ, Phil. 2 : 5, and being thus closely identified with Christ, his character will be similar to the character of Christ, and it will then follow that his walk or conduct will be like the walk and conduct of Christ. Walk in the text means spiritual conduct, or a spiritual course of life resembling the conduct of Christ.

He that saith he is in Christ, or confesses to be in Christ, should have the Lord before him as his example, and make it the one great object of his life to imitate him. He is to walk with Christ. And if he walks with him, and lives with him, and on him, and Christ lives in him, then will he walk as Christ walked, and be a witness to the divine authority and power of Christianity, and prove that he is of God, and that he has the Spirit of God.

In imitating Christ in his walk or conduct, we should look at his conduct, 1, Toward his heavenly Father. This was complete in every particular, and was marked by the most sincere, constant and loving obedience. In a comparison that Paul made between Moses and Christ, he says,

"Moses verily was faithful in all his house as a servant, for a testimony of those things which were to be spoken after; but Christ as a Son over his own house; whose house are we, if we hold fast the confidence and the rejoicing of the hope, firm unto the end." Heb. 3: 5. He was faithful as a Son. 2. His walk toward his brethren was marked with the same faithfulness. What tenderness, forbearance, patience, unselfishness, self-denial, humility, and love characterized all his intercourse with them! "Having loved his own which were in the world, he loved them unto the end." John 13 : 1. How expressive is this language in regard to our Lord's love to his disciples! 3. His walk or conduct to the world, and to his enemies, was marked by great care and circumspection. He was very careful to give no just cause of offense to any. It was a man of the world who said when our Lord was on trial before him, and in reference to the innocency of our Lord, "I find in him no fault at all." John 18: 38. Beloved Christian friends, we have confessed Christ, and profess to abide in him. Then consistency requires that we should walk as he walked.

We conclude our subject with three practical remarks. 1. We are not to be a rule of life to ourselves. We are to walk as Christ walked. His principles and example are to constitute the rule by which we are to be governed. 2. We call your attention to the strictness of the requirements of Christianity. What a holy system it is, as it requires its adherents to imitate the holy Son of God! 3. The Christian life is one of great honor, dignity, usefulness and excellency. It is a life in holy fellowship with, and in imitation of, the life of the holy One of God. And let this thought be a sufficient encouragement to prompt us to do whatever is to be done, to attain unto the Christian life, a life in imitation of that beautiful one lived by our blessed Saviour.

XXXIII.
THE HIGH ENJOYMENT OF THE GOOD.

"But unto you that fear my name shall the Sun of righteousness arise with healing in his wings; and ye shall go forth, and grow up as calves of the stall. And ye shall tread down the wicked; for they shall be ashes under the soles of your feet in the day that I shall do this, saith the Lord of hosts."

The prophet, in closing his prophecies, presents in strong and plain, though in figurative, language, the condition of sinners and saints. After declaring the terrible end of the wicked, he sets forth the blessed state of the good. And our subject will be, *The high enjoyment of the good.* That our blessed Redeemer is referred to by the "Sun of righteousness," there can be no doubt. He is not only presented to us as the "Son of God," and the "Son of man," but he is also presented to us as the "Sun of righteousness." Of all the natural objects that are used in the Scriptures to illustrate the glory, power, greatness and importance of the Saviour to our world, perhaps there is none more suitable to the purpose, or more expressive of his glorious character, than the sun. And though the worshiping of all creatures is idolatry, and we can not but look upon all such worship with disgust and surprise, we can not well help feeling less surprise to see the sun worshiped, than an onion, or some similar object in creation.

The sun is a great body, and the Saviour is a great Saviour. The diameter of the sun is estimated to be 900,000 miles, and it has matter enough in it to make 1,000,000 globes the size of the earth. But who can estimate the greatness of Christ, and where can language be found to express it? He is the brightness of the Father's glory, and the express image of his person, and upholds all things by the word of his power. Heb. 1:3. He is the head of all principality and power. Col. 2 : 10. John thus describes him, as he had seen him in one of his visions: He was "clothed with a a garment down to the foot, and girt about the paps with a golden girdle. His head and hairs were white like wool, as white as snow; and his eyes were as a flame of fire; and his feet like unto fine brass, as they burned in a furnace; and his voice as the sound of many waters." Rev. 1: 14, 15. He is Lord of lords, and King of kings. Rev. 17: 14. And in consideration of his greatness, the shining ranks of heavenly intelligences bow to him and pay their homage to him. " And I beheld, and heard the voice of many angels round about the throne and the beasts and the elders: and the number of them was ten thousand times ten thousand, and thousands of thousands; saying with a loud voice, worthy is the Lamb that was slain to receive power, and riches, and wisdom, and strength, and honor and glory, and blessing." Rev. 5: 11, 12. Such are the Scriptural views of the greatness, the glory and the honor of the Saviour. And justly may he be compared to the sun. All the sun is to the natural world, Christ is to the moral or spiritual world.

In presenting the practical truth contained in the text, we shall present it under the two following heads:

I. A common Biblical characteristic of the good.

II. The blessings received by the good from Christ.

I. A common Biblical characteristic of the good. " But unto you that fear my name shall the Sun of righteousness arise," etc. Saints are here spoken to as fearing the name of the Lord. And this is a very common characteristic of them in the Scriptures. "The whole duty of man" is comprised in fearing God and keeping his commandments. Eccl. 12: 13. This fear is not the slavish fear that makes the slave tremble at the dread of his master's anger and punishment. Neither is it the fear that guilt produces. This was the fear that Adam felt after he had violated the law of

God and stained his pure spirit with sin. His conscience felt the wrong and testified to his guilt, and a terrible fear of God was the result; and to God's question, "Where art thou?" he responded, "I heard thy voice in the garden, and I was afraid." Gen. 3 : 10. The fear of God, that is the peculiar characteristic of saints, is a holy disposition of the regenerated spirit of the believer, that prompts him so to walk that in all things he may please God, guarding against offending him, either by doing what he should not do or by failing to do what he is commanded to do. Such a fear of God will lead to the most cheerful submission to his will, and to the most profound reverence of his character.

The fear that Christians have of God is a filial fear, the fear that the obedient child has of the father. It is a fear mixed with love. The following illustration is an apt one of the fear that the children of God have to their heavenly Father. A little boy was tempted to pluck some cherries from a tree which his father had forbidden him to touch. "You need not be afraid," said his companion, "for if your father should find out that you have taken them, he is too kind to hurt you." "Ah!" said the little fellow, "that is the very reason why I would not touch them, for, though my father would not hurt me, yet I should hurt him by my disobedience."

II. The blessing derived by the good from Christ.

1. He is the light of the soul of the believer. In the night of sin that the believer experienced before he came to Christ, or before Christ arose to dispel the spiritual darkness from his heart, he was in great darkness, and was ignorant of himself, and of God, and of his relation and duty to his God. He walked in darkness and was in the way of destruction, but he knew it not. The god of this world blinds "the minds of them that believe not." 2 Cor., 4: 4. Consequently the condition of such is a dangerous one, as they

know not whither they go. But when they come to Christ and put themselves into the proper relation to him—into the relation of a seeking, penitent soul—then he will arise; and as the rising sun dispels the darkness of night, so will the sun of righteousness dispel the mists and clouds of darkness from the soul, and enable it to see itself just as it is, a guilty and helpless creature before God. But by the light that shines upon it from Christ, "the sun of righteousness," through his word, a way of salvation will also be discovered, and he will hear a voice saying, "This is the way, walk ye in it." Isaiah 30: 21. And by entering the straight gate, and by walking upon the narrow path, Matt. 7: 14, permanent and safe ground will be reached, and pardon and peace found. Christ, "the sun of righteousness" is the true light, in contradistinction to the false lights that are in the world, and that men too often follow to their own ruin. To such false light the prophet alludes in the following language: "Behold, all ye that kindle a fire, that compass yourselves about with sparks: walk in the light of your fire, and in the sparks that ye have kindled. This shall ye have of mine hand: ye shall lie down in sorrow." Isaiah 50: 11.

2. Christ as "the sun of righteousness" has a quickening power by which he quickens the dead soul into life. The similarity between the effect produced by the natural sun upon the earth, and Christ upon the spiritual nature of man, is very striking. The earth for a part of the year sustains a relation to the sun that vegetation apparently dies. During winter the earth seems to be partially dead. The frost in some degree holds vegetation in subjection. But when the earth arrives at a certain point in her annual course around the sun, his power upon the earth increases, and it breaks the power of cold and frost which have held in subjection in some degree the earth, life-giving power is imparted to the earth, and under that power vegetation

springs forth from its grave, and the earth is clothed with life, and that life is manifested on every hand. The seed that has been buried in the earth germinates and grows, and fruitfulness is the result.

And so does Christ, "the sun of righteousness" by his quickening and life-giving power, exerted through his word and Spirit, raise from their spiritual graves the souls that have been dead in trespasses and sins, when they come to him, and put themselves into such a relation to him as will enable him to exert his power in giving them life. Souls that would be made alive by Christ must come to him, and believe on him. They must be planted in him, or grafted into him. He is the vine, and all that will bear fruit unto eternal life must be grafted into him. He then becomes their life. He also matures the fruit of believers. And that fruit is the fruit of righteousness.

3. But the Sun of righteousness is represented as having a healing influence upon his people. There is "healing in his wings." The moral sickness of men is here clearly recognized. And in immediate connection with the truth that men are spiritually diseased, stands the plainly implied truth that Christ is the great physician. And in his redemptive work wrought in believers, he does not only save them from death, but he also saves them from sickness, and restores them to perfect spiritual health. How effectual and complete is his work. "Where sin abounded, grace did much more abound: that as sin hath reigned unto death, even so might grace reign through righteousness unto eternal life by Jesus Christ our Lord." Rom. 5: 20, 21. Dr. Pocock says the Jews have a proverbial saying, "As the sun riseth, infirmities decrease." As the sun has a healthy and invigorating influence upon the bodies of men, so Christ has a healing influence upon the feeble and diseased condition of men's spiritual nature. Reference may

also be made to the physical cures which Christ performed among men while he was upon earth. He is the Saviour of the body and of the soul—of the whole man.

4. He has a binding power, or a power that unites and holds all the good together. In this respect he has a power similar to that of the sun. The sun is understood to be the centre of the solar system, and by virtue of the laws that govern matter, all the planets that revolve around the sun are held to their places by the great law of attraction. So Christ, "the Sun of righteousness" is "the head of all principality and power." Col. 2:10. He is the great corner-stone that binds all the "lively" stones that constitute the great spiritual building of God together. And he is the head of the universal family of the redeemed in heaven and on earth. The apostle, in speaking of the position Christ has been raised to by the Father, says, "he raised him from the dead, and set him at his own right hand in the heavenly places, far above all principality, and power, and might, and dominion, and every name that is named, not only in this world, but also in that which is to come; and hath put all things under his feet, and gave him to be the head over all things to the church, which is his body, the fullness of him that filleth all in all." Eph. 1: 20-23. Such is the great central position that Christ, "the Sun of righteousness," holds in the spiritual universe of God. He is the fountain of light, and of life, and of power, and from him go out in streams of grace ample supplies to meet all the wants of God's great spiritual family.

5. But he is "the Sun of righteousness." He is not only a sun to enlighten, quicken, heal, and attract, but righteousness characterizes all his offices, all his works, and his purposes. While he is represented in our text as "the Sun of righteousness," he is also represented as a King of righteousness. The prophet in alluding

to him in his kingly character, and to the kingdom that he was to establish, says, "Behold, a king shall reign in righteousness, and princes shall rule in judgment." Isa. 32 : 1. And Paul quotes the following expressive language from the psalms and applies it to Christ: " Thy throne, O God, is for ever and ever; a sceptre of righteousness is the sceptre of thy kingdom. Thou hast loved righteousness and hated iniquity; therefore God, even thy God, hath anointed thee with the oil of gladness above thy fellows." Heb. 1 : 8, 9. And, again, it is said of him, "righteousness shall be the girdle of his loins, and faithfulness the girdle of his reins." Isa. 11: 5. Righteousness was a prominent feature in our Redeemer's character, and it should be prominent and controlling in the character of all his people. And so in our text he is very properly declared to be "the Sun of righteousness." And all whom he saves, and over whom he reigns, are distinguished for righteousness as is their head and pattern. Eternal right is enthroned upon their hearts, and it exerts its power over their lives. And they are therefore right in all their feelings, and in all their relations in life. All their passions and words and works are right. They love God supremely, and their neighbor as themselves, according to the divine law.

6. Under the light and influences of "the Sun of righteousness" the good, or those that fear God, are represented as going forth, and as growing up as calves of the stall. This language suggests several beautiful ideas. Those upon whom the Sun of righteousness arises, and who enjoy all the blessed influences of his divine power, increase in knowledge, and grace, and spiritual strength, and go forth victoriously, and successfully on their great mission of life, pressing "toward the mark for the prize of the high calling of God in Christ Jesus." Phil. 3 : 14. They go "from faith to faith," Rom. 1 : 17, thus "leaving the principles of the doc-

trine of Christ, they go unto perfection," and grow up as calves of the stall, strong to labor and suffer in the cause of the Lord. They will be strong to resist the temptations of the wicked, as it is said, "ye shall tread down the wicked; for they shall be ashes under the soles of your feet in the day that I shall do this, saith the Lord of hosts." The good shall be "more than conquerors through him that loved us." Rom. 8: 37.

7. The last general idea suggested by the text that we shall notice is the idea of animation, cheerfulness, and joy. Joy and happiness are associated with light and sorrow and misery with darkness, in the Scriptures. And this agrees with our experience. In regard to the common enjoyments of life, we know that a bright sunny day is more enjoyable and more cheering than a dark and gloomy day. Hence light in the Scriptures is the emblem of joy and happiness. And so it is said, "Light is sown for the righteous, and gladness for the upright in heart." Ps. 97: 11. Here gladness and light are associated together. And in the following passage there is a beautiful cluster of ideas associated with light. "Then shall thy light break forth as the morning, and thine health shall spring forth speedily; and thy righteousness shall go before thee; the glory of the Lord shall be thy reward. Then shalt thou call, and the Lord shall answer; thou shalt cry, and he shall say, here I am. If thou shalt take away from the midst of thee the yoke, the putting forth of the finger, and speaking vanity; and if thou draw out thy soul to the hungry, and satisfy the afflicted soul; then shall thy light rise in obscurity, and thy darkness be as noonday." Isa. 58: 8–10. Here are rich spiritual truths. Even the darkness of the Christian shall be as the noonday. That is, in his darkest hours there is joy. What then must be his hours of light?

In conclusion we remark, 1. What an unspeakable blessing is Christ to those who enjoy him in all his saving power! 2. Christian friends, do you enjoy this light? Has Christ risen with all his brightness upon your souls? If he has not, you are not enjoying what it is your privilege to enjoy. 3. And you, beloved friends, who are yet in darkness, will you not come to Christ, that he may be to you "the Sun of righteousness," turning your night into day, and making you fruitful in every good work? May we all live more constantly in the heavenly light of "the Sun of righteousness," and then will our light shine to the glory of God, and to the honor of our Christianity.

XXXIV.
DIVINE POWER CORRECTING HUMAN MISTAKES.

"And Elisha came again to Gilgal; and there was a dearth in the land: and the sons of the prophets were sitting before him: and he said unto his servant, Set on the great pot, and seethe the pottage for the sons of the prophets. And one went out into the fields to gather herbs, and found a wild vine, and gathered thereof wild gourds his lap full, and came and shred them into the pot of pottage; for they knew them not. So they poured out for the men to eat. And it came to pass as they were eating of the pottage, that they cried out, and said, O thou man of God, there is death in the pot. And they could not eat of the pot. But he said, Then bring meal, and he cast it into the pot: and he said, Pour out for the people, that they may eat. And there was no harm in the pot." 2 Kings 4: 38–41.

We have here one of the miracles performed by Elisha. Elisha was the successor of Elijah. Elijah, before his departure, called Elisha, and gave him to understand that he was to be his successor, and to continue the work of the Lord. Before Elijah's ascension, Elisha kept close to him, and when the eventful period came for Elijah to ascend in a chariot of fire, Elisha saw him go up, and exclaimed "My father, my father, the chariot of Israel, and the horsemen thereof." And he saw him no more: and he took hold of his own clothes, and rent them in two pieces. He took up also the mantle of Elijah that fell from him, and went back and stood by the bank of Jordan: and he took the mantle of Elijah that fell from him, and smote the waters, and said, Where is the Lord God of Elijah? And when he also had smitten the waters, they parted hither and thither: and Elisha went over. And when the sons of the prophets which were to view at Jericho saw him they said, the spirit of Elijah doth rest on Elisha. And they came to meet him, and bowed themselves to the ground before him." The question, "Where is the Lord God of Elijah?" is a suggestive question. And the question was virtually answered in a manner somewhat like the following: "I am with my people, and with my servants, and I will be with you, if you honor the mantle of your father, and are as devoted to me as he was. I will be all to you that I was to him." Elisha took the mantle of Elijah, and smote the waters of the Jordan, and the stream was divided, and he passed over it. He thus had the assurance that God was with him. And this assurance he felt, or had evidence of, in every miracle he performed. He had it at Gilgal, when he performed the miracle recorded in our text.

The sons of the prophets were a class of pious young men that were preparing themselves to fill the places of their seniors when their labors would close and their places be left vacant. They looked up to their spiritual fathers for instruction, and those fathers instructed them in the law, and took much pains, no doubt, to prepare them for usefulness. There was a strong reciprocal feeling of attachment between the old and young prophets of the Lord. Elisha met a number of these young prophets at Gilgal upon his arrival there. They were gathered together with Elisha. And as there was a dearth in the land, it is altogether probable that their supply of food was low, and that they were prevented from doing what their love and respect for Elisha prompted them to do, namely, prepare a good meal for him. And as they had not, apparently, the means of doing what they would like to have done, Elisha helped them. He sent a servant out into the field to gather some vegetables. And he committed a sad mistake, and instead of gathering a wholesome and palatable kind of cucumber or gourd that grew in that country, he gathered a kind that was nauseous and poisonous, which also grew there. And when the pottage was tasted, they discovered the mistake that had been committed, and they supposed they were poisoned, and exclaimed, "O thou man of God, there is death in the pot." The man of God, who was Elisha, as we may readily suppose, sympathized deeply with them in their trouble, and the more so, perhaps, because his servant had brought the poisonous vegetables; he immediately interposed his power and counteracted the influence of the poisonous herb, restored the pottage to a wholesome condition, and thus prepared the way for a very enjoyable time together.

We shall present some practical truths suggested by the text, under the following heads:

I. The mistakes of men.

II. The interposition of God to counteract those mistakes and save men from their effects.

I. The mistakes of men. What is a mistake? A mistake, says Webster, is "*a fault in opinion, judgment or conduct; an error.*" He also says, "a mistake is an interchange or taking of one thing for another, through haste, inadvertence or ignorance." All sins are mistakes but all mistakes are not sins. There may be mistakes that do not necessarily lead to sin or moral evil. That was a sad mistake that the servant of Elisha committed when he gathered the poisonous vegetables. And had not the man of God counteracted the poisonous effect of those vegetables the loss of human life might have been great. And how far the servant would have been responsible had death followed would have depended upon circumstances. There was ignorance, and perhaps carelessness, in what he did. He was not as well acquainted with the character of the vegetables that he gathered as he should have been. We all ought to be careful and not undertake to do what we are not capable of doing. There is either ignorance or carelessness, or both, connected with all mistakes, and so they are connected with all sin.

The history of the human race is made up largely of their mistakes. "The whole world lieth in wickedness." And ignorance and carelessness, and in many cases worse elements combined with these, have produced this wickedness. It has all been produced by mistakes and blunders. How much of the history of the world is made up of the history of war and bloodshed. And mistakes have produced a large amount of the evil that war has inflicted upon our race. The common histories of the world that are written are made up so much of war that the propriety of putting such books into the hands of our youth has led a late author to write history without so much of war being put into it.

As Eve was the mother of our race, so the sad mistake that she committed was the parent of all the mistakes and faults that have afflicted our race since her time. That act of hers that we call the first sin was a terrible mistake. And it had every element of a mistake according to Webster's description of a mistake, when he explains it to be "an interchange or taking of one thing for another, through haste, inadvertence, or ignorance." How true it is that she took "one thing for another." She thought she was taking that which would impart wisdom and pleasure to her. It is said in the Bible account we have of her mistake that "when the woman saw that the tree was good for food, and that it was pleasant to the eyes, and a tree to be desired to make one wise, she took of the fruit thereof and did eat, and gave also unto her husband with her and he did eat." Gen. 3: 6. She thought she was taking that which would make her wise and which would add to her pleasure. But, alas! she was greatly mistaken. She made a mistake and took the wrong fruit, as did the servant of Elisha when he went out to gather the gourds. And there was death in eating of the fruit that Eve partook of as there was in the pottage prepared for the sons of the prophets at Gilgal. The effects in eating the forbidden fruit were not probably the same upon Eve as the eating of the poisoned pottage was upon the sons of the prophets. In the former case the immediate effects were of a moral character, while in the latter case the immediate effects were of a physical character.

But Eve was sadly mistaken in the effects which the eating of the forbidden fruit produced. She expected pleasure but found pain. She thought the fruit would make her wise but it really made her ignorant, for sin is ignorance, or it produces ignorance. Paul, in describing the condition of sinners, says, "Having the understanding darkened, being alienated from the life of God through the ignorance that is in them, because of the blindness of their heart." Ignorance and not wisdom is the fruit of sin. "The fear of the Lord is the beginning of wisdom; a good understanding have all they that do his commandments." Ps. 111: 10. We would say to you, young people, and to all to whom we are speaking, that whenever you expect that sin will add to your interest, or to your real pleasure, you will find yourselves greatly mistaken. "Do men gather grapes of thorns, or figs of thistles?" Surely not. Neither do they receive anything good from sin.

Both nations and individuals have committed sad mistakes. That was a great mistake that the Egyptians committed when they put themselves in opposition to God, and attempted to continue their oppression over his people. "Who is the Lord?" said Pharaoh reproachfully and insultingly, "that I should obey his voice to let Israel go? I know not the Lord, neither will I let Israel go." Ex. 5:2. And as Pharaoh would not hearken to the Lord, nor regard the wonderful works of the Lord performed to show him his mistake, the Egyptians were drowned in the Red Sea, and their dead bodies thrown upon its shore. The Jews committed several sad mistakes in yielding to heathen influences, and in turning from the Lord, and by giving themselves up to idolatry. Solomon committed a great mistake. With all his knowledge and wisdom he stepped aside from the path of rectitude and righteousness, and "did evil in the sight of the Lord, and went not fully after the Lord, as did David his father." 1 Kings 11:6. Peter also committed a mistake when he denied the Lord. How ungrateful and unthoughtful he was! At the very time his Lord so much needed his sympathy and his presence to cheer him in the dark hour of his trial and temptation, Peter forsook him and denied him. There are times, Christian brethren, when there is a special necessity for our testimony and influence to defend and protect the suffering cause of truth. And we ought to be ready at such times to stand up for Jesus. We are sometimes thrown into worldly company when our Christian influence is especially needed to restrain the frivolity, the gaity, and the unbecoming levity of the vain and thoughtless, and we commit a serious mistake when at such times, instead of throwing our influence against such conduct, we help to encourage it.

Oh, how common are the faults of mistakes both with the young and with the old! The former through thoughtlessness, and the latter for the want of the "fear of God before their eyes," are both alike exposed to mistakes, and mistakes are common with them, though many of those mistakes are faults, and if not corrected must lead to ruin. Young men commit mistakes when they indulge in the habit of drinking intoxicating drinks, or in the use of profane language, or any thing of an evil tendency, for such things will grow, and they may lead to ruin. Young men and women, act with wisdom and discretion, and thus avoid mistakes which may lead to ruinous consequences. And let the older, who are less excusable than they because they have more experience, do the same.

II. The interposition of God to save men from their mistakes and their consequences.

The sons of the prophets and all who partook of the poisonous pottage at Gilgal, were in danger of death from the effects of the poisonous gourds. But God in mercy, through his servant Elisha, interfered, and saved their lives. And so he has done in regard to the great mistakes of men involving moral principles and moral character, and thus exposing them to "death of every kind," for death is in the great seething pot out of which we are all eating. "By one man sin entered into the world, and death by sin: and so death passed upon all men, for that all have sinned." Rom. 5:12. Through the guilty mistakes that men have made, they are not only exposed to death, but are actually "dead in trespasses and sins." Eph. 2:1. The moral poison has been taken, and the "whole head is sick, and the whole heart faint." Isa. 1:5. "But God, who is rich in mercy, for his great love wherewith he loved us, even when we were dead in sins, hath quickened us together with Christ." Eph. 2:4, 5. As the prophet put the meal into the pot, and destroyed the poisonous effects of the gourds, so Christ gave his life a ransom for men. He came into the world to save sinners—to save men from the guilt and misery of their mistakes and to give them spiritual light and strength, that they may go on their way after their delivery from death, and "sin no more." There are two things necessary to preserve us from mistakes. First, we need wisdom to enable us to know what evil is. And, secondly, we need spiritual strength to enable us to resist the wrong, when we discover it. All these helps, or necessary means of grace are provided for us in Christ, and we may be delivered from sin and death, and kept by the power of God.

The means by which the prophet Elisha saved the people from death are deserving of our notice. It was simply by throwing meal into the pot. The means were simple. But it should be observed that one of the characteristics of the means which God usually selects to accomplish his purposes is smallness or weakness as looked at by men, and in the light of their own power. It is with the means that God uses, as it is with the agents. Paul, in referring to the Gospel, and those to whom it is committed to preach it, says, "We have this treasure in earthen vessels, that the excellency of the power may be of God, and not of us." 2 Cor. 4: 7. So it is with the means chosen; it is by "the foolishness of preaching," that God saves believers. Some of the means of grace contained in the Gospel, because they are small and simple, they are by some undervalued and set aside. Baptism, feet washing, and other commands of the Gospel, are so regarded by some. But when it is remembered that God usually works by small means, nothing can justly be inferred from them on account of their smallness unfavorable to their character as divine institutions.

In conclusion we notice, that the means used, though small, were effectual. The meal was put into the pot, "and there was no harm in the pot." If the life-giving word of God, the gospel of our salvation, is taken into the heart in humble faith, and carried out in the true spirit of obedience, whatever our faults or mistakes have been, and however near to death we may have been brought, from the danger and guilt of our mistakes we shall be delivered, and an "inheritance among the saints of light" will be the rich reward bestowed upon us by our heavenly Master.

XXXV.
THE STRENGTH OF CULTIVATED CHRISTIAN FEELING.

"Abhor that which is evil: cleave to that which is good." Rom. 12: 9.

1. There are strong religious instincts in man's nature. Among those instincts is prayer. Prayer is asking. And asking is the result of a feeling of want. The infant feels its want, and asks in the only language in which it can make its want known, and that language consists in cries. And prayer is more or less common to persons of all ages. Let man be placed under circumstances of danger, which threaten his life, and how natural it is for him, prompted by his religious instincts, to lift his eyes to heaven and call upon God.

2. Worship is a religious instinct. And hence the many forms and objects of worship that we find in the different nations of men. It has been beautifully said, "Why should it be thought a thing incredible that God should write in the book of our being a record of our childhood and our

need of a Father? Shall the needle turn to the north? Shall the heliotrope follow the sun? And shall the heart of man have no center, where it may rest in safety and peace? Like the tidal marks found in the lowest rocks, there are records even in the stony heart of how high religious emotions may at one time have risen."

While man has religious instincts that incline him to worship and to some form of religion, there is nothing held in higher esteem or estimation by him than his religion, when he is sincere in maintaining his religious principles and forms. And whether those principles and forms are right or wrong, he will tenaciously adhere to them, if he sincerely believes them to be right. But the devout worshiper, however enthusiastic he may be in maintaining and living out his principles, if an idolator, he can not be said in truth to "abhor that which is evil," or to "cleave to that which is good," for he may not be instructed to know what is good and what is evil. And whatever enthusiasm, zeal and sacrificing spirit the superstitious idolator may manifest in his religious devotions and service, the genuine Christian, if he does not show more of these than the idolator does, will possess them in greater efficiency and upon a much firmer basis.

The strength of the cultivated Christian feeling is clearly recognized in our text, and will be seen and felt if the commands contained in it are carried out. And that they can be carried out there will be no doubt on the part of any who believe in God, and in the sufficiency of his grace. Let us consider the attitude of a Christian in regard to evil and good.

I. It is an attitude of abhorrence toward evil.
II. It is an attitude of sincere admiration of good.

I. It is an attitude of abhorrence toward evil. The word used here to express the feelings that Christians are to have toward evil is a strong one. It is one of the strongest that our language affords to express opposition to anything. To remind you of the meaning of the word if you have known it, and inform you of that meaning, if you have not known it, we will give you Webster's explanation of it. He thus defines it: "To shrink back with shuddering from; to regard with horror or detestation; to feel excessive repugnance towards; to hate extremely." You perceive this is making the word "abhor" express a good deal, and all that it expresses is to be felt against evil by Christians. It is not merely to abstain from sinful acts, or from evil thoughts. It is not merely to stand aloof from sin and give it no encouragement. Our attitude toward sin must be decided and positive. It must be one of abhorrence. It has been said that the word abhor always implies *visible* hatred. We are to show an abhorrence to evil.

In the regeneration of man, and in the renewing of the spirit of his mind, all the powers of his mind and the affections of his heart are brought into such a relation to each other as will give them the power to so act upon each other as will give him the full benefit of them all, and as will enable him to do what God requires of him. With such a regeneration and renewing, the Christian is prepared to press forward "toward the mark for the prize of the high calling of God in Christ Jesus." Phil. 3 : 14. And the mark is holiness—the sanctification of "spirit, soul and body." 1 Thess. 5 : 23. When such a state of holiness is attained unto, the whole heart and life will be so imbued with the Holy Spirit, that the entire being will be in a state of antagonism to sin. Holiness and sin are in a state of hostility to one another. And where sin no longer reigns, but becomes subdued by grace, and grace reigns, evil will be abhorred.

To abhor evil there must necessarily be a high state of holiness cultivated.

1. It implies that the judgment must be right. Evil must be looked at from an intellectual standpoint. When Paul reasoned before Felix he reasoned upon righteousness, temperance, and a judgement to come. And when he reasoned of righteousness he no doubt reasoned upon sin likewise. It is very difficult, if not impossible, to treat extensively or successfully any virtue without saying something upon the opposite vice. When there is a willingness to learn, and an open and candid mind to receive instruction, there will be no difficulty in learning what may be understood. And the childlike disposition of the new-born soul is a very favorable state of mind to learn, and especially to learn things of a moral character. And evil only needs to be understood to be abhorred. The great difficulty in regard to the understanding of evil is that it is so hard to put it far enough from us, that we may have an opportunity of seeing it in its true color and real dimensions. To have an object too near the eye, we can not see it so well as if it were farther away. And just so it is with evil persons and evil. It is too near to them for them to see it clearly. But there is another difficulty. While we are in love with evil, we are prejudiced in its favor, and if we do not feel like pitying it we should be slow to condemn it. But when divine truth enters the mind, and lays hold of the mind and begins to work, the true character of evil will begin to appear, and if the approaches of truth are not opposed, but encouraged, light will increase and evil will become more and more apparent in all its hideous forms and terrible effects. As already intimated, it will by no means be difficult to understand the abhorrent character of evil to a mind not in love with it, and that wants to understand it.

Sin is so unnatural that it is strange that it should ever be regarded with any favor by man. When we say that it is so unnatural we mean it is so much unlike and so contrary to the nature of man when possessing the nature in which he was originally formed. Hence to know evil, to know that it has been a curse to our world and the destroyer of our race, as far as it could do so, is to advance an important step in the right direction to abhor it.

2. While the understanding in the performance of its office will enable the Christian to understand evil, the conscience will be ready to condemn it. And in this way its true character will become still more manifest. We may compare the heart to a court. The witnesses are called up and testify. The understanding may be compared to the jury. The jury hears the testimony. It is very plain. The guilt is manifest. And the judge, who may represent the conscience, pronounces the sentence of condemnation, and the criminal is judged worthy of death. So in the case with a Christian man. Evil stands before him as a condemned outlaw. And it will be abhorred.

3. But there is another power in the soul of the Christian to help him to abhor that which is evil. And that power is the moral feeling, and the soul of the Christian, being purified by obeying the truth, according to Peter 1: 22, can not possibly love anything that is impure, and more than this, he will necessarily hate whatever is evil. The Christian in his new-birth and sanctification partakes of the divine nature. And this divine nature can only look upon evil with abhorrence. "Oh, do not this abominable thing that I hate," Jer. 44: 4, is an expression of God's that is instructive, suggestive and admonitory. God hates sin, and he has commanded his people to "abhor that which is evil." And this is saying to his people, in your Christian experience, religious nature, and moral principles, be like me. When the hatred of our renewed nature is aroused, and directed toward evil, the mind is not only enlightened to the great wrong of sin, and conscience is not only awak-

ened to pronounce upon the wrong, but the moral feelings are enlisted against it, and thus the entire being is enlisted against evil, when it is abhorred. And the design of the command "Abhor that which is evil," is to put the Christian into such a state of hostility against evil. Such a state is a state of salvation. While the Christian so regards evil, he will not yield to its open threatening, nor to its deceptive allurements. But we proceed to our second division, the attitude of a Christian toward good.

II. It is an attitude of sincere admiration of good.

"Cleave to that which is good." While the other admonition or command requires the Christian to feel the strongest aversion possible of evil, this requires him to feel a strong attachment to, and the most ardent affection for, what is good. The word *abhor*, used to show the attitude of the Christian to evil, is a very strong word. And the word *cleave*, which expresses the true attitude of the Christian to good, is likewise strong. In a true and genuine conversion, completed by the reception of the Holy Spirit, there is a remarkable assimilation in the feelings of the reformed person to whatever is pure, and holy, and good. As we have seen, the whole being of a Christian abhors sin, and turns away from it with feelings of aversion. So, on the other hand, that whole being, in all its parts, admires what is good, and cleaves to it. The understanding knows what is good, the conscience approves what is good, and there is a sweet consciousness of peace felt within the soul in the possession of what is spiritually good.

And there is a remarkable strength in Christian character when the Christian feeling is properly cultivated. To have our whole being, the intellect, the conscience, and the affections, turn away in abhorrence from evil, and have them all turned to good, is an experience at which angels may well rejoice, and a sight at which Christ may well be satisfied, when he contemplates it as a result of "the travail of his soul." Isa. 53:11.

Our text is a very practical one, and a very instructive one. And we proceed to offer some practical thoughts upon it.

1. What a terrible thing sin must be, that we are called upon to abhor it.

2. How very far are those from being what God requires them to be, who are living in sin, and who love sin. God requires all to abhor sin, but instead of doing so they love it.

3. As sinful as we may be, we are spiritual natures that are susceptible of a very high state of cultivation, under Christian culture. To abhor evil and cleave to good, indicates a high state of holiness.

4. We learn from our text how the yoke of Christ becomes easy and how his yoke becomes light, Matt. 11:29. If we attain unto the experience that is indicated in our text, a Christian life will not only be pleasant, but it will also be easy. Can it possibly be any great trouble to us to abstain from any evil if we abhor it? Certainly not. We do not want to have anything to do with what we hate. Then if a Christian attains unto that strength of Christian feeling indicated in the text, and abhors evil, it will be no difficulty for him to abstain from evil. There has been a great deal said about the evil of drunkenness. And a very strong feeling of abhorrence has been created against it. Now it is not hard for those that abhor the evil of drunkenness to abstain from what will make drunk. So it will be with other evils. Let the practice of lying be studied, and let the evil of it be seen, and then it will be abhorred, and if abhorred, it will not be indulged in. In the same way with pride. Let it be looked at in the light of revealed truth. And if we have a proper Christian culture, we will abhor it, and then there will be no inclination to indulge in it.

And then again, if we have so cultivated our Christian feelings as to live, admire and cleave to what is good, it will be no hardship, but a pleasure, to respond to every duty, and to every work the heavenly Master shall call us to.

Now, my friends, does not our text present Christianity in a very interesting and commendable light? Sin is our worst enemy, and we are to abstain from it. Spiritual goodness, which will make us good, is our best portion, and that we are to love. And in our conversion by and to Christianity, we get a divine nature, which will "abhor that which is evil, and cleave to that which is good." If we are thoroughly imbued with the spirit of Christianity, we can do our duty with ease and pleasure.

XXXVI.
A FATHERLY APPEAL.

"A son honoreth his father, and a servant his master: if then I be a father, where is mine honor? and if I be a master, where is my fear? saith the Lord of hosts unto you, O priests, that despise my name." Mal. 1 : 6.

On another occasion, in an address unto his unfaithful people, the Lord said, "Come now, and let us reason together." Isa. 1 : 18. So in our text the Lord reasons with his people who were again out of the way, as they were in the time of Isaiah the prophet, when the above language quoted was used. They often stepped aside from the path of duty and walked in the way that was not right. Hence the frequent reproofs that they received from the Lord, for as often as they sinned they were reproved by the Lord. This reproof was given to the priests of the Lord, but it applies to the whole Jewish nation. For if there was corruption in the priesthood, it would extend to the body of the people, for "there shall be like people, like priests." Hos. 4 : 9. And though the apostasy was common among the people, the priests were addressed because upon them, as the leaders and teachers of the people, the greatest responsibility rested. The text is a fatherly expostulation on the part of the God of Israel with his disobedient people. And the implied unfaithfulness of the Jews belongs to the Gentiles and to the churches of the Gentiles, more or less, as it belonged, or as it was justly applicable to the Jewish church and nation in the time of Malachi, about four hundred years before Christ. How very imperfectly are the duties which grow out of the relation that we stand in to God as our Father and our Master performed by us! Our subject will be a *Fatherly Appeal.* And in order that the practical application which we may make of the text may be the better understood and remembered, we shall present our thoughts under the following heads:

I. God sustains the relation of Father and Master to the human race, and especially to Christian believers.

II. As there are duties incumbent upon the son and servant growing out of the relation they stand in to the father and master, so there are duties incumbent upon men growing out of the relation they stand in to God as their Father and Master.

III. However common it is for the son and the servant to perform their duties to their father and master, men generally neglect their duties to God.

IV. We shall offer some reasons why the duties that men as the sons and servants of God owe to him should be performed.

I. God sustains the relation of father and master to the human race, and especially to Christian believers.

1. That God sustains the relations here attributed to him, is plainly implied in the text, "If I then be a Father,

where is my honor, and if I be a Master, where is my fear?" This language plainly implies that God sustains the relation of Father and Master to his creatures. That is, it is plain that God himself recognizes such a relationship existing between him and mankind. And if he recognizes such a relationship, it must exist. And he, recognizing the existence of such a relationship to his creatures, exercises a father's care over them, and feels a father's love towards them. And he, performing the part of a kind and loving father, and of a good and merciful master towards his creatures, requires, and he can do so with the greatest propriety and justice, their honor and fear.

2. That God sustains the relationship of father and master to mankind, is not only recognized in the text, but it is also recognized by other passages of Scripture. The universal fatherhood of God over all mankind is plainly recognized and taught by Paul in his able and interesting discourse to the people of Athens, when he took as the basis of his discourse the inscription on their altar, "to the unknown God." In that discourse he declared that God "hath made of one blood all nations of men for to dwell on all the face of the earth, and hath determined the times before appointed, and the bounds of their habitation. . . . In him we live and move, and have our being; as certain also of your own poets have said, for we are also his offspring. Forasmuch then as we are the offspring of God, we ought not to think that the Godhead is like unto gold, or silver, or stone, graven by art and man's device." Acts 17: 26–29. Paul here recognizes the truth of the passage of the Greek poets in which we are all declared to be the offspring of God. Then he is the common father of us all. And in accepting this idea taught by the Greeks, namely, that we are all the offspring of God, Paul makes it the basis of a very logical argument by which he

proves the absurdity of their idols. They acknowledged themselves to be the offspring of God. But they could not possibly be the offspring of gold, or silver, or stone. So Paul tells them that they should not believe the Godhead, that is their acknowledged parent, is like unto gold, or silver, or stone. For if the Godhead was like unto any thing of that kind, they could not possibly be his offspring. Darwinism, as absurd as it may be, is less so than idolatry. For Darwinism recognizes a germ of life as the origin of man, but heathen idolatry in theory recognized man to be the offspring of gods made of gold, or silver, or stone.

So we find the mastership of God is taught in the Scriptures. If we have been made by him we surely are his. And all that we have justly belongs to him. "We are not our own." If then we ourselves belong to God, surely our service belongs to him, and he is properly our master, and justly claims our fear, and all that a faithful servant owes to a good and kind master. When the Saviour washed his disciples' feet, he said to them, "Ye call me master and Lord: and ye say well; for so I am." John 13 : 13. In the parable of the talents we have both the good and bad recognized to be the servants of God. Those represented by the faithful servants served God, and were good. Those represented by the wicked servant were wicked, and served him not. So God is the Father and Master of all men.

Again as a Father and Master God provides for all his creatures. The food that they eat to sustain life, the garments with which they are covered, and the houses in which they are sheltered, are all the result of his gracious providence. All the materials from which the comforts of life are formed are the fruit or production of the benevolent laws by which God governs the world. Man with all his wisdom and power cannot produce, independently of God, what is necessary to promote the life, well-being and enjoyment of his race. The refreshing showers, the fertilizing dews, and the quickening rays of the sun are not under the control of man, but are all under the control of our heavenly Father. It is he that "maketh his sun to rise on the evil and on the good, and sendeth rain on the just and on the unjust." David, when looking at God as we are looking at him, as the great provider for all his creatures, and as the source of all good, says, "The Lord upholdeth all that fall, and raiseth up all those that be bowed down. The eyes of all wait upon thee; and thou givest them their meat in due season. Thou openest thy hand, and satisfiest the desire of every living thing." Ps. 145 : 14-16. Thus as a kind Father and Master God makes timely and suitable provision for all his creatures.

III. As there are duties incumbent upon the son and servant growing out of the relation they stand in to the father and master, so there are duties incumbent upon men growing out of the relation they stand in to God, as their Father and Master.

"A son honoreth his father, and a servant his master." That is, a good son and a good servant will do as is here affirmed of them. It is their duty to do so, and they will do their duty. Just so men should do to God. The obligations, however, that men are under to love, honor and serve God, are much greater than those the son are under to the father, or the servant to the master. The honor which we pay to parents is but a small part of the honor which we owe to God. We are to entertain the most profound reverence and the highest respect for his person, his character, and his will. The son will be likely to have great confidence in his father. What father does, or what our parents do, we commonly think must be right, where there is a proper feeling existing between parents and children. And so the servant will have confidence in his master's judgment, and respect to his master's will. But there are bounds beyond which no human authority extends, and when these are passed, resistance rather than obedience may be our duty. But God's authority is supreme, and it knows no bounds. Whatever he says we are to believe, and whatever he does we are to be satisfied with, and whatever he commands we are to obey without hesitation. Against a divine command there is no excuse for the exercise of carnal reason. Our obedience must be prompt and complete.

The obedience, however, that we render to God as a divine Father and Master, must not be that of a slave rendered to a cruel master, but it must be that of an affectionate child to a loving parent. We like our children to obey us cheerfully as well as promptly. And so we must obey our heavenly Father. He loves a cheerful giver. "God loveth a cheerful giver." 2 Cor. 9 : 7. This applies to all our services, and to all our offerings given to the Lord. We are admonished by Paul to serve one another "by love." Gal. 5: 13. And if we are to serve one another by love, much more are we to serve the Lord "by love."

We have some ideas in the chapter in which our text occurs that should be read in connection with the foregoing remarks in regard to the cheerful, willing and loving spirit in which we are to serve God as our Father and Master. Those ideas to which we refer show how extremely selfish men may become, even in the holy service of God. The following language shows the mercenary and selfish spirit by which the priests were actuated in rendering their service to the Lord: "Who is there even among you that would shut the doors for nought? neither do you kindle fire on mine altar for nought. I have no pleasure in you, saith the Lord of hosts, neither will I accept an offering at your hands." v. 10. The priests would do nothing unless they were paid for it. They would not so much as *shut the doors* or *kindle a fire for nothing*. Provision was made for their support by the Lord. But they would do no extra work without extra pay. They would not even do such little things as are named without receiving some compensation for it, showing clearly that they had no love for the work they were engaged in, nor any love to the Lord. It was the reward they wanted. For this alone they labored. Such mercenary or selfish service the Lord would not accept. He declared in regard to it, "I have no pleasure in you, saith the Lord of hosts, neither will I accept an offering at your hand." Christian ministers should be careful that they do not permit themselves to be governed in their holy labors by a love "for filthy lucre." 1 Peter, 5 : 2. Ministers should be helped, but money must not be their object, or the Lord will have no pleasure in them.

The son that loves the father and honors him will love to be with his father. Some of us will remember how we loved to be with our father, in the field, or in the shop, or in the house, or wherever our father was. If a child is not happy at home there is something wrong. And does not the child of God love to be with his heavenly Father, and with his Father's family, and in his Father's house, in the place where Christians meet to worship? This he does. And he honors his Father by showing such an attachment to his person and to his house and family. The Jew honored God and his holy service when he said in his captivity, "Let my tongue cleave to the roof of my mouth if I prefer not Jerusalem above my chief joy." Ps. 137: 6. The son that properly honors his father will labor to maintain the honor and dignity of his father's family. So the sons of God that honor him as they should, will labor to maintain the honor of the church by laboring to promote its purity, its peace, its soundness of doctrine and its success. And as the servants of

God we should take a proper interest in all that pertains to the great work of righteousness, which is so dear to God, and which he takes so much interest in as the reformatory agent by which he seeks to reform the world. We should pursue our work with all the honesty, diligence, faithfulness and love which characterize the good servants of men.

III. However common it is for the son and the servants to perform their duties to their father and master, men generally neglect their duties to God.

"If I then be a father, where is mine hope? and if I be a master, where is my fear?" As the state of the Jewish nation at the time the text was spoken was very corrupt, as appears from the context, the Lord might well ask the question that he did, and make the complaint that is implied in it. For it appears he was by no means honored and feared as he should have been. And how is it with us at this time? Are we as Christians honoring and pleasing him as we should? Are we honoring him as obedient children honor their parents? And are we fearing him as faithful servants fear their masters? Might he not with much propriety complain of us, or at least of many of us as he complained of the Jews?

And how is it with those who are unconverted? And is he their Father and their Master too? He is as we have clearly seen. And he appeals to them and says, "Where is mine honor? and where is my fear?" Dear friends, awake to your danger and duty, and let your inquiry be, "Lord, what wilt thou have me to do?" You will find that he will have you all to honor and fear him. Do this, and do it now, and you will be blessed in the deed.

IV. We shall offer some reasons why we should honor and fear God.

First, It is right that we should do so. The relation we stand in to him as sons and servants, makes it our duty to do so. Second, If we fail to honor and fear God, while we are his sons and servants, we must meet the punishment that disobedient children and unfaithful servants are doomed to meet. It is a great sin to disobey the lawful commands of a parent and to violate a lawful contract with a master. Consequently, the punishment is to be feared. Third, if we honor God as a son honors the father, and fear him as a servant fears the master, he will, when he "makes up his jewels," own us his, and "spare us as a man spareth his own son that serveth him," and reward us as faithful servants, with an "exceeding great reward."

XXXVII.
THE MISSION OF CHRIST.

"Then the Pharisees went out, and held a council against him, how they might destroy him. But when Jesus knew it, he withdrew himself from thence; and great multitudes followed him and he healed them all; and charged them that they should not make him known that it might be fulfilled which was spoken by Esaias the prophet, saying, behold my servant whom I have chosen: my beloved, in whom my soul is well pleased. I will put my spirit upon him, and he shall shew judgment to the Gentiles. He shall neither strive nor cry; neither shall any man hear his voice in the streets. A bruised reed shall he not break, and smoking flax shall he not quench, till he send forth judgment unto victory. And in his name shall the Gentiles trust." Matt. 12: 14-21.

The text is made up of the language of the evangelist and of the prophet Isaiah. The evangelist in pursuing his narrative or life of Christ comes to that period and work in his life to which the language of the prophet refers. The prophets wrote much of the life of Christ prospectively. The evangelists wrote it retrospectively. And they both agree. There is a remarkable harmony between Isaiah and Matthew. Our subject will be, *The mission of Christ.* His mission or work is presented to us in the Scriptures under a variety of aspects or under various names, all expressive of some prominent feature in his work. In our text his work is said by the prophet to be "to shew judgment to the Gentiles."

1. Our first leading thought, then, will be the work itself which our Lord came to do, which is, as we said, *to shew judgment to the Gentiles.* And what are we to understand by this? By *judgment* we are not to understand calamity and punishment inflicted by the Lord upon individuals and nations on account of their sins, though this is the meaning of the word as it is frequently used in the Scriptures, and it may be a remote meaning of the text, or a meaning that is not primary, as it is a Scriptural doctrine that in the finishing up of his work our Lord will punish the ungodly nations of the earth for their disobedience. "And to you who are troubled rest with us, when the Lord Jesus shall be revealed from heaven with his mighty angels, in flaming fire, taking vengeance on them that know not God, and that obey not the Gospel of our Lord Jesus Christ; who shall be punished with everlasting destruction from the presence of the Lord and from the glory of His power." 2 Thess. 1 : 7-9. But we are to understand it to mean in our text what it means when it is used in the following Scriptures: "My soul breaketh for the longing that it hath unto thy judgments at all times." Ps. 119: 20. "Blessed are they that keep judgment, and he that doeth righteousness at all times." Ps. 106: 3. "But woe unto you, Pharisees! for ye tithe mint and rue and all manner of herbs, and pass over judgment and the love of God; these ought ye to

have done, and not to leave the others undone." Luke 11: 42. Among the definitions which Webster gives of judgment is the following: "The doctrines of the Gospel or God's word." And he refers to the occurrence of the word judgment in our text to justify his definition. We then understand by the phrase, "To shew judgment to the Gentiles," which, according to our text was our Lord's commission, means that he was to shew to the world, in all their plainness, excellence and beauty, the great principles of truth and righteousness as they are manifested both in the character and law of God.

The great principles of truth, justice, and righteousness, which characterize the law of God, and should form the character of men, as they form the character of God and all holy intelligences, though they had been introduced into the world and written, first, upon the human heart in the primitive state of man, and afterward upon the tables of stone in the law which God gave unto his people Israel, nevertheless, but little of those principles was seen in its practical application in governing the dealings of men with one another, or in governing their worship or duty to God. The honest confession of Israel shows the moral state of the Jewish nation in the time of the prophet Isaiah, who thus gives that confession: "For our transgressions are multiplied before thee, and our sins testify against us: for our transgressions are with us; and as for our iniquities, we know them; in transgressing and lying against the Lord, and in departing away from our God, speaking oppression and revolt, conceiving and uttering from the heart words of falsehood. And judgment is turned away backward, and justice standeth afar off: for truth is fallen in the street, and equity can not enter. Yea, truth faileth; and he that departeth from evil maketh himself a prey: and the Lord saw it and it displeased him that there was no judgment." Isai. 59: 12–15. Such is the moral picture of the Jewish world as drawn by the inspired prophet. Our Lord's description of the Jewish nation is as dark as that drawn by Isaiah. The following was one of the charges he made against it: "Thus have ye made the commandment of God of none effect by your tradition." Matt. 15: 6. This was in reference to the duty that children owed to their parents. In the same discourse he shows their delinquency in performing in the proper manner their duty to God. Quoting the language of the prophet Isaiah, he says, "This people draweth nigh unto me with their mouth, and honoreth me with their lips; but their heart is far from me. But in vain they worship me, teaching for doctrines the commandments of men." Matt. 15: 8, 9. And the apostle Paul in his epistle to the Christians at Rome, in showing the necessity of Christ and his righteousness, gives a very low view of the moral character of both Jews and Gentiles, and declares "there is no difference: for all have sinned, and come short of the glory of God." Rom. 3: 22, 23.

Such being the moral condition of the world, there seems to have been a necessity for our Lord's coming into the world as a teacher to teach or "shew judgment to the Gentiles," and also to deliver man from the debilitating effects of sin, that he might have moral strength to do, as well as divine light to know, his duty. And to meet all man's moral wants, Christ "is made unto us wisdom, and righteousness, and sanctification, and redemption. 1 Cor. 1: 30. But why is it that he was to shew judgment unto the Gentiles? From the above view we have given of the Jews, it is evident that these needed, as well as the Gentiles, to have judgment preached to them. And we are not to understand that our Lord was to shew judgment to the Gentiles only. But as the Jews had been the special subjects of God's favors in the former dispensation, and as the religious wants of the

Gentiles had, apparently, or in some degree, been overlooked by the Lord for awhile until the Saviour would come into the world, when his coming is referred to, the Gentiles are mentioned with distinction, because in the Christian brotherhood "there is neither Jew nor Greek, there is neither bond nor free, there is neither male nor female: for ye are all one in Christ Jesus." Gal. 3: 28. The Jews were to have no less privileges than they had before, but the Gentiles were to have many more. Hence these are made so prominent in many of the prophecies which refer to the Christian church and dispensation.

II. *In the second place we shall notice the fitness of our Lord for his work.* 1. He was chosen by the Lord. And we may safely conclude that as he was chosen by God to perform the responsible, laborious, and painful work allotted to him, that he was fitted for the work to which he was called. God is not mistaken in those whom he calls to execute his purposes. If they are not qualified he can and will qualify them.

2. The second qualification we shall notice in the fitness of our Lord for his work, was his servant-like character. "Behold my servant," exclaims the Father. There was nothing whatever dishonorable or low in the office of a servant in our Redeemer's estimation to lead him to reject it. Service in useful and proper work is not dishonorable. Especially is this the case with the servants of God. His servants are employed in doing good. And they have no occasion to be ashamed either of their name or of their work The Saviour in teaching men their duty in all its parts, and in giving them hearts to do it, had a great work to do. He had to deliver them "from the power of darkness." Col. 1: 13. He had also to renew them in the spirit of their mind. Eph. 4: 23. To regenerate and reform guilty and ruined sinners requires work. And Christ had a work to do which

none but he himself could do. And he did it, and he did it cheerfully and successfully. And he could with propriety say, as he did say in his prayer to his heavenly Father, "I have finished the work thou gavest me to do." John 17:4. Yes, he was a servant; and no service was too laborious, too humble, or too painful for him to do, if faithfulness to his calling required it. His humiliation astonished both men and angels. Peter could not entertain the thought that his Lord should wash his feet.

3. *The third qualification alluded to, fitting him for his work, was the receiving of the Spirit.* "I will put my spirit upon him." How fully this promise was accomplished, the wonderful account of his baptism shows. "And Jesus, when he was baptized, went up straightway out of the water; and, lo, the heavens were opened unto him, and he saw the spirit of God descending like a dove, and lighting upon him; and lo a voice from heaven saying, "this is my beloved Son, in whom I am well pleased." Matt. 3:16, 17. He was now anointed with the Holy Spirit, Acts 10:38, and fully fitted for his great work, and how successfully he accomplished it will be seen in the further opening of our subject.

III. *The manner in which our Lord performed his work will be the next point in our subject to be noticed.*

1. He worked very silently, or without noise and ostentation. "He shall not strive, nor cry; neither shall any man hear his voice in the streets." Our Lord's modest and unostentatious manner characterized all his labors. Oh, how unlike the clamorous and noisy world was he! And who will not join in the wish and prayer that his professed embassadors, who claim to be engaged in the same holy and benevolent work, may learn of him to work in the same modest and humble way? How truly has the apostle said, in referring to our Lord's humiliation, " He made himself of

no reputation." Phil. 2: 7. He sought not the honor and applause of the world. We are informed by the evangelist in our text that, after he had healed the multitude, "he charged them that they should not make him known." How different is the spirit that we often see in professing Christians, and even in ministers, to that which the Saviour manifested! His was modest, meek, quiet, and unassuming, while theirs is aspiring after the honor and applause of men. We sometimes find even ministers who are so injudicious as to show an anxiety to know what is thought of their preaching. Our great concern should be to preach to please God, and to acquit ourselves before him, and patiently wait for his approval and honor.

2. Our Lord pursued his work tenderly as well as meekly and unostentatiously. "A bruised reed shall he not break, and smoking flax shall he not quench, till he send forth judgment unto victory." A bruised reed not strong enough to stand erect, or with its head bending toward the ground, and the flame of a lampwick almost extinguished, are very suitable emblems of the weak and discouraging condition of many of the frail sons and daughters of men. Many of that kind probably had been in the multitude that had just been present with our Lord. And perhaps his tender treatment of those physically or morally diseased suggested to the evangelist the prophecy. The statement that our compassionate and merciful Redeemer would not quench the burning wick so nearly extinguished, nor break the reed so easily broken after it was bruised, was a figurative way of saying that he would heal the sick, encourage the desponding, and pardon the humble penitent. Young beginners in a Christian life are often like the bruised reed or smoking flax, and they should be tenderly dealt with by the stronger Christians. The spirit of Christ in his disciples will make them like their Master, "kind one to another, tender-hearted,

forgiving one another, even as God for Christ's sake hath forgiven you." Eph. 4: 32.

IV. *The next point in our text to be noticed will be our Lord's success.* " Till he send forth judgment unto victory." The prophet foresees and foretells the success of Christ's mission. We may look at this success under three aspects. 1. At his success in establishing his church in the world. The opposition he met with from the beginning is known to all who are acquainted with the history of Christianity. The attempt of Herod to kill the infant Saviour is as dishonorable to its author as it is criminal. But it was a failure. When there was such an inhuman slaughter of infants in Judea, the infant Saviour was safe in Egypt. At another time the people were offended at his teaching, "and rose up, and thrust him out of the city, and led him unto the brow of the hill whereon the city was built, that they might cast him down headlong. But he, passing through the midst of them, went his way." Luke 4: 29, 30. Here again his enemies were foiled. And in our text it will be noted there is a statement to the effect that "the Pharisees went out and held a council against him, how they might destroy him." But again the Saviour made his escape. His hour had not yet come. But did not his enemies at length succeed? By no means. His time at length came to die. And his enemies killed him, but they did not destroy him nor his cause. He came from the grave stronger than ever. The hostile spirit of opposition to Christ followed the apostles, and though it killed them, the cause for which they died yet lives, endeared to its friends by the struggles through which it has come, and by the accumulated evidence that it has gathered around it proving that it is a work of God and not of·man.

2. The second aspect under which we may look at the success of Christ is his success over the heart of the sinner. There is often a great struggle in the soul between Satan

and Christ for the victory. But Christ has always proved victorious, and always will do so, if the sinner perseveres. The human heart is desperately wicked, and sometimes will long resist the attempts of Christ to enter, but if the sinner opens the door, he will enter, and bind the strong man, or Satan, and cast him out. Matt. 12: 29.

3. The last aspect under which we should look at the success of Christ, is his final victory over all his enemies, "for he must reign till he hath put all enemies under his feet." 1 Cor. 15: 25. He came to show judgment unto the Gentiles, or to establish justice and righteousness in the earth. And that his principles will finally prevail, is evident from the following: "And the seventh angel sounded: and there were great voices in heaven, saying, the kingdoms of this world are become the kingdoms of our Lord, and of his Christ; and he shall reign forever and ever. And the four and twenty elders, which sat before God on their seats, fell upon their faces and worshiped God, saying, we give thee thanks O Lord God Almighty, which art, and wast, and art to come; because thou hast taken to thee thy great power, and hast reigned." Rev. 11: 15–17.

We close our subject with two remarks. The text closes with the words, "and in his name shall the Gentiles trust." We would then say, 1, let us all trust in Christ, for he is worthy of our confidence, and we need a friend like him to trust in, if we would enjoy the happiness of conscious safety. 2. In our work, as the disciples of Christ, in co-operating with him in showing "judgment to the Gentiles," or in establishing truth and righteousness in the world, let us work in the same meek and unostentatious manner, as none others will secure equal success.

XXXVIII.
AN ADMONITION TO WATCHFULNESS.

A SERMON FOR THE NEW YEAR.

"And that, knowing the time, that now it is high time to awake out of sleep; for now is our salvation nearer than we believed." Rom. 13:11.

The time has suggested our text. We have entered a new year. We are, or ought to be, reminded that time is passing, and the remembrance of this fact should prompt us to diligence in the great work in which we are engaged, for our opportunities for useful labor diminish as time advances. Our subject is "An Admonition to Watchfulness." This seems to be the leading thought of the language of our text.

The admonition is evidently given to Christian believers, for one of the reasons given for watchfulness is the fact that their salvation is said to be nearer than when they believed. And this shows that believers are addressed. It may seem a little strange that believers are addressed as if they were asleep. Did they not awake at the time of their conversion? A similar admonition is given to sinners: "Awake thou that sleepest, and arise from the dead, and Christ shall give thee light." Eph. 5:14. That such an admonition is given to sinners we do not wonder; it is appropriate to their condition. But at first thought it may not seem so appropriate to believers. It might seem to imply that they had fallen asleep again. But such a reflection would not be honorable to the Roman brethren, and therefore we will look for another meaning. We will not suppose that the Roman brethren had gone back " to the weak and beggarly elements " (Gal. 4:9) to which they had been in bondage before their conversion to Christianity. The apostle's admonition does not require us to entertain such an unkind opinion of them. The trouble with them was not that they had gone back to the world. It was that they had not gone on far enough from the world; that the world had not been left far enough behind, considering the length of time that had elapsed since they left the world and came to Christ. This is the case more or less with all who profess the Christian faith. This probably is the case with us who are here to-day. We indulge the hope that none of you have gone back again to the world. We would say as Paul said to his Hebrew brethren, "but beloved we are persuaded better things of you." Heb. 6 : 9. Nevertheless, while we hope better things of you, than to think any of you have gone back to the world, we think it is quite likely none of us have made the distance in the divine life that we might have made, considering the time we have been in the service of the Lord, and the favorable circumstances under which we have been placed, for both of these should be taken into consideration in considering the improvement we have made. It is to be expected that those who have been in the service of the Lord for years will be further advanced in the divine life than those who have but recently entered into it. And then the circumstances by which we have been surrounded should be considered. For instance, we have thought that persons coming into the church, who had not been brought up among the brethren or by the brethren, but under the influences and example of fashionable, worldly people, could not be expected to fall into the order of the brethren in all things, as in the order of plainness of dress, as readily as such that have been brought up by brethren and in the families of brethren. Such have not only failed to enjoy the teaching and influence of the brethren upon many things, but the teaching they have had has been altogether in the opposite direction. These may require more time to see the propriety of all our usages than those of our own families, or who have lived among us.

The power of early education, of habit and custom, and the attachment of people to their first religious sentiments, made much trouble in the churches in the apostolic age. This will be plainly seen by referring to some of the epistolary writings of the apostles, which have many things in them designed to meet those troubles. Such troubles were among the brethren in Rome and Corinth, as well as among those of other localities. Persons who had been brought up in idolatry, as the heathen were, found it more or less difficult to separate themselves from its principles and practice.

We present our thoughts upon the text, under two heads. First, the import of the admonition itself. Second, the reason for the admonition.

First, the admonition itself: "It is high time to awake out of sleep." We have already remarked that the admonition is given unto believers, and that it does not imply that they had gone back to the world or that they had fallen into the moral slumbers that they had been in before their conversion to Christianity. But while this is so, it plainly implies that they were not fully awake, or that they had not fully recovered from the sleep that they had been in ; or, if they had, they were again in some degree under the influence of sin, and were not as wakeful and watchful as they should be, and hence the necessity of the admonition, "it is high time to awake out of sleep." What is sleep, or what moral state does it indicate in such passages as our text? It implies a state of inactivity, thoughtlessness, ease, and unconsciousness. And when applied to sinners it means their inexcusable and guilty unconsciousness and ignorance of the danger they are in. The building may be on fire and the inmates being sleep are altogether ignorant of the terrible danger to which they are exposed. So it is with people who are living in sin. They are exposed to the fire of God's wrath, but are apparently unconscious of it, and therefore easy and unconcerned. As the admonition is more directly addressed to believers, we must understand its application to such. It may have been designed by the apostle for that class of believers, of which there are some in every organized church, and of which there have been some in every age of the general church, namely, those who continue to be babes instead of growing to Christian manhood, and who are tossed about by every wind of doctrine, instead of being established in the principles of the gospel. The admonition of our text, "it is high time to awake out of sleep," is very appropriate to such, and the believers in Rome to whom it so justly applied should have taken it unto themselves, and all slothful believers of this and every age of the church should do the same. But it seems to be designed for the body of believers at Rome, and there is a sense and application of it, which, we think, may justly be made to all Christians whatever may be their attainments.

In the parable of the ten virgins, and in reference to the virgins, it is said, "While the bridegroom tarried, they all slumbered and slept." Matt. 25:5. Different ideas have been suggested as to the meaning of this language, and to reconcile the representation of the virgins in their slumbering and sleeping condition with the condition of true believers. Lange gives the following reading: "They all nodded and fell asleep," instead of "they all slumbered and slept." And he makes these remarks in connection with his reading: "An intimation of weakness indeed, yet expressing the great delay of the bridegroom rather than censure." Alford has the following remarks upon the passage concerning the condition of the virgins: "Being weak by nature, they gave way to drowsiness; as, indeed, the wakefulness of the holiest Christian, compared with what it should be, is a sort of slumber." Dr. Seiss, in his "*Parable of the Ten Virgins,*" has the following: "The essence of this slumbering and sleeping I am disposed to find in a certain dulling and deadening of the church to the specific subject of the bridegroom's coming." The last writer has probably touched the true idea. Even the wise virgins were not fully awake to the glory, and suddenness, and practical effects of the bridegroom's coming. And so we may learn that even the faithful believers, at the coming of our Lord, will not be fully awake to all the practical bearings of that event upon the world. And it was probably this great doctrine of our Lord's second and personal coming, that the believers at Rome were not fully awake to, and hence the apostle's admonition, "And that, knowing the time, that now it is high time to awake out of sleep: for now is our salvation nearer than we believed." The context favors this idea, and especially the verse following our text: "The night is far spent, the day is at hand: let us, therefore, cast off the works of darkness, and let us put on the armer of light." And in the language of Alford, already quoted, we probably may justly say, "indeed the wakefulness of the holiest Christian, compared with what it should be, is a sort of slumber." That is, Christianity in its doctrine, in its facts, in its prophecies, in its hopes and promises, and in its terrible threatenings, and in its everlasting effects upon the destiny of men, is a subject of such transcendent or superior worth, that the most wakeful and enlightened Christians have not grasped it in all its moral dimensions, or fully appreciated it, and hence the propriety of the admonition, "And that, knowing the time, that now it is high time to awake out of sleep: for now is our salvation nearer than when we believed."

Secondly, The reasons for the admonition. These are two. (1) The nature of the time in which believers were then living. (2) The fact that their salvation was nearer than when they believed.

(1) The nature of the time in which believers were then living. We may remark in regard to that time, that it was a very critical time. It was in the first age of the church. It was when Christianity must be established, if established at all, in the face of the most inveterate and formidable opposition. The gospel that revealed Christianity was "to the Jews a stumbling block, and to the Greeks foolishness." 1 Cor. 1 : 23. Every step the believers took in their aggressive movements upon the enemy's works was strongly opposed, and every doctrine promotive of holiness, contradicted. It was then (a) a time of trial for Christianity. Indeed Christianity was on trial before the world. And if it failed, humanity's last hope failed. And if it succeeded, a door of hope would be opened to the sorrowing and troubled, to the guilty and lost to immortality or everlasting life. This time therefore to believers was (b) a very responsible time. To them was entrusted a most important work. The apostle appreciated the position of believers and well knew that there was no time to falter, and none to sleep, and hence his admonition, "it is high time to awake out of sleep." (c) It was also a time that afforded believers an excellent opportunity to do good service for the Lord. And many of them improved the time. And there never was as much work of a spiritual or reformatory character, in the same length of time done, as was done in the apostolic age of the Christian Church. Notwithstanding the disadvantages under which the early Christian workers labored, and the opposition that they had to contend with, their success was great, converts and churches were greatly multiplied. The world felt and showed the effects of the labor of the faithful servants of God. (d) Finally, the early Christian believers felt that the time in which they lived was the last time, or end of the age. And when the apostle said, in the language of our text, "And that, knowing the time, that now it is high time

to awake out of sleep," he probably had reference to the time of the coming of the Lord. The Saviour after he had given his disciples some of the signs which were to precede his coming, said unto them, "Watch therefore; for ye know not what hour your Lord doth come. But know this that if the good man of the house had known in what watch the thief would come, he would have watched, and would not have suffered his house to be broken up. Therefore be ye also ready; for in such an hour as ye think not the son of man cometh." Matt. 24: 42–44. Such solemn warning having been given to the disciples by the Saviour, they felt the time of his absence was very uncertain, and that his coming might be very near. And the apostle feeling that that great event might be near at hand, he admonished his Roman brethren to watchfulness, and said "And that, knowing the time, that now it is high time to awake out of sleep." He would have them awake and ready to meet their Lord.

2. The second reason that the apostle gives for his admonition to his brethren to urge them to watchfulness is the fact that their salvation was nearer than when they first believed. And as they were approaching the consummation of their salvation, and the time when they would receive the prize, the apostle would have them to watch and be ready, for if they would sleep and fail to have their lamps ready when the Bridegroom comes, they would not be received into the marriage, but be left out in the dark.

Our salvation may be represented as consisting of four stages. The first is that stage which brings us into Christ. "Now is our salvation nearer than when we believed." The beginning of salvation, that is of our personal salvation, or of the salvation within us, is connected with our belief. "He that believeth and is baptized shall be saved." Mark 16:16. Thus affirmed our Lord. When we have "repentance toward God, and faith toward our Lord Jesus

Christ," Acts 20:21, and renounce the world, and put on Christ in baptism, Gal. 3:27, and thus show that we believe with the heart unto righteousness, and are ready with the tongue to make a confession unto salvation, Rom. 10:10, and are "born of the water and of the spirit," John 3:5, then does our salvation begin. The second stage of our salvation is our sanctification by the truth, John 17:17. By a sanctified life of obedience to the truth after our baptism, we become more separated from the world, and more assimilated to the divine nature, and more conformed to the mind of Christ, and thereby our salvation becomes nearer to us, or, in other words, we are brought more under its divine power. The third stage takes place at the death of the believer. This is a very important event in the history of a believer. It brings the spirit of the believer nearer to the Lord than it was in the "earthly house of this tabernacle." 2 Cor. 5:1. Hence the apostle desired to depart and to be with Christ, which he knew would be better than to remain in the world. Phil. 1:23. The fourth, or last stage of salvation, is the consummation or completion of salvation, and consists in the redemption of the body from the grave, the reunion of the body and spirit, and the glorification of the whole being. This completion of the work of salvation is thus referred to by Paul: "For our conversation is in heaven; from whence also we look for the Saviour, the Lord Jesus Christ: who shall change our vile body, that it may be fashioned like unto his own glorious body, according to the working whereby he is able even to subdue all things to himself." Phil. 3:20, 21. Our salvation with all its fullness and completeness will be brought near and be given unto us when our Lord shall "appear the second time without sin unto salvation." Heb. 9:28. He will appear, when he comes the second time, to finish what he commenced when he came the first time.

In conclusion, we remark, first, that all the reasons there were to urge the believers at Rome to watchfulness still exist to a considerable degree to urge us to watchfulness. And let us not fail to be watchful and diligent, that when the Lord comes to complete his salvation in his people we may be found among them. Secondly. What a happy and most desirable condition are believers, according to our text, represented as occupying! They are approaching the consummation of their salvation. Every year, and even every day, brings their salvation with all its fullness nearer to them. Our salvation in this sense is nearer than it was a year ago. And if we live to see the year 1882, it will be nearer than it is at the beginning of 1881. And if we die before the year closes, in a certain sense, it will be nearer than if we live. This view of the future connects it with much that is desirable. How different it is with the unconverted! The long, dark night of death is still coming nearer to them, and with death the judgment, and with these their terrible doom. We would say to all, to both saints and sinners, "it is time to awake out of sleep," for there are events great with importance before us.

XXXIX.
THE WORK OF THE CHURCH.
PART I.

"And of some have compassion, making a difference; and others save with fear, pulling them out of the fire; hating even the garment spotted by the flesh." Jude 1: 22-23.

There were unfaithful believers in that day in the Church. There were men and women who had embraced Christianity from improper motives, and had not moral courage and a sufficiency of self-denial to encounter the opposition which they had to contend with, and consequently they proved unfaithful to the holy principles that they had pledged themselves to observe. Our text has special reference to the recovery of these unfaithful members from their apostacy.

While the apostle admonishes his brethren to labor for the recovery of these unfaithful members, that admonition is equally applicable to us, as a Church, to labor for the conversion of all who need it, and not only for the recovery of the luke-warm and back-sliding members of the church. We are to labor to restore all such to holiness and righteousness and to the favor of God.

There are three points that I will open as fully as my time will permit me to do. First, the imminent danger to which sinners are exposed. The expression, "pulling them out of the fire," implies that they were in the fire. If these fallen members of the Christian church are in the fire, because they are in sin, then all persons who are in sin are in the fire. Hence, I make the general statement that the text shows the imminent danger that men and women are in, when they are in sin. Secondly. The work of the church in "pulling them out of the fire," and in recovering them from their lost condition, and in restoring them to God. Thirdly. Some suggestions relating to the manner in which the church is to work. "Of some have compassion, making a difference: and others save with fear; pulling them out of the fire, hating even the garment spotted by the flesh."

First, the imminent danger of the sinner. In the text sin is compared to a fire. There are several Scriptures that present this view of sin. I will notice one. That will be enough to sustain the position which I take. I call your attention to Isaiah 9:18: "For wickedness burneth like a fire: it shall devour the briers and thorns, and shall kindle in the thickets of the forest; and they shall mount up like the lifting up of smoke." Wickedness burned where this church existed, and because these persons did not watch and pray, they fell into the fire of sin, as a little child falls into the fire if not watched carefully. These men and women were in the fire of sin, and it was burning them up. Their Christian friends were to pull them out, lest the fire should burn them up and destroy them. Sin is a fire. I purpose to notice some of the points of similarity and resemblance which exist between sin and a fire. The first point of similarity is in their diffusibility or spreading nature. They both spread very fast. You know how rapidly fire spreads through the material which is burning. It spreads with frightful rapidity. The progress of the flames is onward and it consumes every thing in its way. How rapidly it will go! How soon it will extend over squares, and reach points at a considerable distance from the point at which it started. This spreading tendency of fire is known by all. And how is it with sin? Precisely the same thing is observed. It has the same spreading character. Knowing this, we can see why there are so many and such great sinners in the world. Sin spreads. There was a time when the worst men living were men of innocent character. Men, whose crimes are so great that they can hardly be mentioned in good society, were once innocent babes, as innocent as any child in the room. But when they came to the age of maturity and accountability, instead of pursuing the paths of rectitude, they fell into the fire of sin, and it has spread over them until they are now addicted to drunkenness and licentiousness and many evils. It is from the spreading tendency of sin that it is likened to fire. We know by observation that it is so.

We all remember some of our feelings in childhood—our first remorse of conscience at having broken some of our parents' commands. We perhaps can remember our first feelings when we disobeyed God's demands. When we grew older there was less remorse even when we broke greater commands. The spreading tendency of sin should be guarded against. I want to say to you, who are indulging in any sin, however small, that you are unsafe. I would say to the Christian that we should make a practical application of this principle to ourselves. If we are indulging in any sin, no matter how small it may be, we are unsafe. That one little sin will beget another, and the two will beget a third. Like a fire it will run, and eventually it will bring about our expulsion from the church, unless we die without our sins being exposed. In this case, however, we will be found guilty in the eyes of God, for he knows all things.

My unconverted friends, although you are not in the advanced stages of sin, yet you are unsafe while you are indulging in any sin. It is like fire, and it will burn. Young men and women, you had much better quench the fire of sin while it is in its first stage. Sin will obtain a greater influence over you from time to time, and after awhile it will assume that ugly character which perhaps you can not now bear to think that it ever will.

Our second point of comparison will be the transforming power of sin. Fire, in consuming combustible matter, turns everything into its own character. It matters not what it is, everything is mixed up. The flames transform everything into their own destructive element. So it is with sin. The apostle Paul says: "Unto the pure all things are pure: but unto them that are defiled and unbelieving is nothing pure; but even their mind and conscience is defiled." Titus 1:15. To the sinful person everything is more or less impure. Sin is just the opposite of holiness. While sin transforms everything into its own evil character, holiness transforms everything into its beautiful and glorious character. If we become holy men and live out our principles in our lives, holiness will transform us into its character. All men and women who are trying to do this are becoming more and more assimilated to the pure and holy character of God. There is a transforming power. in holiness. If we have the root of holiness planted in the heart; if we cultivate holiness as we grow older, we will become more and more assimilated to God. The more we associate with holy companions, and practice holy principles, the more we will acquire holiness of character. There will also be the same assimilation if we live with evil associates. The more we live in sin, the more we will become assimilated to it. This is a solemn truth. From this we see the necessity of choosing the ways of the Lord, and of walking therein if we would be holy.

The third point in comparison between these two elements, the element of fire and the element of sin, is seen in the power of the two. You know something of the power of sin. You also know the power of fire. You know that it is said, "Fire is a very good servant, but a very bad master." When it once seizes upon combustible material, how difficult it is to control! The great fires in Philadelphia, Pittsburgh, and New York started from small beginnings. You know of the great fire in London; you have heard of it through history. Many of you can remember the great fire in Chicago. It commenced very small, but grew until it became so large that thousands and hundreds of thousands of people were compelled to fly for their lives. Onward and onward it went in its powerful course of destruction. If some one had poured water upon it when it started, it could have been stopped. But it soon assumed such a powerful force and gigantic magnitude that it defied the power which was brought against it to stop it. Sin is powerful. It is a powerful master when once it gets the mastery over us. It is strong. When once it gets control, how difficult it is to subdue. How hard it is for old sinners to give up sinning, to break away from their sins.

We have a powerful illustration of this. It is only one of the many manifestations of sin. There are many similar manifestations of its power; but as this is one of the most common, I use it. I refer to the sin of drunkenness. When a man has become a confirmed drunkard, how difficult it is for him to change his course of life. I have several cases before my mind as distinctly as your faces come up before me now, of men who have tried for weeks and months to overcome this habit. They meet an old companion and are asked to take a glass of liquor. Then the power of the old habit comes over them, and in many cases they fall. I do not say that it is impossible for a drunkard to reform, but I tell you that it is difficult. Hence, we admonish our young men to abstain from even a temperate use of intoxicating drink. Do not use any beer. Here may be the start of a habit that you may have great trouble to overcome. The power of sin is so great that we do not want to let it get any hold upon us.

Young men and women, there are many old sinners that if they could turn away from their sins as easily and as readily as you can turn from yours, they would do it at once. If they could do it as easily they would be glad to do it. The reason why they do not turn is, because it is so difficult for them to stop sinning. Because they can not do it easily, they are not doing it at all. As in the case of the drunkard I have several persons in my mind. They have long been going to meeting. They have considerable regard for the truth. They pay attention to the preaching. They would like to be members of the Christian community. They would like to share the joys which they see that we have. But they have settled down in their habits. These are fixed upon them. These habits have grown with their growth and strengthened with their age. They may yet come, and they may never come to Christ. The reason why they will not come is because sin has burned so long that it has a great control over them. They are under the power of sin so much that they lack energy to leave it and all its discomforts, and accept holiness with all its joys. I am afraid that death will find them just where they are now.

These two elements are similar with respect to the effect which they produce. The effects of fire upon us are extremely painful. To burn the hand or the finger only a little, to burn ourselves but slightly, is very painful. The slightest burn causes a great deal of pain to us. You know the pain producing tendency of fire upon man's body. You all know that it is very painful. And, how is it with sin? It is sin, and sin alone, that has produced all the pain that is in the world.

Let me call your attention to the remark made by the apostle Paul, with reference to this point. He says in the 22d verse of the 8th chapter of Romans: "For we know that the whole creation groaneth and travaileth in pain together until now." The groaning and travailing of creation in pain is owing to the effect of sin. It is affecting the whole creation. It is affecting universal humanity. It is affecting even the animal creation. You do not yet feel the terrible shock. It has not reached all of us yet in its worst effects. You have not yet fully experienced its painful consequences. What groaning is going on around us! You are in health, but how many invalids are upon their beds suffering with pain. Some disease is preying upon their system, robbing them of sweet sleep and rest. You have plenty upon which to subsist, but in how many hovels of the poor there is groaning and wishing for bread! How much misery arises from that source. You can also see the effect of sin in our penitentiaries and prisons, where the guilty are found wishing for their liberty, and the enjoyments of their old associates of better days. You can supply from your knowledge many instances of the kind to which I have referred. The whole creation groans and sighs with pain of some kind or other. Why is this? Because the fire of sin is at work. It is burning many up. It is burning out what innocency there is left in humanity. It is affecting all in some way or other. There is not a sin but what is followed by pain. That is not the worst. This pain will be everlasting. "And the fifth angel poured out his vial upon the seat of the beast: and his kingdom was full of darkness, and they gnawed their tongues for pain, and blasphemed the God of heaven because of their pains and sores, and repented not of their deeds."—Rev. 16: 10, 11. Whatever mystery there may be about this, whatever difficulty there may be to fix the time of the fulfillment of the prophecy, it shows, my friends, the effects of sin in producing intense misery. It will be fulfilled some time or other, and the ungodly will experience it. The terrible event referred to will come to pass. The judgments of God against sin will some day be visited upon them that are in fellowship with the power of darkness. These threatened judgments show us what a terrible time is coming upon the wicked. But there is a way of escape. If we take timely warning we may escape as Lot did from Sodom, which was consumed with fire from heaven. Sin is God's enemy, and it is a strong one, but he will overcome it and those who will adhere to it must experience an overthrow. So we had much better part with sin, for by so doing we may save ourselves, whereas if we hold on to it we must perish. "For wickedness burneth as the fire: it shall devour the briers and thorns, and shall kindle in the thickets of the forests, and they shall mount up like smoke. Through the wrath of the Lord of hosts is the land darkened and the people shall be as the fuel of the fire: no man shall spare his brother. And he shall snatch on the right hand, and be hungry: and he shall eat on the left hand, and shall not be satisfied: they shall eat every man the flesh of his own arm: Manasseth, Ephraim; and Ephraim, Manasseth: and they together shall be against Judah. For all this his anger is not turned away, but his hand is stretched out still." Isaiah 9:18-21.

Such being the danger to which ungodly professors and sinners are exposed, they should surely become alarmed and make their escape from the burning house before it is consumed, and before they are consumed with it. With what willingness and gladness would the inmates of a house be rescued from the devouring flames, if escape was possible, and if help should be offered them, if the house was on fire! How much more willing and anxious should those burning in sin be to be saved from their perilous position! This can yet be done.

Remember that sin is fire, and that it will burn us up if we are in it. "Escape for thy life; look not behind thee, neither stay thou in all the plain; escape to the mountain, lest thou be consumed." Gen. 19:17. The mountain of safety is Christ.

XL.
THE WORK OF THE CHURCH.
PART II.

"And of some have compassion, making a difference: and others save with fear, pulling them out of the fire, hating even the garment spotted by the flesh."—Jude 1:22, 23.

Our subject will be the work of the Church in saving sinners, which is stated in the text to consist in pulling them out of the fire. This was addressed to the members of the Church for the purpose of telling them how the fallen members might be saved. This is alluded to in that part of Jude where these fallen members are called spots in their lovefeasts or feasts of charity. While our subject has direct reference to the fallen members of the Church, it may be used in reference to all sinners. They are in the same condition whether they are in the Church or not.

Conceive a building to be on fire. It is wrapt in flames. The building is in itself valuable for its excellence; for its beauty of architectural appearance and surroundings. It is a very valuable building. It is not only so in itself, but within it is costly furniture. It is on fire. And suppose in addition to the building itself and its valuable contents, that there are human beings in it. Perhaps they were asleep and only awoke to find themselves enveloped in smoke and flame. Every outlet of escape from the building is closed up. They are in danger of being consumed in the burning building. Those who are outside of the building are now trying to save the inmates of the building.

See the noble firemen laboring to overcome the flame. The men are trying to save the building and the persons who will be burned in the flames by which they are enveloped unless they are taken out. See them working, risking their own lives to save the lives and property of others. They are all around the burning building trying to subdue the flames. Look at the labor and concern with which they work!

We should put forth the same labor in the cause in which we are engaged. What the firemen did in my illustration should be the labors of the Christian Church. The labor of the firemen in trying to save the persons in the building should be the labor of the Church in pulling souls out of sin. The sinner is enveloped in the fire of sin. He will realize terrible ruin and eternal loss if not saved. That is the idea; "And of some have compassion, making a difference: others save with fear, pulling them out of the fire." We should be trying to save and to get them out of the flames which are around them, and which will burn them up if they do not make their escape.

We should have all the intense anxiety and all the self-denial, and should use all the mighty labors which these firemen put forth to save the persons in the burning house. We should do this to save our fellow-men from the flames of sin. The dangers of our fellow-creatures who are in sin are more imminent than the dangers of those who are in that house.

It is the work of the Church to pull sinners out of the fire of sin. It is to be one of the purposes of the Church. Shall I say that it is heaven's design of the Church? I think it was one of heaven's designs in organizing the Church. I might say that there are two designs of the Church. One design is the benefit of the members of the Church. We are organized together that we may be a help to one another, that we may perform the duties growing out of a social relation to one another; that we may aid one another in religion as we help one another in business, and in all the domestic relations in which we stand to one another. Men have organized themselves together into societies that they may mutually help one another; so we are organized together in the Church. We are united together in the Church that we may help one another, sympathize with one another, hold up one another when we are pressed down with burdens. We are to strengthen one another so that we may become strong.

That is an erroneous idea that some have, that we can be as good out of the church as we can be in it. This is a wrong idea. As a general rule, can children do as well if they lose their parents and are turned out into the world without father and mother? Will these children be as good and grow up as well grounded in the principles of right as those who have been brought up under parental influences and had proper surroundings? The Church is a kind of parent to Christians, especially to young converts. And is a widow as able as a woman who has a husband to get along in the world? One of the great principles upon which the family is based is mutual sympathy. This is an important principle in the Church. Do not do away with the Church then by any means. You may, as well do away with the idea of the family and fall into the terrible doctrine of free love which has found many advocates in the world, but thank God is not now on the advance. You might as well talk about the propriety and utility of the family as about the propriety of the Church. Heaven has ordained both the family and the Church. These are both organizations which have been given us by heaven. The propriety, utility and necessity of both, have been recognized by heaven. Both of these must remain.

Heaven has organized the Church and ordained the ordinances belonging to the Church. The ordinances of the Church are of great use. These must be used by the Church.

Another design to the organization of the Christian Church is, that by it the truth may be preserved and circulated. The persons outside of the Church are to be brought under the influence of truth and realize the saving powers of it. We have the following Scriptural declaration: "The Church is the pillar and ground of the truth." 1 Tim. 3:15. What a responsibility rests upon the Church! We are the pillar and ground of the truth. This means the Church is the depository of Christian truth. We are to take care of that gift of heaven—the truth. We are the protectors of it. We are to keep it in its purity. We are to show its divine influence in our lives before the world. We are to hand that truth down to our successors that they may keep it as we have kept it. One generation is to hand that truth to others, and thus it is to be perpetuated. We are to sustain it; we are to love it; we are to keep it; we are to live it. "Beloved, when I gave all diligence to write unto you of the common salvation, it was needful for me to write unto you, and exhort you that ye should earnestly contend for the faith once delivered unto the saints." This is the language of the apostle Jude. We are to hand down the faith in the way in which we have received it from Christ and the apostles. We are to labor to maintain the faith of the primitive Church.

It is the old faith we are to contend for and keep. On the apostolic system of Christian faith and truth no improvement can be made. Any change from the apostolic order should be guarded against. We are to find new enjoyments and new beauties in the truth, and are to make new applications of it as occasions may require; but the truth must stand unchanged. We are to keep it for the coming generations of the people of God. The Church then has a work to perform, besides simply promoting our own enjoyment. Do not forget that. One object is the promotion of our own spiritual enjoyment and our advancement in the divine life. But, my brethren and sisters, there is something else besides this to do. Do not forget that we have another duty to perform. Do not forget that there may be persons in our own families who are in the flames of sin. Do not forget that many men and women are living in sin. They are like the individuals to whom I alluded in my illustration. They are surrounded by the flames of sin, and unless they are rescued they will meet a terrible end. When you pray, remember them in prayer. Remember to pray for the minister who is preaching to them. Pray for the success of the efforts which are being put forth to pull the sinners out of the fire.

We are intrusted with the great work of saving those who are represented as being in the flames. It is the business of the Church to pull them out. How poorly we are performing it! How little does our religious labor resemble that of the daring and working firemen, who are laboring to save the natural lives of men and worldly property! We have a greater object in view. Our work is to save the soul, the entire man or woman. If they are lost there will be universal loss. Said Jesus to the disciples when they began to show signs of fear, "Fear not them which kill the body, but are not able to kill the soul, but rather fear him which is able to destroy both soul and body in hell" (Matt. 10: 28). Soul lost; body lost; all lost. We are to labor for the redemption of those who are in the flames. Well we may labor.

What is the Church? The Church is part of the body of Christ. In speaking of the members of the Christian Church, Paul says: "We are members of his body, of his flesh, and of his bones." Eph. 5: 30. We are members of Christ, and should be like him. Did he not try to save sinners from the flames? He rushed into the burning flames to save them. He was himself consumed in a certain sense. He died that he might rescue the whole human race. He arose from the grave and triumphed over death. He did this that he might rescue the souls of men from the danger to which they are exposed. "Ye are all members of his body, of his flesh, and of his bones." Where is our sympathy for him in his work? Where is our likeness to him in our efforts? Should we not be more or less like him in our labors? Surely we ought.

Whatever benevolence and philanthropy there is among unconverted men and women, their philanthropy will be greatly increased when they become Christians. When we possess the mind and spirit of Christ our benevolence will be broader, and our philanthropy will be deeper. Our self-denial should be more manifest than that of those who are not Christians. The most efficient philanthropists are among the Christians.

In this age there is a good deal of infidelity growing up. You have heard of Robert Ingersoll, the infidel lecturer. You have heard of the unfair representations which he makes of the Bible and of men of piety. A reporter of the *New York Witness* has lately interviewed Hon. G. R. Wendling, who has been lecturing in the Northern States in opposition to Ingersoll. He says, according to the *Christian Cynosure*, from which we quote: "The clergy constitute the most human and self-sacrificing class of men to be found on earth to-day. I have been, in the last year, in nearly every Northern State, from Maine to Nebraska, and everywhere the clergy are doing the most for humanity, not only in the way of religious ministration, but I mean in caring for the poor, the wretched, the homeless, the sick, the weak, the intemperate. They are the men who are at the front in movements designed to alleviate human suffering, working by sunlight and starlight; and four-fifths of them half paid, having poor fare, poor libraries, poor homes, and a portion of every community prejudiced against them. The men, I say, who are doing this are the same preachers whom Ingersoll would cast out. Robert Ingersoll may make pretty speeches about humanity, but here is a class of men whose hats neither he nor I are worthy to hold."

I want you to compare the works of Christianity with those of infidelity, and see whose are the better. When the advocates of infidelity are presenting their position, compare the amount of good done by the former with what has been done by the latter, and you will see who are the greater benefactors of our race. Some of you may, like many others, want to believe in scepticism, in order that you may not have to come out from the world: but remember what effect scepticism would have upon the world if it prevailed, and then remember what effect Christianity has had upon it. That is the way to test the matter. I would modify the language of the lecturer. It would not do for me or any other minister of the Gospel to quote it without some modification of it. These remarks do not only apply to the Christian ministry, but also to the laity. I want you to remember that we have among the laity the most active and zealous workers in the Church. I propose to change it so that it will apply to the active part of the Christian Church. Here, in this body of men and women, we have a power and an influence which is being exerted for the welfare of the world. The Church as a whole is doing the work. Infidels are not doing it; worldly philanthropists are not doing it. This is a work of the Church.

The Church transforms and changes man's entire being. While we clothe the naked and feed the poor, we would also clothe them with the garments of salvation. We are trying to get them ready for eternity while we are sustaining them on earth. This is a work for the Church. The firemen, to whom I have alluded, are trying to extinguish the flames and save the natural body; the Christian Church is pulling the souls of men out of the flames of sin, and are trying to benefit both the souls and bodies of men.

How are we to do this? We are to do it alone by the power of God. The power is not in us. It is derived from God and the Christian truth. We are the pillar and ground of the truth. What is the truth? The truth is another term for the Gospel. Christian truth and the Gospel are synonymous terms. Paul says: "The Gospel is the power of God unto salvation to every one that believeth." Rom. 1:16.

What the fire apparatus is to the firemen, aiding them in quenching the flames of the natural fire, Christian truth and the means of Gospel grace are to the Church, enabling it to quench the flames of sin. And when these means are properly applied by the Church, and in faith received by the sinner, they will accomplish their designed effect without any failure.

It appears from the language of our text that in our work of teaching the truth and saving sinners a difference is to be made. And this difference is to be made, not in the means to be used, but in the manner of using the means. People differ very much in their tempers and dispositions, and we should remember this in dealing with our children or friends and those who are around us. We must study their natures. A careful physician, before he prescribes for any case of sickness, makes a careful diagnosis, a careful examination of the patient. Our medical schools and colleges have dissecting rooms where the human system in all its parts is laid open to the student. In this way he will learn the organization of the human body, and he will then be better able, when he comes in contact with disease, to prescribe.

And those engaged in promoting the moral interests of humanity should try and understand human nature, so that they can more effectually reform and train it. Those having the young under them know very well that they must be dealt with differently. Some require very tender treatment, while others require more rigorous treatment. And so it is in administering spiritual instruction. "If some have compassion" they must be dealt with very tenderly. Harsh measures might discourage and destroy them. "Others save with fear." They must be alarmed and have their fears awakened. They are asleep in sin, and fear no danger. Paul directed Titus to rebuke some "sharply." How tenderly the Saviour spoke to the "weary and heavy laden!" But he dealt more sharply with the hypocritical and hardened Jews. Great discretion should be used in giving Christian instruction. It is said that "Prudence is the queen of graces." It certainly is an important one for the Christian worker. "He that winneth souls is wise." Prov. 11 : 30. In administering the discipline of the Church to members that need it, great discretion should be used. Small offences should not be dealt with as greater ones, and attending circumstances should be considered.

Finally, as the danger is imminent, and the work great, the Church should act with promptness and zeal, and all who are in the danger to which sin exposes them should avail themselves of the offered help and make their escape from the threatening danger. Time is shortening and eternity is approaching. And whatever is done must be done soon. Should the work of salvation be neglected, an irreparable and great loss will be sustained. If it is properly attended to, all will be well, and a glorious immortality will be secured.

www.ingramcontent.com/pod-product-compliance
Lightning Source LLC
Chambersburg PA
CBHW022105290426
44112CB00008B/561